Nelson's Preacher's Sourcebook

APOLOGETICS EDITION

DAVID WHEELER AND
KENT SPANN, EDITORS

THOMAS NELSON
Since 1798

Nelson's Preacher's Sourcebook, Apologetics Edition

© 2010 David Wheeler and Kent Spann

Published in Nashville, Tennessee, by Thomas Nelson. Thomas Nelson is a registered trademark of HarperCollins Christian Publishing, Inc.

Typesetting by Kevin A. Wilson, Upper Case Textual Services, Lawrence, MA

Thomas Nelson titles may be purchased in bulk for educational, business, fundraising, or sales promotional use. For information, please e-mail SpecialMarkets@ThomasNelson.com.

Library of Congress Cataloging-in-Publication Data

Names: Wheeler, David A. (David Alan), 1961- editor. | Spann, Kent, editor.
 | Thomas Nelson & Sons.
Title: Nelson's preacher's sourcebook : apologetics edition / David
 Wheeler, Kent Spann.
Description: Nashville : Thomas Nelson, 2022.
Identifiers: LCCN 2022014488 | ISBN 9780310147442 (paperback)
Subjects: LCSH: Preaching. | Worship programs. | Apologetics. |
 Evangelistic work.
Classification: LCC BV4211.3 .N46 2022 | DDC 251—dc23/eng/20220506
LC record available at https://lccn.loc.gov/2022014488

Table of Contents

Shepherding God's People

Shepherding the Shepherd

Heroes of the Faith

Special Service Registry

Introduction

Sunday's comin'. Are you ready?

For the pastor of the local church, Sunday is always on his mind. You barely get through delivering your current message and the thought hits that you have to get next week's message ready. Sunday is always on the preacher's mind.

Add on top of that the other times you speak, such as Sunday and Wednesday evenings, and you realize preaching is a daunting task. Every pastor remembers the first time he sat down with a calendar and realized he had 52 Sunday mornings and evenings, as well as midweek sermons to prepare. That is 156 sermons a year the average preacher needs to prepare. If you stay with your congregation ten years, you will preach over 1,500 sermons to the same group of people.

Preaching is a demanding task. It is not just preparing messages; it is preparing *fresh* messages that speak to your people. It is not preaching one's favorite passages or messages (sugar sticks); it is declaring the whole counsel of God. It is not entertaining the people; it is speaking the truth of God's Word. It is not just delivering a message; it is delivering a word from God with fire in the preacher's bosom.

That is what makes preaching demanding. Mark Buchanan, pastor of New Life Community Baptist Church in Duncan, British Columbia, in an article at www.preachingtoday.com, described the weekly cycle of preaching well:

> I love preaching. I hate preaching. The best description is Jeremiah's: it is like fire in the bones. It is holy work and dreadful work. It exhausts and it exhilarates, kindles and consumes.
>
> On Mondays, I am charred remains. The hotter I burned on Sunday—the more I preached with fiery conviction and bright hope—the more burned to the ground I am on Monday. I'm restless, but I don't have initiative to do anything or, if I do, the energy to sustain me in it. I'm bone-weary, suffering what the desert fathers called acedia: an inner deadness from the hot sun's scorching.

Worst of all, Monday is lived with the knowledge that I am called to do it all over again next Sunday. Mondays are the days I would rather sell shoes.

How does the preacher go from charred remains on Monday to a holy man of God with fire in his bones? Backdraft preaching! Again I quote Mark Buchanan:

> Backdraft refers to the phenomenon when a fire subsides because it's burned up all the oxygen in the room—then, if somehow the room is breached—a door is opened or the roof bitten through by the fire itself—oxygen-laden air rushes in and sparks an explosion. Fresh wind meets a dying fire, and all again is fiercely ablaze. That's a backdraft.
>
> Backdraft is a good metaphor for the preaching call. It is exactly what I have described: the fire that burns the insides out and almost burns itself out; then, the fire meets fresh wind and breaks out anew.

That fresh wind comes from many directions. It comes in the closet when we are alone with God. It comes when we finally sit down to study the Word for the next week. It comes as we minister to people in the congregation. There are many ways the fire rekindles. It is our prayer that the *Nelson's Preacher's Sourcebook* will be one of those instruments God uses to breathe fresh wind and cause the fire to break out by Sunday in your soul.

In the pages to follow you will find inspiring messages by men who have lived the cycle of preaching and preached with fire in their bones! You will find sermons from the Old Testament and the New Testament, sermons that defend the faith, sermons that instruct and inspire as well call for a deeper walk with Christ. You will find sermons from preachers of old and those who still bring the Word in our postmodern world.

Of course, it is not the words on the page that will stir up the fire; it is the Holy Spirit burning them into the preacher's heart so when he stands up to preach, he preaches with fire. Fred Smith said, "Audiences will listen to a very poor voice, as long as there's fire in it." That means two things as you use the *Nelson's Preacher's Sourcebook:*

1. Let the Spirit of God do a fresh work in your heart. The Bible is not a book of sermon texts; it is the living Word of God that transforms the lives of those who come to it with an open heart (Heb. 4:12), especially the preacher's heart. Nothing is worse than hypocrisy in the pulpit. What is hypocrisy in the pulpit? It is the preacher declaring the Word of God when he hasn't heard it himself.

2. Make the sermon yours. The sermons that follow are not meant to be a substitute for your study of the text and personal preparation of the sermon. You need to let the Spirit make them your sermons. You do that in several ways:

   a. Read the text, meditate on the text, and study the text. Nothing can substitute from time in the Word.

   b. Use your own illustrations. You will notice the sermons do not contain a lot of illustrations. That is because the best illustration is *your* illustration! There are many illustration resources available in books and on Web sites. One of the best illustration Web sites is Preaching Today (www.preachingtoday.com). They provide current life illustrations.

   c. Apply it to your audience. Only you know the real needs of your audience. As you prepare the sermon, keep your people on your heart.

   d. Finally, put the sermon in your own words, language, emotion, and personality. Change the outline to fit your situation and preaching style. These sermons are simply kindling to get the fire going.

We humbly submit this year's volume to you, praying the fires may burn. We (David Wheeler and Kent Spann) would love to hear from you. Your input is always valuable. Your encouragement is always uplifting. Here are our e-mails: David Wheeler (dwheeler2@liberty.edu) and Kent Spann (spann@highlandgrovecity.org).

Dr. Jack Hyles said, "Preaching is truth set on fire." Let the fire burn in your heart this Sunday!

Apologetics Edition Contributors

Dr. Thomas Arnold (1795–1842)

British educator and classical scholar; headmaster of Rugby School from 1827 to 1842, where he preached weekly to the students the convictions of his Christian values.

Week 34

Rev. Jason Barber

Senior pastor of the North Main Baptist Church in Danville, Virginia (www.northmainbc.net).

Week 42

Dr. Carl Barrington

Ethics, apologetics, and Bible teacher at Providence Christian Academy in Lilburn, Georgia.

Weeks 1–10
How to Prepare Sermons with Pizzazz!
Funeral Sermons

Dr. John A. Broadus (1827–1897)

Southern Baptist Seminary president and preacher.

Week 47

Tony Brown

Senior vice president of J. Crew and member of Thomas Road Baptist Church. Also serves on the board of directors for Strategic Renewal.

From the Pew to the Pulpit

John Bunyan (1628–1688)

Author of the greatest allegory ever written, The Pilgrim's Progress. Wrote more than thirty books while imprisoned for preaching the gospel.

Week 35

Dr. David Earley
Chairman of the Department of Pastoral Leadership as well as director of the Center for Ministry Training at Liberty Baptist Theological Seminary. Also serves as the director of the Center for Church Planting at Liberty University.

Funeral Sermons

Jonathan Edwards (1703–1758)
American pastor and third president of Princeton and widely acknowledged as one of America's greatest philosophical theologians. Most famous for his sermon "Sinners in the Hands of an Angry God." He played a key role in the First Great Awakening.

Week 39

Thad Franz
Member of Highland Baptist Church in Grove City, Ohio, and a community clinical pharmacist at Nationwide Children's Hospital.

Mentoring: Passing Along the Faith

Dr. Gary Habermas
American Evangelical Christian apologist, philosopher, theologian, and prolific writer. Has dedicated his professional life to the examination of the relevant historical, philosophical, and theological issues surrounding the death and resurrection of Jesus.

Weeks 17, 18

Dr. Richard G. Halcombe Jr.
Director of Missions for Southern Baptist churches in central Ohio.

Myths and Maxims in Conflict Resolution

Dr. Frank Harber
Senior Pastor and founder of Champions Crossing Church in Dallas, Texas, and co-creator of Got Life? *evangelistic resource.*

Week 20

Dr. Daniel Henderson

Senior pastor for twenty years and now president of Strategic Renewal,
which exists to ignite personal renewal, congregational revival, and
leadership restoration for Christ's glory. Also serves as pastor of prayer
and renewal at Thomas Road Baptist Church and teaches on prayer and
church leadership at Liberty University, and is the author of seven books.

> Weeks 44, 45
> How to Preach on Prayer

Rev. David Hirschman

Chair of Liberty Baptist Theological Seminary's Online Education Program.

> Weeks 1, 2, 4, 5–9, 23–27

Dr. Harry Ironside (1876–1951)

Pastor of Moody Church and prolific writer

> Week 40

John Daniel Jones (1865–1965)

Welsh Congregational preacher who is known for his theological studies.

> Week 41

Rev. Larry Kiser

Senior pastor of Richland Bible Church, located in Richland, Michigan.
Richland has a population of fewer than 1,000, but the church has grown
from a Sunday morning attendance of 125 to more than 1,600 during his
sixteen years there.

> Weeks 28–37

Robert G. Lee (1886–1978)

Former pastor of Bellevue Baptist Church from 1927 to 1960. Most
known for preaching his sermon "Payday Someday," which he preached
more than 1,200 times.

> Weeks 39, 49

Dr. Michael R. Licona

Apologetics Coordinator for the North American Mission Board. Authored, coauthored, or contributed essays in numerous books, including the award-winning book, *The Case for the Resurrection of Jesus.*

Preparing Your Flock to Share Christ with Mr. Skeptic

Robert Murray M'Cheyne (1813–1843)

Scottish minister and poet and a man of deep piety and prayer.

Weeks 44, 51

Dr. Calvin Miller

Professor of Preaching and Pastor Ministries, Beeson Divinity School, Birmingham, Alabama. Artist and author of more than forty books.

Weeks 16, 40–43, 52

Dr. Doug Munton

Senior pastor of First Baptist Church, O'Fallon, Illinois, since 1995. Author of Warriors in Hiding: The Surprising People God Chooses and Uses *and* Seven Steps to Becoming a Healthy Christian Leader.

Week 3
Heroes of the Faith: Dr. J. Edwin Orr

Dr. J. Edwin Orr (1912–1987)

Preacher, revivalist, lecturer, and prolific author; a professor at Fuller Seminary's School of World Missions from 1966 to 1981. He was mightily used to introduce generations to the Great Awakenings.

Weeks 31–33

Josh Saefkow

Pastor of The Hill at West Hill Baptist Church in Wooster, Ohio.

Weeks 38, 40
Heroes of the Faith

A. B. Simpson (1843–1919)

Founder of the Christian and Missionary Alliance and a prolific author, writing more than 100 books.

Week 42

Jack Smith
Former associate in personal evangelism, North American Mission Board, Alpharetta, Georgia.

Week 43

Rev. Mark Smith
Senior pastor of Murdock Baptist Church in Port Charlotte, Florida, where he has served since 2005.

Weeks 44–52

Dr. Kent Spann
Pastor of the Highland Baptist Church in Grove City and coeditor of Nelson's Annual Preacher's Sourcebook.

Weeks 1–39
Funeral Sermon

Rev. Charles Haddon Spurgeon (1834–1892)
Pastor, Metropolitan Tabernacle, London.

Week 36

Dr. Jerry Sutton
Associate professor of Christian Proclamation and Pastoral Theology at Liberty Baptist Theological Seminary in Lynchburg, Virginia. Has ministered as senior pastor for thirty-one years and is the author of three books.

Weeks 46–51

Dr. David L. Thompson
Senior pastor of North Pointe Community Church, which he started in 1999.

Weeks 11–22

Dr. George W. Truett (1867–1944)
Pastor of First Baptist Church in Dallas, Texas, for forty-seven years and the Southern Baptist Convention president from 1927 to 1930.

Weeks 37, 38, 43

Robert Uhle

Founder and director of WellSpring Counseling, a division of Central Ohio Youth for Christ. Currently a clinical counselor and supervisor. Licensed elder in the Fellowship of Grace Brethren churches.

The Lost Art of Encouragement

Dr. Jerry Vines

Pastor of First Baptist Church, Jacksonville, Florida, from 1982 to 2006, and the author of many books.

Week 41

Dr. Vernon Whaley

Director of the Liberty University Center for Worship and chairman of the Department of Worship and Music Studies in Lynchburg, Virginia.

Worship services

Dr. David Wheeler

Professor of evangelism, Liberty University and Liberty Baptist Theological Seminary, Lynchburg, Virginia, and coeditor of Nelson's Annual Preacher's Sourcebook.

Weeks 10–14, 19

Preaching Series

Many of the messages are placed in series. Series offer many advantages. One, they assist the preacher in planning and preparation. Second, they build continuity for the audience. Third, they help the worship leader plan the upcoming worship services. Fourth, if you use PowerPoint, visual aids, or notes, you can create a visual aid for the series instead of one for each individual message.

The user is free to preach individual sermons out of the series, change the order of the sermons, select another time of the year, or change the title of the series.

Getting Ready (Weeks 1–9)

What better way to start off than a series challenging your congregation to get ready for what God is going to do? This inspiring series from the Book of Joshua by Rev. David Hirschman will do just that.

Ephesians (Weeks 1–30)

This edition offers a new feature, a study through a book of the Bible. The thirty messages in this series will take your congregation through a rich study of Ephesians as Paul unfolds the glories of salvation, the mystery of the church, and the church living the Christian life. Preach it as a series or as individual messages.

Real Characters (Weeks 10–13)

Dr. David Wheeler provides a series of sermons looking at some of the important characters in the Old Testament and the most important character in the New Testament, Jesus Christ. Your people will learn how to live a godly life.

Apologetics (Weeks 20–24, 26)

This is one of our featured series in this edition. It is a practical demonstration of the article about preaching on apologetics by Dr. Mike Licona. They will give believers the solid answers they need to defend the faith.

The Big Ten (Weeks 28–38)

The Ten Commandments have become a hotbed of controversy; at least the display of them in public places has. This series teaches believers how to move them from tablets of stone to the table of their hearts.

From Rags to Riches to Reality (Weeks 28–37)

Dr. Larry Kiser provides a ten-sermon series on the life of David, who rose from rags to riches. This is a rich study of the man after God's own heart. Learn from his victories and devastating defeats.

Get Down on Your Knees (Weeks 44–47)

This is the other featured series in this edition. It provides examples of how to preach on prayer as taught by Dr. Daniel Henderson. God loves and responds to the prayers of His people. Challenge your people to pray like never before.

Classics from the Masters (Weeks 34–51)

Learn from some of the classic preachers like John Bunyan, Charles Haddon Spurgeon, George W. Truett, Harry Ironsides, and many other greats.

The Confessions of Christmas (Weeks 48–51)

This edition's Advent series is provided by Dr. Jerry Sutton. Unveil the great confessions made in response to the birth of our Lord, and then make your confessions.

WEEK 1

Getting Ready *to Move*

Joshua 1

By David W. Hirschman

Introduction

God is intent on completing His plan in the lives of His children, and nowhere is this intentional leading more evident than in the account of Joshua and the children of Israel entering the Promised Land. Many important parallels may be applied to churches and individual believers alike as they embrace God's plan for their lives. As the Lord desires to move churches and believers forward, He will begin to reveal important information, information that is vital to the successful start, continuance, and completion of His plan. As God begins to move, we must get ready. We must begin immediately to pay attention and be prepared to follow. We must faithfully follow His leading because the best is yet to come! But before we can move forward, we must:

1. Understand the Plan (1:1–4)

Following the death of Moses, God wanted Joshua to know that His plan for Israel had not changed and that the time had come for Israel to get ready to move. It is important to note that while much had transpired since Israel's failure to believe God at Kadesh Barnea, His plan was still waiting to be accomplished. Certainly, following their departure from Egypt, Israel had attempted their own plans, but God's plan remained His will for His children.

In the light of this, we need to remember that there are many plans—about success, fulfillment, finances, and destinations, but these are frequently based on our incomplete knowledge and understanding of God's plan and our needs.

But God always has *the* plan, based on His complete knowledge and understanding. For the children of Israel, it was to get out of

Egypt, cross the wilderness, enter the Promised Land, and live there experiencing His blessings. For people today, the plan is to leave the former life, enter a new life, live a fruitful life, live experiencing His blessings.

God always has the plan for you!

2. Understand the Power (1:5–9)

Along with His plan, God always supplies the means, or the power, and as we pursue His plans, it must be with the right power!

a. Not the power of personal opinions. God's plans do not work with the power of personal opinions. Remember the tragedy of Numbers 14:1–5.

b. Not the power of group determination. God's plans do not work with the power of group determinations. Remember the tragedy of Numbers 14:40–43. God's plans work only in the simplicity of His own power (1:5, 9).

3. Understand the Prize (1:10, 11)

As God moves churches and believers forward in accomplishing His plan for their lives, it is important to understand His goal. In this case, God wanted Israel to take possession of the land He had promised to them. In order for Israel to accomplish this prize, God issued one order: "*Prepare!*"

a. They had to prepare provisions for the final portion of the trip.

b. They had to prepare their hearts to see God work in a miraculous way—by helping them cross the Jordan.

c. They had to prepare themselves to receive what God wanted them to have.

Conclusion

God wants to see us embrace His plan, His power, and the prize He is directing us toward. To do this, we must get ready. He has a particular goal He wants us to accomplish, and He will provide the power for the process. And along with this, we must get ready to move.

SUGGESTED ORDER OF WORSHIP

Getting Ready Series from Joshua

Prelude—Instrumentalist

> *Great Is the Lord*

Call to Prayer for the New Year—Pastor with all men at the front of church

Call to Praise—Congregation

> CH 353 *Victory in Jesus* (v. 1, chorus, v. 2, chorus)
>
> CH 513 *Thank You, Lord* (2×)

Worship in Prayer—Pastoral Staff

Welcome—Pastoral Staff

Welcome Song *(meet and greet during song)*—Pastoral Staff

> SPW 100 *Bless the Name of Jesus*—Congregation

Scripture Reading—Worship Leader with the Congregation

> CH 698 Selections from Hebrews, 2 Timothy, 1 John, and Psalm 91

Praise and Worship—Congregation

> CH 171 *Come into His Presence* (2×)
>
> BH *Shout to the Lord* (2×)
>
> CH 705 *It Is Well with My Soul* (chorus, last verse, chorus)

Prayer of Dedication and Praise—Pastor

> CH 599 *Jesus Is Lord of All* (2x chorus)

Worship with Our Gifts—Pastoral Staff

Praise and Worship During Offering

> CH *Jesus, Name Above All Names* (2×)

Message—Getting Ready *to Move*

Hymn of Response/ Invitation—Worship Leader and Congregation

      CH 481 *Come, Just As You Are*

Hymn of Benediction—Congregation

      CH *Great Is the Lord*

Postlude—Instrumentalists

      Great Is the Lord

KEY:

CH: Celebration Hymnal (Word Music/Integrity Music, Nashville, TN)

NBH: New Baptist Hymnal (2008)

WH: The Hymnal (Word Music, Nashville, TN)

SPW: Songs for Praise and Worship (Word Music, Nashville, TN)

MSPW: More Songs for Praise and Worship (Word Music, Nashville, TN)

MSPW2: More Songs for Praise and Worship 2 (Word Music, Nashville, TN)

WEEK 1

Introductions

Ephesians 1:1, 2
By Dr. Kent Spann

As we begin this study of Ephesians, it is only fitting that it should begin with introductions.

1. Let me introduce you to the person who wrote the Book of Ephesians (1:1a).

   a. He is Paul the author of Ephesians.

      i. The letter claims to be written by Paul (1:1; 3:1) so the burden of proving otherwise lies with the critics who haven't proved otherwise.

      ii. The letter was widely known and accepted in the early church, and no one disputed it, not even the heretic Marcion, who ripped the New Testament to shreds.

      iii. It is written in Pauline style.

      iv. The letter closely parallels Colossians.

      v. The major themes—justification by faith, grace, atonement by Christ, the place of the Jews, and the Law—agree with Paul's uncontroverted letters.

      vi. The arguments against Pauline authorship are flimsy and based on presuppositions of the critics.

   b. He is Paul the apostle of the Lord.

   c. He is Paul the prisoner of Rome and the Lord.

      He was in prison at the time of this epistle's writing, which would date the letter between A.D. 61 and 63.

2. Let me introduce you to the place Paul wrote to in the Book of Ephesians.

   a. The City of Ephesus

      i. Most important city in the Roman province of Asia

      ii. Located on the west coast of what is now Turkey

      iii. Leading commercial city at the intersection of two major trade routes

      iv. Home to the Temple of Artemis (Diana), one of the Seven Wonders of the Ancient World

  b. The Church at Ephesus

      i. Paul came to Ephesus on his second missionary journey (Acts 18:18–21).

      ii. Paul came back there on his third missionary journey and spent three years ministering there (Acts 20:31).

      iii. He stopped at Ephesus on his way back from his third missionary journey (Acts 20:13–31).

3. Let me introduce you to the people to whom Paul wrote the Book of Ephesians (1:1b).

Who was the letter of Ephesians written to? This may surprise you, but the letter was written to you. This was a circular letter that was sent to Ephesus, but it was intended for a wider audience.

  a. We are saints.

  b. We are believers (the word *saints* can be translated "believers").

  c. We are in Christ.

4. Let me introduce you to the message that Paul wrote in the Book of Ephesians (1:2a).

There are two key themes in Paul's letter.

  a. We can know fully the grace of God, which saves us and provides us all that we need (1:2, 6; 2:5, 7, 8; 3:2, 7, 8; 4:7, 29; 6:24).

  b. We can experience peace with God, which results in peace in our hearts and with one another (1:2; 2:15, 17; 4:3; 6:15, 23).

5. Let me introduce you to the wonderful person that Paul wrote about in the Book of Ephesians (1:2b).

  a. He is God our Father (1:2, 3; 2:18; 3:14; 4:6; 5:20).

  b. He is the Lord Jesus Christ.

WEEK 1

The Greatest Prayer Ever Prayed by Anyone Not Named Jesus

Daniel 9:1–19
By Dr. Carl Barrington

Introduction

A little over 2,500 years ago, an old man was having his quiet time. He happened to read the words of Jeremiah in Jeremiah 29:10–14. In these verses, God describes how His people can go home after seventy years of exile. The seventy years are up! Daniel knows that he must immediately go to the Lord in prayer.

1. True believers understand that they are guilty.

2. God rewards those who humble themselves.

3. God keeps His promises.

Conclusion

As a reward for his humility and faithfulness, God gives Daniel a gift which covers the "seventy sevens" of prophecy. No one until the apostle John would know more of God's plans for the future.

WEEK 2

Getting Ready *to See*

Joshua 2
By David W. Hirschman

Introduction

When God desires to move a believer or group of believers or a church forward in His plan, they must *get ready to move*. You cannot go with God and stay where you are, most certainly spiritually and oftentimes physically. Every believer and church should desire to move in harmony with God and His plan for their lives, but before we can move, we must first understand the plan, the power, and the prize. In Joshua 1, Israel is preparing, or *getting ready*, to move. In Joshua 2, two spies are sent to view the Promised Land as a part of this getting-ready process; however, the land was not the only thing they saw. What they saw as they were getting ready is what we will see as we move with the Lord. They saw:

1. God Already Moving (2:1–11)

As Israel responded to God in faith and prepared to *get ready to move*, they found that God was already moving, setting things in order for the time when Israel would enter the land. As we begin to move, we will find that God does not sit idly by, leaving us on our own to work out details; rather, we will see Him already moving. Once they were in the city of Jericho, the two spies saw God already at work:

  a. Preparing: "For we have heard" (2:10). Where did Rahab and the inhabitants of Jericho hear this news? There may have been travelers who brought the news as they intersected trade routes leading to and from Jericho, or it may have been from God Himself. The important thing is that they knew, and now the spies also knew that God was preparing the way before Joshua and the children of Israel.

b. Ensuring: "Our hearts melted; neither did there remain any more courage in anyone" (2:11a). By Rahab's own confession, the spies witnessed the impact of this news upon the inhabitants of Jericho. Certainly their confidence was building as they witnessed what God was doing.

c. Convincing "For the Lord your God, He is God in heaven above and on earth beneath" (2:11b). This is what the spies knew already, but now the inhabitants of Jericho also knew!

2. Their Faith Increasing (2:12–14)

The spies entered the land ignorantly, not knowing what they would find, perhaps with anxiety or even fear remembering the experiences of their forefathers' last attempt. But with Rahab's words, they see that God has already begun to move ...

a. Their *anticipation* grows: "Since I have showed you kindness, that you also will show kindness" (2:12). Imagine what their thoughts might have been: *What is this that we are hearing? This is a strong city, with soldiers, and she is requesting kindness from us?*

b. Their *expectation* grows: "And ... spare my father, my mother, my brothers, my sisters ... and deliver our lives from death" (2:13). Imagine again the spies thought, *Now she is requesting mercy; does she* know *that they will be defeated?*

c. Their *assurance* grows: "When the Lord has given ... we will deal kindly" (2:14). They were seeing what God can do right before their eyes, and their faith increased by leaps and bounds!

3. Others' Faith Influenced (2:15–21)

The spies are witnessing God at work, and in the process, not only is their own faith increasing but others are choosing to believe and trust in the God of Israel. As we get ready to move and witness the hand of God moving before us, we will see God also moving upon the hearts of others. Rahab is clearly impacted by what is happened and has been changed.

a. Our faith in following God will reveal where He is already working.

b. Where God is working, there are others whom we can influence.

c. Some of these will choose to follow God.

Finally, the spies saw with:

4. Hearts Completely Convinced (2:22–24)

The spies finished their mission as different men, because they saw that God was already moving in front of Israel. They returned home completely convinced of God's plan, His power, and the prize that was waiting for them. "Truly the Lord has delivered all the land into our hands."

Conclusion

As we get ready to move with the Lord, following His plan, in His power, and for His prize, we can count on seeing God already moving in front of us.

SUGGESTED ORDER OF WORSHIP

We Worship Jesus ...

Prelude—Instrumentalists

All Hail the Power of Jesus' Name

As Savior and Lord ...

Call to Praise—Congregation

CH 42 *All Hail the Power of Jesus' Name*

CH *All Hail King Jesus*

Prayer of Praise—Pastoral Staff

Welcome—Pastoral Staff

Hymn of Welcome (*meet and greet during song*)—Congregation

MSPW2 *Lord, I Lift Your Name on High* (2×)

As Shelter and Refuge . . .

Praise and Worship—Congregation

> SPW 39 *In His Time* (2×)

> MSPW 22 *Crown Him King of Kings* (2×)

Worship by Hearing the Word—Pastor

> Psalm 139:1–18; 23, 24

> CH 583 *You Are My All in All* (2×)

> NBH 552 *My Jesus, I Love Thee* (vv. 1 and 4)

Prayer of Praise—Worship Leader

> CH 591 *Have Thine Own Way, Lord*

> *(keyboard play next song during prayer)*

. . . As Tower of Strength!!

Offertory Prayer—Pastor

Offertory Praise—Congregation

> SPW 74 *Isn't He*

Sermon—Pastor

> *Getting Ready—to See*

Hymn of Invitation—Congregation

> CH 481 *Come Just as You Are*

Benediction Hymn—Congregation

> CH 213/214 *We Bring the Sacrifice/He Has Made Me Glad*

Postlude—Instrumentalists

KEY:

CH: Celebration Hymnal (Word Music/Integrity Music, Nashville, TN)

NBH: New Baptist Hymnal (2008)

WH: The Hymnal (Word Music, Nashville, TN)

SPW: Songs for Praise and Worship (Word Music, Nashville, TN)

MSPW: More Songs for Praise and Worship (Word Music, Nashville, TN)

MSPW2: More Songs for Praise and Worship 2 (Word Music, Nashville, TN)

WEEK 2

One Good Blessing Deserves Another!

Ephesians 1:3
By Dr. Kent Spann

We have all heard the statement, "One good deed deserves another." In other words, one deed should set off a chain reaction of subsequent good deeds. I want to change that phrase to say, "One good *blessing* deserves another."

1. God Has Blessed Us

    a. The recipient of the blessings—*us*

    b. The source of our blessings—*God*

    c. The location of our blessings—*the heavenly realms* (1:3, 20; 2:6; 3:10)

    d. The nature of our blessings—*spiritual* (1:3–14)

        i. It means our blessings come to us through the Holy Spirit as we are filled with the Holy Spirit (Eph. 5:18; Gal. 5:22, 23).

        ii. It means our blessings are spiritual in nature (Matt. 6:19, 20).

    e. The magnitude of our blessing—*every*

    f. The sphere of our blessing—*in Christ*

2. We Should Bless God
    God has blessed us, so how can we bless God?

    a. We can *realize* the riches He has bestowed on us.

    b. We can *thank* Him for the riches He has bestowed on us.

    c. We can *praise* Him for the riches He has bestowed on us.

WEEK 2

If I Were Satan

1 Peter 5:8, 9
By Dr. Carl Barrington

Introduction

In various places throughout Scripture, Satan is described as "the prince of this world," "a lion," and "the enemy." Many people see him as a caricature of himself: a dirty old man in long, red underwear with a pitchfork and a pointed tail. If I were Satan:

1. I would deceive people into seeing me as a cartoon character.

2. I would try to convince people that I didn't exist.

3. I would try to keep God's Word away from people.

4. I would try to destroy the power of God's churches.

5. I would try to get Christians to stumble in their daily lives.

6. I would try to sell the world on a gospel other than Jesus Christ.

Conclusion

Satan tries to convince everyone that they have plenty of time to make their decision for Christ, until it's too late.

WEEK 3

The Sanctity of Life:
Life Is a Beautiful Thing

Psalm 139:1–16, especially verses 13–16
By Dr. Doug Munton

Introduction

God made us and greatly values our lives. Our lives are not an accident or a mistake but the result of God's intentional act of creation. Current culture devalues human life. People are, many proclaim, just an arrangement of molecules. Mankind is just an overconsuming animal, according to this line of reasoning. But that is not how God views human life. God created mankind and highly values each life. Every person matters to God because God created us in His image, and every person has great potential.

Let's say you're a new parent, of a bouncing baby boy. Or maybe you've just had your first grandson. You will value that child because of his inherent worth, won't you? He hasn't done anything for you yet. He can't yet say your name or help you with household chores. He doesn't even really know you yet. But he is your pride and joy nonetheless.

In much the same way, God values us for our inherent worth. It is not what we have done for Him. It isn't that we have charmed Him by our goodness or won His love by our righteousness. But God loves us because we are created by Him and in His image. He created us for fellowship with Him and to love Him. God sees mankind through the lens of their worth and their potential.

1. Life has value because God made us with purpose—God put us together (Ps. 139:13).

This passage tells us that God knitted us together in our mothers' wombs. Before we were even born, God cared for us. He created our "inward parts," this verse teaches. God crafted and formed you.

He made the inner you that no one else can see. You are a special creation of the Lord. Every detail of your body was formed by Him. The intricacies of your eye, the details of your blood system, and the marvels of your mind were all crafted by God's own hand.

Modern society has said that life in the womb is merely a choice. God sees that tiny child and sees the masterpiece which He has knit together. That child has great value to God and should have great value to us and to our society. Abortion is an affront to the very nature of God's creative work.

2. Life has value because God made us with promise—God put us together well (Ps. 139:14).

This verse tells us that we have been "remarkably and wonderfully made" (HCSB). God did not just put us together; He put us together well. We are the work of His creation, and His works are "wonderful."

This is God's promise that our lives are not accidents or mistakes. God made us, and He did so in a way that allows our lives to impact the world and eternity. No wonder the Psalmist says, "I will praise You." Our very lives are an opportunity to praise the Creator.

3. Life has value because God made us with plans—God put us together well to fulfill the plans He has for us (Ps. 139:15, 16).

Verse 16 says, "All [my] days were written in Your book and planned before a single one of them began" (HCSB). Before you were born, God planned for your life. He knew everything that you could be and all that you would be. He knew the length of your days and the strength of those days. Your life is not an accident, but a part of God's plan for this world. Your life has been given to you as a great opportunity. You can be part of the plans God has to impact the world and to impact eternity. God has plans for you.

Conclusion

This little boy didn't seem to matter much in the eyes of the world. Born a slave, he was soon orphaned, as well, then traded for an animal—a child for a horse. Growing up, he moved from one foster family to another. As he moved from place to place, he often witnessed horrible things, for example, people—people like *him*—being beaten to death. As a youth, many would have considered his life to be of little worth and no special value. But his life *did* matter. The boy I described was George Washington Carver, famous inventor and scientist. We are still reaping the benefits of his work today. His worth is incalculable.

Modern society has lost touch with the value of life. The lives of others have become insignificant to the eyes of much of our world. But God sees life differently. God sees our intrinsic value and our eternal potential. God values human life more than I cherish my own grandchild or father.

Your life matters to God. God has given you this great gift of life. He has prepared for you and planned for you. Don't miss the great adventure God has in store for your life if you will follow His perfect plan.

SUGGESTED ORDER OF WORSHIP

Theme: I Choose Life

Prelude—Instrumental

Shine, Jesus Shine

Call to Worship—Pastor

Deuteronomy 30:15–20

"See, I have set before you today life and good, death and evil, in that I command you today to love the Lord your God, to walk in His ways, and to keep His commandments, His statutes, and His judgments, that you may live and multiply; and the Lord your God will bless you in the land which you go to possess. But if your heart turns away so that you do not hear, and are drawn away, and worship other gods and serve them, I announce to you today that you shall surely perish; you shall not prolong your days in the land which you cross over the Jordan to go in and possess. I call heaven and earth as witnesses today against you, that I have set before you life and death, blessing and cursing; therefore choose life, that both you and your descendants may live; that you may love the Lord your God, that you may obey His voice, and that you may cling to Him, for He is your life and the length of your days; and that you may dwell in the land which the Lord swore to your fathers, to Abraham, Isaac, and Jacob, to give them."

Call to Praise—Congregation, Choir, and Orchestra

> CH 42/43 *All Hail the Power* (vv. 1, 3)

Prayer of Praise—Pastoral Staff

Welcome—Pastoral Staff

Hymn of Welcome—Congregation

> CH 5 *I Sing Praises*

Praise and Worship—Congregation

> *How Majestic Is His Name* (from *Bless His Name Medley*)
>
> *Blessed Be the Name* (from *Bless His Name Medley*)
>
> *In the Name of the Lord* (from *Bless His Name Medley*)
>
> *Lord, I Lift Your Name on High* (from *Bless His Name Medley*)
>
> *Bless the Lord, O My Soul* (from *Bless His Name Medley*)

Prayer of Praise—Pastoral Staff

Prayer Response—Congregation

> CH 638 *I Need Thee Ev'ry Hour*

Offertory Prayer—Pastor

Offertory Praise—Praise Team

> *God's Own Lamb*

Video

> *Bella–Thought About Adoption* from WingClips.com (http://www.wingclips.com/cart.php?target= product&product_id=16704&substring=Abortion)

Sermon—Choose Life

Hymn of Invitation—Congregation

    CH 481 *Come Just as You Are*

Benediction Hymn—Congregation

    CH 5 *I Sing Praises*

Postlude

    CH 5 *I Sing Praises*

KEY:

CH: Celebration Hymnal (Word Music/Integrity Music, Nashville, TN)

NBH: New Baptist Hymnal (2008)

WH: The Hymnal (Word Music, Nashville, TN)

SPW: Songs for Praise and Worship (Word Music, Nashville, TN)

MSPW: More Songs for Praise and Worship (Word Music, Nashville, TN)

MSPW2: More Songs for Praise and Worship 2 (Word Music, Nashville, TN)

WEEK 3

No Chance

Ephesians 1:4–6
By Dr. Kent Spann

Evolution tells us that we are the product of chance. That is not what the Bible says about us especially concerning our salvation.

1. We were chosen by God in His sovereignty ("He,"1:4).

   a. Our salvation is not the result of random chance but the divine intention and work of God to bring us to salvation (Eph. 2:1–10).

   b. Our salvation was initiated by God.

   c. Our salvation was secured by God.

2. We were chosen by God in love through Christ (1:4, 5).

   a. God chose us in love (1:4).

   b. God chose us in Christ Jesus (1:4, 5).

   c. God chose us in accordance with His will (1:5).

3. We were chosen by God before the foundation of the world (1:4).

   a. Our salvation is not God's last-minute reaction to the sin problem.

   b. Our salvation is not by coincidence or random selection; it was made by God before the foundation of the world.

4. We were chosen by God for a purpose (1:4–6).

   a. God chose us to be holy and blameless (1:4).

   b. God chose us to be sons by adoption (1:5).

   c. God chose us to bring glory to Him (1:6).

WEEK 3

An Attitude of Gratitude

Romans 8:28 and Philippians 4:6, 7
By Dr. Carl Barrington

Introduction

When you study about thanksgiving and gratitude, the first thing you notice is the overwhelming presence in Scripture of verses that remind us that God is in control of our lives.

1. All things that happen to us are not perceived as good, but God can bring about good.

2. I am God's property, and He can do whatever He likes with His own property.

3. Thanksgiving and gratitude have nothing to do with the circumstances of our lives.

4. We can even be thankful for suffering, because suffering is redemptive and helps us appreciate Christ more.

Conclusion

We should have an attitude of gratitude, *not* because we have more stuff, more variety, and an easier life than almost everyone who has ever lived, but because God deserves it.

WEEK 4

Getting Ready *to Experience*

Joshua 3
By David W. Hirschman

Introduction

God can do anything, anytime, anywhere, and in any way, and Joshua and the children of Israel are discovering this firsthand. Consider, if you will, that there is not one thing that God cannot do for His children. Jesus said that "with God nothing is impossible" (Luke 1:37), and "He who did not spare His own Son, but delivered Him up for us all, how shall He not with Him also freely give us all things?" (Rom. 8:32). However, in getting ready to move, and see God at work, there is a preparation work that must take place in the life of the child of God. To experience God at work in our lives and in our ministries, to be a part of what He is doing, is something we should all desire, but also something we must actively pursue. Joshua is an example of one who was willing to get ready to experience what God wanted to do in his life and those around him. Notice the activities/characteristics of his life.

1. He gave himself completely to God's plan: "Then Joshua rose early in the morning" (3:1).

   Joshua was a man who was:

   a. Committed to Giving More Than *Just Enough*

      Notice his commitment to Moses as Moses ascended Mount Sinai to meet with God (Ex. 24:12; 32:15–17; 33:11). As Moses was meeting with God for that extended amount of time, Joshua remained on the mount, waiting for Moses. How was he spending his time? It may have been tempting to return to the camp of Israel, but he remained. Was he praying? Was he seeking the face of God? The Bible does not tell us, but it does reveal that he had a spiritual focus that kept him in close proximity to Moses, rather than returning to the camp.

b. Committed to *Long-term Trust*

Notice how Joshua and Caleb had to wait for forty years to arrive at the point of entering the Promised Land. Certainly it was difficult knowing that they could have taken possession of the land many years before, but instead they had to patiently wait for God's time. Many believers today are impatient and find it difficult to wait on God for forty minutes, much less than forty years.

c. Committed to *Believing for Fulfillment*

Joshua was ready to respond to God's instruction. He did not wait but responded quickly. Why? Perhaps because God's instruction came as no surprise to him. He had given himself completely to God's plan and lived his life anticipating what he believed God had promised to do.

2. He faced his obstacles confidently: "And came to the Jordan" (3:1).

The Jordan River stood between Israel and the Promised Land. It was an obstacle that hindered their advance toward God's plan, yet we see nothing but confidence in Joshua. As we pursue God's plan for our lives, we will encounter obstacles; however, we can and must face these obstacles confidently. Notice some important things about obstacles.

a. Confidence knows there are no unknown obstacles with God.

Joshua and the children of Israel are following God's plan, not their own. God knew where the Jordan was; He knew the time of the year as well. He knew that Israel had to cross the Jordan to enter the land, and He already had the solution to the obstacle!

b. Following God's plan requires that we face our obstacles with confidence.

God can and desires to defeat those things that stand in our way, but He cannot defeat things that we do not face. Frequently, when encountering obstacles, believers try to work out some solution, or alternative. Sadly, some believers interpret obstacles as an indication that they made a mistake somewhere along the process. The Jordan River was no mistake in God's plan, rather an opportunity to see God do what He is so capable of doing, demonstrating that His power is bigger than the obstacle!

c. Confidence in facing obstacles demonstrates our trust.

Remember, there is nothing He does not know, and as He directs us, He will also provide for us, even when huge obstacles stand in the way. God always has the solution!

3. Joshua waited for clear direction: "So it was, after three days" (3:2).

Have you ever wondered what Joshua was doing during the three days of waiting? Again, the Bible does not tell us specifics, but we can draw some reliable conclusions. Remember, Joshua was a man who was wholly committed to God's plan and had waited patiently for forty years to see God fulfill His promise. Therefore, we can conclude that Joshua spent his time:

a. Doing what he was *accustomed* to (praying, trusting).

b. Following what he was instructed (Josh.1:8, 9).

c. Expecting what he knew *God would give* (Why else would God have brought him to this point?).

4. Joshua responded with confidence (3:3–14).

At the right time God gave clear direction, and when Joshua knew what God wanted to do, he also knew what he and the children of Israel had to do—respond with confidence! As a result, Israel began the first step in claiming what God had promise to give!

Conclusion

God wants us to experience what He can do in our lives as we follow His plan for us, but we must give ourselves completely to His plan, be willing to face our obstacles, be willing to wait, and be ready to respond.

SUGGESTED ORDER OF WORSHIP

How Can I Find God's Will for Me?
By Dr. Melvin Worthington

Prelude—Instrumentalist

> CH 213/214 *We Bring the Sacrifice/He Has Made Me Glad*

Prayer of Worship—Worship Pastor

Worship and Praise—Congregation

> MSPW 2 *Holy Spirit Rain Down*

Baptismal Celebration—Pastoral Staff

Prayer—Pastoral Prayer

Welcome—Pastoral Staff

Hymn of Welcome *(meet and greet)*—Congregation

> CH 213 *We Bring the Sacrifice*

Worship and Praise—Congregation

> CH 36 *He Is Exalted* (F)
>
> CH 47 *Jesus, Lord to Me* (F/G)
>
> CH 34 *He Is Lord* (G/Ab)

Scripture Reading from Proverbs 3:1–9

Worship Leader:

1 My son, do not forget my law, but let your heart keep my commands;

Congregation:

2 For length of days and long life and peace they will add to you.

Worship Leader:

3 Let not mercy and truth forsake you; bind them around your neck, write them on the tablet of your heart,

Congregation

4 And so find favor and high esteem in the sight of God and man.

Worship Leader:

5 Trust in the Lord with all your heart, and lean not on your own understanding;

Congregation:

6 In all your ways acknowledge Him, and He shall direct your paths.

Worship Leader:

7 Do not be wise in your own eyes; Fear the Lord and depart from evil.

Congregation:

8 It will be health to your flesh, And strength to your bones.

Worship Leader:

9 Honor the Lord with your possessions, and with the firstfruits of all your increase; 10 So your barns will be filled with plenty! May the Lord add His blessings to the reading of His Word. Amen.

Hymn of Surrender and Worship—Congregation

    CH *Take My Life and Let It Be*

Sermon—Pastor

    Wise Up

Hymn of Response/Invitation

    CH *In My Life, Be Glorified* (3 verses)

Hymn of Benediction—Congregation

    CH 36 *He Is Exalted*

Postlude—Instrumental

KEY:

CH: Celebration Hymnal (Word Music/Integrity Music, Nashville, TN)

NBH: New Baptist Hymnal (2008)

WH: The Hymnal (Word Music, Nashville, TN)

SPW: Songs for Praise and Worship (Word Music, Nashville, TN)

MSPW: More Songs for Praise and Worship (Word Music, Nashville, TN)

MSPW2: More Songs for Praise and Worship 2 (Word Music, Nashville, TN)

WEEK 4

Redeemed

Ephesians 1:7–10
By Dr. Kent Spann

August 25, 1944, was a great day in the life of France. The Allies marched into Paris after fierce fighting and heavy loss of life as the liberator of France. There were celebrations everywhere.

If the people of France had cause for celebration when the Allies marched into Paris, how much more do we as Christians because two thousand years ago Jesus Christ marched into human history and liberated His people? We believers have the greatest cause for celebration. In fact, Paul is leading the celebration of redemption in the letter to the Ephesians. Let's join the celebration.

1. We can praise God for the work of redemption (1:7).

    The word *redemption* is a powerful word. It means "the act of delivering from slavery by making a ransom payment." During the New Testament times the Roman Empire had as many as 6 million slaves. A slave's only hope was redemption.

    All humans are slaves—slaves to sin (Ezek. 18:4; John 8:34; Rom. 6:23; 7:14). We need a redeemer.

    a. We have a redeemer who is *willing* to redeem us (Rom. 3:24; Gal. 3:13; Titus 2:14).

    b. We have a redeemer who is *able* to redeem us (Heb. 9:1–28).

2. We can praise God for the blessings of redemption (1:7, 8).

    a. We have been liberated from the slavery of sin (1:7).

    b. We have been forgiven (1:7).

    c. We have been lavished with the riches of His grace (1:7).

    d. We have been given spiritual discernment (1:8).

3. We can praise God for the consummation of redemption (1:9, 10; Rom. 8:22–25).

WEEK 4

Let the Church Be the Church

1 Peter 2:1–10
By Dr. Carl Barrington

Introduction

There is no greater truth in the Old Testament than the fact that Israel was God's people; chosen to carry His message to the world. They failed repeatedly, however, and God now works through spiritual Israel, the church, to spread His good news.

1. God loves His church.

2. God has redeemed His church from spiritual bondage.

3. God has established His new covenant with His church.

4. God has declared His church to be His new people.

Conclusion

There is a great need for the church to recover its identity as the people of God. The price to pay for being the authentic church is tension: understanding that we have double citizenship, both in this world and in heaven.

WEEK 5

Getting Ready *to Speak*

Joshua 4
By David W. Hirschman

Introduction

In Joshua 3, Israel experienced God's power as they crossed over the Jordan River into the Promised Land. By getting ready to move with, see, and experience, Joshua and the children of Israel witnessed God fulfill His promise to bring them into the land, but before they finish crossing, God makes an important point; He instructs them to leave something behind.

How important is it that we leave something behind us; something that speaks to the faithfulness and power of God; something that speaks of our faith in believing God, facing our obstacles, and our trust in Him? What purpose does leaving something behind us serve? As we journey with God, He can prove Himself in and through us, and we will emerge more convinced and confident. But what impact will it have on others?

In crossing the Jordan River, God instructs Joshua to have the children of Israel leave something behind, a memorial of sorts that could speak to the generations to follow. It would be a noticeable reminder of what God did for Israel when they entered the Promised Land. It doesn't need to be fancy; in this case it was a pile of rocks, but it was enough to be something that could *speak*.

What we leave behind can speak for us. It can speak to those who will follow after us, and give testimony of what was at work in us as people, families, and as a church as we readied ourselves to move with, see, and experience God. In verse 2 God instructs Joshua, "Take for yourselves twelve men from the people, one man from every tribe, and command them, saying, 'Take for yourselves twelve stones from here, out of the midst of the Jordan, from the place where the priests' feet stood firm. You shall carry them over with you and leave them in the lodging place where you lodge tonight.'" This memorial of twelve stones spoke not only of God's power to divide the river so Israel could pass, but also of:

1. Their Faith and What They Did

What did the children of Israel really do? They crossed the river—the entire nation, with all of their belongings. They entered the Promised Land and embraced what God wanted them to have. All of this is true, but is it all they did? More than these things ...

a. They had believed God.

Following the death of their leader (Moses), God picked up (Josh. 1:2–4) where He had left off forty years previously. He had refused to cancel what He had promised to do, even though the promise had been on hold for such a long time.

b. They had disbelieved fact (Josh. 3:15).

The Jordan River was swollen with the runoff of the seasonal rains, and what would have been challenging to cross at other seasons of the year, now was impossible for one million-plus people to cross. However, this is where God had brought them, and His promise lay on the other side. Even though all the facts said it could not be done, Joshua and the children of Israel disbelieved the facts!

c. They had witnessed supernatural truth (Josh. 3:17).

By getting ready to move and see God at work, they experienced the truth that God's plan with God's power gives God's prize!

2. Their Desire and Why They Did It

The twelve stones also spoke of Israel's desire:

a. To *have* what God had promised, through forty years of death and waiting.

The generation that followed those who died in the wilderness embraced a promise that they had only heard secondhand, and even though surrounded by a continual reminder of disobedience, they determined to be obedient and obtain what God wanted them to have.

b. To *fulfill* what God had promised.

Although true in regard to Israel as a whole, this is seen most clearly in the life of Caleb, who refused to forget a promise, but waited to see that promise accomplished (Josh. 14:8–12a).

c. To *complete* and *begin* what God had promised.

God's plan was for Israel to possess the land, not simply enter into it. But the process of possessing began with entering.

3. Their Approach and the Way They Did It

The twelve stones spoke of Israel's obedience and confidence. Their approach to entering the land to obtain God's promise required ...

a. *Obedience*—an obedience to follow Joshua after Moses' death; an obedience to respond to Joshua as he spoke of God's direction, and an obedience to face obstacles that stood in the way of their possession

b. *Confidence* that the God who had directed them to this point, supplied food every day, and had not permitted their clothes or shoes to wear out (Deut. 8:4) was also in this and that He would remove the obstacle

4. Their God and How He Did It (4:22–24)

Supernaturally, by His power, not their own!

Conclusion

We can leave things behind us that can speak for us in the years ahead. What we leave behind should speak of our faith—of how we believe(d) God and of our desire to have, fulfill, and complete God's perfect will for our lives and our ministries. It must speak of our approach—of how we obediently and confidently followed God. And it must speak of our God, who accomplished and accomplishes great things for us! What are you leaving behind? What will you leave behind that will speak for you?

SUGGESTED ORDER OF WORSHIP

The Joy of Giving

Prelude—Instrumentalist

Shine, Jesus, Shine

Call to Worship—Reading Team

Reader's Group

All Readers: Stand up!

Reader One: And praise the Lord your God!

Reader Two: Who is from everlasting to everlasting!

All Readers: Blessed be your glorious name!

Reader Three: And may it be exalted above all blessing and praise.

All Readers: You alone are the Lord!

Reader One: You made the heaven!

Reader Two: Even the highest heavens!

Reader Three: And all their starry hosts!

Reader Four: The earth and all that is on it!

Reader Two: The seas and all that is in them.

Reader Three: You give life to everything,

Reader One: And the multitudes of heaven worship you.

All Readers: Stand up

Reader One: And praise the Lord your God!

All Readers: Blessed be your glorious name!

Reader Three: And may it be exalted above all blessing and praise.

All Readers: You alone are the Lord!

All Readers (Soft): Amen!

All Readers (Loud): Amen!

All Readers (Louder): Amen!

All Readers (Very Loud!): Amen, Praise the Lord! Hallelujah!

From Nehemiah 9:5b, 6

Praise Hymn—Congregation

Majesty (1×) / *Come, Thou Almighty King* (2 verses) / *Majesty* (1×)

Welcome—Pastoral Staff

Welcome Song (*optional—meet and greet during song*)

Shine, Jesus, Shine (2×)

Prayer of Praise—Pastoral Staff

Praise and Worship—Congregation

God Is So Good (3×)

Give Thanks (2×)

Find Us Faithful (2×)

Offertory Prayer—Pastor

Offertory Praise

CH *Great Is Thy Faithfulness* (vv. 1, 2, chorus, v. 3, chorus)

Morning Message—Pastor

The Joy of Giving

Hymn of Response/Invitation—Worship Leader and Congregation

CH *Have Thine Own Way, Lord*

Hymn of Benediction—Congregation

CH *I Love You, Lord*

Postlude—Instrumentalists

Joy Unspeakable and Full of Glory

KEY:

CH: Celebration Hymnal (Word Music/Integrity Music, Nashville, TN)

WEEK 5

A Glorious Inheritance

Ephesians 1:11–14
By Dr. Kent Spann

Imagine for a moment that you received a letter in the mail telling you that you were an heir to a fortune. What would you do? Probably wouldn't believe it, would you? There is a letter written to you that tells of a great inheritance you have.

1. We are heirs of a glorious inheritance (1:11, 12).

The word *chosen* (NIV) can also mean "to obtain an inheritance." Our inheritance is all the promises of God's Word.

   a. This glorious inheritance is reserved for us in Christ ("in Him," 1:11).

   b. This glorious inheritance was planned for us by God ("predestined," 1:11).

   c. This glorious inheritance was for God's glory (1:12).

"I do not go to heaven to be advanced, but to give honor to God. It is no matter where I shall be stationed in heaven, whether I have a high or low seat there, but to live and please and glorify God ... My heaven is to please God and glorify Him, and give all to Him, and to be wholly devoted to His glory."

—David Brainerd

---

2. We are heirs of a guaranteed inheritance (1:13, 14).

   a. The Holy Spirit is God's seal that we are heirs (1:13).

   b. The Holy Spirit is God's guarantee that we will receive the full inheritance (1:14).

WEEK 5

But There Is a God in Heaven

Daniel 2:26–28a
By Dr. Carl Barrington

Introduction

Daniel had a chance to interpret Nebuchadnezzar's dream and claim all the credit for himself. The Babylonian king was ready to give Daniel anything he wanted if he could both interpret his dream and tell him its meaning. Daniel, however, knew that only God could do what the king asked, and gave Him all the credit. Daniel wasn't the only one who learned that there is a God in heaven.

- Moses learned it at the Red Sea.
- Daniel learned it again in the lions' den.
- Peter learned it when he miraculously escaped from prison.
- We truly learn it when we reach the end of our rope and find that He is indeed there.

Conclusion

Only when Christ is all we have do we learn that He is all we need.

WEEK 6

Getting Ready *to Renew*

Joshua 5
By David W. Hirschman

Introduction

Great things are happening for Israel! Joshua and the children of Israel have gotten ready to move, and have moved; they knew the plan, the power, and the prize. They have gotten ready to see and have seen:

- God already moving
- their personal faith increasing
- others' faith influenced
- their own hearts completely convinced

They have gotten ready to experience and have experienced Joshua's principles of:

- giving himself completely to God's plan
- being willing to face the obstacles
- waiting for clear direction
- responding to that direction with confidence

Through that process, they were prepared to speak, and have spoken by leaving something behind that spoke of their faith, desire, approach, and their God. Now they are poised to triumph, but first, they must get ready to renew.

1. Their Renewed Embrace of God's Program (5:2–10)

    a. On Hold

        God's plan for Israel had been on hold because of disobedience and unbelief. Because of the previous generation's failure to trust God and follow Him at Kadesh Barnea, they forfeited entry into the Promised Land and its possession according to God's plan. With that forfeiture, much of Israel's external observances had been on hold as well. Circumcision (v. 5) and Passover (v. 10; cp. Num. 9:1–5) appear to have faded from the national observance (no reference since the rebellion of Numbers 13). Israel had been waiting for the remaining members of the previous generation to pass from the scene.

b. Restarted

Beginning with the death of Moses, God's plan has been resumed, because God intends to finish what He started. With this restarted plan, God once again focuses on the practices that have meaning to a people intent on following Him; and Israel's willingness to move, see, experience, and speak demonstrate their commitment to obedience and faith in their relationship with God.

2. Their Renewed Understanding upon God's Provision (5:11, 12)

God provides what is needed. Once in the Promised Land, the manna stopped, but for this generation, manna was all that they had ever known. It had always been there, a part of God's faithful provision, but now it was gone. However, with their entrance into the land, they discover God's continued provision, "the produce of the land," and they discover that in the same way that God had provided before their entrance, He would provide for them still. This applies in a greater way as well, for God's plan for Israel is to possess all of the land. Soon they will face many unknowns, including Jericho and other obstacles in their way. They will have to trust God's provision.

3. Their Renewed Respect of God's Person (5:13–15)

a. God is holy.

With the restart of God's program for Israel, there had to be a renewed respect for the person of God. Through their lack of faith and willful disobedience, the previous generation demonstrated a disregard for the holiness of God, for which they forfeited entrance into the Promised Land. Before going any farther, Israel had to renew their understanding of God's holiness.

b. God requires holiness.

Israel occupied a unique place among the nations because of their relationship with God: "You shall be to Me a kingdom of priests and a holy nation" (Ex. 19:6), and "For you are a holy people to the Lord your God; the Lord your God has chosen you to be a people for Himself, a special treasure above all the peoples on the face of the earth" (Deut. 7:6). Now that they were where God wanted them to be, they needed to be what He wanted them to because of their relationship to Him.

Conclusion

There are times in our lives that, like Israel, we find that we have been disobedient and unfaithful to God, or simply out of step with what He desires for us. When these times occur, it is time to renew some important commitments and understandings. First, we need to renew our embrace of God's plan for our lives. He is committed to completing what He starts in the lives of His children. Second, we need to renew our understanding of God's ability to provide the things we need; He has promised to meet our needs. And third, we need to renew our respect and submission to His holiness. We can go only so far in His plan without our renewed respect for this essential element of the nature of God. As we do these things, we will find ourselves, like Israel, where God has wanted us all along.

SUGGESTED ORDER OF WORSHIP

Prelude—Instrumentalist

Great Is the Lord

Call to Praise—Congregation

NBH 581 *We Bring the Sacrifice of Praise* (2x in D)

NBH 585 *Count Your Blessings* (v. 1, chorus, v. 3, chorus, chorus)

Worship in Prayer—Pastoral Staff

Welcome—Pastoral Staff

Welcome Song *(meet and greet during song)*—Pastoral Staff

> SPW 100 *Bless the Name of Jesus*—Congregation

Praise and Worship—Congregation

> NBH 133 *Shout to the Lord* (2×)

> NBH 447 *It Is Well with My Soul* (chorus in Bb, last verse, chorus in C)

Prayer of Dedication and Praise—Pastor

> NBH 450 *Precious Lord, Take My Hand* (v. 1 in G)

Worship with Our Gifts—Pastoral Staff

Praise and Worship During Offering

> NBH 448 *Before the Throne of God Above* (v. 1, chorus, v. 2, chorus in D)

Message—Pastor

Hymn of Response/Invitation—Worship Leader and Congregation

> CH 481 *Come, Just As You Are*

Hymn of Benediction—Congregation

> CH *Great Is the Lord*

Postlude—Instrumentalists

> *Great Is the Lord*

KEY:

CH: Celebration Hymnal (Word Music/Integrity Music, Nashville, TN)

NBH: New Baptist Hymnal (2008)

WH: The Hymnal (Word Music, Nashville, TN)

SPW: Songs for Praise and Worship (Word Music, Nashville, TN)

MSPW: More Songs for Praise and Worship (Word Music, Nashville, TN)

MSPW2: More Songs for Praise and Worship 2 (Word Music, Nashville, TN)

WEEK 6

For Your Eyes Only

Ephesians 1:15–23
By Dr. Kent Spann

Paul prays for those who are true believers evidenced by faith in Jesus and a love for the saints (1:15).

1. Paul prays that we will grow in our knowledge of God (1:17).

   Paul wants us to know Him intimately.

   a. Those who know God have great energy for God (Dan. 11:32).

   b. Those who know God have great thoughts of God (Job 38–41; 42:1–6).

   c. Those who know God show great boldness for God (Dan. 3).

   d. Those who know God have great contentment in God (Phil. 4:10–20).

   (The previous four points come from *Knowing God* by J. I. Packer.)

2. Paul prays that we will know the hope of our calling (1:18).

   a. It is the hope of salvation (2 Thess. 2:13, 14).

   b. It is the hope of heaven (1 Peter 1:3–5).

   c. It is the hope of Christ's return (Titus 2:13).

   d. It is the hope of the resurrection (1 Thess. 4:13–17).

   e. It is the hope of future glorification (1 John 2:28—3:3).

3. Paul prays that we will know the riches of God's inheritance (1:18).

   a. It is God's inheritance in us.

   b. It is our inheritance in God.

4. Paul prays that we will know God's awesome power for our lives (1:19–23).

   a. It is an inherent power ("power," 1:19).

b. It is an energizing power ("working," 1:19).

c. It is a conquering power ("mighty," 1:19).

d. It is an enabling power ("strength," 1:19 NIV).

e. It is a resurrection power (1:20).

f. It is an exalting power (1:21).

g. It is a subjugating power (1:22, 23).

WEEK 6

The Top 10 Prayers of All Time

Selected Scripture
By Dr. Carl Barrington

10. 1 Samuel 3:10—"Speak, for your servant hears."

9. Psalm 95:1–7—possibly the most outstanding praise and worship psalm

8. Matthew 8:8—the centurion's prayer of faith

7. Isaiah 6:8—Isaiah's prayer of simple obedience

6. Ephesians 1:15–23—Paul's prayer for the Ephesians

5. John 17:20–23—Jesus' prayer for unity

4. 2 Chronicles 20:12—King Jehoshaphat's prayer of desperation

3. Matthew 26:39—Jesus' prayer of surrender

2. Daniel 9:4–19—Daniel's prayer of confession to God

1. Matthew 6:9–13—The Lord's Prayer

Honorable Mention—the prayer of any sinner when he asks God to save him

WEEK 7

Getting Ready *to Triumph*

Joshua 6

By David W. Hirschman

Introduction

Great things are happening for Israel. Why? Because they were willing to get ready! In getting ready, they have crossed the Jordan in supernatural fashion, and begun to possess the Promised Land, but they are not finished. God is about to teach them additional important principles as they prepare to face their enemies. Following God's plan, agreeing with Him, and living as He intended, do not exempt us from trouble and opposition, but as we follow the Lord's instructions, He sets us up to triumph. Israel will learn this firsthand, and God is going to ensure Israel's triumph over Jericho, but it will not be as Israel expects. Notice what He does and how He does it and how Israel must get ready to triumph.

1. He selects His own way.

Romans 11:33 states, "Oh, the depth of the riches both of the wisdom and knowledge of God! How unsearchable are His judgments and His ways past finding out!" Israel will learn that in understanding God's plan, power, and prize, He frequently will accomplish what He wants to do by unexpected means. Simply put, He selects His own way.

a. At times, His ways go against logic (6:1, 2).

Jericho was an established and functioning city with an organized army. Notice God's description, "the mighty men of valor." Logic states that to fight an army, you need an army, yet God is not obligated to use logic.

b. Many times, His ways go against reason (6:3–5).

Notice God's instruction:

You shall march around the city ... This you shall do six days ... But the seventh day you shall march around the city seven times, and the priests shall blow the trumpets. It shall come to pass, when they make a long blast with the ram's horn, and when you hear the sound of the trumpet, that all the people shall shout with a great shout; then the wall of the city will fall down flat.

c. Oftentimes, His ways go against common sense.

On the surface, this appears to be an impossible situation, but God's ways don't have to make common sense. Israel will learn an important lesson: that in accomplishing His plan, God selects His own way.

2. He states His own outcome (6:5).

With the selection of His own way, God also determines His own results. It is interesting to note, that with God:

a. His outcome is already in view: "And the LORD said to Joshua: 'See! I have given Jericho into your hand'" (6:2).

God saw the triumph as already accomplished. What remained was for Israel to continue to believe, trust, and obey God. This is where it is vital to understand that God's ways do not always match with logic, reason, or common sense, but also with His ways, the outcome is already in view!

b. His outcome is not by chance: "The wall of the city *will* fall down flat" (6:5).

God had not only determined what would happen, but also how the event would turn out. This was not a *maybe* or a *hope-so* outcome, but an outcome of which God was certain. All Israel had to do was follow God's instruction.

3. He sets His own criteria: "*All* the people shall shout" (6:5).

A part of the triumph process is understanding that along with selecting His own way and stating His own outcome, God also sets His own criteria, specifically, who He wants to participate. As Israel pursues possessing the land, God will change the criteria, but for the triumph over Jericho, He wanted to use everyone.

a. God wanted everyone to participate, with the armed men first, then the priests, and then all of the people.

b. God wanted everyone to contribute, to take part in the action. Imagine conversations years later: "Remember when we marched around Jericho?"

c. And God wanted everyone to benefit by seeing what He did, and how He did it!

This is what God wants for you!

4. He provides for a total triumph (6:20, 21).

Israel continued to give themselves completely to God's plan by following His instructions and cooperating with Him in approaching Jericho in the way He prescribed. As a result, they triumphed, opening the way into the Promised Land in anticipation of continued victories.

Conclusion

God desires that His children triumph (experience victory) in their lives, overcoming obstacles that stand in the way of accomplishing His plan for their lives. As we pursue God's plan, we need to understand that He selects His way for us that will frequently go against normal thinking. He will also determine a particular outcome and criteria that oftentimes challenge us in our willingness to cooperate with Him, but it is always for a complete victory. When we cooperate with God, He will cause us to triumph.

SUGGESTED ORDER OF WORSHIP

Theme: We Worship Jesus . . .

Prelude—Instrumentalists

All Hail the Power of Jesus' Name

His Power . . .

Call to Praise—Congregation

NBH 314 *All Hail the Power of Jesus' Name* (v. 1, v. 2 in F)

NBH 295 *All Hail King Jesus* (2x in F)

NBH 314 *All Hail the Power of Jesus' Name* (v. 4 in G)

Prayer of Praise—Pastoral Staff

Welcome—Pastoral Staff

Hymn of Welcome (*meet and greet during song*)— Congregation

MSPW2 *Lord, I Lift Your Name on High* (2x in D)

His Presence ...

Praise and Worship—Congregation

NBH 142 *Worthy, You Are Worthy* (vv. 1 and 2 in Eb, v. 3 in F)

NBH 143 *You Are My All in All* (v. 1, chorus, v. 2, chorus in F)

Worship by Hearing the Word—Pastor, Psalm 145

NBH 130 *Here I Am to Worship* (chorus, v. 1, chorus, v. 2, chorus)

Prayer of Praise—Worship Leader (*keyboard play next song during prayer*)

NBH 552 *My Jesus I Love Thee* (v. 1, v. 4)

... His Person!!

Offertory Prayer—Pastor

Offertory Praise—Congregation

SPW 74 *Isn't He*

Sermon—Pastor

Hymn of Invitation—Congregation

CH 481 *Come Just as You Are*

Benediction Hymn—Congregation

CH 213/214 *We Bring the Sacrifice/He Has Made Me Glad*

Postlude—Instrumentalists

KEY:

CH: Celebration Hymnal (Word Music/Integrity Music, Nashville, TN)

NBH: New Baptist Hymnal (2008)

WH: The Hymnal (Word Music, Nashville, TN)

SPW: Songs for Praise and Worship (Word Music, Nashville, TN)

MSPW: More Songs for Praise and Worship (Word Music, Nashville, TN)

MSPW2: More Songs for Praise and Worship 2 (Word Music, Nashville, TN)

WEEK 7

God's Amazing Grace

Ephesians 2:1–9
By Dr. Kent Spann

John Newton was born in 1725. His father was an infidel, but his mother was a godly woman. When she died, he joined his father's ship to begin the life of a seaman. His early years were spent in rebellion and debauchery and sensuality. He was sold into slavery, living on the crumbs from his master. He escaped and later became a sea captain of several ships and eventually his own slave ship. He was engaged in the capturing, selling, and transporting of black slaves to the plantations of West Indies and America. It was a cruel life.

Newton was converted in 1748 and went on to preach the gospel. When he reflected on what he was and what had happened at conversion, he penned the words to the hymn "Amazing Grace." He never got over God's amazing grace, and neither should we.

1. God's grace is amazing when we remember what we were before we were saved (2:1–3).

    a. We were dead (2:1).

    b. We were disobedient (2:2).

        i. We followed the ways of the world.

        ii. We followed the ways of the devil.

    c. We were depraved ("sinful nature," 2:3a NIV).

    d. We were doomed ("objects of wrath," 2:3b NIV).

2. God's grace is amazing when we remember what God did for us when we were saved (2:4–6).

    a. He loved us and had mercy on us (2:4).

    b. He made us alive with Christ (2:5).

    c. He seated us in the heavenlies in Christ Jesus (2:6).

3. God's grace is amazing when we remember how we were saved (2:7–9).

   a. We were saved by grace (2:8, 9).

   b. We received this gift by faith (2:8–10).

WEEK 7

The Gospel in a Nutshell

Selected Scripture
By Dr. Carl Barrington

Introduction

I love to find those places in the New Testament where the essence of the gospel is summarized in just one or two verses. They are often near the beginning of letters, and it is amazing how much spiritual truth can be found in just a few words.

- Hebrews 1:2, 3: After Jesus finished His work, He sat down.
- Colossians 1:19, 20: His finished work made peace between us and God.
- Revelation 1:5: His finished work proves that He is the King of kings.
- Revelation 5:9–10: His blood redeemed us, or bought us back to our original owner: God.

Conclusion

The essence of the gospel is that without the blood of Christ, there is no possibility of reconciliation with God.

WEEK 8

Getting Ready *to Fail*

Joshua 7–8
By David W. Hirschman

Introduction

When we follow God's ways, we can prepare to receive God's results and triumph as we embrace and pursue His plan. However, Joshua and the children of Israel are about to learn a tragic lesson, that past victories are no guarantee of continued success. Following God's plan requires following it completely. The defeat at Ai involved two miscalculations: the first in Joshua's failure to seek God's direction for the second battle, and the second, in Achan's violation of God's instruction for the battle of Jericho. When we do not follow God's directions/instructions, we get ready to fail. For continued victory in life, we must:

1. Avoid self-confidence—only God knows the right way (7:1–3).

   Joshua reused a tactic that God had instructed him to use previously, perhaps thinking that this was God's accepted way of preparing for battle. Perhaps he was confident having seen this approach used before to accomplish God's plan, but we need to remember that God chooses His own ways, outcomes, and criteria.

   a. Self-confidently but mistakenly, Joshua presumed to know how to approach Ai: "Go up and spy out the country" (v. 2).

   b. Self-confidently but mistakenly, Joshua presumed to know how to fight Ai: "Do not weary all the people there, for the people of Ai are few" (v. 3).

   c. Self-confidently but mistakenly, Joshua presumed to believe he would triumph again: "for they are few."

2. Avoid self-assurance—only God can give continuing victories (7:4–9).

Joshua's self-confidence led him to be self-assured regarding victory over Ai. Unfortunately, he missed one very important aspect of following God's plan: seeking His direction for each step. As a result, Israel's force of three thousand men was routed at Ai, and "the hearts of the people melted and became like water" (v. 5). We need to remember that:

a. God desires to give victory.

God gave victory over Jericho, and the apostle Paul tells us of God's desire to give victories in our lives today. Consider Romans 8:37, "Yet in all these things we are more than conquerors through Him who loved us"; 1 Corinthians 15:57, "But thanks be to God, who gives us the victory through our Lord Jesus Christ"; and 2 Corinthians 2:14, "Now thanks be to God who always leads us in triumph in Christ."

b. God knows every hindrance in our way.

Achan had disobeyed the instruction of God in keeping that which was dedicated to God from the battle of Jericho. Although unknown to Joshua and the rest of the children of Israel, God knew and would have informed Joshua if he had only asked for direction. In failing to ask, Joshua did not wait for God's direction, and instead of victory, there was defeat (Josh.1:1; 3:7; 4:1; 5:2; 6:2).

3. Having failed, return to God-dependence (7:10–26).

Everyone suffered, not only because of one man's sin, but because of Joshua's self-confidence and self-assurance. Failing to seek God's direction, Joshua did not know of Achan's sin, and Israel fell to defeat. There can be no triumph when we fail to seek God's direction. In desperation, Joshua retreated from his self-confidence and self-assurance by seeking God, whereupon God informed Joshua of Achan's sin and provided Joshua with His direction for what to do.

4. We must seek God's direction—He can bring victory from defeat (8:1–29).

a. Armed with God's direction, Joshua knew God's plan: "See, I have given into your hand the king of Ai, his people, his city, and his land" (8:1).

b. With God's plan, Joshua knew how to proceed: "And you shall do to Ai and its king as you did to Jericho and its king" (8:2).

c. When we follow God's plan and seek His direction, God can restore our victories (8:3–29). When Israel learned this, they defeated Ai.

Conclusion

God wants us to triumph as we face the obstacles in our way. When we follow His plan and direction, although they frequently run against human logic, reason, and common sense, we will triumph. However, we must be careful not to lapse into self-confidence and self-assurance. This was the error of Joshua. The plan is always God's, and His plans require His direction, not our assumption based on the way He has done something before. Take the time to seek Him; ask for His specific direction so you are not *getting ready to fail.*

SUGGESTED ORDER OF WORSHIP

Prelude—Instrumental

Redeemed, How I Love to Proclaim It

Call to Worship—Pastor

Prayer *(All deacons/elders/trustees join the pastor at the altar before the service for public prayer)*

Call to Praise—Congregation

Welcome—Pastoral Staff

Hymn of Welcome—Congregation

CH 5 *I Sing Praises*

Praise and Worship—Congregation

NBH 277 *He Is Lord* (chorus in F, chorus in G)

NBH 278 *I Live* (2x in G)

NBH 279 *There Is a Redeemer* (v. 1, chorus, v. 2, chorus, v. 3, chorus in D)

Prayer of Praise—Pastoral Staff

Prayer Response—Congregation

> NBH 276 *Alleluia* (vv. 1, 2, and 4 in G)

Offertory Prayer—Pastor

Offertory Praise—Praise Team

> *Give Me Jesus*

Sermon—Pastor

Hymn of Invitation—Congregation

> NBH 300 *Jesus, Lord to Me* (2x in F, 1x in G)

Benediction Hymn—Congregation

> CH 5 *I Sing Praises*

Postlude—Instrumentalists

> CH 5 *I Sing Praises*

KEY:

CH: Celebration Hymnal (Word Music/Integrity Music, Nashville, TN)

NBH: New Baptist Hymnal (2008)

WH: The Hymnal (Word Music, Nashville, TN)

SPW: Songs for Praise and Worship (Word Music, Nashville, TN)

MSPW: More Songs for Praise and Worship (Word Music, Nashville, TN)

MSPW2: More Songs for Praise and Worship 2 (Word Music, Nashville, TN)

WEEK 8

God's Amazing Work

Ephesians 2:10
By Dr. Kent Spann

Medical advancements enable doctors to do things that are amazing and life-changing. When God saved us, He did an amazing work in our lives.

1. God's work in us is amazing.

We get our word *poem* from the Greek *poiema*, the word translated in this verse as "workmanship." A poem is a composition that is created by a writer.

a. We are the work of God.

b. We are the masterpiece of God.

i. We are the result of His extraordinary skill.

ii. We are His supreme achievement.

c. We are the new creation of God (2 Cor. 5:17).

2. God's work through us is amazing.

a. We were created by God to do *good* works (2 Cor. 9:8; Col. 1:10).

b. We were created by God to do *God's* works ("God-prepared" works).

i. God has given each of us an eternally designed job description.

(1) We see it demonstrated in Christ (John 13:14, 15).

(2) We learn about it in the Word of God (2 Tim. 3:16, 17).

(3) We are enabled to do it through the Holy Spirit (Gal. 5:16, 22, 23).

ii. God has given each of us an individually designed job description (Jer. 29:11).

"It is faith alone that justifies, but faith that justifies can never be alone."

—John Calvin

"Good works are indispensable to salvation—not as its ground or means, however, but as its consequence and evidence."

—John R. W. Stott

WEEK 8

Jesus Has Redeemed Men for God

Revelation 5:9, 10
By Dr. Carl Barrington

Introduction

These two verses summarize the completed work of Christ as well as any in the New Testament. In them, we learn that we have five things that make the redeemed different from the rest of the world.

1. We are servants of God and not masters of ourselves.

2. We are a worshipping people.

3. We have a message of liberation.

4. We have been sent on a mission of freedom.

5. We are truly different and must love with a new quality, care more deeply, and accept more fully.

Conclusion

You *can* be redeemed. *Have* you been redeemed? Are you *willing* to be redeemed?

WEEK 9

Getting Ready to Continue!

Joshua 23–24
By David W. Hirschman

Introduction

In the process of getting ready, first to move, then to see, then to experience, speak, renew, triumph, and fail, Israel had experienced God at work in their midst, working for them and accomplishing things they could never have imagined. In the process, many battles have been fought and many victories have been won. Now, Israel is in her own land. She is living out the reality of God's plan, in His power, and with the prize God wanted them to have all along! Living life God's way, following Him obediently, responding in the fashion He desires, brings His blessing, provision, and ultimate victory. However, change is coming as Joshua prepares to die. How will Israel continue? How will they continue to experience and enjoy God at work on their behalf? How can we continue to experience and enjoy God at work on our behalf?

1. Don't forget how you got to the place of blessing and possession.

Israel entered the Promised Land, defeated their enemies, and obtained God's prize by:

a. Following God's direction/instruction.

Sometimes God's ways fail to make sense; other times they are beyond our comprehension. Yet, God's ways are rooted in His power, knowledge, and wisdom, and as such, are as reliable as He is. Israel learned that they could not fail when they followed the direction and instruction of God.

b. Believing, trusting, and relying upon God.

By not only following God's direction and instruction, but by learning to believe, trust, and rely upon God, Israel came to embrace truths that God wanted them to have. In recounting their shared experiences, Joshua reminded Israel of truths they had come to know: "For the LORD your God is He who has fought for you" (Josh. 23:1–3); "Not one thing has failed of all the good things which the LORD your God spoke concerning you" (23:14); and "I have given you a land for which you did not labor" (Josh. 24:13). The process of believing, trusting, and relying upon God required Israel to learn from God's ways, as at the battle of Jericho, and to learn from their own mistakes, as at the battle of Ai, and in dealing with the Gibeonites.

c. Ultimately, Israel got to the place of blessing and possession by aligning themselves with the plans and purposes of God.

God intended to complete what he had started long ago with a man named Abram, and only when Israel aligned themselves with God's purposes for their lives did they see the plan of God begin to unfold.

2. Don't forget why you are at the place of blessing and possession.

Israel is in their land, the place of promise, provision, power, and presence of God, not because they deserved it or God was obligated to give it to them. In fact, they were in the place of blessing and provision because of:

a. God's mercy: Their previous disobedience hindered their arrival on God's schedule, and should have disqualified them from obtaining the prize. Yet, God in His mercy continued to deal with Israel, making a way for them to obtain the promise.

b. God's faithfulness: God demonstrated His faithfulness to fulfill His plan by not destroying Israel or casting them aside in favor of another plan. Even though they were disobedient and rebellious, God's patience was greater, resulting in a renewed opportunity to obtain what He wanted Israel to have.

3. Don't forget what will keep you at the place of blessing and possession.

At the conclusion of his life, Joshua reinforces the truth that Israel would continue to enjoy God's blessing and favor only by choosing to continue in a right relationship with God. Joshua presents Israel with a choice in Joshua 24:14, 15, and follows with his own example of what he and his family had already chosen to do. Staying in the place of blessing and possession would require honoring God (v. 14a), sincere and honest service (v. 14b), removing anything that stood in the way of their relationship with God (v. 14c), and serving God alone (v. 14d).

Conclusion

God desires to bless His children and bring them to a place of spiritual blessing and possession. He intends to complete what He begins when we first trust Jesus as savior (Phil. 1:6), and He desires that we stay in the place of blessing and possession. However, using the example of Israel, it is easy to become distracted, disgruntled, disobedient, and rebellious, and then lose those things that God intended for us. Only when we remember that it is He who has blessed us by getting us to where we are today, and He who will sustain and keep us in this place, will we ever be prepared to continue on the path that He has chosen for us. Just as we have gotten ready to move, see, experience, speak, renew, and triumph, we must also get ready to continue. Will you continue to follow the One who has brought you this far? Will you get ready to continue?

SUGGESTED ORDER OF WORSHIP

Prelude—Instrumentalist

MSPW2 *Holy Spirit Rain Down*

Prayer of Worship—Worship Pastor

Worship and Praise—Congregation

NBH 98 *Come, Thou Fount of Every Blessing* (vv. 1 and 2, chorus, in D, v. 3 in Eb)

Baptismal Celebration—Pastoral Staff

Prayer—Pastoral Prayer

Welcome—Pastoral Staff

Hymn of Welcome (*meet and greet*)—Congregation

CH 213 *We Bring the Sacrifice*

Worship and Praise—Congregation

> NBH 99 *Forever* (v. 1, chorus, v. 2, chorus, v. 3, chorus)

> NBH 100 *Hallelujah* (Your Love Is Amazing) (2x in G)

> NBH 105 *Grace Greater Than Our Sin* (chorus, v. 1, chorus, v. 3, chorus in G)

Scripture Reading—Worship Leader

Hymn of Surrender & Worship—Congregation

> NBH 112 *Grace Alone*

Sermon—Pastor

Hymn of Response/Invitation—Worship Leader and Congregation

> NBH 109 *There Is None Like You* (2x in G)

Hymn of Benediction—Congregation

> NBH 104 *Amazing Grace* (v. 1, v. 5 in F)

Postlude—Instrumental

> *I Could Sing of Your Love Forever*

KEY:

CH: Celebration Hymnal (Word Music/Integrity Music, Nashville, TN)

NBH: New Baptist Hymnal (2008)

WH: The Hymnal (Word Music, Nashville, TN)

SPW: Songs for Praise and Worship (Word Music, Nashville, TN)

MSPW: More Songs for Praise and Worship (Word Music, Nashville, TN)

MSPW2: More Songs for Praise and Worship 2 (Word Music, Nashville, TN)

WEEK 9

God's Amazing Peace Mission

Ephesians 2:11–22
By Dr. Kent Spann

Sir Neville Chamberlain, then prime minister of Great Britain, upon his return from meeting with Hitler in September of 1938 declared "Peace in our time! Peace with honor!" He thought that he had brokered peace. One year later, Hitler invaded Poland, and on September 3, 1939, Great Britain declared war on Germany. Sir Chamberlain's peace mission failed.

God also embarked on an amazing peace mission, but His mission was not a failure.

1. We were alienated from God because of sin; therefore, we were alienated from one another (2:11–13).

   a. Sin results in alienation from God.

      i. We were separated from Christ.

      ii. We were excluded from citizenship in Israel.

      iii. We were foreigners to the covenants of the promise.

      iv. We were hopeless.

      v. We were without God.

   b. Sin results in alienation from others.

      It causes wars (James 4:1–3), racial problems, marital problems, family strife, alienation of friends, division in churches, etc.

2. We are reconciled to God through the Cross; therefore, we are reconciled to one another (2:14–18).

   a. We have peace (2:14, 15).

   b. We have oneness (2:16).

   c. We have equal access to the Father (2:17, 18).

3. We are united with God through Christ; therefore, we are united with one another (2:19–22).

   a. We are united as citizens of God's kingdom (2:19).

   b. We are united as members of God's family (2:19).

   c. We are united as building blocks in God's temple (2:20–22).

WEEK 9

A Christian Perspective on Death

Psalm 116:15
By Dr. Carl Barrington

Introduction

"Precious in the sight of the LORD is the death of His saints." The Bible has a lot to say about the death of Christians. Most worldly people think about death as a horrible thing, a time of separation from everyone and everything that they love and enjoy. The Bible's attitude regarding the death of one of God's children could not be farther from the world's view. When one of God's children dies:

1. It means a change of environment.

2. It means a change of nature.

3. It proves the reality of our relationship to Him. Our people die well.

4. It draws other Christians closer to God.

5. It means a welcome home for that child.

WEEK 10

Real Characters: Moses

How Do You Face an Uncertain Tomorrow?

Exodus 3:10–15

By Dr. David Wheeler

Introduction

With the collapse of world economic systems and the constant threat of global terrorism finding its way to our neighborhoods, it is a no-brainer to realize that we all face an uncertain tomorrow! Unlike in previous generations, the concepts of safety and security are not guaranteed, nor are they taken for granted.

This catastrophic shift occurred on September 11, 2001, a day that will forever be etched into our psyche. If you think hard enough, I am certain you can remember where you were when you heard about the attacks on the Twin Towers in New York City and the Pentagon in Washington DC.

Since 9/11, one's workplace is always a concern when it comes to facing an uncertain tomorrow. Almost every week there are news reports of disgruntled employees who somehow think that killing their boss and fellow workers will correct the pain of losing their jobs.

The same can be said about attending school. Thirty years ago, acne and hormones were two of the biggest challenges facing high school and college students. Not so today. Look no further than the shootings at Virginia Tech or Columbine High School for more evidence that we *are* facing an uncertain tomorrow!

As if all of this were not enough, consider the recent shootings at churches across America. From Wedgewood Baptist Church in Fort Worth, Texas, where seven lives were snuffed out by a deranged gunman, to the murder on a Sunday morning in the sanctuary of a pastor in Maryville, Illinois. The most sacred concepts of safety and decency are being violated as the world becomes more unpredictable and uncertain.

In many ways, Moses was presented with the same dilemma. Much like many Americans', his life was safe and predictable. He possessed a family, having married Zipporah, the daughter of the priest of Midian. For the first time in his life since miraculously growing up in Pharaoh's courts and escaping sure death as an infant, Moses was settled and happy with his life.

It was then that God intervened in Exodus 3. While Moses was tending his livestock, "the Angel of the LORD appeared to him in a flame of fire from the midst of a bush" (v. 2). Moses saw that though the bush was on fire it did not burn up. So Moses thought, *I will go over and see this strange sight—why the bush does not burn up.*

To Moses's surprise, God informs him,

> I have surely seen the oppression of My people who are in Egypt, and have heard their cry because of their taskmasters, for I know their sorrows. So I have come down to deliver them out of the hand of the Egyptians, and to bring them up from that land to a good and large land, to a land flowing with milk and honey, to the place of the Canaanites and the Hittites and the Amorites and the Perizzites and the Hivites and the Jebusites. Now therefore, behold, the cry of the children of Israel has come to Me, and I have also seen the oppression with which the Egyptians oppress them. (vv. 7–9)

Moses must have been ecstatic. That is, until he heard the Lord's next decree: "I will send you to Pharaoh that you may bring My people, the children of Israel out of Egypt" (v. 10). It was then that he faced his own uncertain tomorrow. After all, how could he return to Egypt after everyone knew that he had killed an Egyptian guard (Ex. 2:14)? Would he, too, be killed upon his return?

With this in mind, how do we face an uncertain tomorrow? Consider the following:

1. Moses could face uncertainty because he was assured, like us, that God was with him (Ex. 3:11, 12).

While Moses initially responds to God with the question "Who am I that I should go to Pharaoh, and that I should bring the children of Israel out of Egypt?" (v. 11), God immediately responds with the affirmation "I will certainly be with you (v. 12). This is not unlike the words from our Lord through the author of Hebrews: "I will never leave you nor forsake you" (13:5). So we say with confidence, "The LORD is on my side; I will not fear. What can man do to me?" (Ps. 118:6).

We, too, can face uncertainty, because we are never alone! God is with us!

2. Moses could also face uncertainty because, like us, he was assured because God is personal (Ex. 3:13–15)

Still not convinced, Moses asks God, "Indeed, when I come to the children of Israel and say to them, 'The God of your fathers has sent me to you,' and they say to me, 'What is His name?' what shall I say to them?" (v. 13). God responds to Moses, "I AM WHO I AM .... Thus you shall say to the children of Israel, 'I AM has sent me to you'" (v. 14).

It sounds odd for Moses to ask God about His name. After all, names are not a big deal to us. However, in biblical days, names defined the person's life and ministry. Moses was actually checking to see if God could deliver if he returned to Egypt.

So ... what did God do? He stamped His name as His promise. The reference to "I AM" is actually *YHWH* in the Hebrew. Based upon the promise of God, the best working definition for *YHWH* is "I will always be what I have been!"

God mentions Abraham, Isaac, and Jacob in Exodus 3:15. He does this to remind Moses, the Israelites, and us, that just as He delivered these heroes of the faith in the past, He also hears our prayers today.

Conclusion

We can face an uncertain tomorrow because when we get to our appointed destination, regardless of joy or devastation, our God is never surprised and will greet us with open arms! For He is, as King David states in Psalm 19:14, "[Our] strength and [our] Redeemer."

SUGGESTED ORDER OF WORSHIP

Theme: Bless the Name of JESUS

Prelude—Instrumentalist

> NBH 77 *Better Is One Day*

Call to Prayer—Pastoral Staff

Call to Praise—Congregation

> NBH 36 *I Exalt Thee* (2x in F) / NBH 37 *Blessed Be the Lord God Almighty* (1x in Bb; 1x in C)

Welcome—Pastoral Staff

Welcome Song (*meet and greet during song*)—Pastoral Staff

> NBH 296 *He Is Exalted* (2x in F)—Congregation

Praise and Worship—Congregation

> NBH 324 *No Other Name* (2x in D)

> NBH 318 *His Name Is Life* (2x in D)

Prayer of Dedication and Praise—Pastor

> NBH 326 *Your Name* (v. 1, chorus, v. 2, chorus, in Ab)

Worship with Our Gifts—Pastoral Staff

Offertory Praise

> NBH 319 *Be Unto Your Name* (v. 1, chorus, v. 2, chorus, in C)

Message—Pastor

Hymn of Response/Invitation—Worship Leader and Congregation

> NBH 325 *In the Name of the Lord* (2x or as needed, in G)

Benediction Hymn—Congregation

> NBH 320 *Jesus, Name Above All Names* (2x in Eb)

Postlude—Instrumentalists
Your Name

KEY:

CH: Celebration Hymnal (Word Music/Integrity Music, Nashville, TN)

NBH: New Baptist Hymnal (2008)

WH: The Hymnal (Word Music, Nashville, TN)

SPW: Songs for Praise and Worship (Word Music, Nashville, TN)

MSPW: More Songs for Praise and Worship (Word Music, Nashville, TN)

MSPW2: More Songs for Praise and Worship 2 (Word Music, Nashville, TN)

WEEK 10

Got It, Give It

Ephesians 3:1–13
By Dr. Kent Spann

Paul gives the reason he is willing to go through imprisonment (3:1). He is a steward ("administration" in the NIV) of God's grace given to him.

1. We are stewards of God's message (3:2–6).

    The mystery is the revealed message (3:2–5).

    a. The message with which we have been entrusted is that the gospel is for all people (3:6).

        i. The gospel transcends national barriers.

        ii. The gospel transcends racial barriers.

        iii. The gospel transcends intellectual barriers.

        iv. The gospel transcends age barriers.

    b. The message with which we have been entrusted is that God is building His church (3:6).

        i. When you accepted Christ, you were made an heir along with all other believers (Rom. 8:17).

        ii. When you accepted Christ, you became a member of Christ's body (Eph. 1:22, 23).

        iii. When you accepted Christ, all the promises of God became yours (2 Cor. 1:20).

2. We are stewards of God's ministry (3:7–12).

    a. We are called to share the message (3:7, 8).

    b. We are empowered to share the message (3:7).

    c. We are designated to share the message (3:10–12).

        i. When we share the message, then the manifold wisdom of

God is displayed to the angels, and God is glorified (3:10).

ii. When we share the message, we fulfill God's eternal purpose in redemption (3:11, 12).

Now that we've got it, let's give it!

WEEK 10

ACTS in Prayer

James 4:2, 3
By Dr. Carl Barrington

Introduction

Although we preachers have used it on many occasions, it is possible that many of our members have not heard and could use an easy acrostic to remember the many varieties of prayer that we find in Scripture.

A is for *Adoration* of God, telling Him how you acknowledge His greatness and His presence with you.

C is for *Confession* of sin, without which no prayer has the right to be heard by God.

T is for *Thanksgiving*, remembering to thank God for previously answered prayer before we ask Him for more.

S is for *Seeking* His help for ourselves and others. Most of us spend most of our time here, but we should seek God's help only after we come to Him in *Adoration*, *Confession*, and *Thanksgiving*.

Conclusion

The poet Alfred Tennyson said it this way: "More things are wrought by prayer than this world dreams of."

WEEK 11

Real Characters: Joshua

The Tragedy of Wasted Possibilities

Joshua 7:2–13, 19–26
By Dr. David A. Wheeler

Introduction

On the heels of one of the greatest miracles of all time, Joshua 7 outlines how quickly a people can fall from God's blessing. Think about it: Joshua 6 describes how the children of Israel obliterated the mighty fortress of Jericho in a week without utilizing any conventional forms of warfare. Surprisingly, all they did was trust God by marching around Jericho as the priests blew their trumpets, and then shouting at the top of their lungs when they were allowed by the Spirit of God on the final day. And as it says in Joshua 6:20, "The people shouted when *the priests* blew the trumpets. And it happened when the people heard the sound of the trumpet, and the people shouted with a great shout, that the wall fell down flat. Then the people went up into the city, every man straight before him, and they took the city."

Imagine what the people of Israel felt after the great victory. As for Joshua, note what it states in Joshua 6:27: "So the LORD was with Joshua, and his fame spread throughout all the country."

Nevertheless, as is with many great spiritual victories, the people forget their blessings and stray from God's will. This is what occurs in Joshua 7. The question is, how? Consider the following steps to disaster:

1. First, the children of Israel relaxed and let down their guard (vv. 2, 3).

Unfortunately, this is what often happens to believers when they are accustomed to walking in God's favor. Note Joshua's arrogance as he instructs his warriors in verse 3, "Do not let all the people go up, but let about two or three thousand men go up and attack Ai. Do not weary all the people there, for the people of Ai are few." It was obvious that his guard was already down and Joshua was feeling his Wheaties!

2. Second, the children of Israel underestimated their *real* enemy (vv. 4, 5).

Based on the misguided instructions of Joshua, according to verse 4, "about three thousand men went up there from the people, but they fled before the men of Ai. And the men of Ai struck down about thirty-six men, for they chased them from before the gate as far as Shebarim, and struck them down on the descent."

It is always dangerous to underestimate one's enemy, especially in spiritual matters against an enemy as formidable as Satan. Keep in mind the words of Jesus in reference to the devil, in John 8:44: He was a murderer from the beginning, and does not stand in the truth, because there is no truth in him ... for he is a liar and the father of it."

3. Third, Joshua lost track of his vision and destination (vv. 6, 7).

The key is the statement in verse 5 when it describes that "the hearts of the people melted and became like water." This is followed up by the revealing of Joshua's clay feet in verses 6 and 7: "Then Joshua tore his clothes, and fell to the earth on his face before the ark of the LORD until evening, he and the elders of Israel; and they put dust on their heads. And Joshua said, 'Alas, Lord GOD, why have You brought this people over the Jordan at all—to deliver us into the hand of the Amorites, to destroy us? Oh, that we had been content, and dwelt on the other side of the Jordan!'"

4. Fourth, Joshua began to focus on self (v. 8).

We call this the dangerous *I* factor. Notice the subtle statement by Joshua in verse 8, "O Lord, what shall *I* say when Israel turns its back before its enemies?" (emphasis added). In the midst of losing thirty-six warriors, Joshua seemed to be worried about himself and his reputation. This was, at best, misguided and narcissistic!

As if this weren't bad enough, Joshua passed the buck of responsibility and began to play the "Blame Game." Look at what Joshua says to God in verse 9: "For the Canaanites and all the inhabitants of the land will hear it, and surround us, and cut off our name from the earth. Then what will *You* do for Your great name?" Before God speaks to Joshua, Joshua is covering his bases by trying to deflect responsibility. The real issue is revealed next . . .

5. Fifth, Joshua and the people forgot the seriousness of sin (vv. 10–13).

The direct approach by God with Joshua is almost comical. While Joshua is apparently clueless as to why all of this had occurred, God intervenes by stating, "Get up! Why do you lie thus on your face? Israel has sinned, and they have also transgressed My covenant which I commanded them. For they have even taken some of the accursed things, and have both stolen and deceived." In case you ever need a reminder, here it is! God always takes sin seriously!

Against the direct commands of God, one man, Achan, chose to disobey, with no regard to consequences (vv. 20, 21). All it took was the sin of one selfish man to derail a whole nation and for thirty-six warriors to lose their lives.

Ultimately, like many people today, Achan forgot the importance of unity and community in the body of believers (vv. 22–26). In the end, Achan died, along with his entire family. His faulty belief that a person could sin in a vacuum without consequences brought devastating results.

Conclusion

One should always be saddened by the tragedy of wasted possibilities. This never occurs by mere accident; rather, it is a progression of missteps that usually begins when a person *lets down his guard*.

SUGGESTED ORDER OF WORSHIP

Theme: The Spirit of God

Prelude—Instrumentalists

    NBH 20 *Great and Mighty*

His Presence to Lead ...

Call to Praise—Congregation

    NBH 335 *Holy Spirit, Rain Down* (2x in F)

Prayer of Praise—Pastoral Staff

    NBH 336 *Come, Thou Almighty King* (vv. 1 and 3 in F, v. 4 in G)

Welcome—Pastoral Staff

Hymn of Welcome (*meet and greet during song*)—Congregation

    MSPW2 *Lord, I Lift Your Name on High* (2x in D)

His Power to Love ...

Praise and Worship—Congregation

    NBH 333 *Where the Spirit of the Lord Is* (2x in Eb)

    NBH 18 *Glorify Thy Name* (vv. 1–3 in Bb)

    NBH 19 *Be Exalted, O God* (2x in Bb)

Prayer of Praise—Worship Leader (*keyboard play next song during prayer*)

    NBH 548 *Seekers of Your Heart* (2x in D)

... His Promise in Living!

Offertory Prayer—Pastor

Offertory Praise—A Cappella Ensemble

NBH 328 *Sweet, Sweet Spirit*

Message—Pastor

Hymn of Invitation—Congregation

CH 481 *Come Just as You Are*

Benediction Hymn—Congregation

CH 213/214 *We Bring the Sacrifice/He Has Made Me Glad*

Postlude—Instrumentalists

Holy Spirit, Rain Down

KEY:

CH: Celebration Hymnal (Word Music/Integrity Music, Nashville, TN)

NBH: New Baptist Hymnal (2008)

WH: The Hymnal (Word Music, Nashville, TN)

SPW: Songs for Praise and Worship (Word Music, Nashville, TN)

MSPW: More Songs for Praise and Worship (Word Music, Nashville, TN)

MSPW2: More Songs for Praise and Worship 2 (Word Music, Nashville, TN)

WEEK 11

The Power Prayer

Ephesians 3:14–19
By Dr. Kent Spann

Paul prays a powerful prayer based on the truth (doctrine) he has shared in chapters 1–3 and what he will share about Christian living (duty) in chapters 4–6.

How do we pray the power prayer?

1. We pray to be strengthened with power through the Holy Spirit (3:16).

   a. We pray for God's endless supply of strength (Is. 40:28–31).

   b. We pray for Holy Spirit power (Acts 1:8).

2. We pray for Christ to be at home in our church and our hearts through faith (3:17a).

   a. We acknowledge His headship (Col. 1:18).

   b. We recognize and welcome His presence (Luke 24:13–35).

   c. We experience the filling of the Holy Spirit (Eph. 5:18).

3. We pray to be rooted and grounded in love (3:17b).

   The logo of the church is to be love (John 13:34, 35).

4. We pray to grasp and experience God's magnanimous love (3:18, 19a).

   "Grasp" means to fully understand the implications of something.

5. We pray to be filled with the fullness of God (3:19b).

   a. We pray to be totally dominated by God in our lives.

   b. We pray to grow up in our faith (Eph. 4:13).

   c. We pray to be filled with the Holy Spirit (Eph. 5:18).

Let's pray the power prayer!

WEEK 11

God's Health Care Plan

Psalm 51
By David Thompson

Have you ever had a nervous stomach or anxiety that made you physically ill? God's health care plan has a lot to do with how one lives.

Your body is affected by your spirit ... and so closely related that they catch one another's disease. Bad health is not always a result of sin—but sometimes it is. Psalm 51 is David's laundry list of things needed to be made right as a result of his sin and discloses how it is committed, confessed, and cleansed.

1. Sin committed affects your health. Three words define sin:

   a. "Transgression" (v. 1) is crossing the line. God drew a line in the sand. David crossed it.

   b. "Iniquity" (v. 2) is twisting and misshaping. David twisted sex into something ugly with Bathsheba.

   c. "Sin" (v. 2) is missing the mark, and David was guilty as charged by Nathan.

2. Sin confessed affects your health (Ps. 32:4, 5).

   a. "Acknowledge" transgression. David acknowledged that his heart, bones, and spirit needed healing.

   b. "Admit" you were sinful from birth (v. 5).

   c. "Against" God you have done evil (Ps. 51:4).

3. Sin cleansed affects your health (Ps. 51:7–9).

   a. "Purge me with hyssop." David refers to the ceremonial cleansing from the blood sacrifice.

   b. "Without shedding of blood" there is no cleansing of sin (Heb. 9:22). The blood of Christ cleanses our conscience from acts that lead to death, namely "sin" (Heb. 9:14).

WEEK 12

Real Characters: Peter and John

There Is No Plan B

Acts 4:8–20

By Dr. David A. Wheeler

Introduction

The story goes that after Jesus' death, burial, resurrection, and ascension back to heaven, He was greeted at the pearly gates by a multitude of angels. It seems that one of the angels was rather inquisitive about how Christ was going to continue His redemptive mission on Earth now that He was back to His rightful place in heaven. Jesus went on to explain in great detail that He had purposely left the ongoing ministry in the hands of several disciples for which He had invested countless hours of mentoring. He smiled as He spoke about the endless possibilities of these men learning to multiply their lives and spreading the gospel as they traveled. Jesus even went as far as expressing His vision for the ages to come as millions of believers would eventually join His redemptive movement and the gospel would saturate the world by way of personal evangelism and biblical multiplication! It was then that the angel asked Jesus, "What if this does not work? What is plan B?" Jesus replied, "There is no plan B!"

Acts chapter 4 gives us a sobering glimpse through the words and actions of Peter and John into how this eternal plan is supposed to unfold through all Christians. Keep in mind that both men were being intimidated, having to address the same religious leaders who had placed them in jail the night before because they preached publicly about Jesus' resurrection from the dead and about five thousand people had believed. So ... what can we learn in order to become multiplying, obedient disciples?

1. We must be filled with the Holy Spirit (Acts 4:8).

The writer of Acts wants us to know in verse 8 that Peter was filled with the Holy Spirit before he addressed the religious leaders. This is the key to all viable ministry. We are nothing without the empowering of God to speak and act as He desires. In other words, we cannot redeem anyone from their sin, but we can, through the power of the Holy Spirit, become mouthpieces to a hurting world!

2. We must know the gospel message (Acts 4:9–12).

It is obvious in verses 9–12 that Peter understands what he is saying. In fact, he is very direct by his use of the personal pronoun "you" on several occasions. He was not concerned with political correctness or offending his audience. On the contrary, he seems much more concerned about speaking truth and defending his Savior. This is evidenced by his bold proclamation in verse 12: "Nor is there salvation in any other, for there is *no other name* under heaven given among men by which we must be *saved*" (emphasis added).

Just like Peter, every Christian should be willing to stand on the name of Christ and proclaim His message of truth! What does this mean to us?

a. Every believer should prepare and be willing to share their conversion testimony. If a person is redeemed and knows Christ on a personal level, knowing their story is a no-brainer. One's story is an amazing tool to communicate Christ in a postmodern world.

b. Every believer should know the basics of the gospel message. A simple and time-tested approach is what many people call the "Romans Road." It goes as follows:

   (1) All have sinned. (Rom. 3:23)

   (2) The wages of sin is death. (Rom. 6:23)

   (3) While we were still sinners, Christ died for us. (Rom. 5:8)

   (4) If you confess with your mouth the Lord Jesus and believe in your heart that God has raised Him from the dead you will be saved. (Rom. 10:9)

   (5) Whoever calls on the name of Lord shall be saved. (Rom. 10:13)

The key: *Do not be ashamed of the gospel!*

3. We must learn to give this faith away (Acts 4:13).

Note what the Bible says in verse 13: "Now when they saw the boldness of Peter and John, and perceived that they were uneducated and untrained men, they marveled. And they realized that they had been with Jesus." Could it be that the religious leaders remembered that Peter and John had walked with Christ? Or, could it be that when they spoke, because of the power of the Holy Spirit, it was as if Jesus were right there with them again?

The bottom line: You have to *be* the message to the world! In other words, you cannot divorce Jesus' message from the man He presented Himself to be as He lived His life out in front of the world.

4. We must not be scared, regardless of the threats and actions of evil men (Acts 4:13–18)

In this case, it is good to remember the words of Paul in 2 Timothy 1:7: "For God has not given us a spirit of fear, but of power and of love and of a sound mind." Even though the religious leaders tried to intimidate Peter and John, they stood their ground and eventually refused to be quiet!

5. We must never be silent (Acts 4:19, 20)!

Note how Peter and John respond to the Gestapo-type approach of the religious leaders. In the face of persecution, they exclaim, "Whether it is right in the sight of God to listen to you more than to God, you judge. For we cannot but speak the things which we have seen and heard." The problem is, too many Christians have stopped speaking about the love and forgiveness of Christ. They are silent . . . and for what good reason?

Conclusion

Like Peter and John, the church must be willing to stand up and proclaim the eternal message of Christ to a hurting world. Note what happens when the apostles return home. They are not shaken or fearful; rather, they are deeply moved by the opportunity to stand up for their Savior. Thus, it is fitting to conclude with Acts 4:31: "And when they had prayed, the place where they were assembled together was shaken; and they were all filled with the Holy Spirit, and they spoke the word of God with boldness." We *must* do the same!

SUGGESTED ORDER OF WORSHIP

Prelude—Instrumental

> *Redeemed, How I Love to Proclaim It*

Call to Worship/Prayer *(All deacons/elders/trustees join the pastor at the altar before the service for public prayer)*—Pastor

Call to Praise—Congregation

> NBH 289 *Days of Elijah* (chorus 2x in Ab)

Welcome—Pastoral Staff

Hymn of Welcome

> NBH 310 *Blessed Be the Name* (chorus, v. 1, chorus, v. 4, chorus in Ab)

> NBH 301 *Crown Him King of Kings* (2x in Ab)

Scripture Reading from Psalms 18:46; 21:13; 34:3; 35:18; 57:11; 138:6; 97:9; 99:2; 145:1

Worship Leader: The LORD lives! Blessed be my Rock! Let the God of my salvation be exalted.

Congregation: Be exalted, O LORD, in Your own strength! We will sing and praise Your power.

Worship Leader: Oh, magnify the LORD with me, and let us exalt His name together.

Congregation: I will give You thanks in the great assembly; I will praise You among many people.

Worship Leader: Be exalted, O God, above the heavens; let Your glory be above all the earth.

Women: Though the LORD is on high, yet He regards the lowly; but the proud He knows from afar.

Worship Leader: For You, LORD, are most high above all the earth; You are exalted far above all gods.

Men: The LORD is great in Zion, and He is high above all the peoples.

ALL: I will extol You, my God, O King; and I will bless Your name forever and ever.

Praise and Worship—Congregation

>   NBH 581 *We Bring a Sacrifice of Praise* (chorus 2x in D)

Prayer—Pastor

>   NBH 279 *There Is a Redeemer* (v. 1, chorus, v. 3, chorus in D)

>   NBH 554 *As the Deer* (v. 1, chorus, v. 3, chorus in D)

Offertory Prayer—Pastoral Staff

Offertory Praise—Praise Team

>   NBH 264 *Worthy Is the Lamb*

Message—Pastor

Hymn of Invitation—Congregation

>   NBH 482 *Draw Me Close* (as needed in Bb)

Benediction Hymn—Congregation

>   NBH 17 *I Sing Praises* (2x in G)

Postlude—Instruments

>   NBH 17 *I Sing Praises*

KEY:

CH: Celebration Hymnal (Word Music/Integrity Music, Nashville, TN)

NBH: New Baptist Hymnal (2008)

WH: The Hymnal (Word Music, Nashville, TN)

SPW: Songs for Praise and Worship (Word Music, Nashville, TN)

MSPW: More Songs for Praise and Worship (Word Music, Nashville, TN)

MSPW2: More Songs for Praise and Worship 2 (Word Music, Nashville, TN)

WEEK 12

Doxology

Ephesians 3:20, 21
By Dr. Kent Spann

The infamous words of the church are "With all due respect, Pastor, what you're thinking can't be done!" Paul shatters those words!

(The preacher should build this message to a crescendo)

1. Our God is able.

   a. Our God is *able*—He has the power.

   b. Our God is able to *do*—He can make, form, or bring about.

   c. Our God is able to do *more*—He is able to do over and above.

   d. Our God is able to do *immeasurably* more—He can do surpassingly, superabundantly, exceedingly, extraordinarily, and quite beyond all measure.

   e. Our God is able do *superabundantly* more than we can ask—He is able to do above and beyond what we ask, and then more on top of that.

   What I have asked for is as nothing compared to the ability of my God to give. I've asked for a cupful, and the ocean remains. I've asked for a sunbeam, and the sun abides. My best asking falls immeasurably short of my Father's giving. It's beyond all that we can ask.

   —John Jowett

   ---

   f. Our God is able do superabundantly more than we can ask or even *imagine*—He can do more than we can even conceive.

   Our God is able!

2. Our God is still able.

He is able throughout all generations, including ours. He wants to demonstrate His superabundant power through us and His church.

    a. Let's partner with God to do great things through us for His glory.

    b. Let's pray for God to do great things through us for His glory.

    c. Let's prepare for God to do great things through us for His glory.

With all due respect, it *can* be done—because our God is able!

WEEK 12

Winner!

Hebrews 12:1, 2
By David Thompson

The Book of Hebrews challenges us to "run with endurance the race that is set before us." God calls us to win the race and gives the three looks of a winner. Like Paul, we are summoned to fight and finish the good fight and thus win the race.

1. Look to the saints (Heb. 12:1).

Saints are the "great cloud of witnesses" in Hebrews 11. The saints are listed in conjunction with one word, "faith." Faith is what made them heroes in God's hall of fame. Look to them not because of their great resources, skill, or popularity. Look because of their faith. That faith made them also "[wait] for a city which has foundations, whose builder and maker is God" (v. 10).

2. Look to the sin (Heb. 12:1).

Sin is the weight that so easily defeats us and keeps us from winning the race. Although we are not sinless, we are to sin less. We are to be holy. Sin is the greatest hindrance to running the race. Look to it and lay it aside.

3. Look to the Savior (Heb. 12:2).

Jesus wrote the book on your faith. He is the finish line. His endurance was due to "the joy that was set before Him." We are winners when Jesus is *our* joy and crown.

Look and win!

WEEK 13

Real Characters: Jesus

Becoming Like Christ in Our Daily Lives!

Part 1
John 4:7–42
By Dr. David A. Wheeler
The Opening Challenge

Who are you most like right now in your actions, attitudes, life habits, and especially your daily responses to a world without Christ? Is it Jesus, or the disciples? In other words, who do you reflect ... God or man?

1. Let's consider Jesus' approach to the unsaved (John 4:7–13).

As you read over this section of chapter 4 in John, the character and compassion of Christ are evident in the masterful ways in which He treats the woman at the well. You will want to take note of the small nuances that verify His commitment to reach out to the unloved and disregarded in culture.

First of all, consider the fact that Jesus *intentionally* traveled through Samaria. While verse 4 states that "He needed to go through Samaria," the truth is that many Jews would have never considered such a detour as a viable option. Rather, they would have chosen to spend precious time traveling *around* Samaria rather than to risk the possibility of mingling with the despised "half-breeds."

According to the actions of Christ, at the very least, the church should intentionally engage with cultural Samaritans. As Jesus states in Matthew 25:40, "Assuredly, I say to you, inasmuch as you did it to one of the least of these My brethren, you did it to Me."

Second, you will note in verse 7 that Jesus *speaks* to the woman. Who would have thought that a simple statement like "Give Me a drink" would have such a profound meaning? The truth is that unlike

His Jewish brethren, Jesus saw this woman in a different light. To Him, she was much more than a social outcast.

From this point, two things are evident about Jesus' actions. First, *His words affirmed the woman's humanity and her value to God.* In addition, unlike the disciples, *He obviously cared more about the woman's soul than His religious traditions.* If this were not true, then why is He in this situation? In fact, beyond His presence in Samaria and His speaking to a woman with questionable morals, there is the nature of His request, "Give Me a drink." Think about it: according to the woman's response, Jesus had "nothing to draw with."

So, what is the point? It is really simple: Jesus was obviously willing to drink from the same container as the woman. Wow! Imagine that! Unlike the disciples or many of us, Jesus was even willing to get Samaritan germs if it resulted in gaining confidence with the woman for the sake of bringing her to faith.

Unfortunately, much like the disciples and us, it bears noting at this point that the church conveniently forgets that reaching out to hurting people is often messy, inconvenient, and outside of established comfort zones and religious taboos.

There is one last observation from this part of the story relating to Christ's approach that will serve to assist in reaching out to an unsaved culture. It is worth observing that *Jesus practiced good, active listening skills with the woman.* That may not sound like much, but in contemporary culture, listening equals love!

This is something that Dr. Jerry Pipes points out in his book *Building a Successful Family.* He makes several observations as he explains different types of listening. For the sake of brevity, Pipes accurately points out that empathetic listening is the deepest level of response. This is exactly what Jesus did with the woman. Before pointing out the woman's obvious sin, Jesus expressed genuine compassion and understanding that eventually led to a Samaritan revival.

2. Let's consider Jesus' presentation (John 4:13–26).

On the heels of Christ's statements in verses 13 and 14 relating to the "fountain of water springing up into everlasting life," note that the woman responds in what appears to be an affirmative manner.

She asks in verse 15, "Sir, give me this water, that I may not thirst, nor come here to draw."

Could this mean that the woman was ready to respond to Christ? Or was she just being sarcastic and still doubted? In either case, unlike most of us, *Jesus was careful not to pick the spiritual fruit too early*. Regardless of the woman's motivation, Jesus was intentional in His actions, yet patient enough to carefully engage the woman in a dialogue that ultimately led to the truth.

Obviously, as it is with anyone else, Jesus knew that the woman must be confronted with her sin before there could be a serious discussion relating to her need of salvation. Jesus does this in verses 15–18 when He addresses the issue of her five husbands.

In addition to dealing with the issue of sin, in verses 21–24, *Jesus calls for the woman to submit her life* and "worship the Father in Spirit and truth." After all, a proper understanding of worship always involves the issue of total submission and surrender to the lordship of the Father.

Another fact that cannot be ignored is that Jesus affirmed in verse 23 that the "Father is seeking such to worship Him." Consider the implications: here is Jesus sharing with a Samaritan woman, and He affirms that God is seeking worshippers, even Samaritans! Wow! Regardless of religious traditions and personal preferences, always be careful not to limit God's grace and mercy to a certain segment of society or culture.

Finally, in verses 25 and 26, in response to the woman's statement "I know that Messiah is coming," Jesus affirms His deity with the words "I who speak to you am He." As a result, the woman *summons the town to come and hear this Man*. She asks in verse 29, "Could this be the Christ?"

At this point, it is worth noting that the woman moves from the natural desire of needing water to sustain her physical body to the spiritual desire of needing water that will feed her soul. She even "leaves her waterpot," an obvious sign that this transition is occurring in her heart, and unlike many Christians today, she would not be silent!

Conclusion

We must pattern our lives after the example of Jesus. After all, He was a Man of compassion; He was a man of love; He is our eternal example! Do your actions and attitudes reflect those of Christ?

SUGGESTED ORDER OF WORSHIP

Prelude—Instrumentalist

CH 213/214 *We Bring the Sacrifice/He Has Made Me Glad*

Worship and Praise—Congregation

NBH 347 *Lord, I Lift Your Name on High* (Chorus 2x in G)

Prayer—Pastor

NBH 322 *Praise the Name of Jesus* (2x in D)

NBH 318 *His Name Is Life* (2x in D)

Welcome—Pastoral Staff

Hymn of Welcome *(meet and greet)*—Congregation

NBH 483 *Friend of God* (2x in C)

Worship and Praise—Congregation

NBH 480 *Step by Step* (2x in F)

NBH 482 *Draw Me Close* (v. 1, chorus, v. 2, chorus in Bb)

Scripture Reading from Philippians 2:6–11 (NIV)

Worship Leader:

Your attitude should be the same as that of Christ Jesus:
6 Who, being in very nature God, did not consider equality with God something to be grasped,

Congregation:

7 but made himself nothing, taking the very nature of a servant, being made in human likeness. **8** And being found in appearance as a man, he humbled himself and became obedient to death—even death on a cross!

Worship Leader:

9 Therefore God exalted him to the highest place and gave him the name that is above every name, **10** that at the name of Jesus every knee should bow in heaven and on earth and under the earth,

Congregation:

11 and every tongue confess that Jesus Christ is Lord, to the glory of God the Father.

> NBH 487 *Knowing You* (v. 1, chorus, v. 2, chorus, v. 3, chorus in C)

Hymn of Surrender & Worship—Praise Team

> NBH 481 *Breathe*

Message—Pastor

Hymn of Response/Invitation

> NBH 542 *In My Life, Be Glorified* (3 verses)

Hymn of Benediction—Congregation

> NBH 296 *He Is Exalted*

Postlude—Instrumental

> NBH 507 *Who Can Satisfy My Soul?* (chorus only)

KEY:

CH: Celebration Hymnal (Word Music/Integrity Music, Nashville, TN)

NBH: New Baptist Hymnal (2008)

WH: The Hymnal (Word Music, Nashville, TN)

SPW: Songs for Praise and Worship (Word Music, Nashville, TN)

MSPW: More Songs for Praise and Worship (Word Music, Nashville, TN)

MSPW2: More Songs for Praise and Worship 2 (Word Music, Nashville, TN)

WEEK 13

The Worthy Walk

Part 1
Ephesians 4:1–6
By Dr. Kent Spann

Paul challenges us to live a life worthy of the calling we received, which is walking in unity (4:1, 4–6).

1. Importance of Unity

    a. It is what Jesus prayed for (John 17:20–26).

    b. It is a powerful witness to the world that Christ is real (John 17:21).

    c. It is the indication of a growing, maturing body of believers (Eph. 4:11–13).

    d. It enables a body to accomplish more than any one individual can (Matt. 18:19; Phil. 1:27).

2. We each must practice humility toward one another if there is to be unity (4:2).

    a. We practice humility when we think properly about ourselves (Rom. 12:3).

        i. We can have too high a view of ourselves.

        ii. We can have too low a view of ourselves.

    b. We practice humility when we think properly about others (Phil. 2:3).

        i. We don't look down on others.

        ii. We don't elevate ourselves above others.

3. We each must practice gentleness toward one another if there is to be unity (4:2).

    a. We practice gentleness by exercising self-control (Prov. 16:32;

Gal. 5:22, 23; 2 Pet. 1:5–7).

    i. We control our tongues (James 3:1–12).

    ii. We control our conduct (Titus 2:12).

    iii. We control our emotions (note Saul's lack of control with his own son in 1 Samuel 20:30–33).

    iv. We control our desires (unlike David in 2 Samuel 11).

    v. We control our attitudes.

b. We practice gentleness by giving up our rights (1 Peter 2:18–25).

c. We practice gentleness by obeying God's Word (James 1:21).

d. We practice gentleness by using our strength for good, not evil (Luke 6:29; 9:51–55; Gal. 6:1; 1 Pet. 3:16).

WEEK 13

Why?

Romans 8:28, 29
By Dr. David Thompson

"Why?" is what's said when you don't get it. The finite will never understand the infinite, yet we are to take comfort in what God says. This beloved promise begins with what "we know" (Rom. 8:28).

There is complete certainty to it. We are not to wonder if or even hope that God is working in our situation. Sovereignty makes it so. There is a certain completeness to it. "All things" means "all things." The good, bad, and ugly are all included.

Many will ask, "Why did God cause or allow that?" Scripture doesn't imply God causes bad things, only that He works even bad things for our good. Why such evil if God is good? Our text doesn't teach that all things are good. Rape and murder are not good. Through the worst thing in life, though, the goodness of God bursts forth.

There are conditions causing the promise to work. It is for those who are "the called," "who love God." That excludes those who don't.

There is an answer to the *why*. It is God's purpose. Paul concludes that those who are called are having "all things work together" ultimately "to be conformed to the image of His Son" (Rom. 8:29). God made you to be like Jesus!

WEEK 14

Real Characters: Jesus

Becoming Like Christ in Our Daily Lives!

Part Two

John 4:27–42

By Dr. David A. Wheeler

The Opening Challenge

You will recall that last week we examined Christ as a man of compassion and love, who reigns as our eternal example! Even though He was placed in a less-than-desirable situation for a Jewish male, He responded to the woman at the well with amazing empathy and compassion, rather than condemnation and disgust. He utilized this awkward situation to demonstrate His love for all people, regardless of nationality. In the end, the woman at the well was so moved by Christ that she rushed back into the town of Samaria to passionately implore the people, "Come, see a man who told me all things I ever did. Could this be the Christ?" (v. 29). So, with all of this as a backdrop ...

Part One: Let's Consider the Disciples' Response (John 4:27–34)

Now let's look at the other side of the equation ... the disciples! Remember that the main issue of this lesson goes back to the Opening Challenge, which asked, "Who are you most like right now in your actions, attitudes, life habits, and especially your daily responses to a world without Christ? Is it Jesus or the disciples? In other words, does your life reflect more about God or man?" As you examine the disciples in light of Christ, keep this personal challenge in mind.

So, how did the disciples respond? First of all, *they would not discuss openly their concerns about Jesus and the woman.* Verse 27 states, "And at this point His disciples came, and they marveled that He talked with a woman; yet no one said, 'What do You seek?' or 'Why are You talking with her?'" There is no doubt that the disciples are uncomfortable with being in Samaria, or that Jesus is publicly speaking with a Samaritan woman of questionable morals. Nevertheless, they are silent.

This may not sound like much, but believe me, their silence speaks volumes. It is almost as if they did not want to say anything that might prolong their stay. One thing is for sure, they obviously ignored the woman as if she did not matter. Unlike Jesus, the disciples did not affirm the woman's humanity or the eternal value of her soul. Their hearts were hardened by years of religious traditions and cultural perceptions. As a result, the disciples' reaction communicated that they did not care about her.

Sadly, unlike the woman and Jesus, it appears the disciples were so distracted by the physical dimension of food that they missed the spiritual point entirely. Consider that the woman was willing to drop her waterpot to pursue a Savior. At the same time, the disciples do not appear willing to drop their prejudice and malice for the Samaritans in order to see the spiritual harvest. What about you?

Part Two: Here Comes the Harvest! (John 4:35–38)

Jesus continues with the theme of doing "the will of Him who sent Me" by responding to the disciples and pointing out the coming harvest. Keep in mind that the disciples are unwilling to grasp the miraculous things that are happening with both the woman and the approaching crowd. In response, Jesus said in verse 35, "Do you not say, 'There are still four months and then comes the harvest'? Behold, I say to you, lift up your eyes and look at the fields, for they are already white for harvest!"

Jesus' excitement is in obvious contrast to the disciples' unconcern about the Samaritans. Nevertheless, He delivers an important lesson about the harvest. He states in verses 36–38, "And he who reaps receives wages, and gathers fruit for eternal life, that both he who sows and he who reaps may rejoice together. For in this the saying is true: 'One sows and another reaps.' I sent you to reap that for which you have not labored; others have labored, and you have entered into their labors."

An understanding of the harvest is essential to the effective ministry of any church. Regardless of the situation, *someone always has to plow (through prayer) and plant (the gospel seed)*! For instance, take a close look at the passage I just read. A paraphrase could be, "Some of you will harvest where you have not plowed or planted; others will plow and plant without directly experiencing the harvest; in either case, someone has to plow and plant for there to be the harvest!"

Part Three: And the Beat Goes On … the Multiplication Principle (John 4:39–42)

There is an essential transition for believers to note in this portion of the story. In verse 39, it states that "many of the Samaritans of that city believed in Him because of the word of the woman who testified." Obviously, this speaks to the imperative that the church must never stop testifying about the works of Christ.

In addition, there is an even greater concept at work. It is the principle of natural multiplication. After Jesus chooses to invest Himself (discipleship) and to stay with the Samaritans for two more days, the ultimate outcome is that the Samaritans grasp salvation and eventually claim it as their own. As it states in verse 42, "Now we believe, not because of what you [the woman] said, for we ourselves have heard Him and we know that this is indeed the Christ, the Savior of the world."

Challenge

This should always be the natural progression of salvation. It begins by way of the Holy Spirit in the hearts of men and women who are redeemed. It must never stop multiplying as the message spreads through the words and deeds of genuine Christ followers!

SUGGESTED ORDER OF WORSHIP

Theme: The Lamb of God

Prelude—Instrumentalist

There Is Power in the Blood

Call to Praise—Congregation

NBH 226 *O The Blood of Jesus* (vv. 1–3 in D, v. 4 in Eb)

NBH 227 *The Blood Will Never Lose Its Power* (v. 1, chorus, v. 2, chorus, chorus)

Worship in Prayer—Pastoral Staff

Welcome—Pastoral Staff

Welcome Song *(meet and greet during song)*—Pastoral Staff

NBH 252 *Down at the Cross* (chorus, v. 1, chorus, v. 4, chorus in G)—Congregation

Praise and Worship—Congregation

NBH 260 *Lamb of Glory* (v. 1, chorus, v. 2, chorus, chorus in G)

NBH 266 *Glory to the Lamb* (2x in C)

NBH 267 *The Lamb upon the Throne* (v. 1, chorus, v. 2, chorus in D)

Prayer of Dedication and Praise—Pastor

NBH 261 *Lamb of God* (chorus only 2x in C)

Worship with Our Gifts—Pastoral Staff

Praise & Worship During Offering

NBH 262 *Behold the Lamb* (2x in Eb)—Solo

Message—Pastor

Hymn of Response/Invitation—Worship Leader and Congregation

> CH 481 *Come, Just as You Are*

Hymn of Benediction—Congregation

> NBH 265 *Hallelujah! Praise the Lamb* (chorus only 1x in G)

Postlude—Instrumentalists

> *He Lives*

KEY:

CH: Celebration Hymnal (Word Music/Integrity Music, Nashville, TN)

NBH: New Baptist Hymnal (2008)

WH: The Hymnal (Word Music, Nashville, TN)

SPW: Songs for Praise and Worship (Word Music, Nashville, TN)

MSPW: More Songs for Praise and Worship (Word Music, Nashville, TN)

MSPW2: More Songs for Praise and Worship 2 (Word Music, Nashville, TN)

WEEK 14

The Worthy Walk

Part 2
Ephesians 4:1–6
By Dr. Kent Spann

The difference between a spotlight and a laser is unity. A laser can be simply described as a medium of excited molecules with mirrors at each end. Some of the excited molecules naturally decay into a less excited state. In the decay process they release a photon, a particle of light. It is here that the unique process of the laser begins.

The photon moves along and tickles another molecule, inviting another photon to join him on his journey. Then these two photons tickle two more molecules and invite two more photons to join the parade. Soon there is a huge army of photons marching in step with each other.

It is this unity that gives the laser its power. A spotlight may have just as many photons, but each is going its own independent way, occasionally interfering with other photons. As a result, much of its power is wasted and cannot be focused to do any useful work. However, the laser, because of its unity, is like an army marching in tight formation and is able to focus all its power on its objective.

[Review points from part 1 of this sermon series.]

1. We must each practice patience toward one another if there is to be unity (4:2).

   a. We tolerate insults instead of striking back.

   b. We make allowance for others' shortcomings, instead of exploding.

   c. We take time with those who aggravate or irritate us.

2. We must each practice forbearance toward one another if there is to be unity (4:2).

    a. We disagree with one another and still love one another.

    b. We still love even when we are sinned against (1 Pet. 4:8).

    c. We take abuse from others while continuing to love them (Prov. 10:12).

3. We must each hold to proper doctrine if there is to be unity (4:4–6).

WEEK 14

Vision

Isaiah 6:1–9
By Dr. David Thompson

God's vision is the key to a healthy church. The preacher must see the Lord, himself, and people, to have a blessed ministry. Isaiah is given the *vision*, *values*, and *victory* for a biblical church.

1. God's *vision* concerns the Lord (Is. 6:1–4).

   God's on His throne because where He does not rule, He overrules. The vision will be consumed with Christ's glory and exalting Jesus. Any heavenly vision will not compromise God's holiness.

2. God's *values* are what matters (Is. 6:5–7).

   God values people, and people matter to God. Personal purity is necessary. The preacher must be right with God before the people will be. Isaiah had core values and clear values. They involved people being reconciled to God. It is solely based on the vision of an exalted Savior.

3. God's *victories* flow out of obedience to a heavenly vision (Is. 6:8, 9).

   This was the key to Paul's success as he planted new churches across the landscape. The voice of God speaks clearly to the one who hates sin and loves Christ. Victory happens when one will go and tell. People will hear your voice when you have heard His voice and tell them about a holy God who can also purge their sins.

WEEK 15

Seeking God: The Desperate Need

Hosea 10:12

By Dr. Kent Spann

Honest Assessment

No doubt everyone here has undergone some kind of assessment in their lives at work, school, or counseling. The purpose of an assessment is to discover where an individual is. Imagine being assessed by God (Jer. 17:9, 10). That is what happened in Hosea.

God's Assessment of Israel (Hos. 10:1–11)

- Israel was prospering (10:1). The analogy of a spreading vine was that of prospering. It was a time of economic prosperity.

- Israel was idolatrous (10:1). The more they prospered, the more unfaithful they became. What an insult that was to God, since He was the one who prospered Israel. Israel forgot the source of their prosperity (Deut. 8).

- Israel had a divided and deceitful heart (10:2). The NIV translates the Hebrew word "deceitful." Its common meaning is "divided." The word was commonly used of parceling out land. Israel had a divided heart. A divided heart is a deceitful heart because it pretends to belong to God when in reality it does not. Their heart was slippery smooth, like a rock in a mountain stream.

- God was going to smash their adulterous idols (10:2).

- Israel would realize the futility of their self-appointed kings to deliver them (10:3).

- Israel would not depend on God to save them because they had rejected Him (10:3). Israel had sealed their own fate by virtue of their choice to trust an earthly king rather than the eternal King.

- Israel was full of deceit and dishonesty (10:4).

- Israel had become a litigious society because of the deceit (10:4). The courts were full of lawsuits. The analogy of the poisonous weeds is that they were popping up everywhere and ruining the field. It was killing Israel.

- Israel was in love with their idols (10:5). The calf-idol of Beth Aven was an idol set up in the city of Bethel. It must have been related to the worship of Baal because of the word translated "priests" later in the verse. They worshipped a heifer, so God called them a stubborn heifer.

- Israel feared the removal of their idols more than God (10:5).

- Israel's gods would be defeated (10:6).

- Israel would be destroyed (10:7).

- Israel's religious shrines would be utterly and completely removed (10:8). The thistle would grow up and cover their once-vibrant altars.

- Israel would be in desperate straits, wanting to die (10:8).

- Israel would now reap what they had sown in God's time (10:9, 10). God made it clear that even though it would be another nation (Assyria) that would conquer Israel, He is behind it all.

- What does He mean by "two transgressions" (10:10)? The text doesn't state it specifically, so we are left to conjecture. I will state two of the commonly held views. The double sin is the sin of Gibeah and now the sin of Bethel—defiant rebellion. Another view is that the double sin is Israel's forsaking God and the house of David (Judah).

- Israel is living a life of unbridled luxury and ease (10:11). The analogy is that of a heifer threshing, which means she is unharnessed, walking around, threshing the corn and eating freely of it. Israel had lived an unbridled life of luxury and ease, doing as she pleased. She was a fat, spoiled heifer. That was all about to change as God put her under the yoke. Her unbridled life of ease was coming to an end.

- Israel would pay a heavy price for her sin (10:11).

A Modern-Day Assessment

There is little difference between Israel and America today. *[The preacher is encouraged to come up with his own comparisons.]*

God's Remedy (Hos. 10:12)

Is the situation hopeless? No. Israel doesn't have to continue down the path of destruction, and neither do we. Right in the middle of His assessment, God tells Israel how to change its destiny. It involves two parallel action steps.

Action Step #1: Sow Righteousness

The righteousness that Hosea speaks of here is two-dimensional.

1. We are to sow righteousness toward God—vertically (Ps. 45:7; Prov. 21:21).

2. We are to sow righteousness toward others—horizontally.

The outward evidence of the person who is living righteous before God is how he or she relates to others.

Action Step #2: Seek God

Parallel with sowing righteousness, there must be seeking of God. The Hebrew word for *seek* here means to seek with care or to inquire. It was something they were to diligently do. This was not a casual seeking; this was earnest seeking of God. See Deuteronomy 4:29; 1 Chronicles 22:19; Isaiah 55:6; and Jeremiah 29:13.

What does it mean to seek God? I would offer some practical applications:

1. We long for Him (Ps. 42:1, 2).

2. We make Him the priority in our lives (Matt. 6:33).

3. We spend time daily with God (Mark 1:35).

4. We run *to* God instead of *from* God (Prov. 18:10).

5. We practice His presence in our daily lives (Ps. 89:15; Matt. 28:20).

What Will You Do? (Hos. 10:13–15)

What would Israel do? God already knew. Israel was stubborn; she refused to turn from her wicked ways and seek God. What happened to Israel? Israel was conquered by Assyria in 722 BC under the rule of Shalmaneser V. The days of Israel as a sovereign nation ended.

It is too late for Israel, but it is not too late for you.

- Will you be stubborn and hardheaded (Hos. 4:16)?

- Will you repent of your stubbornness and instead sow righteousness and seek God (Rev. 2:5)?

SUGGESTED ORDER OF WORSHIP

Prelude—Instrumental Group

> *Come, Now Is the Time to Worship*

Call to Worship—Pastoral Prayer

> NBH 30 *Come, Now Is the Time to Worship* (2x in D)

Call to Worship—Praise Team

> *Jesus, Lover of My Soul*

Welcome—Pastoral Staff

Song of Welcome (*meet and greet*)—Congregation

> NBH 66 *Open the Eyes of My Heart* (2x in D)

Worship and Praise—Congregation

> NBH 579 *I Will Enter His Gates* (2x in D)

> MSPW *Ancient of Days* (2x in D)

> NBH 588 *Sanctuary* (1x in D, 1x in Eb)

Offertory Prayer—Pastoral Staff

Offertory Praise—Praise Team

> *All of the Glory* (Geron Davis-Benson-Brentwood Pub)

Message—Pastor

Hymn of Response/Invitation—Congregation

CH 596 *I Surrender All*

Hymn of Benediction—Congregation

We Bring a Sacrifice of Praise

Postlude—Instrumental Group

I Will Enter His Gates

KEY:

CH: Celebration Hymnal (Word Music/Integrity Music, Nashville, TN)

NBH: New Baptist Hymnal (2008)

WH: The Hymnal (Word Music, Nashville, TN)

SPW: Songs for Praise and Worship (Word Music, Nashville, TN)

MSPW: More Songs for Praise and Worship (Word Music, Nashville, TN)

WEEK 15

Doing Church God's Way

Ephesians 4:7–16
By Dr. Kent Spann

This passage, probably more than any other single passage, sets out the direction God has designed for the church. No plan for church growth that violates the principle of Ephesians 4:11–16 can really be effective and blessed by God.

—John MacArthur

God's Plan for the Church

1. We exercise His gifts for ministry (4:7–10).

   a. We received a spiritual gift when we were saved (Rom. 12:6–8; 1 Cor. 12:7–10; 1 Pet. 4:10).

   b. We each need to discover our spiritual gift.

   c. We each need to exercise our spiritual gift (1 Cor. 12:14–26).

   d. We need to build the ministries of the church around spiritual gifts.

2. We implement His plan for ministry (4:11, 12a).

   a. His plan is for gifted leaders to equip gifted people (4:11, 12).

   b. His plan is for equipped and gifted people to do the work of the ministry (4:12).

      i. It means that every believer is a minister.

      ii. It means the success of the church's ministry depends on the people.

      iii. It means the ministries of the church are to be born out of the heart of the people who make up the body.

The Results of Following God's Plan

- We will be united in doctrine (4:13).
- We will have a deeper relationship with Christ (4:13).
- We will mature spiritually (4:13).
- We will be stable in the faith (4:14).
- We will proclaim the truth in love (15).
- We will experience true unity as we each do our part (16).

WEEK 15

Prescription for the Tongue

James 5:13–20
By Dr. David Thompson

The tongue can be a best friend or worst enemy—a tool for God or Satan. God prescribes four uses for it: to *pray*, to *praise*, to *purge*, and to *proclaim*.

1. Pray (James 5:13)

Call the elders if necessary, but remember that the prayer of a righteous person accomplishes much. God can do more through just one who is just than a group that isn't.

2. Praise (James 5:13)

Sing psalms that instruct us that God lives in such doxology. Praise and prayer are the best uses of that unruly muscle in your mouth. Opera singers live longer because their lung capacity is greater. Praising God in song is fitting for every occasion.

3. Purge (James 5:16)

Purge your conscience and spirit by confessing your faults. Faults are not the same as sins. Do not air your dirty laundry; that glorifies Satan. Pray for others' healing. The planet needed healing after it was cursed. Elijah's prayer (see v. 17) had more impact than all the environmentalists put together. It rained or didn't rain when God's man prayed.

4. Preach (James 5:20)

Preach to the fallen one. God can use your tongue to "save a soul from death." Silent tongues are deadly as well.

WEEK 16

A Communion Service

Blood and Eternity

Hebrews 9:15–22
By Dr. Calvin Miller

Introduction

Only in Christianity does human blood hold a redemptive—really breathtaking—symbolism. God's forgiveness lies at the root of this symbol. Hebrews 9:22 says that without the shedding of blood, there is no forgiveness of sin. Christ provided us with this inheritance, according to Hebrews 9:16. He also gives us daily grace as we mingle the blood of our intention with the blood of his achievement (John 6:53–58).

In Romans 5:8 Paul says we are totally justified by Christ's blood. As we contemplate, we may at first have an automatic revulsion to the whole idea of blood sacrifice. The notion is so unpleasant to so many expositors that they have replaced the "blood of Christ" terminology with "the death of Christ." But all such revulsion is an insult to the power and purity of this symbol.

The Glory of the Blood

The late Paul Brand wrote a magnificent tribute to the metaphor of the saving blood of Christ.

> Sixty *thousand* miles of blood vessels link every living cell; even the vessels themselves are fed by other blood vessels. Highways narrow down to one-lane roads, then bike paths, then footpaths, until finally the red cells must bow sideways and edge through a capillary one-tenth the diameter of a human hair. In such narrow confines the cells are stripped

of oxygen and loaded down with carbon dioxide and urea. If shrunken down to their size, we would see red cells as bloated bags of jelly and iron drifting along in a river until they reach the smallest capillary, where gases fizz and wheeze in and out of surface membranes. From there the red cells rush to the kidneys for a thorough scrubbing, then back to the lungs for a refill. And the journey begins anew. . . .

The pellmell journey, even to the extremity of the big toe, lasts a mere twenty seconds. An average red cell endures the cycle of loading, unloading, *and* jostling through the body for a half million round trips over four months. In one final journey to the spleen, the battered cell is stripped bare by scavenger cells and recycled into new cells. Three hundred billion red cells die and are replaced every day, leaving behind various parts to reincarnate in a hair follicle or a taste bud
. . . .

Blood once repulsed me. I saw it as the most distasteful part of medical treatment. Now, *however* ... I feel like assembling all my blood cells and singing to them a hymn of praise. The drama of resurrection ... takes place without fanfare in each heartbeat of a healthy human being. Every cell in every body *lives at the mercy of the blood*.[1]

But communion speaks of a miracle beyond the ordinary natural miracles of the blood. In communion we celebrate the mercy of the blood of Christ that somehow fills us with redemption. This is so much so that the writer of Hebrews exclaims, "Without shedding of blood there is no remission" (9:22).

Still, his forgiveness is bound up in mystery. How is it that one man dying in the Near East twenty centuries ago can wrap and spindle and twist the centuries together, so that one man's blood becomes a mercy all its own?

Blood, the Inheritance

Not only does his blood forgive, but it also provides for us an inheritance.

---

[1] Paul Brand, *In His Image* (Grand Rapids: Zondervan, 1984), 57–49.

"For where there is a testament, there must also of necessity be the death of the testator. For a testament is in force after men are dead, since it has no power at all while the testator lives" (Heb. 9:16, 17). Two great legacies become ours because of the blood of Christ. One of these two legacies is found in John 16:

> I tell you the truth. It is to your advantage that I go away; for if I do not go away, the Helper will not come to you; but if I depart, I will send Him to you. (v. 7)

When Jesus closed his eyes in death, He knew that He could send the Holy Spirit to live in our lives.

But besides this legacy of the Spirit, one other legacy became ours. Jesus knew He could not provide us an inheritance until His blood was spilled. He knew that for a will to be enforced, the maker of the will must die. God's will for each of us is that we inherit all of heaven and live forever in the eternal presence of Christ.

In the Blood God Provides for His Children

As Jesus closed his eyes in death, He was able to say to His Father, as the last drops of blood fell from His hands, "Look, Father, how I have provided for My children! Everyone who has loved Me in return is provided for eternally. I have spent My blood on this testament, given my life to this legacy."

The Blood of Our Eternity

The final thing the blood of Christ does is to provide us an eternal salvation.

> But God demonstrates His own love toward us, in that while we were still sinners, Christ died for us. Much more then, having now been justified by His blood, we shall be saved from wrath through Him. (Rom. 5:8, 9)

Jesus' death provides for us eternal life and an everlasting inheritance. And He literally overcame death first. It is as though Jesus says to us in point-blank language:

> *Look, today I have suffered; tomorrow you will suffer. Today upon the wood, I bled. Tomorrow you will bleed. Today, I was tempted. Tomorrow you will be tempted. Today I was abandoned. Tomorrow you must stand alone. But today my blood was the blood of the OVERCOMER. Tomorrow, you will spend your own blood as the blood of an overcomer. So when you lift the communion cup, remember this: The only overcomer that counts is the victor whose blood is the purchase of overcoming.*

The late Paul Brand tells about a time on the mission field when his oldest daughter had the measles. He realized that unless she could be free of the measles, she would really suffer. If only he had a dram of serum, an immunization from another bloodstream, she would be spared the coming bout with fever and pain. He said, "What I really needed was just an ounce or less of blood from someone who had already had the measles … what I needed for my little girl was the blood of an overcomer."

Conclusion

In Jesus Christ, we find the inoculation of salvation! We have the victory over death that someone else has already achieved. Ah, this is the mystery that redeems, the blood of our great Overcomer. And what a victory He gave us! What a price He paid! Joy Davidman wrote it all down for us in these words.

> Our generation has never seen a man crucified except in sugary religious art; but it was not a sweet sight, and few of us would dare to have a real picture of a crucifixion hanging on our bedroom walls. A crucified slave beside the Roman road screamed until his voice died and then hung, a filthy, festering clot of flies, sometimes for days—a living man whose hands and feet were swollen masses of gangrenous meat. That is what our Lord took upon himself."[2]

There is a great overcoming in the blood of Christ. There is no cheap

---

[2] Joy Davidson, *Smoke on the Mountain* (Philadelphia: Westminster Press, 1953, 1954), 20.

grace. Every victory of importance is dearly bought. Take the juice and study it. Examine the bread and then your soul. This brief meal is pricey stuff! But look at your legacy and give thanks to the great Overcomer. Then look to the clouds, for what you meet in this cup and on this plate will enable to you to see that crown that Christ the righteous judge shall give to you on that day, and not to you only but to all those also who love His appearing (2 Tim. 4:6).

SUGGESTED ORDER OF WORSHIP

Theme: The Cross of Jesus ...

Prelude—Instrumentalists

The Old Rugged Cross

Purpose of the Cross ...

Call to Praise—Congregation

NBH 237 *I Stand Amazed in the Presence* (v. 1, chorus, v. 2, chorus, v. 4, chorus in G)

Prayer of Praise—Pastoral Staff

Welcome—Pastoral Staff

Hymn of Welcome (*meet and greet during song*)—Congregation

NBH 240 *Mighty Is the Power of the Cross* (2x in Eb)

The Word (Responsive Reading #242 in NBH)—Worship Leader and Congregation

NBH 242 *O Mighty Cross* (v. 1, chorus, v. 2, chorus, v. 4, chorus in D)

Hearing the Word (2 Cor. 13:4; Col. 1:19, 20, 22; Gal. 6:14—Pastor

NBH 239 *The Wonderful Cross* (v. 1, v. 2, chorus, v. 3 in C)

Power of the Cross ...

Prayer of Praise—Worship Leader (keyboard play next song during prayer)

Praise and Worship—Congregation

NBH 232 *The Power of the Cross* (vv. 1, 3, 4 in C)

... Person on the Cross!!!

Offertory Prayer—Pastor

NBH 242 *Hallelujah, What a Savior* (vv. 1–4 in Bb, v. 5 in C)—Congregation

Sermon—Pastor

Hymn of Invitation—Congregation

CH 481 *Come Just as You Are*

Benediction Hymn—Congregation

NBH 252 *Down at the Cross* (v. 1, chorus in G)

Postlude—Instrumentalists

Because He Lives

KEY:

CH: Celebration Hymnal (Word Music/Integrity Music, Nashville, TN)

NBH: New Baptist Hymnal (2008)

WEEK 16

Live the New Life

Part 1
Ephesians 4:17–32
By Dr. Kent Spann

This section of Ephesians is marked off by a call to live (4:17); it is a call to live the new life. It begins with the need to change what we are wearing.

1. We need to put off the garments of the old life (4:17–19).

    a. It is a life of futility (4:17).

    b. It is a life of darkness (4:18a).

        i. They live in darkness because there is no light.

        ii. They become accustomed to the darkness (John 9:40–41).

        iii. They become comfortable with the darkness (John 3:19).

    c. It is a life of alienation (4:18b).

        i. Alienation from the presence of God (Is. 59:2; Eph. 2:12).

        ii. Alienation from fellowship with God (Eph. 2:12; 1 Cor. 1:9).

        iii. Alienation from the life of God (1 John 5:12; Eph. 2:1)

    d. It is a life of callousness (4:18c, 19a).

    e. It is a life of reckless sensuality (4:19b).

2. We need to put on the garments of the new life (4:20–24).

    a. We receive Christ (4:20).

        2 Cor. 13:5; James 4:4; 1 John 2:4, 15

    b. We know Christ (4:21).

    c. We put off the old self (4:22).

        Rom. 6:5–14

    d. We renew our minds (4:23).

    e. We put on the new self (4:24).

        i. We welcome it.

        ii. We appropriate it.

        iii. We act on it.

WEEK 16

Servitude

2 Corinthians 5:8–11
By Dr. David Thompson

The chief of sinners was the chief of servants. Paul served Jesus more passionately than his peers. What was the key to this passion? It was his four *attitudes of servitude*.

1. Anticipation (2 Cor. 5:8)

"Confident" is used often. Paul feared neither death nor impending judgment. It's crazy to anticipate being judged by God. Paul actually was willing and preferred to leave earth and serve Christ in person.

2. Acceptance (2 Cor. 5:9)

Labor was his legacy. Paul worked fervently for Jesus because his attitude was such. We are not saved *by* works but are certainly saved *for* works.

3. Appearance (2 Cor. 5:10)

All appear, and *everyone* receives. There's no escape from the judgment, and it begins in the house of God. This is to stimulate not stifle the servant. We will give an account and then receive what is due. What a motivation. It has been said, "One life to live will soon pass, but only what is done for Christ will last!"

4. Apprehension (2 Cor. 5:11)

Knowing the terror of the Lord, we persuade men. The word translated "persuade" contains the words *through* and *sweetness*. The great Christ servant was a master at that, as He became all things to all men. Mixed emotions coexisted, yet four great attitudes of servitude dominated.

WEEK 17

The Joy of the Resurrection

1 Corinthians 15:58
By Gary R. Habermas, PhD

The resurrection of Jesus occupies the very center of the earliest Christian proclamation. Most treatments concentrate on either its apologetic or its soteriological value as the key to the gospel message. However, the Resurrection is referred to in more than three hundred New Testament verses, where it guarantees the truth of many major doctrines as well as grounding our Christian practice. The focus here is the relation between the greatest miracle and the committed Christian life.

What sort of application follows from the truth of Jesus' resurrection? We will follow the message of what some have called the resurrection chapter in the New Testament, namely 1 Corinthians 15. Here Paul's final move is to point out that, since the Resurrection really occurred, it grounds our motivation for daily living.

1. Paul's Approach in 1 Corinthians 15

    a. The gospel message was preached at Corinth. When the message was accompanied by biblical faith, the individual was saved (15:1, 2).

        Note: In the New Testament, particularly in Paul's epistles and the Book of Acts, the factual content of the gospel is, at a minimum, the deity, death, and resurrection of Jesus (for example, Rom. 10:9). Further, saving faith is more than simply believing that these facts were true. It requires trust in and commitment to Jesus Christ Himself, in light of these truths.

    b. Paul received this gospel message from others, and passed it on (15:3, 4). Most scholars think that Paul received this report from Peter and James the brother of Jesus when he met them in Jerusalem, three years after his conversion (Gal. 1:18–20). This report contained the message of Christ's death, resurrection, and several key appearances to both individuals and groups, to which Paul adds his own appearance (15:5–8).[3] All the apostles were preaching this same message (15:9–11).

c. The Resurrection ensured Christian truths and practices, such as Christian preaching, the forgiveness of sins, and the believer's resurrection (15:12–18). Therefore, far from being the most miserable persons (20:19), believers have a firm foundation for their own eternal futures (15:20–23).

Jesus' resurrection thus becomes both the foundation as well as the pattern for the believers' resurrection (15:35–49). Upon this basis, Paul moves on to further practical considerations.

2. Paul's Conclusion: Grounding Our Most Treasured Christian Beliefs and Practice

a. Paul reaches his crescendo in the last few verses of this chapter. The resurrection of Jesus insures not only the truth of the Christian faith and message, but allows believers to rest securely on this foundation. This allows us to push onward to other areas of commitment.

b. For example, the Resurrection grounds Christian ethics. Earlier, Paul even said that if the dead were not raised, which depends on Jesus' resurrection, then believers may as well revert to a hedonistic lifestyle of eating, drinking, and merrymaking (15:32, quoting Isaiah 22:13)! Absolutely amazingly, apart from Jesus' resurrection, Christians would be living like the world! This wonderful event provides the foundation for our ethical actions as well as our theology.

c. Moreover, Paul wraps up his overall message in 1 Corinthians 15:58 by explaining that because of the Resurrection, believers should stand firmly in the Lord and never be moved. This is crucial in a day when we read about movements like the New Atheism and hear that our young people who head to secular colleges report frequently that they left their faith. But a firm

---

[3] For further details, see Gary R. Habermas and Michael Licona, *The Case for the Resurrection of Jesus* (Grand Rapids: Kregel, 2004).

faith foundation is an incredible blessing, provided by the resurrection.

d. Further, Paul then commands believers to get to work. He sees an argument directly from the Resurrection to our practical commitment to others, for the very next verses (16:1–4) provide instructions for taking an offering for suffering believers. Because Jesus is risen, we should be involved in meeting others' needs. In my opinion, everything we do for the Lord after salvation determines the capacity to which we will enjoy eternity, so our labor is definitely not in vain.

e. Perhaps most crucially, Paul emphasizes the most obvious connection between the risen Christ and believers: we will be raised like our Lord. This truth is mentioned almost twenty times in the New Testament.[4] But Paul actually taunts death in the process: "O, Death, where is your sting? O, Hades where is your victory?" (15:55, quoting Hos. 13:14). Paul gets in death's face! Although he was well aware that death still claimed the lives of believers, Paul also knew that the Resurrection was the beginning of the end; the apostle was clear that one day death's reign would end forever (15:24–26).

Conclusion

For Paul, Jesus' resurrection was more than the greatest evidence for Christianity. It is also relevant to our everyday lives, for it not only guarantees the truth of our most treasured theological beliefs, but it grounds our practical actions and service to God.

---

4 For examples, see John 11:25, 26; 14:19; Acts 4:1, 2; 1 Corinthians 6:14;
   2 Corinthians 4:14–18; 1 Peter 1:3–5; 1 John 3:2.

SUGGESTED ORDER OF WORSHIP

Prelude—Instrumentalist

Celebrate Jesus, Celebrate

Call to Prayer—Pastoral Staff

Worship and Praise—Congregation

NBH 269 *He Lives* (v. 1, chorus, v. 2, chorus in Ab)

Welcome—Pastoral Staff

NBH 269 *He Lives* (v. 3, chorus, chorus in Ab)

NBH 449 *Because He Lives* (chorus, v. 1, chorus, v. 3, chorus in Ab)

Baptismal Celebration—Pastoral Staff

Scripture Reading from Mark 16:1–7 *(Please have prepared for IMAG)*

Worship Leader:

1 Now when the Sabbath was past, Mary Magdalene, Mary the mother of James, and Salome bought spices, that they might come and anoint Him.

Congregation:

2 Very early in the morning, on the first day of the week, they came to the tomb when the sun had risen. **3** And they said among themselves, "Who will roll away the stone from the door of the tomb for us?"

Worship Leader:

4 But when they looked up, they saw that the stone had been rolled away—for it was very large. **5** And entering the tomb, they saw a young man clothed in a long white robe sitting on the right side; and they were alarmed.

Congregation:

6 But he said to them, "Do not be alarmed. You seek Jesus of

Nazareth, who was crucified. He is risen! He is not here. See the place where they laid Him.

Worship Leader:

7 But go, tell His disciples—and Peter—that He is going before you into Galilee; there you will see Him, as He said to you."

> NBH 273 *Christ Arose* (v. 1, v. 2)

Prayer of Thanksgiving—Pastor

> NBH 277 *He Is Lord* (chorus in F, chorus in G)
>
> NBH 278 *I Live* (2x in G)

Offertory Prayer—Pastor

Offertory Praise—Soloist and Praise Team

> *Were You There?*

Message—Pastor

Hymn of Response/Invitation—Congregation

> CH 488 *Just as I Am*

Benediction Hymn—Congregation

> MSPW 12 *The Name of the Lord* (2x in F)

Postlude—Instrumental Group

> MSPW 54 *Christ the Lord Is Risen Today*

KEY:

CH: Celebration Hymnal (Word Music/Integrity Music, Nashville, TN)

NBH: New Baptist Hymnal (2008)

MSPW: More Songs for Praise and Worship (Word Music, Nashville, TN)

WEEK 17

Live the New Life

Part 2
Ephesians 4:17–32
By Dr. Kent Spann

A guy was in his swimming pool, relaxing on a float, when another guy walked up and said, "There you are, lying around in the lap of luxury, while thousands of people around the world are suffering." The fellow lying on the float looked at the guy and said, "Name one of them."

In verses 25 through 32, Paul gets very specific and names what we are to exchange.

1. We exchange lying for truthfulness (4:25).

    a. We stop all forms of lying ("pseudo").

        i. Fabricating a lie

        ii. Embellishing the truth

        iii. Hedging on the truth

        iv. Bearing false witness against other people (Ex. 20:16; 23:1; 25:18)

        v. Living a lie (Matt. 23:27, 28)

        vi. Pretending everything is OK

    b. We speak the truth.

        i. Our word is our bond.

        ii. What we say is unqualifiedly true.

        iii. We are honest.

        iv. We care enough to confront a brother or sister in sin.

2. We exchange unrighteous anger for righteous anger (4:26, 27).

    a. We put off our old unrighteous anger.

      i. Internalized anger

      ii. Intensifying anger

      iii. Irrational anger

      iv. Indiscriminate anger

  b. We put on righteousness anger.

      God's anger (Ex. 4:14; Ps. 7:11) and Christ's anger (Matt. 21:12–17)

      i. It means we get angry about the right things (Ps. 119:53).

      ii. It means that if we get angry, we don't allow it to become sin.

      iii. It means that we deal with our anger quickly.

Assess feelings (Gen. 4:5–8)

Neutralize the emotions (Ps. 103:8; James 1:19, 20)

Gauge the anger (Prov. 29:11; Amos 1:11)

Engage the correct person (Matt. 5:22–24; 18:15)

Resolve the situation (Matt. 5:23, 24; 7:3–5)

> (Acrostic taken from an article by Dr. Richard Berry,
> "Anger Management" on LifeWay.com)

WEEK 17

Right Relationship

Psalm 37:1–7
By Dr. David Thompson

Relationships are the greatest blessing or the greatest curse. The manner we relate to loved ones or friends has everything to do with the way we relate to the Lord. David's psalm gives four keys to right relationships—trust, delight, commit, and rest.

1. "Trust" is the opposite of fret.

People often trust a mechanic or fast food worker more than God. It›s always safe to trust Jesus. Healthy relationships always breed trust. Trust God with everything.

2. "Delight" yourself in Christ.

God wants to fulfill your heart's desire. More important, He wants to be your heart's delight. Delight yourself in your loved one, and trust God with the results.

3. "Commit" to Christ first if you want people to do what's right.

Your relationship to God is the best barometer for your relationship to others. "He will bring it to pass." God requires stewards to be faithful and committed.

4. "Rest" in the relationship.

This is the most difficult. Let go of the wheel. Joyful relationships with others and God are the norm. You can't be angry and rest at the same time. It's OK to rest. "Trust Me," says the Lord!

WEEK 18

What About Emotional Doubt?

Philippians 4:6–9
By Gary R. Habermas, PhD

Virtually all believers struggle at times with questions regarding their faith. In Scripture, similar concerns also plagued God's people. Abraham (Gen. 18:15–17), Job (Job 7:11; 10:3), David (Ps. 13:1, 2), Jeremiah (Jer. 12:1; 15:18), as well as John the Baptist (Luke 7:18–23) and Paul (2 Cor. 12:7–9), all struggled with various questions. This list of heroes includes patriarchs, kings, prophets, as well as apostles. So we are in good company, though this is not an excuse.

But the subject of religious doubt can be a very tricky one. Often simply denied, it is too seldom discussed in ways that can be helpful or provide long-term relief for persons who may suffer horribly. Far too often, we misdiagnose these problems and try to treat it in unhelpful ways.

I will define religious doubt as "a lack of certainty regarding the teachings of Christianity or one's personal relation to them."[5] Examples of this uncertainty can include:

- Questions about our personal assurance of salvation
- Questions concerning the truthfulness of our beliefs
- Questions pertaining to our pain and suffering
- Questions regarding our unanswered prayers

Unfortunately, there are many false beliefs regarding the nature of religious doubt, such as the following:

- Doubt is always sinful, perhaps even the unpardonable sin.
- Doubt never occurs to believers in Scripture.
- Doubt is always solved by studying the evidences.

---

[5] Gary R. Habermas, *Dealing with Doubt* (Chicago: Moody, 1990), 10.

- Doubt occurs most commonly in the elderly.
- Doubt never affects atheists or agnostics.
- Doubt is rare among believers.
- Doubt is always the opposite of faith.
- Doubt usually follows a similar pattern.
- Doubt is usually corrected the same way.
- Doubt never produces positive results.

There are at least three distinct species or types of religious doubt:

1. *Factual doubt* typically raises tough questions of a philosophical, historical, or scientific nature.

2. *Emotional doubt* is usually related closely to our moods or feelings, and often asks what-if questions regarding whether our faith could possibly be mistaken, though usually without any specific evidential reasons for doing so.

3. *Volitional doubt* usually concerns one's lack of will or desire to follow God completely, and is often characterized by lethargy or absence of motivation.

Of these three species, emotional doubt appears to be by far both the most common and the most painful. However, it is usually far less dangerous than we think or tell ourselves. The remainder of this message will deal with this specific type of doubt.

Counselors often suggest treating emotional pain by sound psychological strategies.[6] For example, in spite of what we often think, "It is not, however, either events past or present that make us feel the way we feel, but our *interpretations of those events*."[7] In other words, the painful feelings that we call emotional doubts generally come from how we download things in our minds. Since, as Christians, our faith is crucial to us, if we persist in thinking or telling ourselves, "Maybe I'm

---

[6] For more on this topic, plenty of very readable works by qualified people are readily available. For one of the very best, see William Backus and Marie Chapian, *Telling Yourself the Truth* (Minneapolis: Bethany, 2000), especially chapters 1–3.

[7] Ibid., 17

not really saved," or, "What if it's not true after all?" painful feelings will result. However, if we change our words and thinking, and practice truth,[8] our feelings should change, as well.

Scripture teaches this same truth in dozens of passages. Therefore, it is absolutely essential that we watch what we say (and think) both to ourselves as well as to others.[9] Philippians 4:6–9 promises peace in place of our anxiety. Few texts are more loaded with great advice:

- Paul's language in 4:6 indicates his readers were currently suffering anxiety, perhaps the chief subspecies of emotional doubt.
- Paul commands prayer in the place of the worry (4:6). Peter orders believers to give their anxieties to God (1 Pet. 5:7).
- Paul states that thanksgiving (4:6) and praise (4:8b) are also antidotes to anxiety. Countless believers have personally discovered the same truth.

Paul instructs us, perhaps most crucially, to replace the anxious thoughts with God's truth (4:8a).[6]

6. See also Ps. 39:2; 42:5, 6, 11; 43:5; 55:4–8, 16, 17, 22; 56:3, 4; 73:26; Prov. 14:30; 17:22.

- Paul commands the practice of these principles (4:9).
- Paul twice promises God's peace to those who obey (4:7, 9b).

Conclusion

Doubt is a difficult subject, but the application of God's truth can bring substantial relief.[10] Correcting our thinking is the key to peace.

---

[8] For many suggestions on ways to practice these truths, see Gary R. Habermas, *The Thomas Factor: Using Your Doubts to Grow Closer to God* (Nashville: Broadman and Holman, 1999), especially chapters 6–8.

[9] See Ps. 94:19; 141:3, 4; Prov. 4:23–27; 10:21; 12:18, 25; 15:13–15; 18:21.

[10] Both of the Habermas books listed above on doubt are out of print, but are freely available on his web site: www.garyhabermas.com.

SUGGESTED ORDER OF WORSHIP

Prelude—Instrumentalist

Bless the Name of Jesus

Call to Praise—Congregation

NBH 7 *Come, Let Us Worship and Bow Down* (2x in D)

NBH 451 *In Moments Like These* (2x in D)

NBH 47 *Fairest Lord Jesus* (v. 1, v. 3 in D, v. 4 in Eb)

Worship in Prayer—Pastoral Staff

Welcome—Pastoral Staff

Welcome Song (*meet and greet during song*)—Pastoral Staff

NBH 445 *Yes, Lord, Yes* (2x in Eb)

Worship and Praise—Congregation

NBH 301 *Crown Him King of Kings* (1x in Ab, 1x in A)

MSPW 22 *Crown Him King of Kings* (1x in Bb)

Shout to the Lord (From *God for Us* Book) (1x in Bb, 1x in C)

Worship with Our Gifts—Pastoral Staff

Praise and Worship During Offering

CH 705 *It Is Well with My Soul* (chorus, v. 1, chorus in C, v. 4, chorus in Db)

Message—Pastor

Hymn of Response/Invitation—Worship Leader and Congregation

NBH 411 *Come, Just as You Are*

Hymn of Benediction—Congregation

NBH 20 *Great and Mighty* (1x in Eb with Tag)

Postlude—Instrumentalists

Great and Mighty

KEY:

CH: Celebration Hymnal (Word Music/Integrity Music, Nashville, TN)

NBH: New Baptist Hymnal (2008)

WH: The Hymnal (Word Music, Nashville, TN)

SPW: Songs for Praise and Worship (Word Music, Nashville, TN)

MSPW: More Songs for Praise and Worship (Word Music, Nashville, TN)

MSPW2: More Songs for Praise and Worship 2 (Word Music, Nashville, TN)

WEEK 18

Live the New Life

Part 3
Ephesians 4:17–32
By Dr. Kent Spann

[Review the previous points from this series.]

1. We exchange stealing for hard work and sharing (4:28).

    a. We stop stealing.

    b. We engage in productive labor.

    c. We start sharing (Acts 20:35).

2. We exchange unwholesome speech for wholesome speech (4:29).

    a. Put off unwholesome speech.

    i. Foul speech or cursing (2 Sam. 16:5–8)

    ii. Reckless speech (Prov. 12:18)

    iii. Harsh words (Prov. 15:1)

    iv. Coarse jesting (Prov. 26:18, 19)

    v. Gossip (Prov. 26:20)

    vi. Slander (Eph. 4:31)

    vii. Careless speech (Matt. 12:36)

    viii. Flattery (1 Thess. 2:5)

    ix. Critical speech (James 3:9–12)

    b. Put on wholesome speech.

    i. Restrained speech: "only" (NIV; see also Prov. 10:19)

    ii. Edifying speech: "helpful" (NIV)

    iii. Fitting speech: "according to their needs" (NIV; see also Prov. 15:23; 24:26; 25:11)

      iv. Gracious speech: "that it may benefit those who listen" (NIV)

3. We exchange unforgiveness for forgiveness (4:31, 32)

    a. Unforgiveness (4:31)

        i. Bitterness (Heb. 12:15)

        ii. Wrath (1 Sam. 25:13, 20–22)

        iii. Seething anger (2 Sam. 13:22)

        iv. Clamor (Prov. 9:13; Luke 23:23)

        v. Slander (Ps. 101:5)

        vi. Malice (Ps. 28:3)

"Unforgiveness is like drinking poison and then hoping it will kill your enemies."

—Nelson Mandela

---

    b. Forgiveness (4:32)

There was a man who hated the preacher Henry Ward Beecher but later became his devoted friend. The reason for the change was simple. Beecher was not happy until he had done the offender a good deed. The Proverb in Brooklyn was "If you want a favor from Beecher, kick him."

WEEK 18

Martyr

Acts 6:1–7
By Dr. David Thompson

There is one thing skeptics can't explain. How did the early disciples go from being the faithless, fearful disciples to the fearless, faithful followers of Jesus? The resurrection is the obvious and only explanation. The risen Lord is the difference between Christianity and all other belief systems. Stephen no doubt knew Christ intimately and believed in Him wholeheartedly. This kind of faith made him gladly the first martyr in Christianity.

Two characteristics permeated Stephen and should all Christians, and those are *faithfulness* and *fearlessness*! Christian martyrs are not like the unholy jihadists, who kill innocent women and children. Stephen rose to meet the needs of neglected women. Deacons were chosen for their impeccable integrity. Murder or suicide would be the last thing in Stephen's heart. Instead, the martyr's faithful heart made heaven proud and made Jesus stand to receive him to glory.

This fearlessness in Stephen impacted Philip, the first missionary, and Paul, the great apostle. These men were doubtlessly influenced by Stephen's courage in the face of death. Paul later wrote to Timothy that these "obtain for themselves ... a great boldness in the faith which is in Christ Jesus" (1 Tim. 3:13).

Let us emulate the faithfulness and fearlessness of the Christian martyr that causes men to believe in the Lord Jesus Christ, and for Christ Himself to stand in honor to his boldness.

WEEK 19

Mother's Day

Celebrating Mother's Day: What Does It Mean to Ponder?

Luke 1:26–33, 39–45; 2:6–19
By Dr. David A. Wheeler

Introduction

While most people tend to believe that Mother's Day was created by greedy companies like Hallmark, hoping to cash in by selling millions of greeting cards annually, believe it or not, this is not the case. According to the Website www.123Holiday.net:

> In the United States, Mother's Day started nearly 150 years ago, when Anna Jarvis, an Appalachian homemaker, organized a day to raise awareness of poor health conditions in her community, a cause she believed would be best advocated by mothers. She called it "Mother›s Work Day." ...
>
> In 1905 when Anna Jarvis died, her daughter, also named Anna, began a campaign to memorialize the life work of her mother. Legend has it that young Anna remembered a Sunday school lesson that her mother gave in which she said, "I hope and pray that someone, sometime, will found a memorial mother's day. There are many days for men, but none for mothers."
>
> Anna began to lobby prominent businessmen like John Wannamaker, and politicians including Presidents Taft and Roosevelt to support her campaign to create a special day to honor mothers. At one of the first services organized to celebrate Anna's mother in 1908, at her church in West Virginia, Anna handed out her mother's favorite flower, the white carnation. Five years later, the House of Representatives

adopted a resolution calling for officials of the federal government to wear white carnations on Mother's Day. In 1914 Anna's hard work paid off when Woodrow Wilson signed a bill recognizing Mother's Day as a national holiday.[11]

While at first most people wrote simple, well-meaning letters of appreciation to their mothers, this quickly changed. Jarvis eventually became disgruntled in the 1920s as the day became more commercialized. She even filed a lawsuit trying to get the day removed from the calendar.

Most everyone can relate to the charges of overcommercialization. But still, above all people, mothers deserve the recognition and sincere expressions of appreciation. They are, after all, a very special breed.

As the poet William Ross Wallace once stated in the title of a poem he penned as a tribute to mothers back in 1865, "The Hand That Rocks the Cradle Is the Hand That Rules the World." With this in mind, let's note a few observations from the soon to be mother of Jesus, Mary:

1. A mother always wants to know the details (Luke 1:29).

If I am allowed as a man to make this observation, this was Mary already demonstrating her aptitude as a soon-to-be mother! Even though the angel Gabriel was sent by God to deliver the astounding news, "Rejoice, highly favored one, the Lord is with you" (v. 28), the Bible says that "she was very perplexed at this statement, and kept *pondering* what kind of salutation this was" (v. 29 NASB; emphasis added). Granted, she had to be overwhelmed at the proposition, but like all mothers, she wanted the details because she cared more than we can possibly understand!

2. A mother understands what a father will never comprehend (Luke 1:39–45).

You have heard of Morse code; this is Momma code! Mary goes to visit Elizabeth, the soon-to-be mother of John the Baptist, and as the scripture records, "When Elizabeth heard the greeting of Mary, ... the babe leaped in her womb" (v. 41). Apparently, without Mary saying much more than a simple greeting, Elizabeth "spoke out with a loud voice and said, 'Blessed are you among women, and blessed is

---

[11] http://mothers-day.123holiday.net.

the fruit of your womb! ... But why is this granted to me, that the mother of my Lord should come to me?'" (vv. 42, 43). The key is that both women "believed" that "there [would] be a fulfillment of those things which were told her [Mary] from the Lord" (v. 45).

3. Mothers rule (Luke 2:19)!

Think about it: Mary just had a baby; if she is *pondering* after all that pain, no wonder most women can bring a man to his knees with a simple look! The bottom line is that mothers are a special breed! Mary "pondered" because that is what mothers do:; they remember all the firsts: the first cry, the first smile, the first tooth, the first steps, the first day of school, the first date. I am being facetious, but a normal male finds it hard to keep up with the days on a calendar, much less the child's first potty day, etc. Unfortunately, mothers are often more intense and willing to develop in their spiritual lives than most fathers. This is really sad, as too many mothers are forced to fill the spiritual roles of both mother and father! The key is, Mary *pondered* because she understood the magnitude of the moment. She had spiritual depth to fully appreciate what had just occurred!

Conclusion

So ... what are mothers anyway? Note the acrostic and corresponding adjectives:

M—Memories and soft moments; beautiful melodies; MoM=Maker of Memories

O—Unbelievable optimism; labors in obscurity; demonstrates obedience to God; keeper of order

T—Quality time; daily teaches life skills; treasure to her family

H—Eternal hope; sense of humor; always helpful

E—Demands excellence; energetic and empathetic; picture of elegance

R—Receptive (even of the dumbest ideas); relational (always wants to talk—and listen); respected!

SUGGESTED ORDER OF WORSHIP

Mother's Day

(All women asked to come to front of church for group prayer for service.)

Prelude—Instrumentalist

Shout to the Lord

Call to Worship—Congregation

NBH 104 *Amazing Grace* (vv. 1, 2 in F, v. 3 G)

NBH 105 *Grace Greater Than Our Sin* (chorus, v. 1, chorus in G)

CH 344 *Amazing Grace* (mod. v. 5 in Ab)

Welcome—Pastoral Staff

Recognition of Mothers

Welcome Hymn (meet and greet)—Pastoral Staff

NBH 17 *I Sing Praises* (2x in G)

NBH 18 *Glorify Thy Name* (vv. 1, 2, v. 3 in Bb)

Offertory Prayer—Pastoral Staff

Offertory Praise—Mother's Day Choir

For Our Good (From G3 Music)

Message—Pastor

Mother's Day Sermon

Hymn of Response/Invitation—Congregation

NBH 411 *Come Just as You Are*

Benediction Hymn/Postlude—Congregation

SPW 100 *Bless the Name of Jesus*

KEY:

CH: Celebration Hymnal (Word Music/Integrity Music, Nashville, TN)

NBH: New Baptist Hymnal (2008)

WH: The Hymnal (Word Music, Nashville, TN)

SPW: Songs for Praise and Worship (Word Music, Nashville, TN)

MSPW: More Songs for Praise and Worship (Word Music, Nashville, TN)

MSPW2: More Songs for Praise and Worship 2 (Word Music, Nashville, TN)

WEEK 19

Live a Life of Love

Ephesians 5:1–7
By Dr. Kent Spann

Anatole Lunacharsky, former commissar of education in the USSR, wrote in 1935:

> We hate Christianity and Christians. Even the best of them must be considered our worst enemies. They preach love of one's neighbor and mercy, which is contrary to our principles. Christian love is an obstacle to the development of the revolution. Down with love of our neighbor! What we want is hatred. We must know how to hate. Only thus will we conquer the universe.[12]

Love characterizes the Christian's life to the world. Love contrasts the Christian's life with the world.

1. We reflect the character of God's love in our lives (Eph. 5:1, 2).

    We should love as Jesus loved us.

    a. He loved us sacrificially.

        i. Christ (John 15:13; Gal. 2:20)

        ii. Believers (1 Thess. 2:8; Phil. 2:4)

    b. He loved us forgivingly.

        i. Christ (Matt. 26:28; Eph. 1:7)

        ii. Believers (Eph. 4:31)

    c. He loved us practically.

        i. Christ (Mark 6:30–44)

        ii. Believers (1 John 3:18; James 2:14–17)

---

[12] John M. Drescher, *Spirit Fruit* (Scottsdale, PA: Herald, 1974).

    d. He loved us unconditionally.

        i. Christ (Rom. 5:6–8)

        ii. Believers (Matt. 5:43–47)

    e. He loved us faithfully.

        i. Christ (2 Tim. 2:13; Heb. 2:17; 13:5)

        ii. Believers (1 Cor. 4:2)

    f. He loved us compassionately.

        i. Christ (Ps. 103:13; Matt. 9:35, 36; 1 Pet. 5:7)

        ii. Believers (Col. 3:12; 1 Pet. 3:8)

2. We reject the world's perversion of love in our lives (Eph. 5:3–6).

    a. Sexual immorality

    b. Impurity

    c. Greed or covetousness

    d. Filthiness or obscenity

    e. Foolish talk

    f. Coarse joking

WEEK 19

The Supremacy of Love

1 Corinthians 13
By Dr. David Thompson

The supremacy of love, according to God, far outweighs any spiritual gift. Love is to be practiced biblically because it is the only preeminent thing with permanence.

1. Love is preeminent (13:1–3).

It is greater than all the gifts I have (13:1, 2). Though the slickest talkers have the largest following, Paul says love is better than having an angelic tongue. It is greater than all the gifts I give (13:3). Giving more than Bill Gates or Gandhi counts zero in heaven unless it is marked by love.

2. Love is to be practiced (13:4–7).

Love behaves: it behaves patiently in everything. This is humanly impossible. But the fruit of the Spirit—not the fruit of the Christian—is love. Love doesn't behave: it isn't puffy, provoked easily, nor does it behave unseemly. Love is never a bear, but it bears all things. Love never doubts but believes all things.

3. Love is permanent (13:8–13).

What lasts is what really matters. Nothing else. Perfection is coming. When it does, everything else will fade into oblivion. My preaching will disappear; my love will not. My knowledge and education will dissolve; my love will not. In fact, all faith and hope may abide, but still, the greatest of all is *love*!

WEEK 20

Creation or Accident?

Genesis 1:1
By Frank Harber

Editor's Note: There are varied opinions among Christians as to the time period of creation—seven days, ages, etc. This message addresses the issue of God as the divine Creator, not of how He did it or how long it took Him. It is up to the preacher to communicate his or her view of the time period of creation.

Ask someone if he or she has ever heard the words "In the beginning God created the heavens and the earth," and you will probably get an affirmative answer. The person will likely even know that the statement is found in the opening sentence of the Bible. This most famous of all Bible verses is found, of course, in the book of Genesis. Not surprisingly, the word *genesis* means "origin" or "beginning," and the Hebrew of Genesis 1:1 is a seven-word sentence. For the ancient Jews, seven was the number of perfection.

The Bible's opening statement is simple yet deeply profound in its two premises:

• There is a Designer behind the design, and His name is God.

• There is a design to the heavens and the earth.

It is the answer to debate about origins. It is the answer to the theory of evolution. It is the answer to man's purpose and value as a part of creation. It is the answer to the "green" debate currently raging in the world. It is the answer to creation care.

1. There is a Designer behind the design, and His name is God ("In the beginning God ...").

From the very first verse, Scripture throws down the gauntlet in the debate over the fundamental truth of existence. It calls the question and states its position unequivocally. Is there a Being who created the universe or not? And the answer is yes, and that Being is God. Everyone who has ever lived and ever will live must take one of the two possible positions on the subject: either someone created it all, or it was the product or random chance.

The debate between the evolution view and the creation view is at its core a debate about the existence of God. The late Dr. Henry Morris, founder and president of the Institute for Creation Research, said that evolution is nothing more than "the long war against God." It is a long war that began almost from the beginning. It is not the product of evolution; evolution is just a vehicle for its expression.

The fool has said in his heart, "There is no God." (Ps. 14:1)

Counter the "no God" view of Psalm 14:1 with Romans 1:19, 20.

What may be known of God is manifest in [men], for God has shown it to them. For since the creation of the world His invisible attributes are clearly seen, being understood by the things that are made, even His eternal power and Godhead, so that they are without excuse

John MacArthur, in his sermon "God: Creator and Redeemer," says that God gave man the ability to reason:

Reason is basically a sequence of cause and effect patterns. Anytime you do research you work on cause and effect. Anytime you come to understand a principle, you understand it because there's a cause and effect relationship, there's a sequence of things that builds to a conclusion. That's rationality. Reason is the ability to link things together to come to right conclusions. And God has put in to the mind of man rationality so that he can rationally go back to the fact that there had to be a first cause. That leads him back to God.[13]

---

[13] John MacArthur, "God: Creator and Redeemer" sermon, Grace Community Church, Sun Valley, CA, April 11, 1999.

Legendary British philosopher and atheist Antony Flew turned from atheism at the age of eighty-one. A noted critic of God's existence for several decades, Flew published books such as *God and Philosophy* and *The Presumption of Atheism*. Dr. Gary Habermas, prolific philosopher and historian from Liberty University, debated Professor Flew several times. Still they maintained a friendship despite many years of disagreement over the existence of God.

Habermas interviewed Flew in 2004 after he turned from atheism. A piece of their discussion follows:

HABERMAS: Which arguments for God's existence did you find most persuasive?

FLEW: I think that the most impressive arguments for God's existence are those that are supported by recent scientific discoveries ... I think the argument to Intelligent Design is enormously stronger than when I first met it.[14]

So in the very beginning, the Bible declares Elohim!

2. There is a design to the heavens and the earth ("... God created the heavens and the earth").

Many people assert that this universe is not a creation—it merely happened. Because they believe it was a gigantic accident, there is no Designer. What makes the discussion dicey is that both sides—the God and the no-God folks—have to admit that the cosmos at least *looks* as if it has been designed. Our universe reflects stupendous complexity in which nothing seems to be happenstance. The appearance of design is everywhere. There is no random material floating around without purpose; the universe reflects only very intricate design.

The appearance of design in the universe is undeniable. No matter how committed someone may be to atheism, he or she will not convince us that things do not at least *seem* to be designed. No one could convince us or anyone else of that, which means that the person who chooses to believe that no God designed the universe is left in a very precarious philosophical position. While a theist is free to believe the validity of the observation that everything seems to

---

[14] Found at www.preachingtoday.com.

be designed, the atheist is left only with the awkward assumption that the universe actually exhibits an undesigned design.

Think about that for a minute. What are the logical implications of thinking there could be an undesigned design of some sort? Has anyone ever seen an unpainted painting or an unsculpted sculpture? Has anyone ever lived in an unbuilt house? That's a mind-bending concept—and not only because an elite, intellectually endowed few are capable of grasping the supposed truth of it (although those who maintain the undesigned design position would want us to think our mental capabilities are limited). It's because the idea is simply untenable. It's the emperor's new clothes of philosophy. The idea just doesn't make any more sense than saying there can be dry rain, an elderly newborn, hot ice, or uncooked barbecue. We can pick any analogy, but undesigned design is a world-class oxymoron.

So in conclusion, whether you are speaking biblically, logically, or scientifically, "In the beginning *God created* the heavens and the earth."

SUGGESTED ORDER OF WORSHIP

Prelude—Instrumentalists

Almighty

Call to Praise—Congregation

NBH 4 *Almighty* (chorus, v. 1, chorus, v. 2, chorus w/ coda)

NBH 3 *Worthy of Worship* (chorus, v. 1, chorus, v. 2, chorus, v. 3, chorus in F)

Prayer of Praise—Pastoral Staff

Welcome—Pastoral Staff

Song of Welcome *(meet and greet)*—Congregation

NBH 599 *Soon and Very Soon* (3x in G)

Worship and Praise—Congregation

NBH 126 *Rock of Ages* (2x in G)

NBH 588 *Sanctuary* (1x in D, 1x in Eb)

NBH 44 *He Knows My Name* (2x in Eb)

Testimony of Praise—Pastor's Choice (prefer a 2- to 3-minute video)

Offertory Prayer—Pastoral Staff

Offertory Praise—PT on verse and bridge, Congregation on chorus

NBH 305 *You Are My King (Amazing Love)* (v. 1, chorus, bridge, bridge, chorus)

Offertory Prayer—Pastor

Sermon—Pastor

Hymn of Invitation—Congregation

NBH 552 *My Jesus, I Love Thee* (as needed)

Benediction Hymn—Congregation

NBH 252 *Down at the Cross* (chorus only in G)

Postlude—Instrumentalists

Worthy of Worship

KEY:

CH: Celebration Hymnal (Word Music/Integrity Music, Nashville, TN)

NBH: New Baptist Hymnal (2008)

WH: The Hymnal (Word Music, Nashville, TN)

SPW: Songs for Praise and Worship (Word Music, Nashville, TN)

MSPW: More Songs for Praise and Worship (Word Music, Nashville, TN)

MSPW2: More Songs for Praise and Worship 2 (Word Music, Nashville, TN)

WEEK 20

Living the Light Life

Ephesians 5:8–14
By Dr. Kent Spann
The Trail of Light in the Bible

- God is light (1 John 1:5).
- Christ is light (John 8:12).
- Christians are light (Eph. 5:8).

How do we live the light life?

1. We reflect God's light in the world (5:8–10).

  a. By reflecting goodness in our lives

  God is good (Ps. 34:8; 100:5; Gen. 1:31; James 1:17; Ps. 25:8).

  b. By reflecting righteousness in our lives

  God is righteous in His character (Ps. 119:137; 116:5), His testimonies (Ps. 119:138), His commands (Ps. 119:172), His judgments (Ps. 119:7, 62), His promises (Ps. 119:123), and His acts (1 Sam. 12:7).

  c. By reflecting truth in our lives

  God is the God of truth (Deut. 32:4; Is. 65:16; Ps. 119:160; 2 Sam. 7:28; Ps. 33:4).

  d. By reflecting discernment in our lives

  God is a discerning God, judging between right and wrong (Jer. 17:9, 10; Matt. 7:15–23; 25:31ff)

2. We contrast the darkness in the world (5:7, 11–13).

  - Darkness is the work of Satan (John 8:44).
  - Darkness is the domain of Satan (Col. 1:13; Eph. 6:12; 1 John 5:19).

- Darkness rejects the Christ (John 1:4, 5; 3:19).
- Darkness brings God's penalty (Eph. 5:6; Rom. 1:18).
- Darkness leads to the ultimate destiny of eternal darkness (Matt. 8:12; 2 Pet. 2:17).
- Darkness is no longer who we are (Eph. 5:8a).

a. By avoiding evil (5:7, 11)

b. By exposing evil (5:11b–13)

c. By leading those in the darkness to the light (5:13, 14)

Shine Your Light (5:14)

A train struck a car, killing several youth. At the trial the watchman was questioned: "Were you at the crossing the night of the accident?"

"Yes, Your Honor."

"Were you waving your lantern to warn of the danger?"

"Yes, Your Honor," the man told the judge.

But after the trial had ended, the watchman walked away mumbling to himself, "I'm glad they didn't ask me about the light in the lantern, because the light had gone out."[15]

---

[15] P. L. Tan, *Encyclopedia of 7700 Illustrations: A Treasury of Illustrations, Anecdotes, Facts and Quotations for Pastors, Teachers and Christian Workers* (Garland TX: Bible Communications, 1996, ©1979).

WEEK 20

The Harvest

Matthew 9:35–38
By Dr. David Thompson

The "harvest" is the object of Jesus' compassion. It is to be ours also. Christ healed every sickness, but that was not the focus of His heart. It was that the "multitudes" had no "shepherd" for their souls (v. 36)—they are lost.

Scripture says why they are lost and what to do. Our Savior explains three aspects of the harvest: the *lost*, the *laborers*, and the *Lord* of the harvest.

1. The *lost* of the harvest need the unadulterated gospel preached to them.

    The gospel is the power of God. Biblical healing exists only with the gospel.

2. The *laborers* of the harvest are commanded to pray.

    How? Psalm 126:5 tells us to "sow in tears" if we would "reap in joy." Pray for laborers to be sent with compassion. Dare to ask God to give you a burden for souls.

3. The *Lord* of the harvest is the key.

    God cares for His harvest more than we do. God's Spirit will draw sinners to repentance when His servants faithfully exalt Christ and preach the gospel. The Lord's harvest will be abundant and the laborers plenteous when we seek to follow Jesus' Word and not man's plans.

WEEK 21

The Jesus Controversy

Matthew 16:13–16; John 5:19–40
By Dr. Kent Spann

Controversial People

Have you ever noticed that certain people stir up controversy? George Bush, Paris Hilton, Lindsay Lohan, Arnold Schwarzenegger, Kobe Bryant, Madonna, Hitler, and Napoleon are just a few names that come to mind. Who do you suppose is the *most* controversial figure in human history? The answer to that is simple: Jesus Christ.

If you want to spark a real dialogue at a party or in a college classroom, ask these two questions:

• Who is Jesus Christ?

• What is your opinion about Jesus Christ?

Just consider the Jesus Seminar led by Robert Funk. The scholars decided what Jesus really said as well as examined the historicity of Jesus. Their results were published in three reports from 1993 through 1999. England's Hugh Schonfield wrote a book, *The Passover Plot*, in 1966, alleging that the Crucifixion was part of a scheme by Jesus to fulfill the Messianic expectations rampant in His time and that the plan went wrong. In 1970 John Marco Allegro, a graduate of Manchester University and Oxford University, wrote a book, *The Sacred Mushroom and the Cross*, voicing his opinion that Christian religion was based on a cult practicing frequent drug use (psychedelic mushrooms) and sex. He theorized that Jesus' last words on the Cross were not a lament to God but "a paean of praise to the god of the mushroom."[16]

And who can forget the controversy raised by Dan Brown's book,

---

[16] John Bryan, "John Marco Allegro: 1923–1988," EMuseum @ Minnesota State University, Mankato Web site, http://www.mnsu.edu/emuseum/information/biography/abcde/allegro_john.html.

and later movie, *The DaVinci Code*?

In Ecclesiastes 1:9, Solomon says that there is nothing new under the sun. The controversy surrounding Jesus is nothing new. It is not the product of modern-day science or religion. It is not the result of modern or postmodern thought. It is not due to new discoveries or more astute minds. Jesus has always been at the center of controversy. Even when Jesus walked the face of the earth, He was the source of controversy (Matt. 9:11, 34; 26:65; Mark 3:21; John 7:20; 9:16, 24).

Who Is Jesus?

Jesus was quite aware of the controversy surrounding Him. Once, while in Caesarea Philippi, He engaged the disciples in conversation about public opinion as well as their personal opinion about who He was. It was during this dialogue that Peter made his famous confession, followed by Jesus' affirmation (Matt. 16:13–17). From this incident, we gain great insight into the person of Jesus.

1. Jesus is fully man (Matt. 16:13).

Jesus uses the title "Son of Man" for Himself. It was the most common designation Jesus used for Himself during His earthly ministry. It is found some eighty times in the New Testament. The term "Son of Man" focuses on Jesus' humanity.

Jesus is fully human. Now, that is where liberalism likes to stop— Jesus is human. The problem is that is not where the Bible stops. The clear teaching of Scripture is that not only is Jesus fully human; He is also fully God.

2. Jesus is fully God (Matt. 16:16, 17).

The title "Son of God" is used more than fifty times in the New Testament. What does the title "Son of God" tell us about Jesus and what He believed about Himself? *The Moody Handbook of Theology* says:

A son is of the same nature and essence as a father; in affirming Jesus as His Son, God the Father was saying that Jesus, His Son, is deity because He is of the same essence as the Father.[17]

The apostle John affirms that the term "Son of God" is a declaration of His deity in 1 John 5:20.

Napoleon Bonaparte, the French general, said of Jesus, "I know men, and Jesus Christ is more than a man."

3. Jesus is the promised Messiah (Matt. 16:16).

The title *Christ* is the Greek equivalent of the Hebrew title *Messiah*. The Greek term *Christos* means "anointed" or "anointed one." Notice that Peter says, "You are the Christ." He puts the definite article in front of *Christos*, which is profound. He says to Jesus, "You are *the* Christ, *the* anointed One. You are the one prophesied in the Old Testament who would come to the nation Israel."

Can I Get a Witness?

So the claim is that Jesus is fully God and fully man, the Messiah. Are there any witnesses? In a debate with the Pharisees about who He was, Jesus called forth several witnesses that He is fully God, fully man, the Messiah!

1. The Witness of Himself (John 5:19–31)

Jesus gives a powerful witness about Himself in these verses.

2. The Witness of People (John 5:33–35)

The other person in this passage is John the Baptist. But the list of people who serve as witnesses doesn't stop with him.

a. The apostles gave the ultimate witness by giving their lives based on their belief about Christ.

b. The early church fathers, such as Ignatius of Antioch (50–117), Clement of Alexandria (150–215), Tertullian (160–225), and Origen (185–254) all gave witness that Jesus is fully man, fully God, the Messiah.

c. The early councils, such as the Council of Nicaea (AD 325), the Council of Constantinople (AD 381), the Council of Ephesus

---

17 2. Paul Enns, *The Moody Handbook of Theology* (Chicago: Moody Press, 1989), 87.

(AD 431), and the Council of Chalcedon (AD 451) all in some way affirmed His humanity and deity.

    d. Even unbelievers, such as the centurion at the foot of the Cross, gave a witness to His humanity and deity (Mark 15:39).

3. The Witness of His Work (John 5:36)

Jesus speaks here of the body of His work, which includes miracles of healing and deliverance, preaching and teaching, and the great consummation of His work, His death, burial and resurrection (1 Cor. 15:3–7).

4. The Witness of the Scripture (John 5:39, 40)

    a. The prophecies of Scripture give witness to His humanity, deity, and messiahship.

    b. The teaching of Scripture gives witness to His humanity, deity, and messiahship.

5. The Witness of the Father (John 5:37)

    a. The Father's spoken witness (Matt. 3:17; 17:5; John 12:28)

    b. The Father's affirming witness (John 3:2)

    c. The Father's inner witness (John 6:45; 1 John 5:9–12)

Controversy?

Benjamin Rush (1746–1813), American physician and political leader, member of the Continental Congress, and signer of the Declaration of Independence, said, "Controversy is only dreaded by the advocates of error." Based on that definition we have nothing to dread in the Jesus controversy, because Jesus truly is the Son of Man, the Son of God, the promised Messiah.

SUGGESTED ORDER OF WORSHIP

Prelude—Instrumentalist

    NBH 133 *Shout to the Lord*

Call to Prayer—Pastoral Staff

Welcome—Pastoral Staff

    NBH 129 *Sing to the King* (2x in F)

    NBH 121 *Everlasting God* (2x in Bb)

    NBH 122 *O God, Our Help in Ages Past* (vv. 1–4 in Bb, v. 6 in C)

Baptismal Celebration—Pastoral Staff

Prayer of Commitment—Pastoral Staff

    NBH 132 *Hosanna (Praise Is Rising)* (v.1, chorus, v. 2, chorus in G)

Scripture Reading from Psalm 91:1–7, 9–12, 14, 15
(Please have prepared for IMAG)

1 He who dwells in the secret place of the Most High shall abide under the shadow of the Almighty.

2 I will say of the Lord, "He is my refuge and my fortress; my God, in Him I will trust."

3 Surely He shall deliver you from the snare of the fowler and from the perilous pestilence.

4 He shall cover you with His feathers, and under His wings you shall take refuge; His truth shall be your shield and buckler.

5 You shall not be afraid of the terror by night, nor of the arrow that flies by day,

6 nor of the pestilence that walks in darkness, nor of the destruction that lays waste at noonday.

7 A thousand may fall at your side, and ten thousand at your right hand; but it shall not come near you.

9 Because you have made the Lord, who is my refuge, even the Most High, your dwelling place,

10 No evil shall befall you, nor shall any plague come near your dwelling;

11 for He shall give His angels charge over you, to keep you in all your ways.

12 In their hands they shall bear you up, lest you dash your foot against a stone.

14 "Because he has set his love upon Me, therefore I will deliver him; I will set him on high, because he has known My name.

15 He shall call upon Me, and I will answer him; I will be with him in trouble; I will deliver him and honor him."

Prayer of Thanksgiving—Pastor

> NBH 142 *Worthy, You Are Worthy* (vv. 1, 2 in Eb, v. 3 in F)

Offertory Prayer and Praise

> NBH 143 *You Are My All in All* (v. 1, chorus, v. 2, chorus in F)

Message—Pastor

Hymn of Response/Invitation—Worship Leader and Congregation

> NBH 127 *The Heart of Worship* (2x in Eb)

Benediction Hymn—Congregation

> NBH 139 *Let There Be Glory Honor and Praise* (1x in G, 1x in Ab)

Postlude—Instrumentalists

> NBH 132 *Hosanna* (chorus only, 2x in G)

KEY:

CH: Celebration Hymnal (Word Music/Integrity Music, Nashville, TN)

NBH: New Baptist Hymnal (2008)

WH: The Hymnal (Word Music, Nashville, TN)

SPW: Songs for Praise and Worship (Word Music, Nashville, TN)

MSPW: More Songs for Praise and Worship (Word Music, Nashville, TN)

MSPW2: More Songs for Praise and Worship 2 (Word Music, Nashville, TN)

WEEK 21

The Wise Walk

Part 1
Ephesians 5:15–21
By Dr. Kent Spann

A bishop advised a politician to go out into the rain and lift his head heavenward. "It will bring a revelation to you." Next day the politician reported, "I followed your advice, and no revelation came. The water poured down my neck, and I felt like a fool." "Well," said the bishop, "isn't that quite a revelation for the first try?"

Paul begins a new section in Ephesians about living wisely.

1. We carefully choose the path we travel (5:15: "Be very careful" [NIV]).

    a. We carefully avoid the wrong path.

    i. Easy path (Matt. 7:13)

        ii. Disobedient path (Prov. 2:13)

        iii. Dark path (Prov. 2:13; 4:19)

        iv. Perverse path (Prov. 2:14)

        v. Crooked path (Prov. 2:15)

        vi. Destructive path (Prov. 2:18; 22)

        vii. Hard path (Prov. 13:15)

        viii. Deadly path (Prov. 14:12)

    b. We carefully choose the right path.

        i. Carefully determine what we do (1 Thess. 5:21)

        ii. Carefully choose what we think (Rom. 12:1, 2; Phil. 4:8)

        iii. Carefully watch what we believe (1 John 4:1)

        iv. Carefully guard our hearts (Prov. 4:23)

2. We seize the opportunities God gives us (5:16).

a. We train ourselves to see our God-given opportunities because when they are gone, they are gone

---

"There is in the midst of every great battle a ten to fifteen minute period that is the crucial point. Take that period and you win the battle; lose it and you will be defeated."

—Napoleon

---

b. We learn to use our time wisely.

c. We stop presuming we have tomorrow.

d. We choose the best things.

e. We repent when we fail to seize our God-given opportunities.

WEEK 21

2012

Mark 13:29–37, Acts 1:11, Revelation 22:20
By Dr. David Thompson

The movie *2012* is an apocalyptic movie telling how the world ends in 2012.

Fact: Jesus will return.

Fact: Jesus did not disclose the date.

Fact: Jesus wants us to know when it is near.

Speculators love to postulate the end and subsequent advent of Christ. They're always erroneous. Nonetheless, it is as sinful to prognosticate falsely as it is to *not* watch expectantly for that glorious day.

FACT #1: Jesus will come quickly, says the last page of Scripture. It is the closing thought of the Word of God. The disciples were told immediately at Christ's ascension that Jesus would come back in the same manner that He left. Paul told Titus that it is our blessed hope, and we are to look for it (Titus 2:1, 2).

FACT # 2: Jesus said you do not know the hour of His coming. The year 2012 has been a suggested date for the end and Jesus' return. In 1988 some had their animals put to sleep in fear of an apocalypse. But "that day and hour no one knows" (Mark 13:32).

FACT #3: Jesus said to "watch" and "work" (Mark 13:34). "When you see these things happening, know that it is near" (Mark 13:29). It is nearer than ever. It is imminent. It is soon. It may be today. Jesus said, "I come quickly." Amos's words ring louder than ever: "Prepare to meet your God" (Amos 4:12).

WEEK 22

Is Jesus the Only Way?

John 14:6

By Dr. Mike Licona

The claim that Jesus is the only way to God is difficult to accept for many in modern society. Is God unfair in requiring others to believe only in Jesus to get into heaven? Is it merely Christians interpreting the Bible in this manner?

There is widespread evidence that Jesus claimed to be the only way to God. Not only are His claims multiply attested; His earliest followers taught that He is the only way (Matt. 11:27; Luke 10:22; 12:8, 9; John 3:36; Acts 4:12; Rom. 10:1, 2; 2 Thess. 1:8, 9; 1 Tim. 2:5; Heb. 10:26, 27). There are no claims to the contrary by the earliest Christians. Consider these statements of Jesus:

> "I am the way, the truth, and the life. No one comes to the Father except through Me. (John 14:6)

> "Therefore I said to you that you will die in your sins; for if you do not believe that I am He, you will die in your sins." (John 8:24)

These claims appear as outrageous today as they did to many in Jesus' day. How do we handle it today?

We first ask whether Jesus' claims are true. Jesus said His proof for His claim was His resurrection. If Jesus was truly who He claimed to be, this greatly works towards reconciling His claim to being the exclusive route to God. We can deal with remaining objections by answering three rudimentary questions.

1. What is truth?

A true statement corresponds with reality. For example, let's assess the truth-claims of the Heaven's Gate cult. The earth was not destroyed, as Marshall Applewhite had predicted. While members of the Heaven's Gate cult obtained feelings of peace, hope, and fulfillment from following Applewhite, there is an objective truth that holds true for everyone: Applewhite was a false prophet. Sincere belief to the point of death did not change the truth.

Followers of other religions may claim their religious beliefs and practices give peaceful feelings and purpose for living. However, if Jesus' claim to be the exclusive way to God is true, then the following is false: Muhammad provided a way to be acceptable to God.

While this conclusion is offensive to many, we must not be so captive to our politically correct culture that we are led astray from truth. Since the truth of a statement can be measured by how closely it corresponds with reality, if Jesus claimed to be the exclusive way to God, and rose from the dead in order to confirm that, His claim is true.

2. What is ethical?

Any Christian who has shared his or her faith with others understands that claiming Jesus is the only way can be perceived as being intolerant and offensive. However, when someone claims that saying Jesus is the only way is intolerant and offensive, that person ignores the fact that his or her pluralistic approach is likewise intolerant and offensive. Such individuals are intolerant of exclusivist views and offensive to their holders.

Amy-Jill Levine is a distinguished professor of New Testament Studies at Vanderbilt University and is Jewish. Professor Levine opines that the Christian claim that Jesus is the only way is *not* morally dubious. She adds, "What I would find more 'morally dubious' is my insisting to another that his or her reading or presuppositions, because they are not pluralistic, are somehow wrong.... The evangelical Christian should be free to try to seek to convert me to Christianity: such an attempt is biblically warranted and consistent with evangelical (exclusivist) theology. I remain free to say 'thank you, but no thanks.' I would not want someone telling me that my 'cherished confessional traditions' have only limited value. I would not presume to do the same to another."[18]

---

[18] Amy-Jill Levine, "Homeless in the Global Village" in T. C. Penner and C. V. Stichele, eds., *Moving Beyond New Testament Theology? Essays in Conversation with Heikki Räisänen* (Helsinki: Finnish Exegetical Society/ University of Helsinki, 2005), 195–96.

Moreover, there are times when truth should not be sacrificed for the sake of avoiding offense. With the *Titanic* sinking and lifeboats available, it would have been *unethical* for the crew, in the interest of reducing panic, to have told the passengers to go back to their cabins because everything would be fine in the morning. Truth is important. Decisions of greater importance should drive us to discover the truth, rather than dilute or deny it in the interest of not offending another. However, when sharing your faith with others, remember to do it "with meekness and fear" (1 Pet. 3:15). We should love others and be graceful in our efforts to share the greatest news ever told.

3. What is required?

"It doesn't matter what you believe; the way to heaven is paved with sincerity, goodness, and belief in God." This statement attempts to shed the offense of the exclusivity claims of Jesus, but is problematic. The claim that sincerity, goodness, and belief in a generic God are the true requirements for God's acceptance is a religious claim: "This is how one can appease God." The challenge is, how can this be known? The claimant will need to demonstrate this claim.

Also, how much is required? How good does one have to be to please God? How good is good enough? What will be the standard? Scripture lays out the requirements for God's acceptance: It's nothing any of us can do (Rom. 6:23); it's all in what God has done for us in Jesus (Eph. 2:8, 9); we must entrust our eternal destiny with Jesus (John 14:6); we must believe in Jesus' deity, atoning death, and resurrection (John 8:24; Rom. 10:9).

How can you share the gospel with others, given their aversion to the exclusivity claims of Jesus? *First*, understand answers to the questions we have discussed. *Second*, clothe Jesus' message with love. People don't care how much you know until they know how much you care. *Third*, recognize that timing is important. Some may think you're narrow-minded. However, if a time comes when their lives are falling apart or they have just learned that they have cancer, they may want you to give them *the* answer and will respect you for holding true to your faith.

In conclusion, we can begin to come to terms with the exclusivity claims of Jesus by answering three rudimentary questions: What is truth? What is ethical? And what is required?

SUGGESTED ORDER OF WORSHIP

Prelude—Instrumental Group

NBH 518 *My Life Is in You, Lord*

Prayer of Worship—Pastoral Staff

Welcome—Pastoral Staff

Song of Welcome *(meet and greet)*—Congregation

MSPW 12 *The Name of the Lord* (vv. 1, 2, chorus, v. 3, tag in F)

Worship and Praise—Congregation

NBH 510 *Firm Foundation* (2x in F)

NBH 441 *The Potter's Hand* (2x in G)

NBH 109 *There Is None Like You* (2x in G)

Testimony of Praise (2½-minute video on God's faithfulness in times of war)

Offertory Prayer—Pastoral Staff

Offertory Praise—Trumpet Trio with Congregation

NBH 642 *God of Our Fathers*

Prayer for the Armed Forces *(Pastor select persons to pray for the following)*

The Air Force

The Army

The Marines

The Navy

The Coast Guard

Song for the Nation—Praise Team

    NBH 641 *America, the Beautiful*

Message—Pastor

Hymn of Response/Invitation—Congregation

    CH 487 *Room at the Cross* (as needed)

Benediction Hymn—Congregation

    CH 195 *Bless the Name of Jesus* (2x in C)

Postlude—Instrumental Group

    Evermore

KEY:

CH: Celebration Hymnal (Word Music/Integrity Music, Nashville, TN)

NBH: New Baptist Hymnal (2008)

WH: The Hymnal (Word Music, Nashville, TN)

SPW: Songs for Praise and Worship (Word Music, Nashville, TN)

MSPW: More Songs for Praise and Worship (Word Music, Nashville, TN)

MSPW2: More Songs for Praise and Worship 2 (Word Music, Nashville, TN)

WEEK 22

The Wise Walk
Part 2

Ephesians 5:15–21
By Dr. Kent Spann

[Review previous points from series.]

1. We discover God's will for our lives (5:17).

    a. God has a plan for our lives.

    b. God wants us to understand His will for our lives.

        i. Discovering God's Will

            (1) Submit our lives to God (Rom. 12:1, 2).

            (2) Yield to the Holy Spirit (John 16:13; Acts 13:2).

            (3) Obey His Word (Ps. 119:105; 2 Tim. 3:16, 17) .

            (4) Listen in prayer (Rom. 8:26, 27).

            (5) Pay attention to circumstances (Prov. 3:5, 6; 1 Cor. 16:8, 9).

            (6) Hear counsel of the church (Eph. 4:15, 16; Acts 6:1–7).

            (7) Wait on God (Ps. 5:1–3; 37:7; 38:15).

            (8) Follow our desires (Ps. 37:5).

            (9) Use our minds (1 Cor. 2:16; Col. 3:1–4)

    c. God's will is best for our lives.

2. We live under the control of the Holy Spirit (5:18–21).

    a. How are we filled with the Holy Spirit?

        i. We must desire to be filled with the Spirit (Matt. 5:6; Rev. 3:20).

        ii. We must confess our sin (1 John 1:9).

iii. We must present every area of our lives to God (Rom. 12:1, 2; 2 Tim. 2:20, 21).

iv. We must claim the filling of the Holy Spirit by faith (1 John 5:14, 15).

b. What happens when we are filled with the Holy Spirit?

i. We will be filled with songs of joy (Eph. 5:19).

ii. We will be filled with an attitude of gratitude (Eph. 5:20).

iii. We will be filled with spirit of humility, evidenced in submission (Eph. 5:21).

(1) Husband and wives (Eph. 5:22–33)

(2) Children and parents (Eph. 6:1–4)

(3) Employee and employer (Eph. 6:5–9)

WEEK 22

Broadway

Matthew 7:13: "Broad is the way that leads to destruction …"
By Dr. David Thompson

Evangelism is necessary. Universalism is a lie, and all dogs don't go to heaven. Most souls are going their own way, the wrong way. It is the way of destruction and death. Christians are Jesus' disciples, and He mandates us to evangelize. You are saved to share who were once on the "broad way." A burden for souls on the "Broadway" is a good thing!

Two ironies challenge us to "snatch them from the fire":

1. What is broader than the "broad way"? The broadness of God's love is. Paul prayed for us to know the "width" of God's love (Eph. 3:17–19). God's love is wonderfully wide. Jesus loves Pilate as much as Paul, Judas as much as John, who also reminds us that God loves the whole world. Hell is real, and it is endless. What is more real than that? God's limitless love.

2. What is deeper than the bottomless pit of destruction? God's love is deeper. Paul prayed we would know it. Consider that sinners must crawl over a bloody cross and a loving God to go to hell. How deep? Jesus went from glory to Golgotha to Gehenna. Jesus' love could be no deeper. Evangelize because it was God's loving-kindness that led you to repent, and it is the unfathomable depth of Jesus' love that makes us soul winners.

WEEK 23

Connecting Through Apologetics

1 Peter 3:15
By Michael Licona

Gary Chapman's best-selling book *The Five Love Languages*[19] has helped many marriages. The thesis of the book is that there are five basic ways in which people like to be loved and that each of us has a primary love language. These are (1) words of affirmation, (2) physical affection, (3) quality time, (4) acts of service, and (5) gift giving. Marriages often go awry because we tend to love our spouses in our own primary love language rather than theirs. The result is that we fail to communicate love to them because we are loving them the way we want to be loved rather than the way they want.

A similar mistake is often made when sharing the gospel. In his book *Choosing Your Faith*,[20] Mark Mittelberg describes six ways in which people prefer to receive truth. We tend to communicate truth in the manner we prefer to receive it. If the person with whom we are talking prefers to receive truth in a manner different than we are communicating, they may not *hear* us, just as your spouse may not *hear* you communicate love to him or her if you're not speaking in their love language.

In an increasingly secular culture in North America, including evidence that supports the core beliefs of the gospel, such as Jesus' death and resurrection, is becoming more important. In 1 Peter 3:15, the apostle tells us to be ready always to provide a defense to everyone who asks us to give an account for why we are Christians. The Greek term for providing a defense is *apologia*, from which we get the English term *apologetics*. I think that every Christian should become familiar with apologetics *because* it provides three priceless benefits.

---

[19] Chicago: Northfield, 2010, repr. ed.
[20] Carol Stream, IL: Tyndale, 2008.

1. It informs seekers.

Those who outright reject the gospel usually do so for one of two reasons: intellectual or volitional. If the latter, no amount of evidence will persuade them to accept the gospel. However, if their objection to accept the gospel is intellectual in nature, evidence can provide the answer. Whether Paul was speaking to Jews or Gentiles, he provided the resurrection of Jesus as evidence that Jesus is the Messiah and Son of God. And notice that he did not even appeal to the Scriptures when speaking to the philosophers in Athens, since they would not have accepted them as being divinely inspired (Acts 17). Now that we have entered the second decade of the twenty-first century, it is easy to recognize that we live in a post-Christian culture that is far different than it was in the 1950s. A large percentage of Americans have never read the Bible and don't recognize it as God's Word. Quoting it to others will often have little impact. For example, if I were to say to someone that the Bible teaches that all have sinned and come up short of God's moral standard for them and that this will result in my eternal separation from God apart from God's grace, that person might respond simply that he doesn't believe the Bible. At that point, without compelling evidence for why the Bible should be regarded as historically trustworthy, it will be difficult for the discussion to proceed further. However, if I were to provide a solid case for the historical trustworthiness of the Bible and the person is open-minded, the discussion may proceed.

2. It inoculates the saved.

American football is a sport that is often brutal on the human body. Teams spend a lot of money purchasing protective equipment, the most important of which is the helmet. If one were to play without shoulder pads, an injury could sideline them for the season. However, if one were to play without a helmet, an injury could end their life. So, the greatest precautions must be taken to protect the head.

Isn't it interesting, then, that we often send our children off to a secular university without head protection? Should we be surprised when we learn they are questioning or even abandoning their faith? A 2007 report by two Jewish researchers, titled "Religious

Beliefs & Behavior of College Faculty," revealed that 53 percent of American college faculty had unfavorable feelings toward evangelical Christians, the highest percentage of all religions. Only 22 percent had unfavorable feelings toward Muslims.[21] It is becoming more common to learn of Christian students to whom the professor has openly said during class that his or her objective that semester was to see the Christian student abandon his or her faith. This would never happen to Jewish, Muslim, Hindu, or Buddhist students without severe warnings being issued to the offending faculty member. But no actions are usually taken against the professor when Christian students are the target. Of course, only a fraction of faculty members are so bold. But with more than one-half of American faculty thinking unfavorably of evangelical Christians, doesn't it make sense to provide our Christian students with head protection? Apologetics can do just that!

3. It impacts society.

Nearly a hundred years ago, J. Gresham Machen was a professor at Princeton who recognized a trend toward liberalism at Princeton. As a result, he and a few others formed Westminster Theological Seminary in 1929. A few years prior, Machen wrote the following: "False ideas are the greatest obstacles to the reception of the gospel. We may preach with all the fervor of a reformer and yet succeed only in winning a straggler here and there, if we permit the whole collective thought of the nation ... to be controlled by ideas which ... prevent Christianity from being regarded as anything more than a harmless delusion"[22]

Machen said that our evangelistic efforts would yield increasingly meager results as our culture moved toward regarding Christianity as only a pragmatic system of beliefs not necessarily true. His words have become somewhat prophetic. If the Christian church were to begin adopting a robust use of apologetics, we could begin to turn

---

[21] Gary A. Tobin and Aryeh K. Weinberg, *Profiles of the American University*, vol. 2, *Religious Beliefs & Behavior of College Faculty* (San Francisco: Institute for Jewish & Community Research, 2007), 12, 81, http://www.jewishresearch.org/PDFs2/FacultyReligion07.pdf.

[22] J. Gresham Machen, "Christianity and Culture," *Princeton Theological Review* 11 (1913): 7.

this cultural trend. The results will be greater fruit in evangelistic efforts.

In conclusion, we have seen that every Christian should familiarize themselves with apologetics because it provides three priceless benefits: It informs seekers. It inoculates the saved. And it impacts society.

SUGGESTED ORDER OF WORSHIP

Theme: Rejoice in His Faithfulness ... For Salvation ... For Healing ... For His Provision

Prelude—Instrumentalist

> *He Has Made Me Glad*

Welcome and Announcements—Pastoral Staff

Hymn of Welcome *(meet and greet)*—Congregation

> NBH 491 *Shine, Jesus Shine* (v. 1, chorus, v. 2, chorus, v. 3, chorus in Ab)

Prayer of Worship—Worship Pastor *(keyboard play next song during prayer)*

Song of Worship—Congregation

> NBH 96 *Great Is Thy Faithfulness* (v. 1, chorus, v. 2, chorus, v. 3 in D, chorus in Eb)

Testimony (1 girl—2-minute video)

> *For His Salvation*

Worship and Praise—Congregation

> NBH 89 *Shine on Us* (vv. 1–3, in D)

**Scripture Praise from Psalm 94:19; 117:2; 136:1, 2;
Isaiah 30:18, 22–24**—Pastoral Staff

In the multitude of my anxieties within me,
Your comforts delight my soul....
For His merciful kindness is great toward us,
And the truth of the LORD endures forever.
Praise the LORD! ...
Oh, give thanks to the LORD, for He is good!
For His mercy endures forever.
Oh, give thanks to the God of gods!
For His mercy endures forever....
Therefore the LORD will wait, that He may be gracious to you;
And therefore He will be exalted, that He may have mercy on you.
For the LORD is a God of justice;
Blessed are all those who wait for Him....
You will also defile the covering of your images of silver,
And the ornament of your molded images of gold.
You will throw them away as an unclean thing;
You will say to them, "Get away!"
Then He will give the rain for your seed
With which you sow the ground,
And bread of the increase of the earth;
It will be fat and plentiful.
In that day your cattle will feed
In large pastures.
Likewise the oxen and the young donkeys that work the ground
Will eat cured fodder,
Which has been winnowed with the shovel and fan.

> NBH 98 *Come, Thou Fount of Every Blessing* (vv. 1 and 2
> in D, v. 3 in Eb)

Offertory Prayer—Pastoral Staff

Testimony (1 guy—2-minute video)

For His Healing ...

Song of Praise—Congregation

> NBH 335 *Holy Spirit Rain Down* (2x in F)

Testimony (1 girl—2-minute video)

For His Provisions ...

Song of Praise—Solo

> NBH 93 *His Eye Is on the Sparrow*

Sermon—Pastor

Hymn of Invitation—Congregation

> NBH 94 *He Is Here* (as needed in D)

Song of Benediction—Congregation

> NBH 151 *Bless His Holy Name* (chorus, v. 1, chorus in Eb)

Postlude—Instruments

> NBH 91 *Surely Goodness and Mercy* (1x in Eb)

KEY:

CH: Celebration Hymnal (Word Music/Integrity Music, Nashville, TN)

NBH: New Baptist Hymnal (2008)

WH: The Hymnal (Word Music, Nashville, TN)

SPW: Songs for Praise and Worship (Word Music, Nashville, TN)

MSPW: More Songs for Praise and Worship (Word Music, Nashville, TN)

MSPW2: More Songs for Praise and Worship 2 (Word Music, Nashville, TN)

WEEK 23

The Spirit-Filled Wife

Ephesians 5:22–24
By Dr. Kent Spann
Setting the Record Straight

- Paul's teaching must not be taken out of its context, which is the submission of all believers (5:21).

- Paul is not teaching that women are inferior; in fact, Paul elevates the status of women not degrades them.

- Paul is not calling for a woman to be a man's slave.

- Paul is not telling a woman she has no personal identity and cannot be fulfilled even outside the home.

Getting It Right

1. The Meaning of Wifely Submission

   a. The wife acknowledges and affirms the role of her husband as the primary leader in the home (1 Pet. 3:1).

   b. The wife respects her husband (Eph. 5:32; 1 Pet. 3:2).

   c. The wife primarily focuses on her inward being, not on external things (1 Pet. 3:3).

   d. The wife demonstrates a gentle and quiet spirit (1 Pet. 3:3–5).

   e. The wife puts her hope in God, not in her husband (1 Pet. 3:5).

   f. The wife listens and follows the leadership of her husband (1 Pet. 3:6).

2. The Motive of Wifely Submission

   a. The Spirit-filled wife is motivated by the Holy Spirit (5:18, 21).

   b. The Spirit-filled wife is motivated by the Savior's pleasure (5:22 "as to the Lord").

    c. The Spirit-filled wife is motivated by God's perfect plan established for her protection and security.

3. The Model of Wifely Submission (5:23, 24)

    a. Christ, who submitted himself to the Father to be our Savior (5:23)

    b. The church, which submits itself to Christ as its head (5:24)

WEEK 23

Defining You

1 Corinthians 16:8, 9; Acts 16–17
By Dave Hirschman

Introduction

A definition is something that defines or explains. It is a statement that gives the full picture of someone or something and can be in the form of words, pictures, or concepts. There are items that instantly define corporations and products. What defines chocolate more than a Hershey Kiss, coffee more than Starbucks, computers more than Microsoft or Apple, and cars more than perhaps Mercedes? What defines you? Something will ultimately define you. The church at Corinth allowed immaturity to define them; the Thessalonians, faith; the Philippians, joy, etc. Unfortunately, many churches define themselves with issues (worship style, music, dress, Bible versions, etc., are some of the better examples). What do you want to define you? In closing his first letter to the Corinthians, Paul reveals something interesting, and that provides insight into what defined Paul. Paul was defined by what he believed, and what he believed fueled his spiritual engine. Paul believed in *open doors*, God-authored opportunities to accomplish God's plan wherever he was. Notice how this belief defined Paul.

1. Paul looked for open doors constantly (Acts 16:6–10). Because He expected them, and planned for what he expected (Rom. 1:13; 15:28, Col. 4:3), he kept looking for open doors to share the gospel.

2. Paul pursued open doors repeatedly. People became open doors (Acts 16:11–13); places became open doors; (Acts 17:16–22); and even problems became open doors (Acts 23:10, 11; 24:24, 25 [Felix]; Acts 25 [Festus, Agrippa]).

3. Paul experienced open doors frequently (Acts 14:26, 27, an open door to the Gentiles).

We need to be people who define ourselves as those who look for, pursue, and experience God's open doors, but recognize that open doors are seen only by those who believe they exist, and open doors are pursued only by those who believe they exist fopen doors are experienced only by those who are defined by their belief in God's opportunities.

Conclusion

What defines you? Are you looking for, pursuing, and experiencing God's open doors for you? God has plans for His people, and those plans include open doors of opportunity for you. What will you let define you?

WEEK 24

The Bible: Con Job or God's Word?

2 Timothy 3:16; 2 Peter 1:19-21
By Dr. Kent Spann

What If?

What if the Bible we hold in our hands today and that millions have held in their hands for centuries was a fraud? What if the book that has changed the face of the world and shaped Western civilization was the result of a cover-up? What if the book that has sold not millions but billions was a swindle job? What if the book that men and women have staked their lives on and even lost their lives for was nothing more than a con job?

If it were, it would be the biggest con job in the history of humanity! It would be bigger than Orson Welles's radio broadcast "War of the Worlds," bigger than the Watergate scandal, and more scandalous than the Enron cover-up.

Yet that it is what some would say about the Bible: The Bible is the product of man, not God. The Bible is the result of a selective process spearheaded by a pagan emperor intended to promote a political career and suppress the truth. The Bible we have in our hands is incomplete. All of those claims and more can be summarized in one statement:

> The Bible we hold in our hands today is neither trustworthy
> nor authoritative!

Roman emperors tried to destroy it; Communism ridiculed, banned and burned it; humanists and atheists have scorned it. Why? I will let Voltaire (1694–1778), the French Enlightenment writer and philosopher who was considered to be one of the most influential figures of his time, answer the question:

> If we would destroy the Christian religion, we must first of

all destroy man›s belief in the Bible.

Voltaire is right; if the Bible is false, then the Christian faith crumbles.

Check It Out

Christians need to check out the evidence for the Bible so they can give an answer for what they believe (1 Pet. 3:15).

There are three main issues surrounding the authenticity of Scripture.

1. Inspiration: How did we get the Bible?

2. Transmission: How did we get the Bible we have today?

3. The Canon: What books belong in the Bible?

I. How Did We Get the Bible?

How did we get our Bible? Is it merely the product of man? The clearest verse on the subject of the inspiration of Scripture is 2 Timothy 3:16. The Greek word Paul used here is *theopneustos* which is a combination of two Greek words: *theos*, meaning "God," and *pneustos*, meaning "breath" or "blast of wind." When you put the two words together it means literally "God-breathed," which is how the NIV translates it.

What God-breathed means is that the various writers were moved, led, and guided by God's Spirit to record exactly what God wanted, using each of the authors' backgrounds, vocabularies, and culture. That is why, when you read the Bible, there are different styles of writing—poetry, wisdom, historical, narrative, etc. It is also the reason you can read the same account in two different Gospels and get a different view or added material. Yet each writer still recorded the Word of God exactly as God wanted it to be recorded. That is what makes the Bible such an amazing book.

1. The Bible is a book of God and a book of man.

Erwin Lutzer, pastor of Moody Bible Church, in his book *Seven Reasons Why You Can Trust the Bible*, wrote:

The Bible ... is a book of God *and* a book of man. God's part was to superintend the writing of the books, revealing His will. Man's part was to write this revelation using a human language and style so that God's message was preserved for future generations.[23]

a. God used people to record His revelation.

b. God protected the writers so that they recorded what He wanted (2 Pet. 1:20, 21).

2. The Bible we have is God's Word.

a. It is trustworthy because it is true without any mixture of error.

b. It is authoritative because it is God's Word.

II. How Did We Get the Bible We Have Today?

When we speak of inspiration, we are referring to the original writings. Obviously we don't have the original writings, so how do we know that what we have today is accurate? Here we are dealing with the transmission of Scripture. Can we trust what we have today? Is it reliable? Has it been passed down accurately, or has it been radically altered?

There are many evidences for the reliability of the Bible we have in hand today.

1. The Manuscripts of the Text

a. The Number of Manuscripts

Homer's *Iliad* is second only to the New Testament in the number of manuscripts available. So how do they compare? There are 643 manuscripts for the *Iliad*, while there are 24,970 manuscripts for the New Testament alone.

b. The Date of the Manuscripts

Among the classics the *Iliad* has the manuscript closest to the original. It was written around 900 BC. The earliest copy

---

[23] Erwin W. Lutzer, *Seven Reasons Why You Can Trust the Bible* (Chicago: Moody, 2008), 23, http://www.moodypublishers.com/Media/MediaLibrary/SevenReasonsExcerpt.pdf.

available is from 400 BC, or five hundred years after the original writing. The New Testament was written between AD 40 and 100. The earliest copy available is from AD 125, or twenty-five years after the original writing.

F. F. Bruce (1920–1990), chair of biblical studies at Sheffield University and Ryland's professor of biblical criticism and exegesis at the University of Manchester wrote:

> The evidence for our New Testament writings is ever so much greater than the evidence for many writings of classical authors, the authenticity of which no one dreams of questioning ... And if the New Testament were a collection of secular writings, their authenticity would generally be regarded as beyond all doubt.[24]

2. The Citations of Early Church Fathers

The early church fathers whose original writings we have today quoted from the text we have today.

3. The Protection of God

If God oversaw the giving of the Scripture, why would it be hard to believe that He would protect its transmissions? Consider these passages that speak of God's protection of His Word:

> Forever, O LORD, Your word is settled in heaven. (Ps. 119:89)

> For assuredly, I say to you, till heaven and earth pass away, one jot or one tittle will by no means pass from the law till all is fulfilled. (Matt. 5:18)

> Heaven and earth will pass away, but My words will by no means pass away. (Matt. 24:35)

> But the word of the Lord endures forever. (1 Pet. 1:25)

---

[24] F. F. Bruce, *The New Testament Documents: Are They Reliable?* (n.p.: Wilder Publications, 2009), 15.

III. How Did the Twenty-seven Books Get Selected for the New Testament?

This deals with the subject of the *canon*, or the authoritative list of the books of the Bible.

1. How many gospels were considered?

There were many writings claiming to be gospels, but from the earliest times, only four were considered genuine Gospels.

2. Who decided on what would go in the New Testament?

God, not the church, created the canon; the church merely recognized the books that were inspired from their inception. God guided the process from beginning to end, because it is His book. What were the criteria followed for recognizing the books? There was a pattern.

a. Is it authoritative? Did it come from the hand of God?

b. Is it prophetic? Was it written by a man of God? An apostle?

c. Is it authentic?

d. Is it dynamic? Did it come with the life-transforming power of God?

e. Was it received, collected, read, and used by God's people? Was it accepted by the people of God? What about the councils recognizing the canon?

There were two councils that spoke to the issue of the Canon: the Council of Hippo (A.D. 393) and the Council of Carthage (A.D. 397), both of which confirmed the twenty-seven books in our New Testament as authoritative. They did not decide which books belonged in the canon; they only affirmed what was already believed by the church to be the authoritative books.

Conclusion

So is the Bible a con job, or is it the Word of God? There is no doubt it is the Word of God (2 Pet. 1:19–21).

SUGGESTED ORDER OF WORSHIP

Theme: Great and Mighty Is the Lord

Prelude

Welcome—Pastor

Hymn of Welcome *(meet and greet)*—Congregation

> NBH 584 *Come into His Presence* (2x in Bb)
>
> NBH 20 *Great and Mighty* (2x in Eb)

Great and Mighty in Power . . .

Prayer of Praise—Pastoral Staff

Praise and Worship—Congregation

> NBH 64 *What a Mighty God We Serve* (2x in D)
>
> NBH 666 *We Have Come into His House* (vv. 1, 2 in Eb)
>
> NBH 71 *Holy Ground* (vv. 1, 2 in Eb)
>
> NBH 72 *We Are Standing on Holy Ground* (2x in Eb)

Great and Mighty in Purpose . . .

Worship Through Reading the Scripture (Col. 1:15–22)—
Pastoral Staff

15 He is the image of the invisible God, the firstborn over all creation.

16 For by Him all things were created that are in heaven and that are on earth, visible and invisible, whether thrones or dominions or principalities or powers. All things were created through Him and for Him.

17 And He is before all things, and in Him all things consist.

18 And He is the head of the body, the church, who is the beginning, the firstborn from the dead, that in all things He may have the preeminence.

19 For it pleased the Father that in Him all the fullness should dwell, **20** and by Him to reconcile all things to Himself, by Him, whether things on earth or things in heaven, having made peace through the blood of His cross.

21 And you, who once were alienated and enemies in your mind by wicked works, yet now He has reconciled **22** in the body of His flesh through death, to present you holy, and blameless, and above reproach in His sight.

Prayer of Praise and Call to Obedience—Pastoral Staff

> NBH 487 *Knowing You* (vv. 1–3, chorus in C)

... Great and Mighty in Promise!!!

Offertory Prayer—Pastoral Staff

Offertory Praise—Praise Team or Soloist

> NBH 485 *Psalm 42*

Sermon—Pastor

Hymn of Invitation—Congregation

> NBH 433 *I Surrender All* (as needed in C)

Benediction Hymn—Congregation

> NBH 64 *What a Mighty God We Serve* (1x in D)

Postlude—Instrumental Ensemble

> NBH 20 *Great and Mighty* (1x in D, 1x in Eb)

KEY:

CH: Celebration Hymnal (Word Music/Integrity Music, Nashville, TN)

NBH: New Baptist Hymnal (2008)

WH: The Hymnal (Word Music, Nashville, TN)

SPW: Songs for Praise and Worship (Word Music, Nashville, TN)

MSPW: More Songs for Praise and Worship (Word Music, Nashville, TN)

MSPW2: More Songs for Praise and Worship 2 (Word Music, Nashville, TN)

WEEK 24

The Spirit-Filled Husband

Ephesians 5:25–33
By Dr. Kent Spann

The *Tulsa World*, February 26, 1988, reported, "State House Repeals Law Appointing Husbands as Head of Household":

> After a debate punctuated with Scripture references, the House passed a bill Thursday refuting the law dating back to territorial days that recognized the husband as the head of the household. "I'm asking you to bring Oklahoma from the nineteenth century into the twentieth century before the twenty-first century gets here," said Representative Freddy E. Williams, Democrat from Oklahoma City who has pushed for the law's repeal for years."

We don't need to repeal it; we just need to get it right. What does it mean for the man to be head of the home?

1. The husband is to be a servant-leader of his wife (5:23).

Matthew 20:25–28

True greatness, true leadership, is achieved not by reducing men to one's service, but by giving up oneself in selfless service to them

—Oswald Chambers

---

a. Serve his wife

b. Bring out the best in his wife

c. Help his wife develop and grow as a person

d. Take responsibility for leading the home

e. Dream with his wife

f. Set the tone of his home

True leadership must be for the benefit of the followers, not to enrich the leader.

—John C. Maxwell

---

g. Think of his wife and family first

h. Pray with his wife

i. Lead his wife to a deeper love for God

j. Learn to say, "I'm sorry" and "Forgive me"

2. The husband is to be a sacrificial lover of his wife (5:25–33).

    a. Love her selflessly by giving yourself for her (5:25: "gave Himself for her").

    b. Love her supremely by loving her only (5:28: "their own wives").

    c. Love her satisfyingly by meeting her true needs (5:28: "own bodies").

    d. Love her steadfastly by loving her to the end (5:31).

WEEK 24

Resurrection Morning

Luke 24:1–8
By Dave Hirschman

Introduction

The account of the events of Resurrection morning tells of how the women had prepared the special burial spices and ointments, and how they had returned early in the morning to finish a sorrowful task. In addition, it reveals how they were confused when they arrived at the peaceful garden setting where the tomb is located. Certain things would occur that would change their lives forever, the same things that are changing lives today! On Resurrection morning:

1. The tomb was opened—to show the truth (vv. 1, 2); to show that that the tomb was empty (v. 3); to show why the tomb was empty (v. 4); and to show that He was alive (vv. 5–8).

2. Their eyes were opened—to see the truth (vv. 13–31); to see that the Resurrection was real (v. 31); to see that He was true to His promises (John 2:19, Matt. 12:40); and to see all that His resurrection meant (vv. 32–34, 1 Cor. 15:55).

3. Their hearts and minds were opened—to understand the truth (vv. 36–45); to understand the truth previously hidden (parables), and the truth now clearly presented (Heb. 9:28).

4. The world was opened—to give the truth (vv. 46–8), truth that everyone needs to know.

Conclusion

Many things were opened on resurrection morning, and the truth of that day continues to open eyes, hearts, and minds today; and by His resurrection, Jesus opened the world to the truth as well. Have you opened your eyes, heart, and mind to the truth of Resurrection morning? Will you do so today? Will you help take this glorious truth to a world that has been opened to the truth of Resurrection morning?

WEEK 25

Dad, the Family Teacher

Deuteronomy 6:4–9
By Dr. Kent Spann

In the 1960s, just before the ten o'clock news, television stations would always flash a message that said, "Parents, do you know where your children are?" This morning I want to ask, "Dads, do you know where your kids are today?"

I think we need to focus on the home, and more specifically, the role of the fathers in the home. David Blankenhorn, president of the Institute for American Values, reports on the death of fatherhood and its meaning.

> Much of the national debate about family decline tacitly assumes that the dilemma centers on women's roles, choices and responsibilities. But this assumption overlooks the single most troubling family trend in our era: male flight from family life.

What does the state of fatherhood look like today? Eight thousand men were asked to write epitaphs for their fathers' tombs. Here is what some wrote:

- Here Lies My Dad—Always gone: still is.
- Here Lies My Dad—He did not demonstrate love to his sons.
- Here Lies My Dad—A hardworking man full of pride, who died lonely.
- Here Lies My Dad—If your actions matched your talk, you would be awesome.
- Here Lies My Dad—He had time for the community but not enough for his kids.

Maybe we need to begin this whole discussion of fathers by asking, "What is the main objective of a father?" Is it to teach them manners? Sports? Business? How to be successful? How to fix a car?

Those things are all great, but are they the fundamental things? What is the fundamental thing? It is to teach and train your child the *fundamentals of the faith*!

What are those fundamentals, and how in the world do I teach them to my child? God gave us a strategy three thousand years ago in Deuteronomy 6:4–9.

The Fundamentals

The fundamentals are very simple.
Fundamental # 1: "Who is God?" (v. 4)
Fundamental # 2: "How do we respond to this God?" (v. 5)

Teaching the Fundamentals

Our text provides some insights into how to accomplish this daunting task.

1. Dads, teach your children the fundamentals of the faith by modeling it for them ("your heart," v. 6).

Dad, the good news is, your children will copy you! The bad news, Dad, is your children will copy you! First graders were asked to draw a picture of God in their Sunday school class. Their finished products contained some interesting theology. One child depicted God in the form of a brightly colored rainbow. Another presented him as an old man coming out of the clouds. An intense little boy drew God with a remarkable resemblance to Superman. The best snapshot came from a little girl. She said, "I didn't know what God looked like, so I just drew a picture of my daddy."

A survey confirmed the importance of the dad in the area of Sunday school attendance. When both parents attended Sunday school regularly, 72 percent of the children attended when grown. When just the father attended, 55 percent of the children attended when grown. When only the mother attended, 15 percent of the children attended when grown. When neither parent attended, 6 percent of their children attended when grown.

Dads, your role in spiritual development is critical.

2. Dads, teach your children the fundamentals of the faith by discussing it with them ("talk," v. 7).

Dad, don't leave the religious training of your children to the Sunday school teacher, the preacher, the VBS teacher, etc.

   a. Have a family altar where you read God's Word.

   b. Read spiritual books, and grow in your own faith.

   c. Have a quiet time, and discuss what you learned.

3. Dads, teach your children the fundamentals of the faith by seizing the teachable moments (walking, lying down, getting up, v. 7).

   a. Watch for those events where you can teach them the Word

      i. A problem at school

      ii. A defeat on the ball field

      iii. A rejection by a boyfriend or girlfriend

   b. Watch for those moments when you can interject the love of God and the Word into their lives.

   c. Pray with them about daily events in their lives and the world.

   d. Share experiences from your life—failures and successes.

4. Dads, teach your children the fundamentals of the faith by using object lessons ("Bind them as a sign on your hand, and they shall be as frontlets between your eyes," v. 8).

The Jews took this literally and would actually wear containers with verses in them on their foreheads and their arms. I don't think God was giving them a law as much as saying to them to use creative means to teach your children to love God and His Word.

   a. Use areas of interest for you or your kids.

      If you or they are into sports, look for ways to communicate spiritual truth through sports. If they are into football, talk about being on a team, and relate it to the church team. If you are a hunter, talk about scoping your gun, and then teach them about fixing their eyes on Jesus. Use their favorite author or book.

   b. Nature provides great object lessons.

c. Use things that have happened in your life or theirs.

5. Dads, teach your children the fundamentals of the faith by being creative in communicating them ("Write them on the doorposts of your house and on your gates," v. 9).

Once again the Jews took this literally and attached a container with four verses, called a *mezuzah*, on their door. That was pretty creative, wasn't it? Today's Jews have a beautiful custom that involves their children in a special synagogue service. A drop of honey is placed on a copy of the Torah (their Bible). The child then kisses the drop of honey. It teaches them that the Word is "sweeter also than honey" (Ps. 19:10). That is creative.

Find your own creative ways to teach the faith. Examples:

a. Christian or secular music

b. Literature from church

c. Making up stories

d. Creative games

Conclusion

The bottom line, Dad, is that you are the man charged with the responsibility of teaching your children. Is it going to be easy? No. Will it take a lot of work? Yes. Will it be a stretch for some of you guys? Yep. Will you feel inadequate and uncomfortable at times? Yessiree. Will you botch up sometimes? You betcha. Will some of the things you try flop? Oh yeah. But you know that is okay, because they will still learn.

SUGGESTED ORDER OF WORSHIP

Father's Day

Prelude—Instrumentalists

Call to Prayer—Pastoral Staff (*All men asked to come to front of church for group prayer*)

Call to Praise—Congregation

> NBH 571 *This Is the Day* (2x in Eb)

> NBH 627 *Freely, Freely* (v. 1, chorus, v. 2, chorus in Eb)

Recognition of the Fathers and Families—Pastor

Welcome—Pastoral Staff

Song of Welcome *(meet and greet)*—Congregation

> NBH 568 *I'm So Glad* (vv 1–4 in G)

Scripture Honoring Fathers, from Ephesians 5:25–33—Selected Church Leader

Husbands, love your wives, just as Christ also loved the church and gave Himself for her, that He might sanctify and cleanse her with the washing of water by the word, that He might present her to Himself a glorious church, not having spot or wrinkle or any such thing, but that she should be holy and without blemish. So husbands ought to love their own wives as their own bodies; he who loves his wife loves himself. For no one ever hated his own flesh, but nourishes and cherishes it, just as the Lord does the church. For we are members of His body, of His flesh and of His bones. "For this reason a man shall leave his father and mother and be joined to his wife, and the two shall become one flesh." This is a great mystery, but I speak concerning Christ and the church. Nevertheless let each one of you in particular so love his own wife as himself, and let the wife see that she respects her husband.

Prayer of Praise—Pastoral Staff

Worship and Praise—Congregation

> NBH 555 *I Love You, Lord* (vv. 1 and 2 in F)

> NBH 556 *We Fall Down* (2x in F)

NBH 557 *More Precious Than Silver* (2x in F)

Testimony of Praise—Pastor's Choice (prefer a 2- to 3-minute video)

Offertory Prayer—Pastoral Staff

Offertory Praise—Men's Ensemble or Choir

A Few Good Men

Sermon—Pastor

Hymn of Invitation—Congregation

NBH 566 *Father, I Adore You* (as needed)

Benediction Hymn—Congregation

NBH 560 *Oh, How I Love Jesus* (chorus only in G)

Postlude—Instrumentalists

NBH 571 *This Is the Day*

KEY:

CH: Celebration Hymnal (Word Music/Integrity Music, Nashville, TN)

NBH: New Baptist Hymnal (2008)

WH: The Hymnal (Word Music, Nashville, TN)

SPW: Songs for Praise and Worship (Word Music, Nashville, TN)

MSPW: More Songs for Praise and Worship (Word Music, Nashville, TN)

MSPW2: More Songs for Praise and Worship 2 (Word Music, Nashville, TN)

WEEK 25

The Spirit-Filled Family

Ephesians 6:1–4
By Dr. Kent Spann

The Vatican in June 2006 issued a report stating that the traditional family is under attack:

> Man of modern times has radicalized the tendency to take the place of God and substitute him. Never before in history has human procreation, and therefore the family, which is its natural place, been so threatened as in today's culture.

Children (6:1–3)

1. Children must obey their parents (6:1).
   a. Listen attentively (Prov. 1:8; 4:1, 20)
   b. Respond positively
   c. Obey promptly
2. Children must honor their parents (6:2, 3).
   a. Respect them
   b. Listening to their wise counsel
   c. Cherish and value their parents
   d. Provide and care for their parents in their old age (1 Tim. 5:4; Matt. 15:3–6)
   e. Living morally upstanding lives (Prov. 10:1)

Parents (6:4)

1. Parents should treat their children respectfully.
   a. Deal with them in a right spirit.

b. Don't smother or excessively control them.

c. Avoid unreasonable discipline.

d. Live what they teach.

e. Refrain from overprotecting them.

f. Value each of their children.

g. Encourage rather than discourage them.

h. Keep their promises.

i. Resist pushing achievement beyond reasonable bounds.

j. Make sure each child knows he or she is important to them.

k. Love their spouses.

2. Parents should nurture their children spiritually.

  a. By training them ("train")

    i. Moral development (Matt. 22:37–39)

    ii. Mental development

    iii. Personal development (Prov. 22:6)

  b. By teaching them ("instruction")

    i. Correct them when they are wrong.

    ii. Tell them what they have done wrong, why it is wrong, and how to do it right.

    iii. Affirm them when they are right.

    iv. Seize the teachable moments (Deut. 6:4–6).

WEEK 25

Finishing Approved

1 Corinthians 9
By Dave Hirschman

Introduction

Time flies! Have you accomplished everything you set out to do in this year? We start out with good intentions but it's easy to get off track, lose momentum, and run out of gas. It happens spiritually too. What did you set out to accomplish spiritually this year? Perhaps to develop consistency in reading His Word, or to begin a memorization program? Hopefully, you had some spiritual goals this year and accomplished some of them, and are finishing the year sensing God's approval. The apostle Paul uses the figure of a race to describe the life of a follower of Jesus (Acts 20:24; Phil. 3:13, 14). Is it possible for a runner to be disapproved or disqualified from the race? Certainly. Paul used a similar expression in 1 Corinthians 9:27: "Lest, when I have preached to others, I myself should become disqualified" (*adokimos*:"disapproved, disqualified"). One day it will be life and not the year that ends, and then the race will be over. Does it matter how we run? Does it matter if we run at all? It should be our desire to run and finish approved! To run and finish approved we must:

1. Be fit ("Therefore I run thus: not with uncertainty. I fight: not as one who beats the air. But I discipline my body and bring it into subjection," 1 Cor. 9:26, 27).

   Physical fitness is the result of physical conditioning (running, sit-ups, weight training, etc). Spiritual fitness is the result of spiritual conditioning (1 Cor. 3:1, 2; Heb. 5:12–14). Prolonged spiritual running requires ongoing spiritual fitness. Many believers avoid spiritual conditioning, and are spiritually unfit. Spiritual fitness develops by focusing on eternal truth, applying God's principles, developing endurance.

2. Understand the course (1 Cor. 9:25).

Before a runner runs, he checks the track, to be completely familiar with every part, to know it. It is a lifetime course—not just when it is sunny or convenient, or when young or older. It is a challenging course—there are trials, temptations, troubles, and an adversary! It is a course with distinct rules—it requires righteousness, faithfulness, and submission.

3. Run to finish (1 Cor. 9:24).

There is a physical prize—"crown" (2 Tim. 4:7, 8; James 1:12); there is a spiritual prize—"Well done, good and faithful servant" (Matt. 25); and there is the ultimate prize—the presence of God!

Conclusion

We should all want to finish life with God's approval. Are you striving to become and stay spiritually fit? Are you following the divine instructions as you are running? Many believers are distracted with the things of this world, but finishing approved should motivate us to run well. We need to run (live) with determination, stay in a constant state of training, and run to finish. You are already a winner in Jesus; live like it; run to finish approved!

WEEK 26

Does God Exist?

Jeremiah 9:23, 24

By Dr. Kent Spann

What is the greatest thing in the entire world to you? The answers will vary among people. How can you tell what really is the greatest thing to a person? By their boasting. People boast about what is important.

What is the greatest thing in the entire world? According to Jeremiah 9:23, 24, it is knowing God. In this passage, three powerful truths emerge.

Truth #1: God is real.

How can you know and understand someone you do not believe is real? For many the existence of God is where the journey of knowing and understanding God begins. What do I mean when I say He is real? I mean two things: (1) God exists, and (2) He is absolutely supreme.

God exists. There is a view of God that thrives in our world today called *atheism*. Atheism says there is no God. When we think of atheism, we automatically think of Communist China, North Korea, or Cuba, but folks, it exists and thrives in our society. In our world, we call it *naturalism*. At the heart of naturalism is atheism—there is no God.

In response to those who deny the existence of God, either practically or philosophically, God says in verse 24, "I am." There are tremendous evidences for the reality of God that we can give to those who declare there is no God.

1. Scripture declares that He exists (Gen. 1:1).

Now, some would look down on this evidence because they don't believe the Bible to be true. When we deal with those who do not believe the Bible is true, we have to go back to the evidence for the truth of Scripture. When a person comes to acknowledge the truthfulness of Scripture, and if he is intellectually honest, then he will have to acknowledge that there is a God.

2. Nature declares that He exists (Rom. 1:20).

As we look out at the universe, there is a great awareness that there is a God who has created all that we know. A look at the universe confirms this in our hearts.

One of the world's most loved comic strips is BC. In one strip we find a caveman kneeling in prayer. "It's not easy to believe in you, God. We never see you. How come you never show yourself? How do we know you even exist?" What follows is a flower springing to life beside him; a volcano erupting in the distance; an eclipse of the sun, turning the sky black; a star shooting across the stratosphere; a tidal wave rushing over him; lightning flashing; a bush beginning to burn; and a stone rolling away from the entrance to a tomb. The caveman pulls himself from the mud, dripping wet, surrounded by darkness. "OK, OK. I give up! Every time I bring up this subject, all we get are interruptions."

Many are like the caveman. The evidences are everywhere around them, but they can see God in it. Their minds have been trained to see nature through the lens of naturalism.

3. Man's heart declares that He exists (Rom. 1:21).

A small boy was flying a kite high in the sky one April afternoon when a low drifting cloud encircled the kite and hid it from view. A passerby asked the little boy what he was doing with that string in his hand. "I'm flying my kite," the child responded. The man, looking up and seeing only the cloud in an otherwise clear sky, said, "I don›t see a kite up there anywhere."

"Mister," the little boy replied, "I don›t see it either, but I know it's up there because every once in a while there's a tug on my string."

We feel that tug in many ways. From the very beginning there is awareness in people's mind of God, whether you are talking of a sophisticated Westerner or a person who comes out of the jungle for the first time. Where did that come from?

One of the arguments for God is called the *moral argument*. It points out man's sense of right and wrong that spans time and culture, and the need for justice to be done. Where did the sense of right and wrong come from? The moral argument says that God is the source of right and wrong, and He will someday mete out justice to all people.

4. Reason declares that He exists (Ps. 14:1).

The atheist says that Christians have to leave reason at the door to believe there is a God. The truth is the opposite, according to Psalm 14:1. What is a fool? It is somebody who has lost his or her reason or can't reason properly. Folks, it is more unreasonable to deny the existence of God than it is to acknowledge the existence of God.

There are two great arguments from reason.

    a. The cosmological argument proves the reality of God from cause and effect.

        1) The universe had a beginning.

        2) Anything that has a beginning must have been caused by something else.

        3) Therefore, the universe was caused by something else, and this cause was God.

    b. The teleological argument proves the reality of God based on evidence for intelligent design.

        1) All designs imply a designer.

        2) There is a great design in the universe.

        3) Therefore, there must be a Great Designer of the universe.

God is absolutely supreme. He is absolutely supreme—the Lord. There is another worldview that has gained great popularity: *polytheism*. Polytheism says there is a plurality of gods. Polytheism is at the heart of Hinduism, from which many New Age religions evolve; Buddhism, which is on the rise in the U.S.; and Mormonism. It is also at the heart of the statement, "It doesn't matter which religion you adhere to, just as long as you sincerely believe." It implies that there are many gods and all are equal. God makes it clear in Jeremiah that He is absolutely supreme; that is, there is no other God besides Him (Deut. 4:35; 6:4; 1 Tim. 2:5).

Truth # 2: God is revealed.

There are many in our world today, even in our churches, who acknowledge the reality of God but would say that you cannot know this God. In Jeremiah 9:24, God makes it clear that we can know Him. We don't have to go out and create our ideas of God; we don't have to hold panels to guess what God is like—we can know Him. Now, here is the key: *we can know Him because He has chosen to reveal Himself.* I want to share the two primary ways He reveals Himself to us.

1. He reveals Himself through Jesus Christ (Matt. 11:27; John 14:5–14; Heb. 1:1–4).

2. He reveals Himself through the Scriptures.

We can know God. We can't know everything about God, but we can know Him as He has revealed Himself. That leads to the most important question—why has the incomprehensible God chosen to reveal Himself? Let's examine truth #3.

Truth # 3: God is relational.

God reveals Himself because He is relational and wants to have a relationship with us.

There is another view of God that, while acknowledging that God truly exists, says that He is distant and removed from creation. He started creation, wound up the clock, and then left. He is sort of an absentee Father. This is known as *deism*.

Nothing could be farther from the truth. The Hebrew word translated "knows" in Jeremiah 9:24 means far more than intellectual knowledge. It means an intimate and personal knowledge.

What is God telling us here?

1. He wants us to know Him individually.

2. He wants us to know Him intimately.

3. He wants us to know Him increasingly.

Conclusion

God is real, and He has chosen to reveal Himself to us because He is relational.

SUGGESTED ORDER OF WORSHIP

Prelude—Instrumentalist

    NBH 121 *Everlasting God* (2x in Bb)

Call to Prayer—Pastoral Staff

Welcome—Pastoral Staff

    NBH 322 *Praise the Name of Jesus* (2x in D)

    NBH 325 *In the Name of the Lord* (2x in D)

    NBH 326 *Your Name* (v. 1, chorus, v. 2, chorus in Ab)

Baptismal Celebration—Pastoral Staff

Prayer of Commitment—Pastoral Staff

    NBH 330 *Spirit of the Living God* (2x in F)

Scripture Reading from 1 Peter 1:3–9 *(Please have prepared for IMAG)*

Blessed be the God and Father of our Lord Jesus Christ, who according to His abundant mercy has begotten us again to a living hope through the resurrection of Jesus Christ from the dead, to an inheritance incorruptible and undefiled and that does not fade away, reserved in heaven for you, who are kept by the power of God through faith for salvation ready to be revealed in the last time. In this you greatly rejoice, though now for a little while, if need be, you have been grieved by various trials, that the genuineness of your faith, being much more precious than gold that perishes, though it is tested by fire, may be found to praise, honor, and glory at the revelation of Jesus Christ, whom having not seen you love. Though now you do not see Him, yet believing, you rejoice with joy inexpressible and full of glory, receiving the end of your faith—the salvation of your souls.

Prayer of Thanksgiving—Pastor

NBH 516 *Like a River Glorious* (v. 1, chorus, v. 2, chorus in F, v. 3, chorus in G)

NBH 528 *I Give You My Heart* (v. 1, chorus, chorus in G)

Offertory Prayer and Praise

NBH 529 *Change My Heart, O God* (v. 1, chorus, chorus in C)

Message—Pastor

Hymn of Response/Invitation—Worship Leader

NBH 143 *You Are My All in All* (v. 1, chorus, v. 2, chorus in F)

Benediction Hymn—Congregation

NBH 518 *My Life Is in You, Lord* (1x in G)

Postlude—Instrumental Only

NBH 519 *Because We Believe*

KEY:

CH: Celebration Hymnal (Word Music/Integrity Music, Nashville, TN)

NBH: New Baptist Hymnal (2008)

WH: The Hymnal (Word Music, Nashville, TN)

SPW: Songs for Praise and Worship (Word Music, Nashville, TN)

MSPW: More Songs for Praise and Worship (Word Music, Nashville, TN)

MSPW2: More Songs for Praise and Worship 2 (Word Music, Nashville, TN)

WEEK 26

The Spirit-Filled Worker

Ephesians 6:5–9
By Dr. Kent Spann

A Word About Slavery

- There were many different forms of slavery in Rome, not all of which were bad.
- Paul's purpose in writing this was not to comment on whether slavery was right or wrong.
- Paul's focus was on the heart of the Christians who found themselves either as slaves or masters.

The Spirit-Filled Employee (vv. 5–8)

1. The Spirit-Filled Employee's Responsibility

    a. Submit to their authority

    b. Listen to their authority

    c. Respect their authority

2. The Spirit-Filled Employee's Attitude

    a. Be respectful (v. 5)

        David (1 Sam. 24)

    b. Be sincere (v. 5)

        Joseph (Genesis 41:39-57)

    c. Be wholehearted (v. 7)

3. The Spirit-Filled Employee's Motivation

    a. Work for their earthly master as they would to the Lord (v. 5)

    b. Work for their earthly master to ultimately please the Lord

(v. 6)

c. Work for their earthly master as an act of service to the Lord (v. 7)

d. Work for their earthly master in anticipation of the Lord's reward (v. 8)

The Spirit-Filled Employer (v. 9)

1. The Spirit-Filled Employer's Responsibility

They are to treat those under them the way they want their employees to treat them (Matt. 7:12).

2. The Spirit-Filled Employer's Attitude

a. Treats employees with respect, recognizing they are in the image of God (6:5; Gal. 3:28, 29).

b. Treats employees with sincerity by being faithful to them (v. 5).

c. Treats employees with wholeheartedness by doing them good (v. 7).

d. Treats employees with kindness (v. 9).

e. Treats his employees with equality (v. 9; see also Acts 10:34; Rom. 2:11; James 2:9).

3. The Spirit-Filled Employer's Motivation

a. Exercises oversight as to the Lord (vv. 5–8)

b. Exercise oversight knowing they will be accountable to God for how they treat employees (v. 9)

WEEK 26

Refuse to Lose Your Focus

2 Kings 2
By Dave Hirschman

Introduction

Focus is important. A football kicker attempting a field goal must keep his focus in the face of the opposing team. A pilot preparing to land his aircraft must remain focused to land safely. A couple desiring a lasting marriage must remain focused to accomplish their dream. Second Kings 2 demonstrates this principle in the account of Elijah and Elisha. This account reveals that Elisha refused to do anything that would cause him to lose his focus. Paul understood this principle when he expressed his desire in Philippians 3:13, 14. As Jesus followers, we must not allow anything to distract us from our Master. Notice this principle at work in the life of Elisha. Elisha refused to lose focus, and he:

1. Pursued what he knew (2:1–6), refusing any other direction, because he was pursuing what he knew

    He knew he was called (1 Kin. 19:16); he knew he had made an irreversible decision (1 Kin. 19:19–21); He knew he had a specific purpose (replace Elijah (1 Kin. 19:16)); he knew he had seen God work (when Elijah called for a drought, defeated the prophets of Baal, and brought rain again). Elisha refused to lose focus because of what he knew.

2. Expected what he pursued (2:7–12), refusing to think any other way

    He expected something to happen, because God is always about something. He expected that he could participate because God delights to use men and women in His work. He remained focused, expecting that God was at work.

3. Received what he expected (2:13, 14)

He was in a position to see God work; he witnessed God at work, and Elisha received what he expected—the assurance that God was still there and would use him after taking Elijah.

4. Used what he received (2 Kin. 3–13)

God used the servant who refused to lose his focus—miracles of oil, a son, victory over death, victory over Israel's enemies, and a voice to continue proclaiming the word of God

Conclusion

If we will refuse to lose our focus, pursuing what we know, expecting God to work, and be ready to use what we receive, God will bring us through and use us beyond your imagination! But we must refuse to lose focus! In the midst of the unexpected and difficulties, will you refuse to lose focus, and expect that your God is at work so you can receive what He has for you and He can use you to accomplish His plan?

WEEK 27

Is America a Christian Nation?

Proverbs 11:10, 11
By Dr. Kent Spann

As a senator in June 2007, Barack Obama told CBS:

> Whatever we once were, we're no longer a Christian nation. At least not just. We are also a Jewish nation, a Muslim nation, and a Buddhist nation, and a Hindu nation, and a nation of nonbelievers.[25]

Later asked to clarify his remarks, Obama wrote an e-mail to CBN News senior national correspondent David Brody.

> I think that the right might worry a bit more about the dangers of sectarianism. Whatever we once were, we're no longer just a Christian nation; we are also a Jewish nation, a Muslim nation, a Buddhist nation, a Hindu nation, and a nation of nonbelievers.[26]

As President Barack Obama, at a press conference in Turkey on April 6, 2009, he said:

> One of the great strengths of the United States is ... we have a very large Christian population—we do not consider ourselves a Christian nation or a Jewish nation or a Muslim nation. We consider ourselves a nation of citizens who are bound by ideals and a set of values.

President Obama is not the only one saying that America is no longer a Christian nation. Jon Meacham, the Pulitzer Prize–winning editor of *Newsweek* magazine, wrote a piece in the April 13, 2009, edition entitled "The End of Christian America."

---

[25] http://www.wnd.com/index.php?fa=PAGE.view&pageId=67735.

[26] http://www.worldnetdaily.com/index.php?fa=PAGE.view&pageId=67735.

Is America a Christian Nation?

What do we mean when we say that America is a Christian nation? Let's consider what it does *not* mean.

- All citizens are Christians, because in our nation one is free to be whatever he wishes.
- Christianity is the established religion, because the Constitution prohibits the establishment of a religion.
- All politicians must be Christian, because that would be unconstitutional.
- All laws in our land reflect Christian values and beliefs, because that is not the case.

So what does it mean? Supreme Court Justice David Brewer (1837–1910) said that America was "of all the nations in the world ... most justly called a Christian nation" because Christianity "has so largely shaped and molded it." Christianity made America what she is today. Most of our cherished traditions are derived from Christianity. That America is a Christian nation in this sense has been confirmed by presidents, Congress, and the courts numerous times.

Why All the Hoopla?

Why are people getting all stirred up by comments like President Obama's and others? Is it really that big a deal? Isn't it just semantics? Is it really that important?

Listen to these words from Orthodox rabbi Daniel Lapin of the Jewish Policy Center:

> [I] understand that I live ... in a Christian nation, albeit one where I can follow my faith as long as it doesn't conflict with the nation's principles. The same option is open to all Americans and will be available only as long as this nation's Christian roots are acknowledged and honored.[27]

[27] http://www.wallbuilders.com/LIBprinterfriendly.asp?id=23909.

Again he gives a solemn warning:

> Without a vibrant and vital Christianity, America is doomed, and without America, the west is doomed. Which is why I, an Orthodox Jewish rabbi, devoted to Jewish survival, the Torah, and Israel am so terrified of American Christianity caving in. God help Jews if America ever becomes a post-Christian society! Just think of Europe![28]

Proverbs 11:10, 11 makes it very clear why this is so important. Solomon contrasts the effect of the righteous versus the wicked on the life of a nation.

The Righteous and Their Nation

Who are the righteous? The righteous are those living in accordance with the proper standard as revealed in God's Word, because true righteousness is defined and derived from God.

This righteousness speaks to ethical and moral behavior of individuals and a nation. It reaches into one's personal spiritual life, the business community, and the political scene. Solomon is speaking thus of those who adhere to God's standard for *all of life*.

What does it mean that the righteous prosper? It means they do well. It does not mean that the righteous always prosper economically; rather, they do well in the land. They abound in the land. The way of the righteous is embraced. Sadly, in American culture today, the righteous are condemned, blamed, and put down.

What is the impact upon a nation when the righteous do well?

1. The nation rejoices (11:10).

The Hebrew means to rejoice, be jubilant, or to triumph (Prov. 28:12). Why is this so? Because justice and righteousness prevail. Things go better when God's righteousness prevails.

2. The city is exalted (11:11).

When the city is exalted, it means it is elevated or honored (Prov. 14:34; 29:4).

---

[28] http://www.etpv.org/2007/acwuyua.html.

The Wicked and Their Nation

Now contrast the impact of the wicked versus the righteous on a nation

1. The people are oppressed (11:10).

Thus the cause for rejoicing when the wicked fall. The image that comes to my mind is the Allied troops rolling into France and other countries that had been held in the grip of Nazi tyranny. It brings up pictures of celebration when the regime of Saddam Hussein was toppled.

2. The city is destroyed.

   a. It is destroyed by its own conduct.

   Abraham Lincoln, in a speech to the Young Men's Lyceum of Springfield, Illinois, January 27, 1838, entitled "The Perpetuation of Our Political Institutions," made a telling statement concerning the need to maintain the rule of law.

   How, then, shall we perform it? At what point shall we expect the approach of danger? By what means shall we fortify against it? Shall we expect some transatlantic military giant, to step the Ocean, and crush us at a blow? Never! All the armies of Europe, Asia and Africa combined, with all the treasure of the earth (our own excepted) in their military chest; with a Bonaparte for a commander, could not by force, take a drink from the Ohio, or make a track on the Blue Ridge, in a Trial of a thousand years.

   At what point then is the approach of danger to be expected? I answer, if it ever reach us, it must spring up amongst us. It cannot come from abroad. If destruction be our lot, we must ourselves be its author and finisher. As a nation of freemen, we must live through all time, or die by suicide.[29]

   b. It is destroyed by God.

---

[29] For the full speech go to http://teachingamericanhistory.org/library/index. asp?document=157.

Examples abound in Scripture: Sodom and Gomorrah (Gen. 19), Jerusalem (Is. 3:8, 9; Jer. 19:7; Luke 21:24) or any nation (Rom. 1:18–32).

Ladies and gentlemen, the vitality, if not the survival, of our nation is at stake. The greatest danger is not the enemies out there, but those inside our borders. We must return to our Christian roots or we will see the demise and destruction of this land we love and for whom many have shed their blood to begin and preserve.

What Should Be Our Course of Action?

- Christians must pray for our nation, our churches, and ourselves (Joel 2:12–17).

- Christians must engage the culture by standing up for what is right and even getting involved in the political process (Matt. 5:13–16), but more important, by carrying the gospel message to the unconverted (2 Cor. 5:18–21).

- Christians must repent of their personal sins, including their apathy (2 Chron. 7:14).

- Unbelievers need to repent of their sin and confess Christ as their Savior (Acts 2:36–38).

SUGGESTED ORDER OF WORSHIP

Celebrate America

Prelude—Instrumental Group

*Americana Overture**

Celebrate America in My Life—Solo with Track

I Love the USA

Welcome and Call to Worship—Pastoral Staff

Welcome Song—Congregation

> NBH 579 *He Has Made Me Glad*

Presentation of the Colors—Armed Forces Color Guard (Air Force or National Guard)

Pledge of Allegiance—Led by Worship Pastor

The National Anthem—Soloist or Congregation

> NBH 644 *Star Spangled Banner*

Tribute to Our Armed Services (From the Procession of the Patriots**)—Army, Navy, Coast Guard, Air Force, Marines

> *Salute to Our Fallen Heroes**

Praise for Divine Guidance—Congregation

> NBH 645 *Battle Hymn of the Republic*

Scripture Reading from Deuteronomy 8:11, 12, 14, 16–18; Job 8:8–13; 1 Peter 5:6–8; 10, 11

"Beware that you do not forget the LORD your God by not keeping His commandments, His judgments, and His statutes which I command you today, lest—when you have eaten and are full, and have built beautiful houses and dwell in them; ... when your heart is lifted up, and you forget the LORD your God who brought you out of the land of Egypt, from the house of bondage; ... who fed you in the wilderness with manna, which your fathers did not know, that He might humble you and that He might test you, to do you good in the end—then you say in your heart, 'My power and the might of my hand have gained me this wealth.' And you shall remember the LORD your God, for it is He who gives you power to get wealth, that He may establish His covenant which He swore to your fathers, as it is this day." ... For inquire, please, of the former age, and consider the things discovered by their fathers; for we were born yesterday, and know nothing, because our days on earth are a shadow. Will they not teach you and tell you, and utter words from their heart? Can the papyrus grow up without a marsh? Can the reeds flourish without water? While it is yet green and not cut down, it withers before any other plant. So are the paths of all who forget God; and the hope of the hypocrite shall perish ... Therefore humble yourselves under the mighty hand of God, that He may exalt you in due time, casting all your care upon Him, for He cares for you. Be sober, be vigilant; because your adversary the devil walks about like a roaring lion, seeking whom he may devour... But may the God of all grace, who called us to His eternal glory by Christ Jesus, after you have suffered a while, perfect, establish, strengthen, and settle you. To Him be the glory and the dominion forever and ever. Amen.

Prayer for America—Pastor

Offertory Prayer—Guest Member of the Armed Services

Offertory Praise—PT or Choral Ensemble

NBH 430 *If My People Will Pray*

Message—Pastor

Hymn of Invitation—Congregation

NBH 434 *I Have Decided to Follow Jesus*

Benediction Hymn—Congregation

God Bless America

Postlude—Instrumental Group

I Love the USA

KEY:

CH: Celebration Hymnal (Word Music/Integrity Music, Nashville, TN)

NBH: New Baptist Hymnal (2008)

WH: The Hymnal (Word Music, Nashville, TN)

SPW: Songs for Praise and Worship (Word Music, Nashville, TN)

MSPW: More Songs for Praise and Worship (Word Music, Nashville, TN)

MSPW2: More Songs for Praise and Worship 2 (Word Music, Nashville, TN)

Americana Overture and *Procession of the Patriots* were written, arranged, and orchestrated by Camp Kirkland and published by Praise Gathering Music

**Salute to Our Fallen Heroes*, by Randy Vadar, is arranged and orchestrated Jay Rouse for Praise Gathering Music. A video track for use with solo and choir is available from the publisher.

WEEK 27

We Are at War

Part 1
Ephesians 6:10–20
By Dr. Kent Spann

In an article for *Youth Ministries* magazine, a fourteen-year veteran of the Navy SEALs described the color-code system used to indicate levels of combat readiness. Each stage has a parallel in spiritual warfare.

- **Condition White**: The soldier is relaxed and daydreaming, unaware of his surroundings. A Christian in this condition is easy prey for Satan.

- **Condition Yellow**: The soldier is relaxed physically but alert mentally. A believer at this level may sense trouble coming, but he's not ready to confront it.

- **Condition Orange**: The soldier is physically prepared, mentally alert, and ready to fight. A believer at this stage has on the full armor of God.

- **Condition Red**: As in condition orange, the soldier is ready to fight. The difference is experience. A battle-seasoned Christian knows quickly what to do because of his experience and familiarity with Scripture.

1. We must heed our Commander's exhortation (vv. 10, 11a).

   a. Be strong in the Lord's mighty power (v. 10; Phil. 4:13; 2 Tim. 4:17).

      i. Immeasurable power (Eph. 3:20)

      ii. Resurrection power (Eph. 1:19–21)

      iii. Glorious power (Col. 1:10, 11)

   b. Get dressed for battle (v. 11)

        i. Put on the full armor of God.

           (1) In prayer

           (2) In faith

           (3) In totality

        ii. Stand firm in the full armor of God (James 4:7; 1 Pet. 5:8, 9).

2. We must know our enemy (vv. 11b, 12).

    a. His identity

        i. The devil (v. 11b)

        ii. The demons (v. 12)

    b. His schemes (2 Cor. 2:11)

        i. He knows your name.

        ii. He is relentless.

        iii. He is bent on your destruction.

WEEK 27

An Anointed Nobody!

1 Samuel 15—1 Samuel 16:13
By Rev. Larry Kiser

Introduction

Imagine this scenario. You're an elementary-aged kid, and you're outside for recess. You and a bunch of other kids have gotten together for a game of softball.

The two hunkiest guys appoint themselves captains, and they begin choosing sides. The rest of the kids, including you, line up against the playground fence while the two self-anointed captains choose their respective teams. Now let's say you're a kind of chunky kid, and you're never the first one chosen. As usual, you stand there while the choosing goes on, hoping you will not be one of the two last ones picked. The longer you stand there and watch others being chosen in front of you, the more longingly you look into those captains' faces, begging to be chosen next. You feel like a nobody.

If you have ever been in such a situation, then you can take great courage in knowing that David experienced exactly that kind of situation, and today, you can go away knowing that God loves to anoint nobodies!

To understand the story today, we must begin with a brief story about King Saul, the first king of Israel, whom David replaced. Saul was the kind of guy who never had to stand along the fence at the playground, hoping to be the next one chosen, because he was usually the one doing the choosing. The Scriptures tell us he was tall, handsome, and athletic, which in that culture or ours is a pretty slick ticket to popularity and success.

[Tell the story of the Amalekites and God's command to Saul.]
But King Saul disobeyed God by not obeying him completely.

[Read 1 Samuel 15:13.]

The fact of the matter is, partial obedience is simply disobedience that feels better!

When Samuel further presses Saul, Saul gives a reason for his disobedience.

[Read 1 Samuel 15:14–21.]

Saul feared his followers, the people he was leading. We fear more what people think than we do what God knows!

Our fears are based on an earthly value system.

Even Samuel was surprised at God's selection of David, because our earthly value system is completely different from God's eternal value system. Attractive appearance impresses people; submissive hearts impress God!

[Read 1 Samuel 15:22.]

As Samuel anoints David after turning down all of David's handsome and strong brothers, he demonstrates a beautiful combination of faith and obedience. Submitting to God's sovereignty requires uncomfortable faith!

Conclusion

Biblical faith will rarely be comfortable. The very essence of Biblical faith is submission and obedience. Biblical faith is the pathway to God's amazing anointing.

God delights in transforming earthly nobodies into eternal somebodies!

WEEK 28

The Big Ten Overview

Exodus 20:1–17
By Dr. Kent Spann

The State of the Ten Commandments

• They are controversial.

Alabama chief justice Roy Moore was removed from office on November 13, 2003, by the State Court of the Judiciary, which said that Moore violated the state's code of judicial ethics by not obeying a federal judge's order to remove a monument bearing the Ten Commandments. Its display was seen by the American Civil Liberties Union (ACLU) and liberal interpreters of constitutional law as a violation of the Constitution's First Amendment.

The Supreme Court in 2005 heard two cases originating in Kentucky and Texas. In Kentucky, two counties had moved to display the Ten Commandments, along with other documents, in 1999. Controversy quickly ensued, and lawsuits were filed claiming that the displays represented an unconstitutional establishment of religion. In Texas, a monument that included the text of the Ten Commandments had stood for forty years on the grounds of the Texas capitol. The original plaintiff in that case charged that passing by the monument with the Ten Commandments represented a violation of his own constitutional rights.

• They are no longer seen as relevant.

In the book *The Day America Told the Truth*, by James Patterson and Peter Kim, using a survey technique that guaranteed the privacy and anonymity of the respondents, the authors were able to document what Americans really believe and do. The results were startling. They found that there was no moral authority in America. "Americans are making up their own moral codes. Only 13 percent of us believe in all the Ten Commandments. Forty percent of us believe in five of the Ten Commandments. We choose which laws of God we believe in. There is absolutely no moral consensus in this country as there was in the 1950s, when all our institutions commanded more respect."

The Relevance of the Ten Commandments

What was the place of the Ten Commandments in Israel? The Ten Commandments were Israel's constitution. They were foundational to everything else in Israel's national life. They were not merely a set of laws to be followed; they were the foundation of the society that God was establishing. They would provide the framework for the moral fabric of a just and godly society.

God saw these as the foundational principles for his people to live by. They would be later summarized as loving God (Deut. 6:4, 5) and loving others (Lev. 19:18).

Are they still relevant today? Absolutely!

1. They reveal God's character.

    a. The first commandment reveals that there is only one God, and He is jealous (20:2, 3).

    b. The second commandment reveals that He is the true and living God (20:4–6).

    c. The third commandment reveals that He is to be honored and obeyed by His people. It also shows that He is righteous; therefore His people should be righteous (20:7).

    d. The fourth commandment reveals that He is the Creator and owner of all, and thus sovereign over daily events (20:8–11).

    e. The fifth commandment reveals that He has all authority and has ordained order and authorities in our lives. We are to respect these authorities because it teaches us to respect His authority (20:12).

    f. The sixth commandment reveals that He is the God of life and our final judge (20:13).

    g. The seventh commandment reveals that He is faithful and pure (20:14).

    h. The eighth commandment reveals that He owns everything and that He blesses our labor (20:15).

    i. The ninth commandment reveals that He is truthful and trustworthy (20:16).

    j. The tenth commandment reveals that He is our provider and the One who satisfies our needs (20:17).

2. They govern our relationship with God.

3. They govern our relationships with other people.

4. They provide the moral and ethical framework for a nation as well as the individual.

5. They reveal man's sinfulness.

6. They restrain man's sinfulness.

> *If God would have wanted us to live in a permissive society He would have given us Ten Suggestions and not Ten Commandments.*
>
> —Zig Ziglar

7. They reveal our need for a Savior (Gal. 4:1–7).

What About the New Testament Believer?

Weren't we set free from the law? Didn't Christ abolish the law? See Ephesians 2:14, 15.

You need to know that there were different kinds of law in Israel.

• The Ceremonial Law (Col. 2:13–17; Heb. 10:1)

    It consisted of God's regulations for Israel's worship and the sanctuary. It is no longer in effect because it was a foreshadower of Christ, who has fulfilled it all.

• The Civil Law

    It consisted of those laws that governed Israel as a nation. It does not apply to the believer, because the church is not a state. America is not a theocracy. It can act as a guide or insight for our own civil law.

- The Moral Law

It consisted of those laws that govern our moral conduct. It is the righteous and eternal standard for our relationship with God and with others. The moral law is a fixed position, like the North Star. It is to this law that Jesus referred in Matthew 5:17–19.

The Ten Commandments obviously fall under the category of moral law, so they still apply to believers today.

P. G. Ryken and R. K. Hughes, in their book *Exodus*, wrote:

> The Ten Commandments were written in stone because they would remain in effect for as long as time endured. When would it ever be permissible to worship another god, to misuse God's name, to lie, murder, or steal? Never, because these things are contrary to God's very nature.
>
> So to summarize, God's law was in effect in various ways long before the Israelites ever reached Mount Sinai. What, then, were the Ten Commandments? Think of them as a fresh copy. They were a republication, in summary form, of God's will for humanity. As Peter Enns comments, "The 'giving' of the law at Sinai is not the first time Israel hears of God's laws, but is the codification and explicit promulgation of those laws." This makes perfect sense when we remember that the Ten Commandments express the character of God, who does not change. (*Exodus: Saved for God's Glory* [Wheaton, IL: Crossway Books, 2005])

Applying the Ten Commandments

- They must be interpreted in light of all Scripture.
- They need to be applied externally and internally (Matt. 5:21, 22, 27–30).
- They have a negative and a positive application.
- They have an order of priority, with the first four taking precedence over the last six.
- They are to be grounded in love (Matt. 22:37–40).

- They are to be lived in the spirit of Christ and the grace of God.
- They are to be obeyed.

SUGGESTED ORDER OF WORSHIP

Big Ten Overview

Prelude—Instrumentalist

NBH 426 *Open Our Eyes, Lord*

Call to Worship—PT or Ensemble

NBH 157 *In This Very Room* (v. 1, chorus, v. 3, chorus in Bb)

Call to Prayer and Worship—Pastor

Worship in Song—Congregation

NBH 147 *Jesus, What a Wonder You Are* (2x in F)

NBH 156 *Jesus! What a Friend for Sinners* (v. 1, chorus, v. 2, chorus, v. 4, chorus, in F, v. 5, chorus in G)

Welcome Song (meet and greet)—Pastoral Staff

NBH 26 *Blessed Be Your Name* (v. 1, chorus, v. 4, bridge, chorus in A)

NBH 424 *I Must Tell Jesus* (v. 1, chorus, v. 4, chorus, chorus, in D)

Prayer of Intercession—Pastor

NBH 426 *Open Our Eyes, Lord* (vv. 1 and 2 in D)

Offertory Prayer—Pastoral Staff

Offertory Praise—Congregation

NBH 66 *Open the Eyes of My Heart* (2x in D)

Message—Pastor

Big Ten Overview (Ex. 20:1–17)

Hymn of Response/Invitation—Congregation

> NBH 423 *I Need Thee Every Hour*

Benediction Hymn—Congregation

> SPW 100 *Bless the Name of Jesus* (1×)

Postlude—Instrumentalist

> SPW 100 *Bless the Name of Jesus* (1×)

KEY:

CH: Celebration Hymnal (Word Music/Integrity Music, Nashville, TN)

NBH: New Baptist Hymnal (2008)

WH: The Hymnal (Word Music, Nashville, TN)

SPW: Songs for Praise and Worship (Word Music, Nashville, TN)

MSPW: More Songs for Praise and Worship (Word Music, Nashville, TN)

MSPW2: More Songs for Praise and Worship 2 (Word Music, Nashville, TN)

WEEK 28

We Are War

Part 2
Ephesians 6:10–20
By Dr. Kent Spann

Not only must we heed our Commander's exhortation and know our enemy; we must also be properly be dressed for battle.

1. We must get dressed for battle (6:13–20).

   a. The Belt of Truth (6:14)

      A Roman soldier wore a tunic, which was a large, square piece of material that had holes for the head and arms. It hung loose on his body. When time came for battle or a long march, he would gird up his loins by gathering up the loose tunic and tuck it in the belt so that he could go to battle or make the march. He would be a fool to go to battle with the tunic loose because he would trip and fall or his enemy would grab him. The belt with which he girded himself was a large leather belt.

      i. The strategy of the enemy is lies and distortions (John 8:44; Gen. 3:5; Matt. 4:5, 6; 2 Cor. 2:11; 11:14).

      ii. The armor of the Christian is truth.

         (1) We have a settled conviction about the truth.

         (2) We know and practice the truth (John 8:32).

         (3) We live a life of integrity so the enemy has no fodder for attack (Acts 24:16).

   b. The Breastplate of Righteousness (6:14)

      The breastplate covered the chest area. John MacArthur points out that "no Roman soldier would go into battle without his breastplate, a tough, sleeveless piece of armor that covered his full torso. It was often made of leather or heavy linen, onto which were sewn overlapping slices of animal hooves or horns or pieces of metal. Some were made of large pieces of metal molded or hammered to conform to the body. The purpose of that piece of armor is obvious—to protect the heart, lungs, intestines, and other vital organs."[30]

    i. The strategy of the enemy is to ensnare us in sin and then condemn us (Gen. 3; Rev. 12:10).

    ii. The armor of the Christian is righteousness.

        (1) We receive Christ's imputed righteousness—salvation (Rom. 4:6; 2 Cor. 5:21).

        (2) We practice Christ's imputed righteousness—sanctification (Eph. 4:20–32; Phil. 2:12, 13).

c. The Boots of the Gospel of Peace (6:15)

Paul uses the image of the Roman soldier's boot, called the *caliga*. It was a half boot, which the legionnaire regularly wore while on duty. It was an open-toed leather boot with a heavily nail-studded sole, which was tied to the ankles and shins with straps.

This piece of the soldier's armor was obviously very important. It helped him maintain steady footing. It protected his feet.

    i. The strategy of the enemy is to alienate (opposite of peace) us from fellowship with God and cause us to live in fear.

    ii. The armor of the Christian is peace.

        (1) Peace with God (Eph. 2:11–22)

        (2) Peace of God (John 14:27; 2 Thess. 3:16)

---

[30] John MacArthur, *Ephesians* (Chicago: Moody Press, 1996, c1986), 351.

WEEK 28

A Giant Killer!

1 Samuel 16:14—17:54
By Larry Kiser

Everyone loves it when an underdog wins. *[Use appropriate illustration of such an experience.]* There are rich lessons for each of us as we live as victors but seeming underdogs in our worlds.

All of us have different giants in our lives.

You Can't Kill Giants without the Holy Spirit's Power! (1 Sam. 16:13)

In the Old Testament, the Holy Spirit came upon people for very specific purposes (Ex. 31:1–5; Num. 24:2; Judg. 3:10; 6:14; 11:29; 13:25; 14:6; 1 Sam. 10:10; 2 Chr. 15:1; 2 Chr. 24:20).

David expressed extreme confidence. Why? Confidence is the fruit of faith (1 Sam. 17:34–37).

David's big public demonstration of faith with Goliath here didn't happen suddenly. Big public faith always rests on small personal faith (1 Sam. 17:34–37).

After Saul gave David permission to fight Goliath, he tried to get David to use his battle gear. He was well-intentioned, but David had to go with what he was comfortable with, a sling and some stones. The lesson for us is clear: you don't defeat your giants with someone else's spiritual strength (1 Sam. 17:39)!

Conclusion

David moved toward the giant. He didn't wait for the giant to come to him. And faith in our lives must always move us forward. Our faith must be a daily, moving-forward kind of faith.

Daily faith eventually moves mountains and kills giants!

WEEK 29

God and God Alone

Exodus 20:2, 3
By Dr. Kent Spann

What America Needs

There is a lot of talk about what America needs. In 1999 a conservative talk show host declared. "What America needs is more God!" He got it right, but that raises an important question.

Which God?

If America needs more God, then the question needs to be asked, "Which God?" *Time* magazine had an article about God in America.

> It seems amazing now that there was a time when science was supposedly the "enemy" of faith, and religion was deemed hostile to technological investigation. The end of atheism and agnosticism became inevitable as soon as computer calculations made improbable the odds that random natural selection could be the sole explanation for the ever increasing intricacies found in biology. Equally influential was the discovery of multiple universes, which astronomers found at the macrocosmic level and physicists detected in the microcosmic. Science thus established the current Age of Faith, re-creating the Creator. Nowadays, only the fool says in his heart, "There is no God." The question now becomes which God: the amorphous Soul of fashionable cults, the antiseptic First Principle of science, or the personal God who still inspires awe and commands commitment? (Fall 1992, 61)

So which God? The god of Jehovah's Witnesses, Mormonism, Scientology, Native Americans, Hinduism, Buddhism, Islam, New Age, liberalism, or the more practical gods, like sports, sex, self, materialism, etc.? It can be very confusing, living in our god-filled world.

It was just as confusing for Israel when they stood at the foot of Mount Sinai. Israel had been a part of a god-filled culture. There was Aker, the earth-god and helper of the dead; Amon, the wind-god; Horus, the sky-god; Isis, the goddess of healing; Ptah, the Creator-god; and others ad nausem.

Israel didn't have a Bible to know about God, so which God? The first commandment was God's answer to the question.

God's Answer

1. God reveals who He is (20:2).

God doesn't leave it to chance. He doesn't wait for the philosophers and the great thinkers in the camp to get together and figure out who He is and what He is like. We know what happens when that takes place: you get a golden calf (Ex. 32:1–6). God chose to reveal Himself to Israel.

a. He is the self-existent God.

The word translated "Lord" in this passage is the Hebrew word *Yahweh*. It is sometimes called the *Tetragrammaton* because in the Hebrew it was written without any vowels—YHWH. This name would become the most sacred of all of God's names because it was the name that God revealed to Israel. It was so sacred that Jews didn't even speak it.

i. God is mysterious.

ii. God is and will always be.

iii. Everything in life owes its existence and being to God.

iv. God is independent.

b. He is the sufficient God.

He says, "I AM." What does that mean?

i. He is all He needs. God doesn't need anything from creation or any other source to exist.

ii. He is all we need.

c. He is the supreme God.

The word translated "God" is *Elohim*. This is one of the common names for God.

i. He is the mighty God. The name often implies the "fullness of might."

ii. He is the Creator God.

iii. He is the triune God.

The word *Elohim* is the plural form of the word *El*, which means "God." Although Israel would not fully understand this, God was revealing Himself as the plural God, or the triune God. We now know Him as the Father, the Son, and the Holy Spirit.

iv. He is the covenant God.

d. He is the sovereign God.

He reminded Israel that He was the God who brought them out of slavery. It is how He brought them out of slavery that demonstrated His sovereignty. Each of the plagues was a demonstration of God's sovereignty over the Egyptian deities.

i. Nile to blood (7:20) vs. Hapi, god of the Nile; and Khnum, giver of the Nile.

ii. Frogs (8:6) vs. Heket, the frog-head goddess.

iii. Lice (8:17) vs. Geb, god of the earth; and Aker, the earth god.

iv. Flies (8:24) vs. Khepri, the god of the dung beetle. He failed to stop the breeding of the flies, which takes place in the dung.

v. Livestock disease (9:6) vs. Apis, the sacred bull god; Mnevis, the bull-god and symbol of fertility; Hathor, the cowlike mother goddess; and Isis, queen of the gods, who wore a cow's horns on her head.

vi. Boils (9:10) vs. Sekhmet, the goddess of war and sickness; and Heka, the god of magic.

vii. Hail (9:23) vs. Shu, the god of the air; and Nut, the sky goddess.

viii. Locusts (10:13) vs. Osorapis, the agriculture god; and

Seth, god of chaos, desert, storms, and crops.

ix. Darkness (10:22) vs. Ra, the god of the earth and sky. One of the most universally worshipped gods

x. Death of the firstborn (12:29) vs. Pharaoh, who was considered a god; and Meskhenet, the goddess protector of the newborns and destiny.

God showed His sovereignty over the gods of Egypt. He is still sovereign over all the gods of this world.

e. He is the sole God.

God tells His people they are to have no other gods before him. Why? Because He is the sole God. All those false gods were not really gods. They were just demons.

This commandment speaks against the trends of our culture, such as pluralism, tolerance, and syncretism.

This first commandment reveals who God is. But there is a message for God's people.

2. God reveals what He expects of His people (20:3).

a. He expects our loyalty.

God expects His people to be loyal to Him. If you are married, do you expect your spouse to be loyal? Why of course. An unfaithful spouse is called an adulterer.

When we are not loyal to God we are spiritual adulterers (Hos. 4:12; 5:4; 7:4).

God expects loyalty, and rightfully so.

b. God expects our love.

It is important to be loyal, but loyalty is not enough; there must be love. A husband can be loyal to his wife but not really love her. God wants our love (Deut. 6:4, 5)

Conclusion

Camp Quest West, just north of Sacramento, California, is no church camp. Designed for children of agnostics, atheists, freethinkers, and humanists, the mission of the camp is to "promote respect for others with different viewpoints, values, and beliefs." It goes one step further to say, "We deplore efforts ... to seek to explain the world in supernatural terms and to look outside nature for salvation." The camp ends with what director Chris Lindstrom calls "a competition for the kids to create their own religion that everyone can believe in and that will be good for all, for all time."[31]

God makes it clear that religion is not up for grabs in a camp competition; He is God and God alone and therefore worthy of our loyalty and love.

SUGGESTED ORDER OF WORSHIP

God and God Alone

Prelude—Instrumentalists

> NBH 52 *How Majestic Is Your Name*

Call to Praise—Congregation

> NBH 19 *Be Exalted, O God* (2x in Bb)
>
> NBH 297 *Majesty* (2x in Bb)
>
> NBH 5 *How Great Thou Art* (chorus, v. 4, chorus in Bb)

Prayer of Praise—Pastoral Staff

Welcome—Pastoral Staff

Song of Welcome *(meet and greet)*—Congregation

> NBH 618 *I've Got Peace Like a River* (vv. 1–3 in G)

Worship and Praise—Congregation

> NBH 51 *God of Wonders* (v. 1, chorus, v. 2, chorus, bridge, chorus, in G)
>
> NBH 53 *Lift Up Your Heads* (2x in G)

Offertory Prayer—Pastoral Staff

---

[31] Richard Chin, "Camps sign up free thinkers," www.usatoday.com (April 11, 2007).

Offertory Praise

NBH 31 *We Bow Down* (v. 1, chorus, v. 2, chorus in D)—
PT or Congregation

NBH 68 *Holy, Holy, Holy* (vv. 1 and 2 in D, v. 4 in Eb)—
Congregation

Sermon—Pastor

God and God Alone (Ex. 20:2, 3)

Hymn of Invitation—Congregation

NBH 552 *My Jesus, I Love Thee* (as needed)

Benediction Hymn—Congregation

NBH 52 *How Majestic Is Your Name* (2x in C)

Postlude—Instrumentalists

NBH 31 *We Bow Down* (2x in D)

KEY:

NBH: New Baptist Hymnal (2008)

WEEK 29

We Are at War

Part 3
Ephesians 6:10–20
By Dr. Kent Spann

1. We must get dressed for battle (6:13–20).

   a. The Shield of Faith (v. 16)

      This is not the small shield carried on the forearm and used for hand-to-hand combat. Paul is talking about the long, oblong shield measuring four to four and a half feet tall and two and a half feet wide. It was made of two layers of laminated wood, covered first with linen and then with hide, and then bound top and bottom with iron, with an iron ornament decorating the front of it. A soldier could stand behind it and be protected from arrows or lances. These shields could be joined together to form a huge phalanx extending as wide as a mile. The archers would stand behind a line of these shields and fire upon the enemy.

      i. The strategy of the enemy is temptation (Gen. 3:1; 1 Chr. 21; Matt. 4:3; 1 Cor. 7:5; 2 Cor. 11:3; 1 Thess. 3:5).

      ii. The armor of the Christian is faith (1 John 5:4).

   b. The Helmet of Salvation (v. 17)

      The helmet had a band to protect the forehead, and plates for the cheeks, and extended down in back to protect the neck. The purpose of the helmet was to protect the soldier from the blows of the two-handed, double-edged sword that measured three to four feet long. The soldier would swing it at the other soldiers' heads to split their skulls or decapitate them. Virtually the only weapon that could penetrate this helmet was a battle axe.

      i. The strategy of the enemy is doubt and discouragement.

ii. The armor of the Christian is salvation.

(1) Past tense—we have been saved—justification (Rom. 5:1; Gal 3:24).

(2) Present tense—we are being saved—sanctification (Rom. 6:14, 18–22; Phil. 1:6).

(3) Future tense—we will be saved—glorification (Rom. 8:30; Phil. 3:21; 1 Pet. 3:10; 1 John 3:2).

c. The Sword of the Spirit (v. 17)

This sword was 6–18 inches long. It was the common sword carried by the Roman foot soldier and was the principal weapon in hand-to-hand combat. He would carry it in a sheath or scabbard attached to his belts.

i. The strategy of the enemy is to make us to believe what he says (Gen. 3:4. 5).

ii. The armor of the Christian is God's Word as a defensive (Matt. 4:1–11) and offensive weapon (Heb. 4:12).

d. The Power of Prayer (vv. 18–20)

i. The strategy of the enemy is for us to be self-sufficient.

ii. The armor of the Christian is God-dependency in prayer.

(1) Pray in the Spirit.

(2) Pray in all occasions.

(3) Pray all kinds of prayers.

WEEK 29

A Humble Hero!

1 Samuel 17:53—19:9
By Larry Kiser

Introduction

We all love a humble hero. *[Use Tim Tebow, the Heisman trophy winner, as an example.]* It's a wonderful thing to see someone who is a hero demonstrate genuine humility in reference to his gifts or achievements.

David had captured the hearts and imagination of the Israeli people with his courageous victory over Goliath. But as we read the story today, we will see that he maintained an incredibly authentic humility in the midst of his stardom.

[Read 1 Samuel 17:53–58.]

1. The honoring of parents is the first lesson of authentic humility and biblical obedience (1 Sam. 17:53–58; Eph. 6:2, 3).

    Recognizing that our very life itself is owed to our parents is reason enough to have a basic humility. David was always careful to speak and act honorably toward his parents.

    David was on the fast track to success as a result of his victory over Goliath, but he was careful to build deep and authentic relationships with both friends and family.

    David developed an incredible friend relationship with Jonathan. Even though he was the next anointed king of Israel, David maintained a humble posture toward Jonathan, the first prince of Israel.

2. Faithful relationships are more valuable than personal promotions (1 Sam. 18:1–5).

    [Read 1 Samuel 18:6–11.]

    When everyone else was applauding David, Saul became jealous and plotted against David.

3. God can use even unjust opposition to keep us authentically humble (1 Sam. 18:6–11).

Saul was wrong in his opposition to David, but it kept David from becoming intoxicated with this newfound fame.

[Read 1 Samuel 18:12–16.]

As David became more popular, Saul became more fearful of David. Why would this powerful King of Israel fear this upcoming young warrior? Because the Lord was with him.

4. When the Lord is with you, fear is your opponent's problem (1 Sam. 18:12–16).

Even though David was incredibly popular, he demonstrated sincere respect for the king and authentic humility in himself.

[Read 1 Samuel 18:17–19.]

David did not consider himself worthy to have Saul's daughter Merab as a wife, so she was given to another.

[Read 1 Samuel 18:20–27.]

But Saul had another daughter, Michal, who was in love with David, so Saul was delighted to give her to David, as long as David would prove his love by killing two hundred Philistines. Saul's secret hope was that David would be killed in the battle, but he wasn't, so David and Michal were married.

5. The Plans of the Most Powerful King can't compete with the purpose of God (1 Sam. 18:20–27).

[Read 1 Samuel 18:28–30.]

Conclusion

God's anointed presence is the most powerful asset one can possess. God's anointed presence always follows humility and obedience. The more danger David faced, the more favor God bestowed.

God's favored presence is an irresistible power!

—1 Samuel 18:28–30

WEEK 30

Worship Wars

Exodus 20:4–6
By Dr. Kent Spann

What Will Lead to America's Downfall?

Will it be hatred and violence, the Democrats or Republicans, global warming, materialism, illegal immigration, etc? The Bible makes it very clear what will lead to America's downfall—*idolatry*. This has always been the cause of the downfall of a nation, because it is the downfall of man (Rom. 1:18–25).

At its very core idolatry is a worship issue. People were created to worship. The question is, who do we worship? Our answer begs the question, "What do we believe about the one we worship?

Idolatry

1. Idolatry is worshipping the wrong God.

   Every man has a god or believes in a god. Blaise Pascal (French mathematician, philosopher, and physicist, 1623–1662) said, "There is a God-shaped vacuum in the heart of every man." The problem with the God-shaped vacuum is that we can fill it with any number of gods.

   Idolatry, then, is giving our worship to any god other than the God of the Scripture revealed in Jesus Christ.

   America is rampant with idolatry. I will go a step further and say that even within the Christian church idolatry is rampant.

   It comes in many forms.

   a. Religious idolatry happens when a person worships a declared deity, as in Hinduism or Islam.

   b. Secular idolatry occurs when people search for or find meaning, success, happiness, security, peace, or wholeness in anything other than the God of Scripture revealed in Jesus Christ.

- It can be addictions, such as gambling, overeating, pornography, alcoholism, etc.
- It can take the form of family. A 2007 study by the Barna Group found that seven out of ten adults choose their earthly family over their heavenly Father when asked to choose the most important relationship to them. Of the 1,004 adults over the age of eighteen that were surveyed, one-third said their entire nuclear family is more important than God.
- It can be a career.
- It can be a relationship.
- It can be material stuff.

I could go on and on.

2. Idolatry is worshipping God the wrong way.

This is the main focus of this passage. In the first commandment the Father made clear which God; in the second commandment He made clear how they were to worship Him. God was commanding His people not to pervert their worship of God.

3. Idolatry is the perversion of the true God.

    a. When we distort God, we are guilty of idolatry.

        During his long career as pastor of New York's Riverside Church, the late H. E. Fosdick spent many hours counseling students from nearby Columbia University. One evening a distraught young man burst into Fosdick's study and announced, "I have decided that I cannot and do not believe in God!"

        Fosdick said, "All right, but describe for me the God you don't believe in." The student sketched out his idea of God. When he was finished, Fosdick said to him, "Well, we're in the same boat. I don't believe in that god either."

    b. When we dethrone God, we are guilty of idolatry.

        How do we dethrone God? We dethrone God when we trust

something or someone more than Him; when we fail to obey Him; when we enjoy anything more than God.

c. When we dishonor God, we are guilty of idolatry.

d. When we denigrate God, we are guilty of idolatry.

To *denigrate* means to treat God with little respect or importance. We denigrate God when we fail to engage in worship or listen to the preaching. We also do it when we treat God glibly.

We are just as guilty of idolatry today, if not more, than Israel of breaking the second command. Tim Keller, author and founding pastor of Redeemer Presbyterian Church in New York City, says, "Sin isn't only doing bad things; it is more fundamentally making good things into ultimate things. Sin is building your life and meaning on anything, even a very good thing, more than on God. Whatever we build our life on will drive us and enslave us. Sin is primarily idolatry."[32]

God's View of Idolatry (20:5)

What is God's view of idolatry? He hates it and will judge it. It just doesn't get any clearer than that. Again read Romans 1:18–32.

Take an Inventory

- Are you worshipping the one true God?
- Are you worshipping God in the right way?
- Is there anything or anyone more important to you than God?
- Is there anything that consumes you?
- Is there anything you choose over God?
- Is there anything that you allow to interfere with your relationship with God?
- Is there anyone or anything that keeps you from worshipping God?

---

[32] Tim Keller, *The Reason for God* (Dutton, 2008), 275–76, and Tim Keller, "Talking About Idolatry in a Postmodern Age," www.thegospelcoalition.org.

True Worship

So how do we worship God in a way that pleases Him? Jesus gave us great insight in John 4:19–26.

1. We worship Him in spirit (4:25). That means we do not get caught up in external conformity to religious rituals. Worship is a matter of the heart.

2. We worship Him in truth as revealed in Scripture (4:25).

3. We worship Him in Christ (4:25, 26).

If any athlete was known for focus, it was Michael Jordan. In Jordan's book, *Driven from Within*, Fred Whitfield, president and chief operating officer of the NBA's Charlotte Bobcats basketball team, tells a fascinating story about something Jordan did while getting ready to go out one evening. When Jordan asked if he could borrow a jacket from Whitfield, he found that Whitfield's closet was filled with both Nike and Puma products. The Nike outfits had been given to Whitfield because of his relationship with Jordan, who had a lucrative contract with the company. The Puma outfits had been given to Whitfield because of his relationship with ex–basketball player and Puma representative Ralph Sampson. Whitfield recalls that Jordan walked into the living room, laid all the Puma gear on the floor, and went into the kitchen to grab a butcher knife. When Jordan returned to the living room, he proceeded to cut all of the Puma clothes to shreds. He then picked up the scraps and carried everything to the dumpster. Once Jordan came back inside, he turned to Fred and said, "Don't ever let me see you in anything other than Nike. You can't ride the fence![33]

It's time to take the knife to all the false gods in our closet!

---

[33] Thom S. Rainer and Eric Geiger, *Simple Church* (Nashville: B&H Publishing Group, 2006), as found at www.preachingtoday.com.

SUGGESTED ORDER OF WORSHIP

"Worship Wars" (with optional Baptismal Celebration)

Prelude—Instrumentalist

>NBH 39 *Let There Be Praise*

Call to Prayer—Pastoral Staff

Welcome—Pastoral Staff

>NBH 35 *Sing Hallelujah to the Lord* (2x in D)

>NBH 36 *I Exalt Thee* (2x in F)

>NBH 37 *Blessed Be the Lord God Almighty* (1x in Bb, 1x in C)

>NBH 38 *Awesome in This Place* (v. 1, chorus, chorus, in C)

Baptismal Celebration—Pastoral Staff

Prayer of Commitment—Pastoral Staff

>NBH 34 *O Lord, You're Beautiful* (vv. 1–3 in D)

Scripture Reading from Psalm 27:1–6 *(Please have prepared for IMAG)*

The LORD is my light and my salvation; whom shall I fear? The LORD is the strength of my life; of whom shall I be afraid? When the wicked came against me to eat up my flesh, my enemies and foes, they stumbled and fell. Though an army may encamp against me, my heart shall not fear; though war may rise against me, in this I will be confident. One thing I have desired of the LORD, that will I seek: that I may dwell in the house of the LORD all the days of my life, to behold the beauty of the LORD, and to inquire in His temple. For in the time of trouble He shall hide me in His pavilion; in the secret place of His tabernacle He shall hide me; He shall set me high upon a rock. And now my head shall be lifted up above my enemies all around me; therefore I will offer sacrifices of joy in His tabernacle; I will sing, yes, I will sing praises to the LORD.

Prayer of Thanksgiving—Pastor

Offertory Praise—PT with Congregation

NBH 16 *I Worship You, Almighty God* (2x in F)

Message—Pastor

Worship Wars (Ex. 20:4–6)

Hymn of Response/Invitation—Congregation

NBH44 *He Knows My Name* (as needed in Eb)

Benediction Hymn—Congregation

NBH 320 *Jesus, Name Above All Names* (2x in Eb)

Postlude

NBH 321 *Blessed Be the Name of the Lord* (2x in F)

KEY:

NBH: New Baptist Hymnal (2008)

WEEK 30

Farewell to Ephesians

Ephesians 6:21–24
By Dr. Kent Spann

Final Words (6:20–24)

1. Paul introduces Tychicus, the bearer of the letter (vv. 21, 22).

    a. He is a dear brother and a faithful servant.

    b. He has two missions.

        i. Report about Paul to the Ephesians (v. 21).

        ii. Encourage the Ephesians (v. 22).

2. Paul blesses the Ephesians (vv. 23, 24).

    a. He wants them to know God's peace in their lives (Eph. 1:2; 2:14–17; 4:3; 6:15).

    b. He wants them to experience God's love in their relationships (Eph. 1:4, 5, 15; 2:4; 3:17–19; 4:2, 15, 16; 5:2, 25, 28, 33).

    c. He wants them to exercise great faith toward God (Eph. 1:15; 2:8; 3:12, 17; 4:5, 13; 6:16).

    d. He wants them to receive God's grace not only in salvation but also in daily living (Eph. 1:2, 3–7; 2:5–8; 3:2, 7, 8; 4:7).

Final Review

- We learned that we have been richly blessed in Christ (1:3–14).
- We learned how to pray for spiritual insight and power (1:15–23).
- We learned about God's amazing grace and plan for our lives (2:1–10).
- We learned that we are one in the body of Christ (2:11–21).
- We learned that we are stewards of God's message and ministry (3:1–13).
- We learned how to pray for spiritual fullness (3:14–19).

- We learned that God's power working on our behalf is beyond any power we know (3:20, 21).

- We learned that doctrine and duty, belief and behavior go hand in hand.

- We learned how to live in unity as believers (4:1–16).

- We learned how to live the new life we have in Christ (4:17–32).

- We learned how to live a life of love (5:1–7).

- We learned how to live as children of light in a dark world (5:8–14).

- We learned how to live wisely in a foolish world (5:15–21).

- We learned how to live as Spirit-filled believers in our various relationships (5:22—6:9).

- We learned that we are at war and how to dress for battle (6:10–20).

WEEK 30

Resisting Revenge!!!

1 Samuel 24
By Larry Kiser

Introduction

Revenge makes for great stories. The great classic *The Count of Monte Cristo* is a story of amazing revenge. The book is filled with dozens of redemptive images and lessons, but it really is a book about the sweet taste of revenge. Whenever there is injustice, we love it when injustice is not only corrected, but when sweet revenge is taken on the perpetrators of that injustice. Revenge makes for a great story, but it doesn't make for a strong or obedient Christian. All of us have been the victims of injustice at some point in our lives. How we handle that injustice is essential to our spiritual growth. Our natural tendencies are usually exactly the opposite of God's biblical promptings.

Saul had grossly mistreated David. He knows it. He feels an overwhelming sense of guilt for his own disobedience, which led to David's anointing, and for his selfish attitude and actions toward David. Important lesson here:

1. Unresolved guilt leads to unnecessary and sometimes irrational fears (1 Sam. 18:28, 29).

    In fact, we all know that fear is the great enemy of both faith and love. We have seen how fear interferes with love, but we also must remember that ...

2. Perfect love will defeat fear (1 John 4:18).

    Fear leads us to take things into our own hands. We want to protect ourselves, from others, from pain, from whatever. And when we retreat into our pain, we become unwittingly driven by it. And our pain drives us toward revenge.

3. Revenge feeds the flesh and destroys the soul (Rom. 12:17–19).

David lived long before this was written, but since he was led by the Spirit of God, who wrote this truth, he lives it out beautifully in the story today.

[Tell story of David being pursued by Saul.]

[Read 1 Samuel 24:1–10.]

Even though David knew that Saul was trying to kill him, he was still able to respect God's sovereignty enough to realize that God had allowed Saul to remain as king of Israel at this point and that he should not interfere with God's timetable.

David's men encouraged him to kill Saul. They believed that God had delivered Saul into David's hands for that purpose. But David respected God and His timing more than he respected the advice of carnal friends.

4. Respecting a person's position will often protect us from the wrong response of revenge (1 Sam. 24:6).

What incredible respect for God! David respected God's sovereignty over his own pain and suffering. His own circumstance was terrible, and it was largely because of the injustice of King Saul, but David respected God's sovereignty enough to endure continuing discomfort at Saul's hand.

When given a perfect opportunity for revenge, David exercised amazing mercy and unconditional love toward Saul by sparing his life. What a testimony this was to David's men!

The bottom-line reminder to each of us when we are prone to seek revenge is this: let us be grateful that God did not seek revenge with us.

Conclusion

When we are tempted to choose revenge, let us choose to be like God. Like David:

God chose mercy and love toward us,
rather than judgment and justice!

WEEK 31

Reverence God

Exodus 20:7
By Dr. Kent Spann
Are You Guilty of Copyright Infringement?

According to Christian economist Gary North, in *Chronicles: A Magazine of American Culture*:

> One way for a modern American to begin to understand this commandment is to treat God's name as a trademarked property. In order to gain widespread distribution for His copyrighted repair manual—the Bible—and also to capture greater market share for His authorized franchise—the Church—God has graciously licensed the use of His name to anyone who will use it according to His written instructions. It needs to be understood, however, that God's name has not been released into the public domain. God retains legal control over His name and threatens serious penalties against the unauthorized misuse of this supremely valuable property. All trademark violations will be prosecuted to the full limits of the law. The prosecutor, judge, jury, and enforcer is God.[34]

God's name is copyrighted!

What's in a Name?

We don't attach a lot of weight to the importance of a name. It is primarily an identification tag. That is not the case in Scripture. The name of God is not just a name; it is who He is.

---

[34] Gary North, *Chronicles: A Magazine of American Culture* (December 1992), 15, quoted in P. G. Ryken and R. K. Hughes, *Exodus: Saved for God's Glory* (Wheaton, IL: Crossway Books, 2005).

- It validates His existence.
- It represents His character.
- It promotes His reputation.
- It communicates His dignity.
- It declares His worth.
- It identifies who He is.

Look at Exodus 3:14, 15.

God's name is to be reverenced.

The ancients Jews took the name of God revealed to Moses very seriously. A Jew wouldn't even say the name that God gave to Moses. Instead Israel used another name.

Today there is no respect for God's name.

Misusing the Name of God

How is God's name misused in our society and even by Christians?

1. We misuse God's name when we use it in profane ways.

Little Mary, attending Sunday school for the first time one Christmas season, eagerly listened as her teacher told of the birth of God's Son. She was thrilled to hear the story of the angels, wise men, the star, and the gifts. Then the teacher added, "And they shall call His name Jesus." Mary looked over at the person beside her and asked "Why did they have to name such a sweet baby a swear word?" It was the first time she had ever heard His name used outside of a curse.

People can blatantly misuse God's name in profanity, and you know what I mean. But there are less obvious ways, for instance, when in anger or frustration, we say "Jesus Christ, what is wrong with you?" We need to be careful how we use God's name.

2. We misuse God's name when we carelessly invoke His name.

People use God's name when it has no real significance in their lives. Yale Law School professor Stephen Carter makes this point in a book on the role of religion in public life, suitably titled *God's Name in Vain*:

In truth, there is probably no country in the Western world where people use God's name quite as much, or quite as publicly, or for quite as many purposes, as we Americans do— the Third Commandment notwithstanding. Few candidates for office are able to end their speeches without asking God to bless their audience, or the nation, or the great work we are undertaking, but everybody is sure that the other side is insincere ... Athletes thank God, often on television, after scoring the winning touchdown, because, like politicians, they like to think God is on their side. Churches erect huge billboards and take out ads in the paper ... God's will is cited as a reason to be against gay rights. And a reason to be for them. God is said not to tolerate poverty. Or abortion. Or nuclear weapons ... Everybody who wants to change America, and everybody who wants not to, understands the nation's love affair with God's name, which is why everybody invokes it.[35]

3. We misuse God's name when we engage in meaningless worship (Is. 29:13).

4. We misuse God's name when we make false oaths and promises.

Presbyterian pastor Philip Ryken, in his book *Written in Stone*, wrote:

> What does it mean to "lift up" God's name? This term had a fairly technical meaning. It was used in legal situations to refer to the taking of an oath. When witnesses needed to confirm their testimony, instead of swearing on a Bible, they lifted a hand and swore by God's name.[36]

It was a common practice among Jews to invoke the name of the Lord when making an oath. Leviticus 19:12 warns against swearing falsely and profaning God's name. Jesus did the same in Matthew 5:33–37.

---

[35] Stephen L. Carter, *God's Name in Vain: The Wrongs and Rights of Religion and Politics* (New York: Basic, 2000), 12, 13.

[36] Philip Graham Ryken, *Written in Stone: The Ten Commandments and Today's Moral Crisis* (Wheaton, IL: Crossway Books. 2003), 87.

5. We misuse God's name when our profession doesn't match our lifestyle.

It is one thing to *say* you are a Christian; it is quite another to *be* a Christian. Many people claim to be Christians, but there is no evidence of it in their lives.

When we are not living in obedience, we call ourselves hypocrites. But even more serious, we are taking God's name in vain (Rom. 2:22–24).

6. We misuse God's name when we don't give God our best.

Look at the words of Malachi 1:6–14. What was Israel guilty of doing? Giving God the leftovers. We are guilty of this when God gets the leftovers of our time, money, life, and service.

Honoring the Name of God

So, how can we honor God's name?

1. We honor God's name by reverencing Him (Matt. 6:9).

2. We honor God's name by praising Him (Ps. 8:1; 135:1; 148:5).

3. We honor God's name by giving Him the credit He deserves.

4. We honor God's name by living a life that brings glory to His name.

5. We honor God's name when we proclaim His glory to the unbeliever.

6. We honor God's name when we exalt the name of Jesus (Phil. 2:9–11).

7. We honor God's name when we *genuinely* call upon the name of the Lord for salvation (Acts 4:12; Matt. 7:21–23).

SUGGESTED ORDER OF WORSHIP

Reverence God

Prelude—Instrumental Group

NBH 7 *Come, Let Us Worship and Bow Down*

Prayer of Worship—Pastoral Staff

Worship and Praise—Congregation

NBH 99 *Forever* (v. 1, chorus, v. 2, chorus, v. 3, chorus in G)

Welcome—Pastoral Staff

Song of Welcome *(meet and greet)*—Congregation

NBH 116 *I Could Sing of Your Love Forever* (chorus, verse, chorus, chorus in F)

NBH 162 *Wonderful, Merciful Savior* (v. 1, chorus, v. 2, chorus, v. 3, chorus in Bb)

NBH 101 *How Deep the Father's Love for Us* (vv. 1–3 in F)

Testimony of Praise

Offertory Prayer—Pastoral Staff

Offertory Praise

NBH 133 *Shout to the Lord* (2x in Bb)

Message—Pastor

Reverence God (Ex. 20:7)

Hymn of Response/Invitation—Congregation

NBH 18 *Glorify Thy Name* (as needed)

Benediction Hymn—Congregation

NBH 8 *Bless the Lord, O My Soul*

Postlude—Instrumental Group

NBH 13 *Joyful, Joyful, We Adore Thee*

KEY:

NBH: New Baptist Hymnal (2008)

WEEK 31

Forgiveness of Sins

1 John 1:5–9
By Dr. J. Edwin Orr

Jesus paid the price for the forgiveness of sins. This forgiveness is the basis of our salvation and our healthy fellowship with others. While we cannot pay the price for our own forgiveness, we can reap the benefit of the forgiveness offered by Christ's sacrifice on the cross.

1. Principles of Forgiveness

    a. Someone must pay for forgiveness.

    b. The one who forgives is the one who suffers.

2. The Cross is the basis of forgiveness.

    a. The condition of forgiveness for the unbeliever is conversion.

    b. The condition of forgiveness for the believer is confession.

The unbeliever receives forgiveness of sin by placing faith in the work of Christ on the Cross. Believers need to confess their sins as a means of continued healthy fellowship with the Savior who forgives sins.

WEEK 31

Saul's Fall and David's Rise!

1 Samuel 31–2 Samuel 1
By Larry Kiser

Introduction

It's always sad to see someone who was once a strong and courageous fighter become weak and vulnerable. Examples here can range from personal examples of aging to the more contemporary example of Tiger Woods's fall from greatness. That final fall is one of the saddest dramas in the human experience.

In 1 Samuel 31, we read the sad story of Saul's final battle and death. *[Tell story or read 1 Samuel 31.]*

1. When leadership fails, followers suffer (1 Sam. 31:1).

Saul had wandered far away from following God. He had consulted with the witch at Endor. He had repeatedly tried to kill David, even though he had promised David he would cease doing so each time he was caught. But finally, God allows him to suffer defeat from foes that he had many times conquered in the past.

2. The enemy uses public failure to advance his cause (1 Sam. 31:2–10; 2 Sam. 1:1–12).

Even though Saul had become David's worst enemy, David realized that they both served the same God. David not only resisted the temptation for revenge in the past, but he resisted the temptation to profit from Saul's fall.

David's respect for God and for God's servants was stronger than his personal agenda. My, how we need to remember that in today's Christian world. All too often, because of differences in style or insignificant theological issues, we treat fellow servants of God as our personal enemies. David had this abiding respect for Saul, because of God's anointing on Saul's life, even though Saul actually opposed David personally. What an important lesson for us.

3. Our respect for God and His work through others must overrule our personal opinions and positions (2 Sam. 1:13–16).

The man who came to David tried to curry David's favor by reporting Saul's death to David in a certain way. Be wary of anyone who tries to curry favor with you by being critical of someone else, even one of our perceived enemies. Loyalty must be based on solid principles and integrity, not the whims of popular opinion or political power.

4. True respect of one person is never built upon the disrespect of another.

That kind of respect is simply cheap and fickle favor. I know many Christians who move from church to church, currying favor with the new church by speaking disrespectfully or critically about the former church.

Don't come here like that. If I sense that in someone coming to this church, I will tell them directly, "Go and make sure you have done your best to remedy your problems with the old church before you come here. I will not allow people to be here and be openly critical of another good church or pastor!" And that is something we must do because of *principle*, recognizing that other pastors and churches may not return the favor when people leave here and go there.

The platform of future success must be built upon personal and ministry integrity. David knew that he must ascend to the throne in an honorable manner. He could not disrespect the Lord's anointed and expect people to respect him as the Lord's new anointed.

Conclusion

The same is true of our personal success. It must be built upon personal integrity and relational authenticity.

True success is built only upon integrity and relational fidelity!

Our relationship with God is based on the integrity of the Word of God and the unconditional love of Jesus Christ for us.

WEEK 32

Time-Out

Exodus 20:8–11

By Dr. Kent Spann

Time-Out

The term has many different applications. Parents use it as a disciplinary tool. A coach uses it to stop the game for a short time. The idea of time-out is stopping, ceasing, or taking a break.

Long before the idea of time-out was thought of for child discipline or made a sports staple, God called for a time-out in Exodus 20:8–11.

Israel and the Sabbath

Israel has a very long and storied history with the Sabbath. Let's take a quick look at the Sabbath in Israel's history.

The Institution of the Sabbath

- The practice began a week before the giving of the Ten Commandments (Ex. 16:23).

- God gave it as a new law, a *lex nova*—on Mount Sinai (Ex. 20:8–11).

The Importance of the Sabbath

- It had a humanitarian purpose—a day of rest.

- It had a covenant purpose—Israel is a theocracy (Ex. 31:16).

- It had a spiritual purpose—to remind Israel that Yahweh is the God who delivered them (Deut. 5:15).

- It had a salvific purpose—it foreshadowed the rest that the Messiah would give them (Heb. 4:1–13).

The Abuse of the Sabbath

Tragically Israel lost sight of the purpose of the Sabbath and turned it into a legalistic nightmare. By the time of Jesus, the Jewish lawyers had developed thirty-nine classifications of work forbidden on the Sabbath. There were more than fifteen hundred laws to follow for the Sabbath. The Sabbath became a horrible burden for Israel.

Christ and the Sabbath

Is it any wonder that Jesus clashed with the Pharisees over the Sabbath so often? Jesus wasn't diminishing the Sabbath; rather, He was moving it back to its original intent.

Let's summarize what Jesus did in regard to the Sabbath.

- He protested the idolatry of the Sabbath.
- He proclaimed the true function of the Sabbath (Matt. 12:1–14; Mark 2:23–27; Luke 13:10–17).
- He declared Himself to be Lord of the Sabbath (Matt. 12:8; Mark 2:28).
- By His death and resurrection, He changed the Sabbath into the Lord's Day (Acts 20:7; 1 Cor. 16:2; Rev. 1:10).

The New Testament Christian and the Sabbath

Does this commandment have any relevance or application for us today? Some would say no, pointing out that the other nine are commanded in the New Testament, but this one is not. In fact, Colossians 2:16–18 says we are not under the Sabbath law.

You have to remember that there were three kinds of laws in Israel.

- The Ceremonial Law (Col. 2:13–17; Heb. 10:1)

  The ceremonial law is no longer in effect, because it was a foreshadow of Christ, who has fulfilled them all.
- The Civil Law

  It consisted of those laws that governed Israel as a nation. Israel was a theocracy. We do not live in a theocracy, so the Sabbath as a civil law doesn't apply.
- The Moral Law

It consists of those laws that govern our moral conduct. It is the righteous and eternal standard for our relationship with God and with others. It is the spirit of the law. Is there a universal principle that applies to the believer even today? I believe there is. We are not under the law but under grace, which means we can live out the law as God intended it.

1. We engage in hard, productive work six days.

Many people see work as part of the curse. Sin certainly cursed our work, but work is not a curse.

The fourth commandment dignifies and celebrates productive labor. It commends and applauds hard work. It elevates the work ethic.

See your work as an act of worship to God.

2. We set aside one day for the Lord.

God says that the Sabbath is "to the Lord." It is something that we are to give to Him. How do we give a day to the Lord? What do we do?

a. We rest.

We have become so addicted to activity that we don't know how to stop anymore. If our bodies stop, our minds are racing, and if our minds stop, our bodies are fidgeting. Hurry Sickness is the disease of the twenty-first century. All those things created to free up time have only made us busier.

This addiction to speed comes with horrendous consequences. It has been said that you will get your rest in one of three places—your bed, the hospital, or the grave.

We have totally misunderstood the Sabbath command. It is not God trying to put a crimp on our lifestyle; it is God bringing sanity to our lives.

b. We reflect.

The Sabbath is also a call to reflect on God and life. In verse 11 God says to reflect on God and what He has done. One of the tragic consequences of our hurried lifestyle is that people don't have time for God. They can't slow down long enough.

Let me give some practical reflections from our text to help us regain the idea of the fourth command.

 i. God is our Creator.

  In our busyness, we have forgotten who made us. He knows what is best for us.

 ii. God is our Provider.

  Setting aside a day to the Lord requires us to trust God.

 iii. God is our Sovereign.

  Taking that day when everything else is screaming for our attention declares who is our Lord.

 iv. God is our Redeemer.

  It is a time to remember that God is our Savior.

 c. We revere.

We spend time in worship with God's people. Corporate worship needs to be an important part of keeping the spirit of this command. Jesus thought so (Luke 4:16).

Now, we could stop right here, but there is more than meets the eye in this command. There is a deeper application of this command.

3. We enter into the Sabbath rest of Christ (Col. 2:16–17; Heb. 4:1–11).

 Aren't you tired of the striving? The turmoil? The chaos?

When billionaire Bill Gates was asked why he didn't believe in God, he said, "Just in terms of allocation of time resources, religion is not very efficient. There's a lot more I could be doing on a Sunday morning."[37]

Bill missed it. Don't *you* miss it!

---

37 Bill Gates, quoted by Walter Isaacson, "In Search of the Real Bill Gates," *Time* (January 13, 1997), 7.

SUGGESTED ORDER OF WORSHIP

Time-Out

Prelude—Instrumentalist

NBH 1 *Praise to the Lord, the Almighty*

Call to Worship—PT or Ensemble

NBH 1 *Praise to the Lord, the Almighty* (v. 1, v. 3, in F, v. 4 in G)

Call to Prayer and Worship—Pastor

Worship in Song—Congregation

NBH 30 *Come, Now Is the Time to Worship* (2x in D)

NBH 7 *Come, Let Us Worship and Bow Down* (2x in D)

NBH 588 *Sanctuary* (1x in D, 1x in Eb)

Welcome—Pastoral Staff

Welcome Song *(meet and greet)*—Pastoral Staff

NBH 8 *Bless the Lord, O My Soul* (1x in G, 1x in Ab)

NBH 23 *Thou Art Worthy* (2x in Ab with tag)

Offertory Prayer—Pastoral Staff

Offertory Praise—Solo

NBH 536 *Lord, I Want to Be a Christian* (vv. 1–4 in Eb)

Message—Pastor

Time-Out (Ex. 20:8–11)

Hymn of Response—Congregation

NBH 22 *We Will Glorify* (v. 1, v. 2, in D, v. 4 in Eb)

Benediction Hymn—Congregation

NBH 518 *My Life Is in You* (1x in G)

Postlude—Instrumentalist

    NBH 510 *Firm Foundation* (1x in F)

KEY:

NBH: New Baptist Hymnal (2008)

WEEK 32

Sins of the Spirit

Selected Scripture
By Dr. J. Edwin Orr

Introduction

Most Christians are startled when they learn that the sins of the spirit are a far greater hindrance to spiritual revival than the sins of the flesh. This contrast can be seen in the attitude of our Lord, who was doubly lenient with the woman taken in adultery, and triply severe with the pride of the Pharisee. This does not mean that adultery is less culpable than pride, but rather that one who gives way to pride is harder to help than one who gives way to adultery.

1. Pride (1 Pet. 5:5)

   The heart of pride is egotism, self-centeredness.

2. Hypocrisy (Matt. 23:28)

   Hypocrisy is a spiritual sin for which Christ reserved His strongest condemnation.

3. Neglect of Prayer

   By neglect of prayer, a Christian becomes prey to a hundred vices.

4. Neglect of Devotions

   Prayer, devotional reading, and family reading are critically important.

5. Neglect of Witness

   Better called cowardice or indifference, this is a besetting sin of spiritual Christians.

6. Lovelessness (Mark 12:30)

   Lovelessness is the greatest sin of all.

7. Unbelief (Heb. 3:12)

It is impossible to exaggerate the importance of faith in the very Word of God.

WEEK 32

The Traps at the Top

2 Samuel 6:1–23
By Larry Kiser

Introduction

Have you ever had an experience where you said, "Wow! Now this is how the other half lives!" *[Tell example of such personally.]* Most of us have had that kind of experience at one time or another. The fact of the matter is, the people at the top do face different kinds of challenges than the rest of us. Most of us would like more occasions when we could wrestle with those kinds of problems, because most of us aspire to move closer toward the top, whether it is in terms of professional advancement or any other endeavor. The fact of the matter is, there are special traps at the top that many of us are ill equipped to deal with, and God knows it, so most of us are, by God's grace, kept from often being at the top of a lot of things.

David finds himself at the top of Israel. He is their king and finally has the authority to make many things right that were wrong. One of those things was the location of the ark of the covenant. David wanted to bring the ark of the covenant back to the royal city and make it the centerpiece of his worship and use it as a means to bring a wayward Israel back to true worship.

[Read verses 1–7.]

There were very strict rules given by God regarding the handling and moving of the ark of the covenant. Uzzah violated those divine rules, but he did so with the best of intentions. Important lesson for all of us.

1. Good intentions are a trap and can be no substitute for complete obedience (2 Sam. 6:1–7).

    Perhaps God allowed this to happen during the early part of David's reign to remind David of that important lesson. Remember

Saul's good intentions regarding the handling of the Amalekites, and instead of completely obeying God, he with good intentions, only partially obeyed God. Let's look at David's response to the death of Uzzah.

There is another lesson for us in this troubling story, and it is this: our love for God must be tempered with a deep and abiding respect for His Word and holiness.

2. Love for God without the fear of God produces no abiding fruit for God (2 Sam. 6:1–7; Prov. 9:10).

David was both angry and afraid of God at the same time: angry about what God had done, and afraid to respond because of who God is. The fact of the matter is, the ark of the covenant did not return to the royal city for three months, while David struggled with understanding God's ways and purposes.

Another trap at the top is our desire and ability to *make things happen* and *make them happen now*. We need to remember that:

3. The "now" trap can cause us to forget that there is no substitute for time and struggle in our understanding of God's ways (2 Sam. 6:8–11).

[Read verses 12–23.]

David was anointed with a new joy and freedom as he embraced God's truth and ways in a new and fresh way. He meticulously honored and worshipped God in his moving of the ark of the covenant to the royal city.

But his wife had become enamored with the applause of the people, and she was embarrassed at David's exuberance and undignified worship. Abigail was more interested in pleasing people than she was worshiping God with abandon!

4. The trap of people pleasing leads to relationships that are shallow and divinely displeasing!

This lesson applies to all of us in our relationship with God. *You can't be who Christ died for you to be as long as you're dying to be who the world wants you to be!*

David was not showing off in his worship of God. He was simply worshiping God with his whole heart and body. One of the most dangerous traps at the top is the trap of people pleasing, because people at the top have larger potential audiences.

Conclusion

Regardless of the size of our audience, we really all have the same essential audience.

We live, love, worship, and serve for an audience of one!
Josh. 24:16; 2 Sam. 5:19–23

WEEK 33

Live Long and Prosper

Exodus 20:12
By Dr. Kent Spann

It was in 1967 in *Star Trek*'s second season that Mr. Spock raised his hand and gave the Vulcan salute with these words: "Live long and prosper." That phrase became popular with the rise in popularity of the *Star Trek* series. Actually, it is a Hebrew priestly blessing.

Our world is obsessed with living long and prospering. The problem is, they are looking in all the wrong places. Exodus 20:12 and Ephesians 6:1–3 give the clear answer to the individual and national question of survival. Exodus 20:12 makes it clear that the health of a nation is directly tied to the family. Ephesians 6:1–3 comes at it from a different angle—quality of life.

Paul is not saying that if you live a short life, it is because you did not honor your parents; neither is he saying that if you honor your parents, you are guaranteed a long life. The focus here is on the quality of life. Those who honor their parents enjoy a prosperous life. It is also a promise to a nation.

What does the word *honor* mean in the Exodus text? The Hebrew word *kābēd* means "to be heavy, or weighty." It describes people that are heavy. In this text, it means to give weight to our parents, or to honor them.

What's the Connection?

What is the connection between honoring our parents and living a long and prosperous life as an individual or a nation? *The respect of authority!*

It is in the home that we first learn to respect authority. If children do not learn to respect authority in the home, they will not respect authority anywhere—school, workplace, government, etc. Pope John Paul II said, "As the family goes, so goes the nation and so goes the whole world in which we live."

But it has ramifications beyond the school, workplace, and government. If children don't learn to respect authority in the home, they will not respect God's authority in their life.

Listen how James Montgomery Boice, the late pastor of Tenth Presbyterian Church, drives home the connection.

> The dark background of this commandment is to be found in the natural human dislike for authority. That is why the family is so important in God's economy. If children are not taught to respect their parents but allowed to get away with disobeying and dishonoring them, later in life they will rebel against other valid forms of authority. If they disobey their parents, they will disobey the laws of the state. If they do not respect their parents, they will not respect teachers, those who possess unusual wisdom, elected officials and others. If they do not honor their parents, they will not honor God.[38]

Is it any wonder that America is in trouble? I want to read from Annie Gottlieb, one of many writers who identifies the Sixties as "the generation that destroyed the American family." She wrote:

> We might not have been able to tear down the state, but the family was closer. We could get our hands on it. And ... we believed that the family was the foundation of the state, as well as the collective state of mind ... We truly believed that the family had to be torn apart to free love, which alone could heal the damage done when the atom was split to release energy. And the first step was to tear ourselves free from our parents.[39]

Oh yeah, they tore themselves free from their parents, all right, and look where it has gotten us!

God Is Serious

God is serious about this, as made clear in His Word (Ex. 21:15, 17;

---

[38] James Montgomery Boice, *Foundations of the Christian Faith*, rev. ed. (Downers Grove, IL: InterVarsity, 1986), 237.

[39] Annie Gottlieb, *Do You Believe in Magic?* (New York: Time, 1987), 234, 235.

Deut. 21:18–21; Prov. 30:17; Rom. 1:18, 28–32; Col. 3:20). Honoring our parents is no laughing matter. Our national and individual well-being rises and falls with honoring our parents. This is serious stuff.

Honoring Our Parents

Let's consider practically how to honor our parents.

1. We obey our parents.

Obey and honor go hand in hand; in fact you can't have one without the other. Obedience is what we do; honor is the attitude motivating our obedience.

2. We respect our parents.

Leviticus 19:3 commands children to respect their parents. Again what does that look like?

a. We speak kindly *to* our parents.

b. We speak kindly *of* our parents.

A little girl was very unhappy because her parents had refused her wishes. That evening her mother was amused to hear her pray, "Please, Lord, don't give her any more children; she doesn't know how to treat the ones she's got now."

Now, I know someone out there is saying, "But Pastor, you don't know my parents!" What if your parents don't act respectable? *Respect their God-given position.*

3. We listen to our parents' counsel.

Shaquille O'Neal, one of the most dominant players in the history of the NBA, attributes his success to his father. "Thank God, I listened to my father. I would have been dead otherwise. He raised me the old-fashioned way. He taught me how to play basketball. He taught me about life. He loved me. He whipped me when I needed it. And things have turned out good."[40]

4. We live wisely (Prov. 10:1).

5. We forgive our parents.

---

[40] *Chicago Sun-Times*, June 24, 1992, 93.

Parents will make many mistakes; children must learn to forgive them (Eph. 4:32).

6. We care for our parents.

Jesus sternly rebuked the Pharisees for a practice called *Corban* (Mark 7:9–13). Corban meant that something of material worth had been devoted to God and could not be given even to a needy parent. Jesus made it clear that it was morally wrong not to care for aging parents.

A good illustration is the story "The Old Man and His Grandson" from *Grimm's Fairy Tales*, the story of a very old man who was feeble and nearly blind. He lived with his spoiled son and the young man's uppity wife. The couple, disrespectful of the old man's age and unsympathetic with his trembling hands, were disgusted and scolded him when, at mealtime, he frequently spilled his food. Finally, they made him sit in the corner on the floor and eat out of a bowl, like a dog.

Now, the couple had a toddler son. One day they saw the boy gathering up bits of wood. "What are you doing, son?" they asked. The little boy said, "I'm making a trough for you," he answered, "for you to eat out of, when I grow up."

In shame, the couple began to cry. They brought the aged father back to the table for every meal, and never complained again about his spilled food.

Live Long and Prosper

God has given us the key to national and individual prosperity. It begins when we are but children and continues as we grow old.

Honor your parents, that you may live long and prosper!

SUGGESTED ORDER OF WORSHIP

Live Long and Prosper

Prelude—Instrumentalists

NBH 124 *Jehovah Jireh*

Call to Praise—Congregation

NBH 510 *Firm Foundation* (chorus, v. 1 chorus, v. 2, chorus, in F)

NBH 511 *The Solid Rock* (v. 1, chorus, v. 2, chorus, v. 4 in F)

NBH 519 *Because We Believe* (v. 1, chorus, v. 2, chorus, v. 3, chorus, in C)

Prayer of Praise—Pastoral Staff

Welcome—Pastoral Staff

Song of Welcome (*meet and greet*)—Congregation

NBH 118 *He Is Jehovah* (v. 1, chorus, v. 2, chorus in E minor)

NBH 124 *Jehovah Jireh* (2x in E minor)

Scripture Reading from Psalm 86:12, 13; Romans 8:38, 39—Pastoral Staff

I will praise You, O LORD my God, with all my heart, and I will glorify Your name forevermore. For great is Your mercy toward me, and You have delivered my soul from the depths of Sheol....

For I am persuaded that neither death nor life, nor angels nor principalities nor powers, nor things present nor things to come, nor height nor depth, nor any other created thing, shall be able to separate us from the love of God which is in Christ Jesus our Lord.

Worship and Praise—Congregation

NBH 170 *Oh, How He Loves You and Me* (vv. 1 and 2 in Ab)

NBH 171 *O the Deep, Deep Love of Jesus* (vv. 1–3 in Ab)

NBH 172 *Love Divine, All Loves Excelling* (v. 1, v. 3, in Ab, v. 4 in Bb)

Offertory Prayer—Pastoral Staff

Offertory Praise—Ensemble or Solo

NBH 169 *What Wondrous Love Is This* (vv. 1, 2, and 4 in D minor)

Sermon—Pastor

Live Long and Prosper (Ex. 20:12)

Hymn of Invitation—Congregation

NBH 552 *My Jesus, I Love Thee* (as needed)

Benediction Hymn—Congregation

NBH 146 *Praise You*

Postlude—Instrumentalists

NBH 139 *Let There Be Glory, Honor and Praises*

KEY:

NBH: New Baptist Hymnal (2008)

WEEK 33

Confession of Sins

Selected Scripture
By Dr. J. Edwin Orr

Introduction

Clear teaching concerning the confessing of sins by Christians is one of the most neglected doctrines of today. As a general rule, the circle of the offense committed should be the circle of the confession made.

1. Specific Confession (Lev. 5:5)

2. Responsible Confession (Josh. 7:19)

3. Thorough Confession (Prov. 28:13)

4. Private Confession (Matt. 5:23, 24)

5. Open Confession (James 5:16)

6. Cleansing Confession (1 John 1:9)

Conclusion

Confession of sin leads to the blessings of God. The price of blessing involves the heart-searching of the Spirit, candid admission of failure, immediate confession to God, and subsequent confession to persons involved.

WEEK 33

The Power of Divine *Noes*!

2 Samuel 7:1–29
By Larry Kiser

Introduction

Have you ever had an urge to do something really significant for God? A vision that is just so wonderful that you would be happy to give your life to it?

Pastors often feel such urges. For instance, there was one pastor who was sure that God wanted him to aspire to the pulpit of the wonderful church where he was the associate. This associate pastor enjoyed a wonderful relationship with the senior pastor and had learned so much from him. He believed with all of his heart that he was the heir apparent to that pulpit. But God had other ideas completely. He sent the young minister to an obscure town and a small church and allowed him to witness how He could build a large church, as he grew its new pastor in the process. At the time that God said no to the young man's first dream, he had no way of seeing His superior substitute.

Have you ever had someone come to you with grand visions for the kingdom? While you should never just shoot them down, always be careful to advise them that God sometimes gives big visions so that we will experience the reality of His saying no to our carrying out that vision personally. It isn't the divine masochism that it appears to be, but rather a very practical lesson in expanding our hearts and shrinking our egos!

[Read 2 Samuel 7:1–3.]

King David is at peace with his enemies. He looks around at his beautiful palace and desires to build God an even more beautiful house. He consults his best friend and prophet at the time, and is told that it's a good idea, and that he should pursue it.

That vision and desire flowed out of a sincere heart. David bounced the idea off his friend and prophet and got an initially positive response. Important lesson here:

1. The affirmation of friends is no substitute for the approval and direction of God (2 Sam. 7:1–3).

   David felt that it is only right for God to dwell in a place superior to God's leader. This was a valid assumption, but one based on earthly reasoning.

2. Our godly visions are often built on godly assumptions rather than godly promptings (2 Sam. 7:1–3).

   [Read 2 Samuel 7:4–7.]

   God is saying here, "Did I tell you I wanted a better house built?" *[Illustration here about how husbands often give their wives what they think they want rather than what they really want]*

3. We must learn to love the way the object of our love desires to be loved, and not how we think He should want to be loved (2 Sam. 7:4–7).

   Nathan goes back to tell David all that the Lord said, and in essence, the Lord simply said no to David. He didn't give him a clear, logical reason here. He just said no.

   But Nathan does tell David that God promises him all kinds of stuff, mainly that David's house and name would be established eternally. Rather than David building a house of brick and cedar for God, God promises to make the house of David an eternal house of blessing (2 Sam. 7:8–16).

4. God's eternal love is lots better than a logical reason (2 Sam. 7:8–16; Ps. 136).

   David responds in worshipful gratitude to God's promises. It's like God saying, "David, I know you wanted this, but instead, I'm giving you something else, better than what you wanted!"

Let's admit that God does not always give us what we want, even when we want wonderful things for His name's sake. But He always gives us what we need.

Conclusion

God's ways don't always make sense to us. But the bottom line is this: God always makes grace for when life doesn't make sense!

He often uses NO to make us learn to say yes to His sovereignty.

WEEK 34

The Sanctity of Human Life

Exodus 20:13
By Dr. Kent Spann

A Sunday school teacher was discussing the Ten Commandments with her class of five- and six-year-olds. After explaining the commandment to honor thy father and thy mother, she asked, "Is there a commandment that teaches us how to treat our brothers and sisters?" Without missing a beat, one little boy answered, "Thou shalt not kill."

There is a positive and a negative message. That is true of all the Ten Commandments. The Ten Commandments are not a list of "don'ts"; it is a list of "dos" as well!

Let's talk about the sixth commandment.

God Proclaims the Sanctity of Human Life

This is the positive message of the sixth commandment.

In the late Pope John Paul II's 2000 Christmas message, he warned of a "culture of death" threatening the world. Looking around the world at the violence in the Middle East, as well as many other places in the world, he saw a culture of death. Little did he know that nine months later, the world would witness the barbaric taking of three thousand lives on September 11, 2001.

We see the culture of death everywhere—in daily life, movies, video games, schools, etc.

God speaks to our culture of death in this simple command. He is saying that murder is wrong because human life is sacred. Why is human life sacred in contrast to animals? Because we are made in the image of God (Gen. 9:4–7).

Why is there a culture of death? Because our culture has forsaken the biblical teaching that man is made in the image of God

Have you ever heard of Planned Parenthood? Margaret Sanger, its founder, said, "The traditional view of the sanctity of human life will

WEEK 34 / 289

collapse under pressure from scientific, technological and demographic developments." That has happened in Western civilization.

As believers, we must proclaim the sanctity of human life. We must counter the prevailing philosophy being taught in our schools and institutes of higher learning that says that people are no different from animals. We must do everything we can to promote and protect human life.

God Prohibits the Murder of a Human Being.

What is God forbidding here? I want to address right off the bat what it is *not* talking about.

- It is not forbidding the taking of a life in war.

   A Christian soldier is not violating this command. Neither Jesus nor Paul condemned soldiers as murderers.

- It is not addressing the taking of a life in self-defense.

- It is not addressing the taking of a life by a police officer in the line of duty.

- It is not forbidding the killing of animals (Gen. 9:2–3).

- It is not forbidding capital punishment.

There are no fewer than eighteen crimes for which the Bible calls for the death penalty. To put a criminal to death is not murder, but justice. This, according to Paul, is the role of government (Rom. 13:1–5).

Philadelphia pastor Philip Ryken wrote:

> The Hebrew language has at least eight different words for killing, and the one used here has been chosen carefully. The word *ratzach* is never used in the legal system or in the military. There are other Hebrew words for the execution of a death sentence or for the kind of killing that a soldier does in mortal combat. Nor is the word *ratzach* ever used for hunting and killing animals. So the King James Version, which says, "Thou shalt not kill" (Exod. 20:13), is somewhat imprecise. What the commandment forbids is not killing,

but the *unlawful* killing of a human being.[41]

What is God forbidding here?

1. Intentional Murder

Intentional murder is the malicious, unjust murder of a legally innocent life. There are many examples of intentional murder.

a. Homicide

b. Suicide

c. Euthanasia

d. Abortion/Infanticide

How can people justify the taking of an unborn life? In his book *Practical Ethics*, Dr. Peter Singer, professor of bioethics at Princeton University, says:

> The fact that a being is a human being, in the sense of a member of the species Homo sapiens, is not relevant to the wrongness of killing it; it is, rather, characteristics like rationality, autonomy, and self-consciousness that make a difference. Infants lack these characteristics. Killing them, therefore, cannot be equated with killing normal human beings, or any other self-conscious beings.[42]

That is sick but is the logical conclusion of evolution. A fetus, or for that matter, an adult, is not much different from a dog or a deer that you shoot. But abortion, no matter what stage or for what reason, is the taking of a human life.

2. Invisible Murder

This is the most common and yet heinous of all murders. It is almost the most devious kind of murder. It occurs on a daily basis at the hands of non-Christians and Christians alike. Some of you are

---

[41] Philip Graham, *Exodus: Saved for God's Glory*, gen ed. R. Kent Hughes (Wheaton, IL: Crossway Books, 2005), 616.

[42] Peter Singer, *Practical Ethics* (Cambridge: Cambridge University Press, 1999), 182.

murderers this morning. Invisible murder is murder from the heart. Jesus teaches in Matthew 5:21, 22 that if you harbor hatred and bitterness in your life, you are committing invisible murder. If you are angry with someone, without a cause, you are guilty of invisible murder. If you harbor resentment, you are guilty of invisible murder. If you slander another person, you are guilty of invisible murder.

3. Insidious Murder

"Pastor," you may tell me, "I am feeling pretty good right about now. I have never intentionally murdered anyone, nor have I invisibly murdered anyone that I know of. I am not a murderer." Ah, but you are wrong. You are guilty of the most insidious murder in all of human history—the murder of Jesus Christ. Peter, on the Day of Pentecost, told the gathered crowd:

> "Men of Israel, hear these words: Jesus of Nazareth, a Man attested by God to you by miracles, wonders, and signs which God did through Him in your midst, as you yourselves also know—Him, being delivered by the determined purpose and foreknowledge of God, you have taken by lawless hands, have crucified, and put to death ..." (Acts 2:22–23)

We put Jesus to death because it was our sin that nailed Him to the Cross. But God conquered death with life. Peter went on:

> "... whom God raised up, having loosed the pains of death, because it was not possible that He should be held by it." (v. 24)

The death, burial, and resurrection of Jesus Christ are God's clear, unmistakable message to *all people*, regardless of nationality, skin color, age, etc., that life is sacred! They are God's personal word to you that your life has value and worth.

SUGGESTED ORDER OF WORSHIP

Sanctity of Human Life

Prelude—Instrumentalist

NBH 498 *I Will Call Upon the Lord*

Call to Prayer—Pastoral Staff

Welcome—Pastoral Staff

NBH 498 *I Will Call Upon the Lord* (v. 2x, chorus 2x in C)

NBH 480 *Step by Step* (2x in F)

Baptismal Celebration—Pastoral Staff

Prayer of Commitment—Pastoral Staff

NBH 509 *My Faith Looks Up to Thee* (vv. 1, 2, 4 in D)

Scripture Reading from 1 John 5:1–5; 1 Corinthians 15:50–57 *(Please have prepared for IMAG)*

Whoever believes that Jesus is the Christ is born of God, and everyone who loves Him who begot also loves him who is begotten of Him. By this we know that we love the children of God, when we love God and keep His commandments. For this is the love of God, that we keep His commandments. And His commandments are not burdensome. For whatever is born of God overcomes the world. And this is the victory that has overcome the world—our faith. Who is he who overcomes the world, but he who believes that Jesus is the Son of God? ...

Now this I say, brethren, that flesh and blood cannot inherit the kingdom of God; nor does corruption inherit incorruption. Behold, I tell you a mystery: We shall not all sleep, but we shall all be changed—in a moment, in the twinkling of an eye, at the last trumpet. For the trumpet will sound, and the dead will be raised incorruptible, and we shall be changed. For this corruptible must put on incorruption, and this mortal must put on immortality. So when this corruptible has put on incorruption, and this mortal has put on immortality, then shall be brought to pass the saying that is written: "Death is swallowed up in victory. O Death, where is your sting? O Hades, where is your victory?" The sting of death is sin, and the strength of sin is the law. But thanks be to God, who gives us the victory through our Lord Jesus Christ.

Offertory Prayer—Pastor

Offertory Praise—Congregation

> NBH 506 *In Christ Alone My Hope Is Found* (vv. 1–3 in D, v. 4 in Eb)

Message—Pastor

> *Sanctity of Human Life* (Ex. 20:13)

Hymn of Response—Congregation

> NBH 470 *Without Him* (v. 1, chorus, v. 2, chorus in F)

Benediction Hymn—Congregation

> NBH 320 *Jesus, Name Above All Names* (2x in Eb)

Postlude—Instrumentalist

> NBH 491 *Shine, Jesus Shine*

KEY:

NBH: New Baptist Hymnal (2008)

WEEK 34

Alive in God

Matthew 22:32
By Thomas Arnold

Introduction

In this passage the Lord Jesus is answering the Sadducees; He has brought in one of the most solemn truths—"God is not the God of the dead, but of the living."

1. Dead: God not being the God of the dead signifies two things:

    a. They who are without Him are dead.

    b. They who are dead are also without Him.

2. Alive in God

    a. God is the living God from the past.

    b. God is the living God of the present and future.

Conclusion

Behold then, life and death are set before us; not remote, but even now present before us; even now suffered or enjoyed. Even now, we are alive unto God, or dead unto God.

WEEK 34

Sex, Lies, and Sin's Red Tape!

Part 1
2 Samuel 11:1–27
By Larry Kiser

Introduction

Have you ever been amazed at the capacity for evil that man has? Review some of history's most heinous actions toward humanity. *[Illustrations: Holocaust, Saddam Hussein, etc.]* But each of these illustrations was carried out by human beings. So, the first lesson we must learn today, and it is a lesson so tragically illustrated in this part of David's life is this:

1. In Christ we have the potential for amazing goodness; in our flesh, we have the potential for amazing badness (2 Sam. 11:1–27).
   [Read verses 1, 2.]

   Now, much has been made of this passage regarding David's idleness. And to be sure, from the way it is written, we must assume that David should have been out with his troops. So:

2. Idleness is a breeding ground for self-indulgence (2 Sam. 11:1, 2).

   But I wonder why David did not go. Was he afraid? No. Was he lazy? No. Why, then, did he not go with his armies?

   I have a possible reason that fits with his personality, I believe. Remember, David was not immediately given a reason for why he could not build the temple, but we do find a reason recorded in 1 Chronicles 22:6–8.

   [Read 1 Chronicles 22:6–8.]

   David was about fifty years old here. He had seen a lot of war. He also knew that the reason that God didn't want him to be the one to build the temple was because he was a man of war and had shed much blood.

I believe David was subtly resisting continuing to extend his reputation as a man of war. He had such a soft side. He loved poetry and music. He had been thrust into a life of war, and I believe he secretly resented his reputation as a man of war. War may be glamorous on the silver screen, but to those who have lived it, it is not glamorous at all.

[Use Douglas MacArthur quote.]

I know war as few other men . . . know it, and nothing to me is more revolting. I have long advocated its complete abolition, as its very destructiveness on both friend and foe has rendered it useless as a method of settling international disputes!"

—General Douglas MacArthur

But regardless of why, the fact remains, David did not go to war with his armies as he should have.

[Read 2 Samuel 11:2–4.]

David saw—no sin there. But then he stopped, and the table of sin was set. Then he stared, because it says that he saw that she was very beautiful. That stare allowed desire to be born, and when we allow desires to be embraced, we go into action.

The sequence of lust and sin:

SAW → STOPPED → STARED → SOUGHT → SIN

Once he stared, he allowed *desire* to set in. He then *sought* what he had stared at.

And once desire is in the driver's seat, sin is the next turn. No amount of human reason can change our direction.

We become a captive of the desires we embrace (see James 1:13–15).

[Talk about the dangers of lust on the Internet, in movies, etc.]

We might say, "How could that happen to David, such a godly man?" The fact of the matter is, godliness is not a protection from temptation, but rather an attraction for it.

Godliness attracts temptation!

The enemy seeks to send temptation in the direction of Godly people.

Conclusion

Once the boundary of sin has been breached, the cloak of hypocrisy seems to be the only way out. Covering our sin is the first impulse of our flesh.

Covering our sin is the impulse of the flesh; confessing our sin is the impulse of the spirit! David chooses the former, and not the latter.

WEEK 35

The Scarlet Letter

Exodus 20:14
By Dr. Kent Spann

What do you think of when you hear the name Tiger Woods? You used to think golf, but after news broke of his multiple affairs against his wife, Elin Nordegren, you probably think *adultery*.

What is adultery? Listen to this amusing story of a children's pastor in Nebraska:

> As children's pastor, I listened as a fourth-grade Sunday school teacher shared a concern. Completing a quarter's lessons on the Ten Commandments, he had asked the kids, "What is the hardest Commandment for you to keep?" to which most of them responded, "Thou shalt not commit adultery."
>
> We couldn't understand why fourth graders would find that command a problem until a mother quizzed her son on what he thought committing adultery meant. Without blinking, the boy replied, "Thou shalt not sass back to adults."[43]

The Hebrew word for *adultery* means "having sexual intercourse with someone other than one's spouse."

Sex therapist Peggy Vaughan, author of *The Monogamy Myth*, conservatively estimates that about 60 percent of married men and 40 percent of married women will have an affair at some time during their marriage. It is almost expected. In the tabloids it is certainly celebrated. It is the stuff money is made of. We are definitely on a downward spiral morally.

---

[43] Sheryl Tedder, "Kids of the Kingdom," *Christian Reader* (Omaha, NE), quoted in Charles S. Mims, "Grazing the Greener Grass: Realizing Revival by Following the Rules" (sermon), Christian Network Web site, http://www.cnetwork.co.uk/charles36.html.

God's View on Marriage and Sex

Exodus 20:14 makes God's view of marriage and sex very clear. He is not like the politicians hemming and hawing as they try to avoid taking a stand for fear they will lose some voter base. God just says it, and what He says, He means.

1. God declares that marriage is sacred.

This commandment is as much about marriage as it is about sex. It is God making clear what is essential for a healthy and prosperous society. Remember the context in which these words are spoken. It is the establishment of the nation of Israel. God is laying down the rules for a strong and prosperous nation.

Why is marriage so sacred? Look at Genesis 2:2–24.

a. God ordained marriage (Gen. 2:20):

   i. for His glory

   ii. for companionship (Gen. 2:18a)

   iii. for mutual assistance (Gen. 2:18b)

   iv. for bearing, nurturing, and training children (Gen.1:28; Deut. 6:4–7)

   v. as the proper context of human sexuality (Gen. 2:25; Heb. 13:4)

b. God designed marriage (Gen. 2:24).

   He told the first couple to leave, cleave, and become one flesh.

c. God blessed marriage (Gen. 1:27, 28; Matt. 19:4–6).

What does a person do when he or she commits adultery? The adulterer:

- desecrates God's order
- defies God's command
- subverts God's design for marriage
- violates the covenant of marriage (Prov. 2:16, 17; Mal. 2:10–16; Matt. 19:9)
- causes great pain and suffering (Prov. 2:18; 2 Sam. 12; Ps. 51)

God was making a statement to this band of people gathered around Mount Sinai, who were embarking on the creation of a new nation: marriage is sacred.

2. God declares that sex is sacred.

A father was once telling his little boy about the facts of life. About halfway through the father's explanation, the boy interrupted him and asked, "Do you think God knows about all this?"

Folks, not only does God know about it; He *created* it. It was His idea! We have heard that, but it doesn't always translate. A biblical view of sex has been a bit of a stumbling block for Christians. Augustine taught that procreation was the only non-sinful end of the sex act. If a couple had sexual relations for pleasure, it was venially sinful. Sadly, the church and Christianity have been stigmatized as antisex.

Sex is not dirty; it is beautiful. It is not a necessary evil; it is God's blessing. Sex is a pure and wonderful thing—when it is practiced God's way, between one woman and one man in a marriage relationship.

Why did God give this commandment to the Jews of that time? Because much like our culture, Canaan's culture was sex crazed. Sex was a religion. The Canaanites had gods and goddesses of sex. Sex symbols were everywhere. They even had cult prostitutes, male and female. The act of sex was an act of worship to their god. It was not sex as the true God ordained it. Sounds like twenty-first-century America. God wanted to make it clear that Israel was to have no part of the pagan culture around them. The pagans' view and practice of sex and its practice could not coexist with God's.

The seventh commandment is God's declaration that *all sex* is to be confined to the marriage relationship. Remember the definition of adultery—having sexual intercourse with someone other than one's spouse. God is forbidding premarital sex, cohabitation, affairs, and any other sexual relationship outside the bonds of marriage.

The Scarlet Letter

The Scarlet Letter is Nathaniel Hawthorne's classic story of Hester Prynne, a young woman who gives birth to a child after committing adultery. For her punishment she is made to wear a scarlet A on her bosom as she is paraded down the streets, holding her baby. It is the stigma she is forced to wear—for life—for her wrong. The scarlet letter was a sign of shame.

There was a time when there was at least some shame for sexual immorality, but not now. Today the scarlet letter is *v* for *virgin* or *p* for *pure*. You are shamed for not being sexually active.

People proudly are sexually active in or out of marriage! In the 2005 movie *Hitch*, Will Smith plays a guy who wins fame as a relationship expert. In real life, Smith is married to actress Jada Pinkett Smith. His real-life views won't win hearts. Talking about his relationship with his wife, he explained to the *New York Post*:

> "In our marriage vows, we didn't say 'forsaking all others.' ... The vow that we made was that you will never hear that I did something after the fact."

He went on to say:

> "If it came down to it, then one [spouse] can say to the other, 'Look, I need to have sex with somebody. I'm not going to if you don't approve of it—but please approve of it.'"[44]

We need to return to the view that adultery is a scarlet letter, not something to celebrate.

On Guard

As believers, we must stand up against the attack on marriage. We must resist the current of society that would sweep us away in a flood of immorality. We must champion God's plan and purpose for marriage and for sex. We must remain pure in a sin-sick world.

---

[44] Russell Scott Smith, "'Hitch' a Switch for Big Willie—Lights, Camera, Love! Man-of-Action Smith Becomes Sweet Talker on Silver Screen," *New York Post*, September 6, 2006, http://www.nypost.com/p/entertainment/silver_switch_ screen_becomes_willie_kqD0rJSF59oGT4yvMiNPCN.

SUGGESTED ORDER OF WORSHIP

"The Scarlet Letter"

Prelude—Instrumental Group

NBH 570 *The Trees of the Fields*

Prayer of Worship—Pastoral Staff

Worship and Praise—Congregation

NBH 134 *O Magnify the Lord* (v. 1, chorus, v. 2, chorus in D)

NBH 456 *How Firm a Foundation* (vv. 1, 2 in G, v. 4 in Ab)

Welcome—Pastoral Staff

Song of Welcome *(meet and greet)*—Congregation

NBH 483 *Friend of God* (2x in C)

NBH 499 *Victory in Jesus* (v. 1, chorus, v. 3, chorus in F)

NBH 507 *Who Can Satisfy?* (chorus only 2x in C)

Testimony of Praise (Prerecorded video of a recent convert)

Offertory Prayer—Pastoral Staff

Offertory Praise

NBH 448 *Before the Throne of God Above* (vv. 1–3 in D)

Message—Pastor

"The Scarlet Letter" (Ex. 20:14)

Hymn of Response—Congregation

NBH 529 *Change My Heart, O God* (as needed)

Benediction Hymn—Congregation

NBH 434 *I Have Decided*

Postlude—Instrumental Group

NBH 560 *Oh, How I Love Jesus*

KEY:

NBH: New Baptist Hymnal (2008)

WEEK 35

The Heavenly Footman

1 Corinthians 9:24: "Run in such a way that you may obtain."
By John Bunyan

Introduction

The apostle Paul writes to the Corinthian believers that they would not run to be content with themselves with every kind of running, but says, "Run in such a way that you may obtain."

- *Fleeing*. Running [that you may obtain] is not the ordinary running; it is to be understood as the swiftest sort of running.

- *Pressing*. Running means, "pressing towards the mark," which signifies they will have heaven.

- *Continuing*. Running is a continual way of life.

Conclusion

We must run by studying the Word of God every day and to lay aside anything that would hinder us from running to the Cross. Where is your heart? Where are you running?

WEEK 35

Sex, Lies, and Sin's Red Tape!

Part 2
2 Samuel 11:1–27
By Larry Kiser

Introduction

The cover-up is always the thing that gets you. I remember that happening as a child. Give personal example. Also, use Watergate as an example. The cover up is always worse than the infraction. And such is the case with David's sin. We are reminded of our foundational lesson on this topic: In Christ we have the potential for amazing goodness; in our flesh we have the potential for amazing badness (2 Sam. 11:1–27).

[Review story from 2 Samuel 11:1–27.]

David had stepped over a major sin boundary, but rather than embracing confession and forgiveness, he chose pride and covering. Covering one sin will always lead to another sin.

1. Hypocrisy is habit-forming!

In this day and age, technology has made it incredibly easy to produce fraud.

[Use Photoshop to produce a picture that looks like it was taken by a lake, even though it was actually taken inside.]

Technology has allowed us to produce imitations of the real thing so effectively that we can no longer tell the real thing from the fake thing.

That may be great in the world of technology, but it's a dangerous thing in the world of morality and relationships. We can produce a life that looks good, but really isn't at all what it looks like.

So, what does King David do after his sin? How does he attempt to cover it?

[Read 2 Samuel 11:4–13.]

David assumed that Uriah would go home to his wife. He assumed that Uriah would make love to his wife. What he misjudged was the great loyalty that Uriah had to his comrades in the field and in an indirect way to King David as his commander. The first proposed cover-up failed. David must have thought to himself, *I can't believe this. This man's wife is a knockout, and he doesn't take advantage of her love?!*

2. God often gives us more than one chance to come to confession (2 Sam. 11:4–13).

   In light of Uriah's failure to unite with his wife, David now decides to take even more drastic measures in covering his sin.

   [Read 2 Samuel 11:14–27.]

   So, lust led to adultery, and adultery led to murder. Uriah, the only innocent party in this sinful set of events, ends up paying the ultimate price. There's an important lesson here for all regarding the consequences of sin:

Innocent people are always caught in the crossfire of selfish sin!

—2 Samuel 11:14–27

In our day and age, it's usually the children who are the innocent victims in a husband's or wife's selfish sin. But finally, Uriah is dead, David and Bathsheba are married, and things are just fine from man's perspective.

Conclusion

When sin has been covered up, things may appear to be okay from man's perspective, but if God's not pleased, things aren't right.

If God's not pleased, what seems good isn't!

WEEK 36

Stop, Thief!

Exodus 20:15

By Dr. Kent Spann

It's Okay to Shoplift

Tim Jones, parish priest of St. Lawrence and St. Hilda, told his congregation in York, Northern England, "My advice, as a Christian priest, is to shoplift," according to a CNN report December 22, 2009. He went on to explain: "I do not offer such advice because I think that stealing is a good thing, or because I think it is harmless, for it is neither. I would ask that they do not steal from small family businesses, but from large national businesses, knowing that the costs are ultimately passed on to the rest of us in the form of higher prices."

We must be reading from different Bibles, because in my Bible, Exodus 20:15 says, "You shall not steal." Again, this command is a simple, two-word Hebrew phrase with a wide application even for our world today. It is especially applicable to Christians.

The Prohibition

This command prohibits taking something from another without permission. Let's think about some of the forms of stealing:

1. Robbery
2. Kidnapping
3. Shoplifting, often called the "Five-Finger Discount"
4. Identity theft
5. Employee theft

Employee theft is called the fastest-growing crime in America, according to the FBI. The U.S. Chamber of Commerce estimates that 75 percent of employees steal from the workplace and that most do so repeatedly. One-third of all U.S. corporate bankruptcies are directly caused by employee theft.

    a. We can steal time from our employers.

    b. We can steal goods from our employers.

6. Fraud, which is deception for personal gain or to damage another

    a. Insurance fraud

    b. Telemarketing fraud

    c. E-mail fraud—e-mails telling you that there is a large sum of money available

    d. Political fraud

7. Theft of one's purity

When you engage in sex before marriage, you are taking away something that doesn't belong to you—the other person's virginity. It is something you can never replace or give back. Not only have you stolen it from the person that you have sex with; you have also stolen it from the individual's future husband or wife.

8. Cheating

    a. Cheating on tests

According to surveys in *U.S. News and World Report*, 80 percent of "high-achieving" high school students admit to cheating, while 51 percent of high school students did not believe cheating was wrong. The article said 75 percent of college students admitted cheating. Almost 85 percent of college students said cheating was necessary to get ahead.[45]

    b. Cheating on taxes (Matt. 22:21)

9. Plagiarism, which is the use or close imitation of the language and thoughts of another author and the representation of them as one's own original work

Joe Biden had to drop out of the presidential race against Bill Clinton for plagiarizing after using passages from British Labour Party leader Neil Kinnock in one of his speeches, without attributing them to Kinnock.

---

[45] *U.S. News & World Report*, November 22, 1999.

10. Copyright theft

Downloading music and movies on the Internet without paying fees or without permission from the owner is copyright theft. The same is true of copying CDs to give to friends.

11. Failure to pay debts

12. Gambling

Gambling is nothing more than legalized stealing where a person takes from another without giving anything in exchange.

These are just a few of the ways we can steal.

The Theology of Stealing

Whether you know it or not, there is a theology that underlies stealing.

- I cannot trust in God's provision; therefore, I will take whatever I want or need, when I want to and how I want to.

- I do not love other people; therefore, I will take what God has given to them so I can have it.

Think about it for a moment. Those two underlying theological premises are in diametric opposition to the two great commands Jesus gave in Matthew 22:37–40.

Biblical Theology

What two important theological principles can we glean from this passage?

1. Private property is a biblical concept.

The right to private property did not originate with capitalism; it originated and derives its authority from God.

a. We need to respect the private property of others

b. We need to return or make restitution for goods that we have taken without permission.

No wonder Karl Marx hated religion so much. It countered his social philosophy.

2. Hard work has been and always will be God's plan for our lives

Work is not the result of the Fall. Before the Fall, God made it clear that the man and woman were to work in the garden of Eden (Gen. 2:15).

3. Hard work provides us with the opportunity to share with those in need and accomplish God's purposes (Eph. 4:28).

Evangelical Christian author Jerry Bridges has observed that there are three basic attitudes we can take toward possessions. The first says, "What's yours is mine; I'll take it." This is the attitude of the thief. The second says, "What's mine is mine; I'll keep it." Since we are selfish by nature, this is the attitude that most people have most of the time. The third attitude—the godly attitude—says, "What's mine is God's; I'll share it."[46]

Before we close our look at the eighth commandment, I want to look at one very serious form of theft.

Grand Theft: Stealing from God

- We steal from God when we fail to give Him our worship (1 Chr. 16:27, 28; Ps. 95:6).

- We steal from God when we do not give our tithes to Him (Mal. 3:7–9).

- We steal from God when we receive His saving grace and then do not tell others about Him (2 Cor. 5:11–21).

- We steal from God when we don't use the gifts and talents He has given us to honor Him and minister to others (1 Pet. 4:10).

- We steal from God when we fail to use our time wisely for His glory (Ps. 90:12; Eph. 5:15, 16; Col. 4:5).

- We steal from God when we claim ownership of what we have instead of acknowledging that all we have is from God (1 Chr. 29:14; Ps.

---

[46] Jerry Bridges, *The Discipline of Grace: God's Role and Our Role in the Pursuit of Holiness* (Colorado Springs: NavPress, 1994), 88.

24:1).

- We steal from God when we fail to bring glory to God (Is. 43:7; Prov. 30:9).

The Ultimate Thief

We steal from God, but I want you to know that someone is stealing from you, and you may not even know it.

"The thief does not come except to steal, and to kill, and to destroy. I have come that they may have life, and that they may have it more abundantly."

—John 10:10

Satan wants to steal your life and take it to hell. Jesus wants to give you eternal life. Would you rather follow a life-stealer or a life-giver?

SUGGESTED ORDER OF WORSHIP

"Stop, Thief"

Prelude—Instrumentalist

NBH 134 *O Magnify the Lord*

Call to Worship—PT or Ensemble

NBH 528/529 *I Give You My Heart/Change My Heart, O God*

Call to Prayer and Worship—Pastor

Worship in Song—Congregation

NBH 386 *Brethren, We Have Met Together* (vv. 1 and 2 in G. v. 4 in Ab)

NBH 23 *Thou Art Worthy* (2x in Ab)

NBH 78 *I Stand in Awe* (2x in Ab)

Welcome—Pastoral Staff

Welcome Song *(meet and greet)*—Pastoral Staff

  NBH 27 *Rise Up and Praise Him* (2x in D)

  NBH 25 *Let It Rise* (2x in G)

Offertory Prayer—Pastoral Staff

Offertory Praise—Solo or PT

  NBH 50 *Indescribable*

Message—Pastor

  Stop, Thief (Ex. 20:15)

Hymn of Response—Congregation

  NBH 84 *Lead Me, Lord* (as needed in D)

Benediction Hymn—Congregation

  NBH 91 *Surely Goodness and Mercy* (v. 1, chorus in Eb)

Postlude—Instrumentalist

  NBH 95 *Come Thou Fount*—Warrenton Tune (2x in C)

KEY:

CH: Celebration Hymnal (Word Music/Integrity Music, Nashville, TN)

NBH: New Baptist Hymnal (2008)

WH: The Hymnal (Word Music, Nashville, TN)

SPW: Songs for Praise and Worship (Word Music, Nashville, TN)

MSPW: More Songs for Praise and Worship (Word Music, Nashville, TN)

MSPW2: More Songs for Praise and Worship 2 (Word Music, Nashville, TN)

WEEK 36

Watching, Waiting, Writing

Habakkuk 2:1–4
By Rev. Charles Haddon Spurgeon

Introduction

Here was the old problem of King David in another form. "Why do you look on those who deal treacherously?" (Hab. 1:13) is but a repetition of "I was envious of the boastful, when I saw the prosperity of the wicked" (Ps. 73:3). This same problem occurs to us, and this text may help us.

1. The sense in which there is a delay in the promise

2. The attitude of a believer while the promise delays

3. The work of the Lord's servant while the promise delays

4. The difference seen in men when the delay of the promise tests them

Conclusion

Let us settle this in our hearts, that He must and will fulfill His promises. Our text shows us a punctual God, a patient waiter, and a published confidence; but it finishes up with a proud believer.

WEEK 36

Spiritual Labor Day

1 Corinthians 3:1–11
By Dave Hirschman

Introduction

Labor Day was celebrated first on Tuesday, September 5, 1882, in New York City. By 1894, twenty-three states had adopted the holiday, and on June 28, 1894, Congress passed an act making the first Monday in September of each year a legal holiday. Paul addressed the importance of spiritual labor in 1 Corinthians 3, stating that spiritual labor is a part of God's plan, that we should labor for the Lord, and that our labor yields a spiritual reward. What does spiritual labor entail for you and me? Simply this: participating in God's plan for this age; telling others about Jesus Christ, making God known, and directing the way to eternal life. We also labor in prayer, in faith, in enduring difficulties. Spiritual labor should be a way of life for every follower of Jesus (Matt. 9:37, 38, 1 Thess. 1:2, 3, 1 Tim. 4:10, Heb. 6:10). Consider Paul's teaching on spiritual labor in 1 Corinthians 3:1–11. Spiritual labor is:

1. The Product of Spiritual Maturity (3:1–4)

    a. Physical/spiritual infants are too weak to work—verse 2: "not able to bear it" (KJV).

    b. Physical/spiritual infants think only of themselves—verse 3: "envying, strife, and divisions."

    c. Physical/spiritual infants are preoccupied with childish things—verse 4: "I am of Paul, ... Apollos."

2. The Proof of Spiritual Relationship (3:5–7)

    a. Through spiritual labor, someone brought you to Jesus—verse 5: "Paul" and "Apollos."

    b. But God did the work—verse 6: salvation, sanctification, satisfaction.

    c. God at work is the proof of relationship (v. 7) (Phil. 2:13; 4:20).

3. The Process of Spiritual Operation (3:8, 9)

    a. God works in and through His spiritually mature children (v. 9b; Col. 1:27–29).

    b. His children never work alone (v. 9a), and God will reward His children for their spiritual labor (v. 8).

4. The Project of Spiritual Motivation (3:10, 11)

We are to build upon a precious foundation (v. 11), Jesus, and our spiritual labor should be our best work for the Lord (v. 10).

Conclusion

When we mature spiritually, our focus turns from self to the things of God, including participating in spiritual labor for the Lord. If there is no spiritual labor, can there really be a relationship? We can only work as we permit the Lord to work in us; how is the process working? How is your project progressing?

WEEK 37

Truth, Justice, and the American Way

Exodus 20:16

By Dr. Kent Spann

How many of you grew up watching *Superman*? Was he your favorite superhero? Wasn't he just the coolest? Do you remember the opening statement, that said he fights for "truth, justice, and the American way"?

What has happened to truth in America? I am not talking about propositional truth; I am talking about telling the truth. Truth is no longer important.

Lying is a way of life in America. Film producer Linda Obst described Hollywood culture this way: "Inhale. Lie. Exhale. Lie."[47]

On the Internet are some of the biggest lies ever told:

- "The check is in the mail."

- "You get this one; I'll pay next time."

- "My wife doesn't understand me."

- "Trust me; I'll take care of everything."

- "Of course I love you."

- "It's not the money; it's the principle of the thing."

- "I never watch television except for PBS."

- "But we can still be good friends."

- "She means nothing to me."

- "I'll call you later."

- "I've never done anything like this before."

- "Sorry, we can't come to the phone right now."

---

[47] *Los Angeles Times*, February 13, 2001; reprinted in *Citizen* magazine, May 2001, 9, as found at www.preachingtoday.com.

Lying has now become America's favorite pastime.

Help, LORD, for the godly are no more; the faithful have vanished from among men. Everyone lies to his neighbor; their flattering lips speak with deception.

(Ps. 12:1, 2 NIV)

Christian leader Charles Colson wrote a column for *Christianity Today* that called our society a "Post-Truth Society" because lying is so prevalent.[48]

Truth, Justice, and God's Way

The obvious and direct application of Exodus 20:16 were the court system and process. God says you shall not give a deceptive witness about your neighbor. God made it clear that in this new society, false testimony against a neighbor was anathema (Deut. 17:7; 19:15–21).

Lying is an abomination to God (Prov. 6:16–19; 12:22).

Why does God so hate lying and dishonesty?

- Because Satan, His enemy, is the father of lies (John 8:44).
- Because God is the God of truth (Ps. 31:5; John 14:6; 1 John 4:6).
- Because lying is sin.

Oliver Wendell Holmes said, "Sin has many tools, but a lie is the handle that fits them all."

Variations on Lying

- Outright lies (Ps. 34:13)
- Rumors (Ex. 23:1)
- Gossip (Prov. 20:19; Rom. 1:29)
- Slander (Lev. 19:16; Ps. 15:1–3; James 4:11; 1 Pet. 2:1)
- Silence (Lev. 5:1)

---

[48] Charles Colson, "The Back Page: Post-Truth Society," *Christianity Today*, March 11, 2002.

- Flattery (Rom. 16:18; 1 Thess. 2:5)
- Exaggeration and boasting (James 3:5, 14)
- Hypocrisy (Matt. 23:13, 15, 23; Titus 1:16)
- False teaching (2 Pet. 2:1–3)

Honesty Is the Best Policy

George Orwell said, "In a time of universal deceit, telling the truth is a revolutionary act."

God calls us to be revolutionary (Prov. 12:22; Eph. 4:25).

1. Commit to live a life of integrity.

Seven-year-old first baseman Tanner Munsey never thought he'd end up in *Sports Illustrated*, but he did. While playing T-Ball in Wellington, Florida, Tanner fielded a ground ball and tried to tag a runner going from first to second base.

The umpire, Laura Benson, called the runner out, but young Tanner immediately ran to her side and said, "Ma'am, I didn't tag the runner." Umpire Benson reversed herself and sent the runner to second base.

Two weeks later, Laura Benson was again the umpire, and Tanner was playing shortstop. This time Benson ruled that Tanner had missed the tag on a runner going to third base, and she called the runner safe. Tanner, obviously disappointed, tossed the ball to the pitcher and returned to his position. Benson asked Tanner what was wrong, and Tanner quietly said he'd tagged the boy.

Umpire Benson's response? "You're out!" She sent the runner to the bench. When the opposing coach rushed the field to protest, Benson explained what had happened two weeks before, saying, "If a kid is that honest, I have to give it to him."[49]

Speak the Truth in Love

Here is a great acrostic to help you evaluate how you speak. Ask, is it:

---

[49] Craig Neff, ed., "Scorecard," *Sports Illustrated*, July 10, 1989, http://sportsillustrated.cnn.com/vault/article/magazine/MAG1068563/3/index.htm.

True?
Helpful?
Inspiring?
Necessary?
Kind?

2. Own up to your actions, no matter what it costs.

One of the most tragic stories is that of David and Bathsheba. The whole affair turned into a huge web of deceit, because David was unwilling to own up to his own action and admit his sin. The Bible is replete with examples of people failing to own up to their actions.

Speaking the truth in love means we own up to our actions, whether they are decisions we make, which may or may not be bad, or sins we commit.

3. Think and say the best about people.

Paul tells us in 1 Corinthians 13:7 to think the best about people. Our propensity is to go negative.

4. Don't gossip.

"Without wood a fire goes out; without gossip a quarrel dies down" (Prov. 26:20 NIV).

5. Keep your word.

One of the best testimonies you can have in today's society is that you are a man or woman of your word.

"Let your 'Yes' be 'Yes,' and your 'No,' 'No.' For whatever is more than these is from the evil one" (Matt. 5:37).

6. Be honest in your dealings with others.

Being honest with others would seem to be simple, but it is not for fallen creatures like us. American politician Adlai Stevenson defined a lie as *"an abomination unto the Lord, but a very present help in time of trouble."* Unfortunately, that is how many even Christians define lies.

a. We need to admit our dishonesty.

b. We need to think honestly; that is, make honesty our mind-set.

c. We need to be honest in the small things.

7. Believe the truth.

This is where the rubber really meets the road. Being truthful begins with believing the truth. I would point out truths you need to come to grips with.

a. The Truth About Your Heart

"The heart is deceitful above all things, and desperately wicked; who can know it? I, the LORD, search the heart, I test the mind, even to give every man according to his ways, according to the fruit of his doings." (Jer. 17:9, 10)

As long as you think you are not that bad, you are living in a world of deceit.

b. The Truth About Christ

You need to come to grips with the truth about Christ. That could be a whole other sermon, but one verse will suffice now.

Jesus said ... "I am the way, the truth, and the life. No one comes to the Father except through me." (John 14:6)

SUGGESTED ORDER OF WORSHIP

"Truth, Justice, and the American Way"

Prelude—Instrumentalists

Jesus Saves (Travis Cottrell Tune)

Call to Prayer—Worship Pastor

Call to Praise—Congregation

NBH 54 *Agnus Dei* (2x in A)

NBH 548 *Seekers of Your Heart* (2x in D)

NBH 65 *We Declare Your Majesty* (2x in G)

Prayer of Praise—Pastoral Staff

Welcome—Pastoral Staff

Song of Welcome *(meet and greet)*—Congregation

NBH 63 *Awesome God* (1x in G, 1x in Ab)

Worship and Praise—Congregation

NBH 326 *Your Name* (v. 1, chorus, v. 2, chorus in Ab)

NBH 365 *Song for the Nations* (vv. 1–5 in Ab)

NBH 326 *Your Name* (chorus only in Ab)

Offertory Prayer—Pastoral Staff

Offertory Praise—Solo, PT, or Ensemble

NBH 431 *The Lord's Prayer* (1x in Bb, tag from "For Thine")

Sermon—Pastor

"Truth, Justice and the American Way" (Ex. 20:16)

Hymn of Invitation—Congregation

NBH552 *My Jesus, I Love Thee* (as needed)

Benediction Hymn—Congregation

NBH 388 *Make Us One* (2x in C)

Postlude—Instrumentalists

NBH 390 *Bind Us Together* (2x in F)

KEY:

CH: Celebration Hymnal (Word Music/Integrity Music, Nashville, TN)

NBH: New Baptist Hymnal (2008)

WH: The Hymnal (Word Music, Nashville, TN)

SPW: Songs for Praise and Worship (Word Music, Nashville, TN)

MSPW: More Songs for Praise and Worship (Word Music, Nashville, TN)

MSPW2: More Songs for Praise and Worship 2 (Word Music, Nashville, TN)

WEEK 37

The Conquest of Fear

Revelation 1:17, 18
By George W. Truett

Introduction

The message concerning the conquest of fear is both the mission and the message of Jesus to deliver mankind from servile, enervating, down-dragging fear.

1. Jesus bids us to be unafraid of life.
2. Jesus bids us to be unafraid of death.
3. Jesus bids us to be unafraid of eternity.

Conclusion

Are you trusting Christ as your personal Savior, and do you gladly bow to Him as your rightful Master?

WEEK 37

Confrontation and Confession!

2 Samuel 12:1–23
By Larry Kiser

Introduction

It's amazing how our sense of morality and justice can be crystal clear when looking at another person's life or situation, yet be just as blind when analyzing our own lives and situations.

[Read 2 Samuel 12:1.]

God sent Nathan to David to confront him. I imagine that was one of the worst prophetic assignments Nathan had ever been given. Confronting the king with his sin was the business of the prophet, and Nathan had no choice.

Confession is often the result of confrontation. God sent Nathan to David to confront him about his sin. Confronting people about their sin has become a lost ministry.

All Christians are called upon to be prophets at times. We must accept the prophetic role of confronting those we love with their sin. Confrontation is unpleasant, messy business.

1. Confrontation is messy business; ignoring sin is messier business (2 Sam. 12:1).

   How we confront is important. None of us want to be perceived as judgmental or holier-than-thou. So, we can learn something from Nathan the prophet about how he confronted the king of Israel, a man powerful enough to have him killed on command.

   [Read 2 Samuel 12:1–4.]

2. Stories are a powerful form of communication (2 Sam. 12:1–4).

   Nathan used a story to confront David, a story involving a dear lamb, since David knew what it was like to love lambs, being a keeper of sheep in his youth.

Look at how David responded to this story of injustice.

[Read 2 Samuel 12:5, 6.]

3. We're really tough on other people's sin (2 Sam. 12:5, 6).

The truth trap has been set. David jumps into the trap with an angry sense of righteousness.

[Read 2 Samuel 12:8–12.]

Nathan not only spells out David's sin, but also spells out the consequences of David's sin. The consequences of David's sin will affect his children and their children.

4. The consequences of sin always outlast its pleasure (2 Sam. 12:8–12).

The consequences of David's sin would be long lasting, affecting his key relationships for years. David responds well to Nathan's confrontation.

5. Honest confession brings immediate forgiveness.

[Read 2 Samuel 12:13.]

What an amazing picture of God's readiness to forgive! That same forgiveness is available to all of us. In fact, that is exactly what Paul meant when he said in Romans 5:20 that where sin increased, grace increased all the more. *Grace does its most powerful work in the midst of man's greatest failures!*

What an amazing picture here of God's grace. God's grace is amazing, but it doesn't take away our pain or the sting of sin's consequences.

The baby still died, but David was restored to a place of God's richest blessing.

[Read 2 Samuel 12:24.]

When God forgives, He also restores!

Conclusion

When we confess our sins, God is delighted to forgive and to quickly restore us to a place where we can once again feel the delight of His unconditional love!

WEEK 38

King George and the Ducky

Exodus 20:17
By Dr. Kent Spann

In Veggie Tales' *King George and the Ducky*, an animated children's film, Larry the Cucumber stars as King George, and Bob the Tomato is his faithful servant, Lewis. The privileges of royalty—kingdom expansion, castles, power, and treasures—do not appeal to King George, but he loves to bathe with his rubber duck. Splishing and splashing, he sings an ode to his rubber duck called—what else?—"I Love My Duck."

One day, while standing on the royal balcony in his purple robe and golden crown, King George peers through binoculars, and his eyes grow wide with desire. He spies something wonderful—a rubber duck. But it belongs to Billy, who happens to be bathing with his rubber duck on his own balcony. Billy's rubber duck looks exactly like King George's rubber duck. Nonetheless, the king covets it, exclaiming, "I want it."

Lewis reminds him that he already has a duck and that the other duck belongs to someone else.

"Are you saying I shouldn't have whatever I want?" asks the king.

Lewis opens a large wardrobe overflowing with hundreds of identical rubber ducks and says, "If I could just jog your memory, you already have quite a few ducks."

King George's rationale is simple. He shoots a condescending look at his unlearned servant and replies, "Those are yesterday's ducks."[50]

Someone else had a new duck, and King George wanted it.

Grapes of Wrath

That reminds me of the tragic story of Ahab in 1 Kings 21. Ahab saw Naboth's vineyard and decided he wanted it. When Naboth refused to give or sell it to Ahab, Ahab went home pouting to his wife, Jezebel.

---

[50] "King George and the Duck" (Big Idea, 2000), not rated, written by Jennifer Combs, directed by Mike Nawrocki. as found at www.preachingtoday.com.

Jezebel hatched a plan to get it, resulting in Naboth's death. Finally Ahab had what he wanted, but the joy of it was short-lived, because Elijah showed up to pour cold water on his party.

When you dig deep into the story, you see how covetousness led to the violation of almost all of the Ten Commandments.

- Ahab put the land ahead of God (first commandment).
- Ahab worshipped the land (second commandment).
- Jezebel misused the name of the Lord by proclaiming a fast (third commandment).
- Ahab dishonored Naboth's family by taking the family inheritance (fifth commandment).
- Jezebel murdered Naboth (sixth commandment).
- Ahab stole the vineyard (eighth commandment).
- Jezebel arranged false testimony (ninth commandment).
- All because Ahab coveted (tenth commandment).

A Daily Tragic Story

What a tragic story! But no more tragic than what goes on every day in our own country and in most of our lives. It is called coveting, and it is the desire to have something or someone that belongs to another person. It is life in twenty-first-century America.

One of the most popular movies of 1991 was a horrific thriller called *The Silence of the Lambs*. The movie, directed by Jonathan Demme, was about a serial killer named Hannibal Lecter and his strange friendship with a young FBI trainee named Clarice Starling. In the beginning Lecter is being held by the FBI in a special cell designed to prevent any possibility of escape. As Starling gets to know him, she asks for his help in capturing another serial killer. He agrees to help, and in a climactic scene set in Memphis, Tennessee, Lecter explains to Starling where she should begin to look. In the process he gives her what amounts to a lecture in biblical theology. The conversation went something like this:

"What was the original sin, Clarice?"

"Excuse me?"

"What was the original sin in Eden?"

"I don't know, and I don't have time to play games."

"Think. What was the sin that Adam and Eve committed?"

"I don't know."

"It was coveting. They wanted something they couldn't have."

"So what?"

"That's the answer, Clarice."

"What do you mean?"

"The man you are looking for is a covetous man. He wants something he can't have." Then Lecter explains what he means in a sentence of pure spiritual truth: "We covet what we see every day. Go back," he says. "Go back and find his hometown. Go back and see what he sees every day. There you will find your answer."

Coveting is the original sin. The first couple coveted the forbidden fruit and sinned against God.

God Speaks

Once again God speaks to our covetous society in Exodus 20:17. The commandments were given by God at the time of Israel's founding. God was giving the Israelites their constitution. He did it personally from Mount Sinai.

No society can thrive when it is eaten up with covetousness.

- Covetousness is never satisfied (Eccl. 5:10–12).
- Covetousness engrosses the heart (Ezek. 33:31; 2 Pet. 2:14) and even comes from the heart (Mark 7:22, 23).
- What we covet becomes an idol (Eph. 5:5; Col. 3:5).
- Covetousness leads to:
  - injustice and oppression (Mic. 2:2)
  - murder (Prov. 1:18, 19; Ezek. 22:12)
  - great temptations (1 Tim. 6:9)
  - harmful desires (1 Tim. 6:9)
  - ruin and destruction (1 Tim. 6:9)
  - departure from the faith (1 Tim. 6:10)
- Covetousness ruins homes and marriages (Prov. 15:27).

- Covetousness is the cause of war and conflict (James 4:1–4).
- Covetousness results in God's judgment upon a nation (Josh. 7:1–26; Mic. 2:2, 3).

The Antidote to Covetousness

How can we fight covetousness?

1. Desire the right things the right way.

I state this one first because we need to know that all desire is not wrong. God created us to desire. A person without desire is no longer a person.

How do we keep desire in check?

a. We desire the right things—God (Ps. 42:1, 2; Phil. 3:7–14), His kingdom (Matt. 6:33), His approval (Matt. 25:21, 23), and others' good (1 Cor. 13:4–7).

b. We desire the right way by avoiding excess and rejecting illegitimate, exploitative, or selfish desires.

2. Love our neighbor (Matt. 22:39).

3. Cultivate gratitude (Ps. 100:4; Col. 2:7; 1 Thess. 5:18).

4. Choose contentment (Phil. 4:10–19; Heb. 13:5).

A man was tired of his friends owning nicer homes than his, so he went to see a realtor and put his home on the market and began to search for a new one. One day, as he was reading the paper, he came across a listing for a home that was just what he was looking for. He called his realtor. The realtor replied "Sir, that is your house. That is the house we are trying to sell for you."

5. Give generously (Acts 20:35; Rom. 12:13; 2 Cor. 8, 9).

A Tale of Two Lives

The story of Howard Hughes, who lived between 1905 and 1976, is tragic. There was only one thing he wanted in life—more. He wanted more money, so he parlayed inherited wealth into a billion-dollar pile of assets. He wanted more fame, so he went to Hollywood and became a filmmaker and star. He wanted more sensual pleasures, so he paid handsome sums to indulge his every hedonistic urge. He wanted more thrills, so he designed, built, and piloted the fastest aircraft in the world. He wanted more power, so he secretly dealt political favors so skillfully that two U.S. presidents became his pawns. All he ever wanted was more.

And yet Howard Hughes ended his life emaciated, colorless, with a sunken chest. His fingernails resembled grotesque, inches-long corkscrews. His teeth were black and rotten, and innumerable needle marks covered his body from his drug addiction. Howard Hughes walked around nearly naked most of the time, with his beard and hair to his waist. He lived in darkness, wore rubber gloves, and sterilized everything in his junk-filled room. He spent most of his time watching old movies and drinking soup. He talked on the phone for ten to fifteen hours a day, because he was so lonely. He died weighing ninety-five pounds. The only way the Treasury Department could identify him was by his fingerprints.

Now contrast that to the apostle Paul, who lost everything but needed nothing (Phil. 3:7–14).

Let me put it in simple terms.

Enough is enough when God is enough!

SUGGESTED ORDER OF WORSHIP

Prelude—Instrumentalist

   NBH 350 *Shout to the North*

Call to Prayer—Pastoral Staff

Welcome—Pastoral Staff

   NBH 349 *Great Is the Lord Almighty* (2x in Bb)

   NBH 522 *In His Time* (2x in Eb)

   NBH 385 *They'll Know We Are Christian* (v. 1, chorus,
   v. 2, chorus, v. 3, chorus, v. 4, chorus in Ab)

   NBH 359 *People Need the Lord* (2x in C)

Baptismal Celebration—Pastoral Staff

Prayer of Commitment—Pastoral Staff

> NBH 415 *Room at the Cross* (chorus, v. 1, chorus, v. 2, chorus in G)

Scripture Reading from Psalm 100 *(Please have prepared for IMAG)*

> Make a joyful shout to the LORD, all you lands!
> Serve the LORD with gladness;
> Come before His presence with singing.
> Know that the LORD, He is God;
> It is He who has made us, and not we ourselves;
> We are His people and the sheep of His pasture.
> Enter into His gates with thanksgiving,
> And into His courts with praise.
> Be thankful to Him, and bless His name.
> For the LORD is good;
> His mercy is everlasting,
> And His truth endures to all generations.

Prayer of Thanksgiving—Pastor

Offertory Praise—PT with Congregation

> NBH 426 *Open Our Eyes, Lord* (vv. 1 and 2 in D)

Message—Pastor

> *"King George and the Ducky"* (Ex. 20:17)

Hymn of Response/Invitation—Congregation

> NBH44 *He Knows My Name* (as needed in Eb)

Benediction Hymn—Congregation

> NBH 320 *Jesus, Name Above All Names* (2x in Eb)

Postlude

> NBH 321 *Blessed Be the Name of the Lord* (2x in F)

KEY:

CH: Celebration Hymnal (Word Music/Integrity Music, Nashville, TN)

NBH: New Baptist Hymnal (2008)

WH: The Hymnal (Word Music, Nashville, TN)

SPW: Songs for Praise and Worship (Word Music, Nashville, TN)

MSPW: More Songs for Praise and Worship (Word Music, Nashville, TN)

MSPW2: More Songs for Praise and Worship 2 (Word Music, Nashville, TN)

WEEK 38

A Promise for Every Day

Deuteronomy 33:25
By George W. Truett

Introduction

This promise comes to reinforce us to be faithful unto the Lord Jesus every day.

1. Whose Promise?

   a. Man's promises

   b. God's promises

2. Limitation of the Promise

   a. "As your days ..."; nowhere does it say, "As your desires."

   b. What is it? "Your days," not as one's weeks, months, or years, but days.

3. Security of the Promise

   a. God is with you.

   b. Fret not.

Conclusion

Will you take this promise today and make it yours? There is one concern for every one of us to have, and that concern is to be faithful to Jesus Christ.

WEEK 38

The Love of God

John 3:16a
By Josh Saefkow

Introduction

Martin Luther called John 3:16 "the mini gospel"; A. T. Robinson said John 3:16 is "the gospel in a nutshell." The existence of God is under attack in today's society. It is vitally important to allow one of the most popular verses in the Bible to embed in your heart.

1. The Opening of God's Love: "For God"

2. The Overflow of God's Love: "so loved the world"

Conclusion

There is nothing you can do to escape the love of God. There is neither beginning nor end to His precious love for you. Before eternity you were not; before your parents conceived you, you were not. But from the moment of your conception, you will always be; where will you be?

WEEK 39

Ordination Sermon for a Minister

Christ, the Example of Ministers

John 13:15, 16

By Jonathan Edwards

> *[The following is a summary of the message delivered by Jonathan Edwards. The preacher is encouraged to take the message and put it in his own words to reflect the times.]*

When we read of our Savior calling on His disciples to imitate the example He had given them in what He had done, we are to understand Him, not merely by the example He gave in the emblematical action, in washing His disciples' feet, in itself considered, but more especially, of that much greater act of His that was signified by it, in abasing Himself so low and suffering so much for the spiritual cleansing and salvation of His people.

1. Then, I would show wherein ministers of the gospel ought, in the work of their ministry, to follow the example of their great Lord and Master, Jesus Christ.

    a. *First*, in general, ministers should follow their Lord and Master in all those excellent virtues, and in that universal and eminent holiness of life that He set an example of in this human nature.

    b. *Second*, more particularly should ministers of the gospel follow the example of their great Master in the manner in which they seek the salvation and happiness of the souls of men.

2. Some reasons why ministers of the gospel should follow the example of their great Lord and Master, Jesus Christ:

    a. *First*, they should follow His example because He is their Lord and Master.

    b. *Second*, ministers of the gospel are in some respects called and devoted to the same work and business that Christ Himself was appointed to.

c. *Third*, the example of Christ is most worthy of ministers' imitation.

d. *Fourth*, ministers should follow that example of Christ because if they are fit to be ministers, and are such as have any right to take that work upon themselves, Christ has set them this example in what He has done for their souls.

3. I now proceed, as was proposed, in the third place, to apply what has been said to myself, and others that are employed in this sacred work of the gospel ministry, and to such as are about to undertake it, or are candidates for it; and particularly to him that is now to be solemnly set apart to this work in this place.

a. That we may thus follow Christ's example, and be partakers with Him in His glory, we need to be much in prayer for His Spirit.

b. In order to imitate Christ in the work of the ministry, in any tolerable degree, we need not have our hearts overcharged and our time filled up with worldly affections, cares, and pursuits.

c. Another thing that is of very great importance, in order to do the work that Christ did, is that we take heed that the religion we promote be that same religion that Christ taught and promoted, and not any of its counterfeits and delusive appearances, or anything substituted by the subtle devices of Satan, or vain imaginations of men, in lieu of it.

4. And last thing at first proposed, namely, to show what improvement should be made of what has been said, by the people of this church and congregation, who are now about solemnly to commit their souls to the charge of him whom they have chosen to be their pastor, and who is now about to be set apart to that office:

a. And you, my brethren, as all of you have immortal souls to save, if you have considered the things that have been spoken, cannot but be sensible, that it not only greatly concerns your elect pastor to take heed how he behaves himself in his great work, wherein he is to act as a coworker with Christ for your salvation; but that it infinitely concerns you how you receive him, and behave toward him.

b. And as it is your duty and interest well to support your minister, so it concerns you to pray earnestly for him, and each one to do what in him lies in all respects to encourage and help him, and strengthen his hands, by attending diligently to his ministry, receiving the truth in love, treating him with the honor due to a messenger of Christ, carefully avoiding all contention with him, and one with another.

SUGGESTED ORDER OF WORSHIP

Prelude—Instrumental Ensemble

Jesus Is All the World to Me

Call to Prayer—Pastor

Song of Welcome—Congregation

NBH 599 *Soon and Very Soon* (2x in G)

Prayer of Love and Worship—Pastoral Staff

Worship and Praise

CH 517 *I Will Sing of My Redeemer* (1x verse, 2x chorus in G)

NBH 588 *Sanctuary* (1x in D, 1x in Eb)

NBH 44 *He Knows My Name* (2x in Eb)

Scripture of Encouragement from 1 Thessalonians 3:1–8—Pastoral Staff

Therefore, when we could no longer endure it, we thought it good to be left in Athens alone, and sent Timothy, our brother and minister of God, and our fellow laborer in the gospel of Christ, to establish you and encourage you concerning your faith, that no one should be shaken by these afflictions; for you yourselves know that we are appointed to this. For, in fact, we told you before when we were with you that we would suffer tribulation, just as it happened, and you know. For this reason, when I could no longer endure it, I sent to know your faith, lest by some means the tempter had tempted you, and our labor might be in vain. But now that Timothy has come to us from you, and brought us good news of your faith and love, and that you always have good remembrance of us, greatly desiring to see us, as we also to see you— therefore, brethren, in all our affliction and distress we were comforted concerning you by your faith. For now we live, if you stand fast in the Lord.

Prayer for the Fellow Servants—Pastoral Staff

Praise and Worship—Congregation

> CH 87 *Fairest Lord Jesus* (vv. 1 and 2)
>
> CH 88 *More Precious Than Silver* (2x in F)
>
> NBH 566 *Father, I Adore You* (2x in F)
>
> SPW 220 *You Are My All in All* (1x in F, 1x in G)

Offertory Prayer (Praise for God as Provision and All in All)—Pastoral Staff

Offertory Praise—Congregation

> CH 497 *I Will Praise Him* (chorus, v. 1, chorus, v. 3, chorus, v. 4, chorus in D)
>
> NBH 346 *The Church's One Foundation* (2x in D, 1x in Eb)

Message—Pastor

Hymn of Invitation/Response—Congregation

> NBH 628 *He Touched Me*

Postlude—Instrumental Group

> *No Other Name*

KEY:

CH: Celebration Hymnal (Word Music/Integrity Music, Nashville, TN)

NBH: New Baptist Hymnal (2008)

WH: The Hymnal (Word Music, Nashville, TN)

SPW: Songs for Praise and Worship (Word Music, Nashville, TN)

MSPW: More Songs for Praise and Worship (Word Music, Nashville, TN)

MSPW2: More Songs for Praise and Worship 2 (Word Music, Nashville, TN)

WEEK 39

The Only Begotten of the Father

John 3:18; 1 John 4:9
By Robert G. Lee

Introduction

Jesus has many names, and among the greatest is "the only begotten Son." Consider this name in the glory of His:

1. Pre-Incarnation (John 17:5, 24)

2. Prophecy (Luke 24:27)

3. Presentation (Is. 7:14)

4. Pain (Matt. 26:38)

5. Preeminence (Col. 1:18; John 3:31)

Conclusion

Jesus Christ was smitten; we are shielded. Christ was lacerated; we are liberated. He was slain, and we are secured. Christ's was the judgment, and ours is the joy. Christ's was the condemnation; ours is the justification. How can mankind have the heart to reject such a lover of their souls?

WEEK 39

A Rare Find!

Genesis 39–50; Proverbs 20:6
By Dr. Kent Spann

In 1947, young Bedouin shepherds, searching for a stray goat in the Judean Desert, entered a long-untouched cave and found jars filled with ancient scrolls. That initial discovery by the Bedouins yielded seven scrolls and began a search that lasted nearly a decade and eventually produced thousands of scroll fragments from eleven caves. What they found is known as the Dead Sea Scrolls, which are the oldest manuscripts of the Old Testament that we have. Folks, it was a rare find.

As rare as that find is, I want to tell you about an even more rare and valuable find. Turn to Proverbs 20:6. God is looking for a faithful person, and when He finds them He will bless them. Joseph was one of those rare finds.

1. Joseph was faithful to do what he was told by those whom God placed over him (37:12, 13).

2. Joseph was faithful when he was entrusted with responsibilities (39:2–6).

3. Joseph was faithful when it was costly to be faithful (39:6b–10).

4. Joseph was faithful when he was given big responsibilities in the limelight or little ones in obscurity (39:19–23).

5. Joseph was faithful when times were good and when they were bad (39:22, 23).

It is easy to be faithful when everything is going great, but what about when things aren't? The faithful person sticks to it because he knows that there will come bad and good times, but if he will remain faithful, God will eventually bless. They are faithfully optimistic.

6. Joseph was faithful when opportunities were given to Him by God (41:16).

Many a man claims to have unfailing love, but a faithful man who can find? Are you one of those rare finds?

WEEK 40

Two-a-Penny

Matthew 10:24–30
By Dr. Calvin Miller

Are not sparrows two-a-penny? Yet without your Father's leave, not one of them can fall to the ground.

Introduction

I am touched by the love of God. When I see the suffering of so many in this tortured world of ours, I am prone to ask myself, "Where is there even an iota of justice?" But I rarely ask myself, "Where is God?" I know God is there, and He is in love with His world. He has promised His presence, and that is adequate for me. But He has declared His love in the most simplistic and proverbial way. God loves sparrows, and if sparrows, why not us? Sparrows in Jesus' day were sold for a penny, yet not one of them could fall to the ground without the Father's leave.

One day an old preacher was walking down the street with a fellow preacher who had his three-year-old son along. As they walked, the little boy looked down and saw a penny lying on the sidewalk. The child became so excited he reached down and grabbed it. He could have been no happier if it were a thousand dollars. "Daddy, Daddy," he cried, "Look what I found … a penny!"

His excitement fascinated the old preacher. He could not imagine getting so excited about so little. He ran his hand into his pocket and found that he had a whole pocketful of change, mostly pennies. He hurried his step to walk just ahead of the child, and for the next few moments he dropped pennies for sheer joy of watching the boy's excitement as he found them. Knowing that pennies buy so little, the preacher didn't even feel any sense of sacrifice in what he was doing. But to the little boy the retrieval of every one of them was over and again erupting with joy.

The God of Pennies

I doubt if I would even stop to pick up a penny, yet the thing that I do not treasure was clearly celebrated by the child in this story. I have been overwhelmed time and again by what seems to be God's sense of wonder. Treasuring the seemingly worthless is somehow like our God.

Could it be that we all become too dull to esteem the ordinary values of life that leave us so unlike God? Does God have a low value system, or just a highly developed esteem for the ordinary? It must be the latter or God would never have stopped to save us. Does it bother God that Idi Amin killed a quarter of his own countrymen? Does he care that the Ayatollah Khomeini executed ruthlessly those who stabilized his own early regime and called for his homecoming? Does God grieve over Stalin's execution of sixty million of his own countrymen, or that terrorists murder so many in His name?

When I am prone to think like this, I stop to consider the story I told, of a little boy's excitement over finding pennies. Then I know that things seemingly worthless, with better vision, have real worth. As long as God cares so much for sparrows, knowing that they sell two for a penny, maybe the Cross is God's finest shopping spree, for at Calvary He spent all He had to buy the souls of those who put Him to death. So much for so little! In the midst of our senseless human circus, God goes on deliberately picking up pennies.

Jesus, the Picture of a Caring God

God's Son, let us not forget, was a peasant. No doubt in the learning of His trade, Jesus caught His thumb in the vise or was forced to pull the rough-wood splinters from His hand. Jesus very likely grieved at Joseph's funeral, and probably saw one or two of His infant brothers or sisters die, when a dram of penicillin—had it been invented—would have saved them. God's perfect boy cried over the plight of urban Jerusalem, with its thousands of lost citizenry. Finally, of course, they hung Him by His hands. And while He hung there, He asked the howling gales about His Father's concern. "Do You care, Father?"

"Eloi, Eloi, lama sabacthani?
My God, My God, why have You forsaken Me?" (Matt. 27:45)

Perhaps at this very moment of suffering, the emperor Tiberias was getting a rubdown by a Nubian slave, and Pilate was involved in a board game with one of the Praetorian Guard. Perhaps the Jews at that very time were so busy with Passover shopping to even notice how much all their apathy was costing God.

Jesus suffered and died during a week when there was a multiplicity of things going on. And even then He must have known His penny-loving Father was grieving over all He was undergoing on that horrible, dark day. Such a God is even in the height of Jesus suffering counting sparrows and judging them to be of worth. Jesus says in this great passage that the very hairs of our head are numbered, so thorough is God's love and concern for us (Matt 10:30).

One of the greatest evidences of thoughtful care of a loving God can be heard in an old spiritual. Perhaps you've heard it:

> I sing because I'm happy.
> I sing because I'm free.
> For His eye is on the sparrow
> And I know He watches me.

When the Pain Comes

When the pain comes, God cares. Oh, there are moments when we are prone to say that God lives in heaven, above a brass sky, protected from all human pain by a kind of godly apathy. We cry and look around for Him, but He is silent, and we wish He would show up for just a moment of compassion for all we are feeling. And our prayers don't seem to be getting the thorough reading we want them to have when they reach His drowsy throne.

But oh, He does care! Remember Adoniram Judson:

He asked God to send him to India, and God sent him to Burma.

He asked God to give him the security of a warm family, and his devoted wife died of fever.

He asked God that his fevered child might live, and she died.

He asked God to give him many converts so he could feel that God was blessing his ministry, and he struggled for seven empty years to win his first convert to Christ.

And what did he do to keep his sanity while his every prayer seemed to fall on a deaf heaven? He remembered the principle that God is the God of sparrows. He goes on numbering the loss of the old sparrows and counting the eggs in the nests of those new ones as each of them hatches.

The hard times of life are the very province of God's most impressive miracles. There is God, who didn't avoid the human question marks. He hovers above the Cross, weeping, crying over the anguish of His Son. And maybe we are too prone to forget this. We rail at God for ignoring our hurt, when, if we are honest, God passed Pain 101 with flying colors and many tears. Why indeed should we feel that our cross is more special than that carried by Christ? No servant is above his Lord (Matt. 10:24). Where did we ever get the idea that when we became disciples, God said, "Way to go! Thank you so much for believing. I'm so flattered. Here's your very own Hardship Exempt card! If you ever get in trouble, just flash this card, and I'll have you back on your bed of roses in no time."

Rejoice! You Are Loved!

Look at the Cross and try to remember that God will not superstitiously deliver you from either great suffering or death. As many Christians suffer as do non-Christians. Indeed, atheists and devoted saints also die at the same rate. But God is still a sparrow lover. Why do Christians find such preoccupation with the Cross? Because the Cross is evidence that God means it when He says He cares for us and loves us.

The most famous verse of the Bible is also evidence that when God says He cares about us, He really means it: "For God so loved the world that He gave His only begotten Son, that whoever believes in Him should not perish but have everlasting life" (John 3:16).

The Cross has become a tribute to a love that means business. And if you are prone to ask, "How much does God love me?" just remember the words that long ago fell from the poet's pen:

> Could we with ink the oceans fill
> And were the skies of parchment made,
> Were every stock on earth a quill,
> And every man a scribe by trade,

> To write the love of God above
> Would drain those oceans dry,
> Nor would the scroll contain the whole,
> Though stretched from sky to sky

Conclusion

God cares for you. You may count on His concern. Remember the birds: "Are not sparrows two-a-penny? Yet without your father's leave, not one of them may fall."

If God so loves us, we live under requirement, and here is what God requires: "The very hairs of your head are all numbered. Do not fear, therefore; you are of more value than many sparrows" (Matt. 10:30, 31).

As our fathers sang this old hymn, they placed their faith in God's loving care:

> Come ye disconsolate, where ere ye languish.
> Come to the mercy seat fervently kneel.
> Here bring your heartache. Here bring your anguish.
> Earth has no heartache that heaven cannot heal.

Here is an old hymn worth singing, because it helps us remember that we are loved.

> We are pursued by the sparrow lover.
> We are loved by the one who loved us all the way to Calvary.
> So, stand! Stand and declare that love:
>> to the God of sparrows,
>>> to the God of lavish care,
>>>> to the God of the cross.

SUGGESTED ORDER OF WORSHIP

Two-a-Penny

Prelude—Instrumentalist

    NBH 491 *Shine Jesus, Shine*

Call to Worship—PT or Ensemble

    NBH 330 *Spirit of the Living God* (2x in F)

Call to Prayer and Worship—Pastor

Worship in Song—Congregation

    NBH 296 *He Is Exalted* (2x in F)

    NBH 295 *All Hail King Jesus* (2x in F)

    NBH 297 *Majesty* (2x in Bb)

Welcome—Pastoral Staff

Welcome Song *(meet and greet)*—Pastoral Staff

    NBH 299 *Victory Chant* (vv. 1–3 in G)

    NBH 325 *In the Name of the Lord* (2x in G)

    NBH 312 *Jesus, Your Name* (vv. 1–3 in C)

Offertory Prayer—Pastoral Staff

Offertory Praise

    NBH 279 *There Is a Redeemer*—Solo with PT

Message—Pastor

    Two-a-Penny (Matt. 10:24–30)

Hymn of Response—Congregation

    NBH 277 *He Is Lord* (1x in F, 1x in G)

Benediction Hymn—Congregation

    NBH 275 *Celebrate Jesus* (2x in F)

Postlude—Instrumentalist

    NBH 510 *Firm Foundation* (1x in F)

KEY:

NBH: New Baptist Hymnal (2008)

WEEK 40

Samson, the Castaway

Judges 16:18–21; 1 John 1:9
By Harry A. Ironside

Introduction

While a child of God can never lose eternal life, there is a great deal he can lose. Samson's life demonstrates a life of a castaway.

1. Samson Marrying a Philistine (14:2: "I have seen a woman in Timnah of the daughters of the Philistines; now, therefore, get her for me as a wife.")

    He is going to please himself, whether it pleases God or not.

2. Samson Messing with Delilah (15–18)

    Every time Samson gives her a compliment, she wants to know where his strength lies.

3. Samson Making a Confession upon Death (19–31)

    He was appointed by God to destroy the Philistine enemies of God, and now he calls out for one more opportunity to do what he should have done before.

Conclusion

A castaway? Yes, but now in mercy restored, and still used for the blessing of God's people (1 John 1:9).

WEEK 40

Counting the Cost

Luke 14:25–35
By Josh Saefkow

Introduction

Jesus wants those who are contemplating a relationship to count the cost. There are three areas one should consider before becoming a follower of Jesus.

1. Two Costs of Discipleship (14:25–32)

    a. Family (14:26)

    b. Suffering (14:27)

2. Third Cost of Discipleship (14:33–35)

    a. Possessions (14:33)

    b. Conclusion About Saltiness (14:34, 35)

Conclusion

Will you count the cost today and receive Jesus into your heart? Say yes today, and become a faithful follower of Christ.

WEEK 41

The Nobody Savior of a Nobody World

Isaiah 11:1–9
Adapted from a sermon by Dr. Calvin Miller

Introduction

Isaiah rings with power, breaking into joy that Jesus, still eight hundred years unborn, is the branch, a root out of Jesse, a Savior for the nobodies of this world. In this passage Isaiah paints Him as "a nobody Savior for a nobody world." Not recognized in His time, dying ignominiously ... even anonymously, so that anonymous men and women, whom the world might never take note of, might be saved.

Robert Browning took the Pied Piper of Hamelin and set it down in a glorious, near-lyrical kind of verse:

> Into the street the piper crept,
> Smiling first a little smile
> As if he knew what magic slept
> In his quiet pipe ...
> And out of the house the rats came tumbling
> And the grumbling grew to a mighty rumbling.
> Great rats, small rats, lean rats, brawny rats,
> Brown rats, black rats, gray rats, tawny rats
> Grave old plodders, gay young friskers,
> Fathers, mothers, uncles, cousins,
> Cocking tails and pricking whiskers,
> Brothers, sisters, husbands, wives
> Families by tens and dozens,
> Followed the piper for their lives.

Browning is not so much talking about rats as he is an infected world, hungry for a piper who lures us toward decent values with a redeeming message. Rats, rascals, children, scamps, and all the people of the whole world—all the nobodies who have ever lived are looking for a worthy piper.

Always Pick the Proper Piper

Why would any thinking person ever want to follow such a tyrant as Adolf Hitler? If you were to talk to someone who lived in Germany during the World War II era, you may find that, especially if it was an older person, he or she is a bit embarrassed to admit that the whole nation wholeheartedly followed such a heinous piper.

In *The Man in the Glass Booth*, Adolf Eichmann stands to defend himself before his Jewish jurors. He shouts out through the bulletproof glass of his box, "People of Israel, had he chosen you, you too would have followed."

Contrast such a megalomaniac as Hitler with Jesus. Isaiah said, "He has no form or comeliness; and when we see Him, there is no beauty that we should desire Him" (52:2). Christ was seen truly as a nobody in His own time.

In 1900 Albert Schweitzer published his epic, *The Quest of the Historical Jesus*, and the book literally rocked the world. Schweitzer clearly stated that if Jesus Christ was really as almighty as the Gospels proclaim Him to be, surely there would be some mention of Him in the secular histories of His day. Surely, he reasoned, some historian would have mentioned such a mighty man as Jesus, yet none of His contemporaries did. The German physician searched the Roman annals of the day (which the Romans kept faithfully year by year—hence the name *annals*) and found not one mention of Jesus between 7 BC and AD 27, the years of Christ's earthly life. So Schweitzer concluded that nothing official could be known of His years upon the earth.

Jesus Christ, according to Schweitzer, was a historical nobody! But what a nobody! Isaiah spoke of Him eight hundred years before He came into the world, calling Him a root out of Jacob. Job thought of Him in much the same way; he saw a burned-out stump (Job 14:7) that, at the scent of water, budded and sent a sprout out of the deadness of its charred soul. So uncomely was this Jesus that the historians of the world missed Him, somehow. Yet mighty became the sprout out of Jesse.

God Saving Nobodies

Some believe that Matthew 1 is a waste of time up to verse 18. The initial seventeen verses include what has been called (under the force of the King James Bible) the "begat" passages. But what you must realize is that Matthew 1:1–17 is about Jesus' ancestors. What was so notable about His ancestry? Perhaps the whole point is that there is not a great deal that is notable about His forebears. Jesus came from a long list of largely non-historical nobodies. But then that is exactly the meaning of grace. God loves, saves, and then uses nobodies, and the combined force of the faith of these nobodies in the end rewrote the history of the world. These nobodies followed their "non-Schweitzer" Lord until the world was filled with charity: hospitals, orphanages, universities, and a million charitable industries that gave what people could never pay for—grace and forgiveness, health and education.

But let us turn to this table of nobodies that occupy the first seventeen verses of the New Testament.

Consider Matthew's list of the nobodies whom, throughout biblical history, God found the grace to save and use to create the kingdom of God. Abraham comes first on the list. Who was he, after all? A onetime moon worshiper perhaps, who took a concubine to try to hurry God along with his promise of an heir. Then there was Isaac, blessing the wrong son, to the odd right purposes of God's plan. Then there was Jacob, "the Supplanter," whose crooked dealings would have landed him in prison in our time. Then there was Rahab, the Arab harlot, whose profession may have been less chaste than God would have preferred it to be, but there she shows up as one of the ever-so-great-grandmothers of Jesus.

Well, all these people on Matthew's list suggest that ultimately Jesus came from a long line of scalawag sand scoundrels, to live the perfect sinless life, in order to redeem scalawags and scoundrels.

A Closer Look at the Savior

"Well," says Isaiah, "this family tree isn't as crucial as we might wish, because when the Messiah comes, He will literally be a root out of dry ground." The hope of God is never to be listed among the beautiful people. God can draw from a stump of nobodies a root of life, a nobody Savior for a nobody world.

Here's how Isaiah really defined the faith:

The Spirit of the LORD shall rest upon him,

The Spirit of wisdom and understanding,
The Spirit of counsel and might,
The Spirit of knowledge and of the fear of the LORD.

(Is. 11:2)

Here's how James Moffatt translates the next two verses:

He will not judge by appearances,
    nor decide by hearsay,
But act with justice to the helpless
    and decide fairly for the humble;
He will strike down the ruthless with his verdicts
    And slay the unjust with his sentences.
Justice shall gird him up for action,
    he shall be belted with trustworthiness

(Is. 11:3, 4 Moffatt).

So what is the ultimate impact of this Christ? This Savior of a nobody world will delight in the power of God and the fear of the Lord. When God's kingdom, in its merciful peace and joy, is finished, "the wolf shall ... dwell with the lamb, [and] the leopard shall lie down with the young goat" (Is. 11:6). One day the whole animal kingdom will be tamed, brought to oneness with the power of God. Infants will play over the den of the cobra.

This great Jesus, having tamed the whole of nature at one time, now invites you to His heart. In John 10:7 He says, "I am the door of the sheep." It is an invitation to join Him and dwell with Him in His great heart of love. It is a lovely respite, precisely because it is the only eternal respite. Cherish this invitation to enter into the Christ life, for there is no "other name under heaven given among men by which we must be saved" (Acts 4.12). This Christ is the great Messiah of Isaiah 11, who creates His colony of grace from His army of nobodies:

They shall not hurt nor destroy in all My holy mountain,
    For the earth shall be full of the knowledge of the Lord
        As the waters cover the sea.

(Is. 11:9)

Conclusion

Your fullest self—your greatest destiny—all begins with a simple confession, "Lord, I am a nobody in great need of the Somebody that can change my life, and make from its tawdry values system a disciple of Yourself." And this peace begins the moment you say, "Lord, I am weary with my own nobody status. I give You my life, this nothing that I am. Receive my warring soul into Your peace. May the Rod out of Jesse cause my own deadness to live for reasons beyond myself. I stand in repentance and await the renovation that will make me usable for greater purposes than I could ever know without You.

I wait for grace with just one simple plea:
Deliver me from self, to what you'd have me be.

SUGGESTED ORDER OF WORSHIP

The Nobody Savior of a Nobody World

Prelude—Instrumentalists

NBH 162 *Wonderful, Merciful Savior*

Call to Praise—Congregation

NBH 625 *I Will Sing of the Mercies of the Lord* (2x in C)

NBH 129 *Sing to the King* (v. 1, chorus, v. 2, chorus in F)

NBH 120 *Made Me Glad* (v. 1, chorus, v. 2, chorus, v. 3, chorus in Bb)

Prayer of Praise—Pastoral Staff

Welcome—Pastoral Staff

Song of Welcome (*meet and greet*)—Congregation

NBH 453 *Leaning on the Everlasting Arms* (v. 1, chorus, v. 3, chorus in G)

Worship and Praise—Congregation

NBH 374 *The Longer I Serve Him* (chorus, v. 1, chorus, v. 2, chorus in G)

NBH 440 *Here I Am, Lord* (v. 1, chorus, v. 2, chorus, v. 3, chorus in G)

Offertory Prayer—Pastoral Staff

Offertory Praise

NBH 232 *The Power of the Cross* (v. 1, chorus, v. 2, chorus, v. 3, chorus, v. 4, chorus in C)

NBH 130 *Here I Am to Worship* (v. 1, chorus, v. 2, chorus in F)

Sermon—Pastor

The Nobody Savior of a Nobody World (Is. 11:1–9)

Hymn of Invitation—Congregation

NBH411 *Come Just as You Are* (as needed)

Benediction Hymn—Congregation

NBH 151 *Bless His Holy Name* (2x in Eb)

Postlude—Instrumentalists

NBH 20 *Great and Mighty* (2x in Eb)

KEY:

NBH: New Baptist Hymnal (2008)

WEEK 41

How Jesus Closed the Book

Luke 4:20

By Rev. John Daniel Jones

Introduction

Every reader who has read on previous Sabbaths has closed the book when the lesson is done; no one has ever closed it as Jesus did. There is finality about the act of Jesus, which does not belong to any other closing.

1. Jesus is the completion and fulfillment of the prophet Isaiah (Luke 4:18, 19).

2. Jesus is the completion of the Old Testament.

3. Jesus is the completion of divine revelation.

Conclusion

Jesus closes the book on the world and every human soul. And what a happy and beautiful ending to the Book our Lord supplies!

WEEK 41

The Heart of a Soul-Winner

Acts 20:1–27
By Dr. Jerry Vines

The greatest soul-winner in history is Jesus Christ Himself. I guess the next greatest soul-winner has to be the apostle Paul.

From Paul we learn certain ingredients of being a successful winner of the lost (Acts 20:18–20).

1. The Attitude of a Soul-Winner

   a. Dependability (20:18)

   b. Humility (20:19)

   c. Sincerity (20:10)

   If you have someone on your heart, if you have a burden for them, you will be surprised what God will do when you start praying. Ask God to break your heart for those people. Submit yourself to Him, and you may have the joy of seeing those people saved. Wouldn't that be wonderful? That's the attitude of a soul-winner.

2. The Approach of a Soul-Winner

   How did Paul approach the matter of soul-winning? There is a threefold approach in verse 20.

   a. Personal Conviction (20:20, 27)

   Here is Paul's personal conviction—the need of the human heart.

   b. Public Instruction (20:20)

   Paul often conducted large public meetings. It is a stirring time when people gather together and the gospel is publicly preached.

   c. Private Presentation (20:20)

   Private presentation is going into homes and presenting the

gospel, probably the best place to present the message.

3. The Appeal of the Soul-Winner

   a. Turn from sin (20:21)

      That is the meaning of *repentance*—an about-face, a change of mind about yourself, your sin, and Jesus.

   b. Turn to Jesus (20:21)

      When you turn from your sin, then you turn to the Lord Jesus Christ. The very moment you invite Jesus into your heart, you are saved!

WEEK 42

Call His Name ... Let's See ... Bill!

An Evangelistic Sermon
Joshua 6:1–6, 20; Matthew 1:21–25
By Dr. Calvin Miller

Introduction

For most parents, naming their first child can present some difficulty. Do we go with something everyday—Anna, perhaps? Or something less common, like Nirvana or Flannery? What if it's a boy? Old-school, like Robert or Richard? Or a more modern name, like Ace? The choices are endless, and the decision can be a real struggle of soul. Every mom and dad wants to be sure that the name they select is one that their child can live with for life.

Unlike us, Mary and Joseph had the baby-naming problem solved well ahead of time.

Jesus, the Common Name (Matt. 1:21)

What happens in Matthew 1:21 is a beautiful thing. An angel comes to the waiting mother and father with a specific name: Jesus. This may have surprised Mary and Joseph, since theirs was to be a very special baby, while Jesus was not a very special name. Every Tom, Dick, and Harry in Israel was named Jesus! There were so many Jesuses that it's incredible that the angel would come in with such an utterly commonplace name! It would be the equivalent of an angel flapping into your room and saying, "Your baby will rule the nations—name him Bill!"

Well, the angel gives the instruction to name this baby Jesus, the most common name of a common Savior, "the Savior named Bill." "Thou shalt call His name Joshua (*Jesus* is a transliteration of the Hebrew name *Joshua*.), because He's going to save His people from their sin," shouts the angel.

Jesus, a Messiah in Common Clothes

How could this high drama come in such a simple way? Can you tell me that this great Jesus entered through something as common as a womb? A birth canal? The Jesus who was born as the "Lamaze Jesus," was it He who would redeem us? Wrapped in Pampers or Huggies, was this the Jesus who would redeem us? The all-too-human, all-too-common Son of God?

Poet Luci Shaw wrote:

> After
> The bright beam of hot annunciation
> Fused heaven with dark earth
> His searing sharply-focused light
> Went out for a while
> Eclipsed in amniotic gloom:
> His cool immensity of splendor
> His universal grace
> Small-folded in a warm dim
> Female space—
> The Word stern-sentenced
> To be nine months dumb—
> Infinity walled in a womb
> Until the next enormity—
> The Mighty, after submission
> To a woman's pains
> Helpless on a barn-bare floor
> First-tasting bitter earth.[51]

Jesus, the Ever-Present Incarnation

Some years ago, a coal mine collapsed in West Virginia. A group of men were trapped deep in the bowels of the earth for a long period of time. All the people were trying to get through to see if there were any left alive, and they were sinking a new shaft in a hopeful rescue attempt. Finally, by God's grace, these men were all set free at the zero

---

[51] Luci Shaw, "Made Flesh," *Listen to the Green* (Wheaton, IL: Harold Shaw Publishers, 1971), 77.

hour. Bystanders asked them how they kept their minds together. One man replied, "I have a secret. It's the Redeemer who will not leave men long in dark places." Viewers were amazed as he quoted his secret of survival on national television:

> Such knowledge is too wonderful for me;
> It is high, I cannot attain it.
> Where can I go from Your Spirit?
> Or where can I flee from Your presence?
> If I ascend into heaven, You are there;
> If I make my bed in hell, behold, You are there.
> If I take the wings of the morning,
> And dwell in the uttermost parts of the sea,
> Even there Your hand shall lead me,
> And Your right hand shall hold me.
>
> (Ps. 139:6–10)

This Jesus named by an angel didn't leave us comfortless for long. A Savior named Bill. The great commoner! Not saying, "I'll live up here, at a safe, secure distance," but "I will be involved, and not one of My children will ever go through any nightmare experience where I will not be with them."

Jesus' Great Namesake (Josh. 6:12–14)

I want to show you how faith works. Joshua 6 contains the picture of Jesus' great namesake—the man after whom He was named! Joshua was given a most unusual assignment. In Joshua 6, Joshua could not inhabit the great promised land of Canaan, because the enemies owned it. And there, in the middle of the enemy's encampment, was a great walled city named Jericho. Joshua could not possibly hope to set up a nation in a land where there was already another kingdom.

Joshua 6:12 says, "Joshua rose early in the morning, and the priests took up the ark of the Lord." Now, one can almost hear these priests say, "Oh, not again! Let's all sleep in! Not one more mindless march around this city!" Yet they did it day after day. The Bible says in verse 13, "Then seven priests bearing seven trumpets ... went on continually and blew with the trumpets. And the armed men went before them.

But the rear guard came after the ark of the Lord, while the priests continued blowing the trumpets." Now, I can visualize the people in this city, standing up on the walls, wondering, *What in the world is going on? They're not attacking the city, but they're just marching around it.* As they march, you can almost see these people laughing and making fun of them.

God has never yet saved anybody without asking for a participation of faith: the Israelites would march around the city, trusting that God somehow had a reason for what he asked of them. So they marched around six days until, on the seventh day, the walls collapsed. Marching ... playing trumpets ... marching ... playing trumpets ... marching ... playing trumpets!

I want to ask you to imagine the priests marching around the city, incessantly blowing on the horns, until finally there's a bad case of jitters in Jericho, and then God redeems.

Jesus the Deliverer (Josh. 6:20, 21)

When the angel said to Mary and Joseph, "Name this boy Jesus," it was as if the Lord Himself were saying, "I'm enclosing My life in an event. And the event is this: if you trust Me and do what I say, I will provide you a way out."

Who is Jesus? What is Jesus? He is the *Exodus*, the way out.

One of the most important verses in the Bible is 2 Corinthians 5:19: "God was in Christ reconciling the world to Himself ... and has committed to us the word of reconciliation." This verse tells us that there's a way out. When life doesn't work, just remember: God noticed a long time ago and sent Jesus.

Conclusion

Charles Swindoll told about a boy who colored all his pictures black. Someone finally asked him, "Why don't you use pretty colors?" He said, "Oh, I would love to have a colored picture. But my desk is in the far corner of the room, and when I go up to get the colors out of the box, the only one left is the black crayon."

And that's how life works. We don't have it all like we want. But the truth is, there's a way out. Jesus Christ has come, Jesus, the commoner, born of a woman to make life as special as you will let Him. "Call his name Jesus—*Yeshua*—the Great Commoner. Immanuel, God with us, reminds us that if He hadn't come to be with us—we'd be alone, with no way out.

SUGGESTED ORDER OF WORSHIP

Call His Name ... Let's See ... Bill!

Prelude—Instrumentalist

NBH 347 *Lord, I Lift Your Name on High* (2x in G)

Call to Prayer—Pastoral Staff

Welcome—Pastoral Staff

NBH 342 *Thy Word* (chorus, v. 1, chorus, v. 2, chorus in F)

NBH 527 *The Greatest Thing* (vv. 1–3 in F)

NBH 344 *Ancient Words* (v. 1, chorus, v. 2, chorus in F)

NBH 349 *Great Is the Lord Almighty* (chorus, v. 1, chorus, v. 2, chorus, v. 3, chorus in Bb)

Baptismal Celebration—Pastoral Staff

Prayer of Commitment—Pastoral Staff

NBH 451 *In Moments Like These* (2x in D)

Scripture Reading from Joshua 6:1–17, 20, 21, 27 (*Please have prepared for IMAG*)

Now Jericho was securely shut up because of the children of Israel; none went out, and none came in. And the LORD said to Joshua: "See! I have given Jericho into your hand, its king, and the mighty men of valor. You shall march around the city, all you men of war; you shall go all around the city once. This you shall do six days. And seven priests shall bear seven trumpets of rams' horns before the ark. But the seventh day you shall march around the city seven times, and the priests shall blow the trumpets. It shall come to pass, when they make a long blast with the ram's horn, and when you hear the sound of the trumpet, that all the people shall shout with a great shout; then the wall of the city will fall down flat. And the people shall go up every man straight before him." Then Joshua the son of Nun called the priests and said to them, "Take up the ark of the covenant, and let seven priests bear seven trumpets of rams' horns before the ark of the LORD." And he said to the people, "Proceed, and march around the city, and let him who is armed advance before the ark of the LORD." So it was, when Joshua had spoken to the people, that the seven priests bearing the seven trumpets of rams' horns before the Lord advanced and blew the trumpets, and the ark of the covenant of the LORD followed them. The armed men went before the priests who blew the trumpets, and the rear guard came after the ark, while the priests continued blowing the trumpets. Now Joshua had commanded the people, saying, "You shall not shout or make any noise with your voice, nor shall a word proceed out of your mouth, until the day I say to you, 'Shout!' Then you shall shout." So he had the ark of the LORD circle the city, going around it once. Then they came into the camp and lodged in the camp. And Joshua rose early in the morning, and the priests took up the ark of the LORD. Then seven priests bearing seven trumpets of rams' horns before the ark of the LORD went on continually and blew with the trumpets. And the armed men went before them. But the rear guard came after the ark of the LORD, while the priests continued blowing the trumpets. And the second day they marched around the city once and returned to the camp. So they did six days. But it came to pass on the seventh day that they rose early, about the dawning of the day, and marched around the city seven times in the same manner. On that day only they marched around the city seven times. And the seventh time it happened, when the priests blew the trumpets, that Joshua said to the people: "Shout, for the LORD has given you the city! Now the city shall be doomed by the LORD to destruction, it and all who are in it. Only Rahab the harlot shall live, she and all who are with her in the house, because she hid the messengers that we sent.... So the people shouted when the priests blew the trumpets. And it happened when the people heard the sound of the trumpet, and the people shouted with a great shout, that the wall fell down flat. Then the people went up into the city, every man straight before him, and they took the city. And they utterly destroyed all that was in the city, both man and woman, young and old, ox and sheep and donkey, with the edge of the sword.... So the LORD was with Joshua, and his fame spread throughout all the country.

Prayer of Thanksgiving—Pastor

Offertory Praise—PT with Congregation

> NBH481 *Breathe* (2x in A)

Message—Pastor

> *Call His Name ... Let's See ... Bill* (Josh. 6:1–6; Matt. 1:21–25)

Hymn of Response/Invitation—Congregation

> NBH 460 *His Strength Is Perfect* (2x in F)

Benediction Hymn—Congregation

> NBH 480 *Step by Step* (2x in F)

Postlude—Instrumentalist

> NBH 498 *I Will Call Upon the Lord* (2x in C)

KEY:

NBH: New Baptist Hymnal (2008)

WEEK 42

Under the Shadow of the Cross

Luke 22:19

By A. B. Simpson

Introduction

The Lord's Supper is a sort of microcosm, or miniature, of the believer's life, and over every moment, every word, and every action, we may well inscribe, "Do this in remembrance of Me." Let us contemplate the Cross in its practical relation to our actual Christian life.

1. Refuge for the Sinner

When a sinner recognizes his guilt, what refuge can he take apart from the Cross?

2. Refuge for the Tempted

When temptation comes and the newborn soul has found its first stumbling stone, what can bring deliverance and victory but the Cross of Calvary?

3. Salvation from the Effects of Sin

Sometimes our past comes back like an ocean of misery and overwhelms us.

4. Sanctification Through the Cross

When we come to the great conflict with inbred sin, we find once more that the Cross has made provision not only for our justification but also for our sanctification

5. Healing Through the Cross

The shadow of the Cross touches our mortal frame; our very bodies have been redeemed; our liability to sickness because of sin has been canceled by Christ's death.

Conclusion

What significance will the Cross have in connection with the crown? There shall be no joy, there shall be no glory, there shall be no crown for us there that did not come from some surrender, some sacrifice, some renunciation, and some crucifixion here. God help us, therefore, to stamp upon all our life below and our crown above the passion sign of the Cross.

WEEK 42

Tell Them Your Testimony

Acts 26:1–23

By Jason H. Barber

Introduction

God desires that we use our own story of life change to share the gospel. Every opportunity to speak to men is an opportunity to speak of Christ.

1. Recount your condition before knowing Christ (26:4, 5, 9–11).

    Paul was:

    a. A Pharisee (v. 5)

    b. A persecutor (vv. 9–11)

2. Recall your conversion to Christ (vv. 12–18).

3. Recommend your commission by Christ (vv. 16–18).

    a. Jesus sent Paul as a minister and witness in order to:

    i. Open their closed eyes (2 Cor. 4:4, 6)

    ii. Turn them from darkness to light (1 Pet. 2:9)

    iii. Turn them from the power of Satan to the power of God

    b. That they may receive:

    i. Forgiveness

    ii. An inheritance

    iii. Christlikeness of life

4. Reaffirm your commitment to Christ (v. 19: "I was not disobedient"; v. 22: "to this day I stand").

Conclusion

Success in evangelism is sharing God's good news of salvation in the power of the Holy Spirit and leaving the results to God. Was Paul unsuccessful (v. 28)? He was successful because he was faithful. Like Paul, faithfully tell your story.

WEEK 43

The Evangelist Is a Rebel Lover

2 Samuel 15:1–5; 18:5–9, 14, 33
By Dr. Calvin Miller

Introduction

Absalom was the rebel son of a king—a prince who stabbed at his father's love. In 2 Samuel 15 the heart of this rebel is disclosed. What lay in his heart? What drove his rebellion? Just this hidden cry of pride: "If only I were king, I would do things better!" Arrogance is the engine that drives most rebellions. It is always easy to see how we would do it, until it is our time to do it!

"If only I were king, I would do it better," cried Absalom. He, of course, never lived to be king, so we have no idea how he actually would have managed. But rebels are often such shallow dreamers that all they envision is grandeur. As the rebel Lenin would improve on Czar Nicholas II, or Castro would improve on Batista, or Ortega on Somoza, so Absalom as king would improve upon the reign of his father, David.

To complete their dreams rebels usually are more savage than kind. They pick the moments when the establishment is napping, and they are wide-awake and ready for the fight.

So Lenin rode through Sweden on a sealed train when the czar had resigned and the imperial army was in rags.

Mao moved against Chiang when Japan had China at bay.

Absalom, too, moved his war against a father whose age and house had lost their taste for war. It was then that he came to test his father's stamina.

The Care of the Father

But never mind the son—what was the father doing? Did he rage and rail against his self-serving son? Did he want to crush him in the coils of war, of hate and destruction?

Hardly.

As the soldiers left, he whispered to his high general, Joab, "Deal gently with the young man Absalom, for my sake. No matter his hostility—answer him only in love." (2 Sam. 18:5, paraphrased).

"Care, Joab!" cried the weeping king.

Joab curled his lip against the rebel and moved out to lead the army.

The helmets caught the sun. The king cried over the battlements in a voice made faint by iron rims on cobblestone, and winding, dusty distance.

"Care, Joab!"

What David really cried was, "Every rebel is loved," but his cry was swallowed up by Absalom's self-concern.

Thus the tragedy is formed; the rebel must pay.

We, Too, Are Rebels Against Love

And who are we? We are Absalom burn anew. Christ entered the pain of this world. If we desire to help Christ with His rescue plans, we must go with Him and enter the world beyond our church. We must carry out our conquest of love with our loving Commander at the helm. But we are the lazy envoys. We would rather do our saving work where almost no one is lost—inside the church. So we sing thirty-two verses of "Just as I Am" for three struggling primary children who are standing in the pew, trying to think what Big Bird would do. But at last they come, saving not just their little souls but our sleepy reputations. Then at last we can go to the evangelism conference with some baptisms to report.

Children are precious to God, but are they our best shot at evangelistic reputation? Are there rebels with more stature? Is there not someone not already wooed by a gospel cable network? Is there not a genuine non-cable-watching sinner not traumatized by overexposure—a macho sinner with a one-*Playboy*, three-wife, four-martini-per-day aroma about him? What of these class-A renegades, these lost-forever rebels?

Where are they? How did we miss them? Why, they are all around our churches, yet never come inside them. Between margaritas, they are often sober enough to answer the doorbell and ask, "What must we do to be saved?"—if ever we go there to ask.

What, Really, Are the Two Questions?

But our first question in caring is not, "If you were to die, do you know for sure?" The first question is, "How are you?"

"How are you?" I ask you! Are you not struck dumb that no plan of salvation out there teaches us to ask three questions, instead of only two? But those who care begin by asking, "How are you?" and after "How are you?" "How are Madge and the kids?"

"Madge and the kids?" I ask you.

Simple and lovely niceties show how much we care, and as the cliché goes, people don't care how much we know till they know how much we care. Rebel-catching is rarely done by our clever schematics. We waste a lot of time trying to question and answer people into the kingdom of God. Maybe we ought to try caring people into Christ.

Rebels Rarely Ask for Rescue

Rebels rarely ask for rescue. There is something in them that cries out for it. Absalom would likely have it different. Do you not see that some of Absalom longed for his father? In his mind, and only in his mind, would he help seize the royal palace and kill his father? In his heart there was a yearning to embrace the very father his heart would kill. Rebels always have two forces tearing their insides out—they want to fight, and yet they want to be loved.

Can you not remember that awful struggle of your rebel heart against God? You fought Him as He tried to lift you from your sin, yet you reached for His embrace. You did not want God, yet at the same time you wanted all of God that you could hold. "Crucify" we cry against Christ even as we try to choke the words to silence. We are rebels and hateful lovers, the loving haters of the great Almighty who loves us.

We are Christians, little Christs—little rescuers of a sinking world. How do they tell us they are sinking? How do they cry out to us by ignoring us? They speak their needs in hidden phrases. Listen to their crying hearts, and know their self-protective rhetoric. "If you died today, would you . . ."

"Please, I think my spiritual life is a very personal thing."

"I never discuss religion!"

"I'm quite happy in the church I never go to."

"I'm Episcopalian, you know—thoroughbred—registered, papers and all."

"I gave my heart to Brother Moseby when I was ten. It is enough."

"I send ten dollars to Brother Cable every time his makeup gets thin."

"I don't believe in organized religion."

"My father was a Baptist, my mother was a Methodist, and I'm a somnambulist."

Still, there is something to this question-and-answer business. People are there, longing for the encounter, if we can get the questions right. These needy rebels are loved, and we are their lovers—we bear the word of faith—saving faith.

But hear the last thing our King whispers over the battlements as we choke down the last donut and leave the evangelism training room: "Please care. Deal gently with the young rebel, for My sake."

The Great Sin of the Church

Apathy is the great sin of the church.

If there was anything that Absalom prided himself on, it was his Afro. How do I know he had an afro? I don't, I just wonder if he might have. Rebels sometimes have a way of wearing their hair a little funny. If the straights have long hair, they get crew cuts. If the straights have crew cuts, they wear it long. The key thing is just don't look like the establishment.

Naturally, his father's cabinet had protested. Most of the time when they passed Absalom in the corridors of the palace, and Absalom said, "Shalom," they said, in a strong Hebrew imperative, "Galech"—which, being interpreted, is, "Get a haircut, you wild kid!" Absalom got a little tired of it all.

It amazed King David how no one saw Absalom's finer points. He was a child of God! He was unaccepted, ridiculed, and a social outcast. Yet his very name, Absalom, meant "Father of Peace." And it is funny that the king never noticed how long his hair was! My, how God loves those who we feel are so odd and so different. God loved him from the womb, and so it is with all rebels.

Rabindrinath Tagore wrote, "Every child comes with the message that God is not yet discouraged of man." And even as the king, like every father with a new son, looks at his baby, his heart, too, hopes.

"My son will do it better than I have. He will run where I have stumbled. He will love where I have lusted. He will serve God where I have served only myself!"

Now the child, all bright with hope, is a lost rebel.

Still, rebels have dreams. They are beautiful dreams, plans, life-sized blueprints that always spell success.

What Happens When Our Rebellion Fails?

Absalom's day ended in tangled shame. He was hanging by his hair in the tree. His rebellion was now dreamless. And then Joab listened, and the very breezes whispered the old king's words, "Care, Joab ... care, Joab ... care, Joab!"

But Joab took three spears and drove them through the heart, and the rebel died. He was dead, caught in the tangled thickets of his lost dreams.

But the rebel was not the only thing that died; along with him died the major part of the old man's heart. And as each messenger came, he asked again, "Is the young man Absalom safe?" Ahimahaz was sure they had won the battle. But that is not what the old man wanted to know. The Cushite came in at last to tell the rebel's final tale: "May the enemies of my lord the king, and all who rise against you to do harm, be like that young man!" (2 Sam 18:32).

And the father wept.

> Then the king was deeply moved, and went up to the chamber over the gate, and wept. And as he went, he said thus: "O, my son Absalom—my son, my son Absalom—if only I had died in your place! O Absalom my son, my son!" (2 Sam. 18:33).

And thus is the unclaimed love of a father, like a great diamond, Star of India, exposed in the window of a pawnshop. A thing of great value made cheap and lost.

God alone grieves the loss of rebels! Apathy—who comforts a king when a rebel dies? No one does that much. They saw only the rebel's long hair and remembered his Bolshevism. But not the king! He wept. Apathy ... it bakes casseroles for church fellowships while battles rage in the woods of Ephraim. And turnpike-wide, they drive forward like lemmings into hell. Churches don't cry. Seminaries don't cry. Only God cries.

For the rebels are lost ... perished and gone! Not just lost, but hanging in the tangled thickets of life, trying in their last moments or first to make meaning of it all. Waiting for a kinder Joab who can weep with God. We shoot our wounded too—Joab-like, in the thickets of Ephraim.

Conclusion

Drugs, booze, the cancer ward, the divorce courts ... *the cities themselves are the thickets!* And God weeps and waits, and Jesus, levitating from Olivet, cries out ... "Into all the world ...."

> Please care ... please care ... please care.
> Don't take a plan of salvation ... or any other plan.
> Take Me, the dying Christ, and get to the hurting world.
> For they hang by the millions, dying in tangled woods, with tangled minds!

We can clear the thickets. We must tell each hurting and lost person of God's extravagance; we must tell them that God offers every rebel:

> More sky than he can see
> More seas than he can sail,
> More sun than he can bear to watch
> More stars than he can scale.
> More breath than he can breathe,
> More yield than he can sow.
> More grace than he can comprehend.
> More love than he can know![52]

---

[52] Ralph W. Seager in *The Treasure Chest*.

SUGGESTED ORDER OF WORSHIP

The Evangelist Is a Rebel Lover

Prelude—Instrumental Group

NBH 271 *My Redeemer Lives* (2x in D)

Prayer of Worship—Pastoral Staff

Worship and Praise—Congregation

NBH 264 *Worthy Is the Lamb* (2x in A)

Welcome—Pastoral Staff

Song of Welcome *(meet and greet)*—Congregation

NBH 271 *My Redeemer Lives* (2x in D)

NBH 66 *Open the Eyes of My Heart* (2x in D)

NBH 318 *His Name Is Life* (2x in D)

NBH 83 *Be Thou My Vision* (v. 1, v. 3 in D, v. 4 in Eb)

Testimony of Praise (2-minute video)

Offertory Prayer—Pastoral Staff

Offertory Praise

NBH 87 *My Lord Is with Me All the Time* (v. 1, chorus, v. 2, chorus, v. 3, chorus in D)

Message—Pastor

The Evangelist Is a Rebel Lover (2 Sam. 15:1–5; 18:5–9, 14, 33)

Hymn of Response/Invitation—Congregation

NBH 435 *Just as I Am* (as needed)

Benediction Hymn—Congregation

NBH 102 *Think About His Love* (2x in Eb)

Postlude—Instrumental Group

    NBH 13 *Joyful, Joyful, We Adore Thee*

KEY:

CH: Celebration Hymnal (Word Music/Integrity Music, Nashville, TN)

NBH: New Baptist Hymnal (2008)

WH: The Hymnal (Word Music, Nashville, TN)

SPW: Songs for Praise and Worship (Word Music, Nashville, TN)

MSPW: More Songs for Praise and Worship (Word Music, Nashville, TN)

MSPW2: More Songs for Praise and Worship 2 (Word Music, Nashville, TN)

WEEK 43

The Door to Heaven

Revelation 4:1
By George W. Truett

Introduction

What does the Bible teach about heaven?

1. Heaven is a place.

2. Heaven is a holy place.

3. Heaven is a busy place.

4. Heaven is a populous place.

Conclusion

O church, I love you as I love no other institution in all the earth. Christ's masterpiece is the church. I am not depending on the church one iota to get me to heaven. O baptism, beautiful symbol of the burial and resurrection of our glorious Lord, I delight in thee, but I am not depending one iota on baptismal waters to get to the land above the stars. Oh, good men all about me, whose fellowship is sweet, and whose counsels priceless, I treasure them all, but there is just one door to heaven and that door is Christ Jesus. Have you chosen that door?

WEEK 43

Seven Reasons Christians Share the Gospel

2 Corinthians 5:1–20
By Jack R. Smith

1. Reasons Christians Are Not Sharing the Gospel

    a. There is opposition by the forces of the devil, because in soul-winning, you are, in effect, invading the enemy camp to free hostages.

    b. There is fear of failure, partly because of a misunderstanding of the mandate.

    c. There is fear of rejection by the lost person.

    d. There is even occasional opposition from non-witnessing fellow believers.

    e. Low self-esteem causes Christians who sincerely want to witness to feel like failures, because they think they can't do it as well as others.

    f. Many Christians do not witness simply because they do not know what to say.

    g. Church members who have never been exposed to a happy, witnessing believer—who have no mentor, no role model—have a hard time imagining themselves in that role.

2. Reasons for Sharing the Gospel

    In 2 Corinthians 5, at least seven compelling reasons are given for telling the good news.

    a. Christians share the gospel because of its worth (5:1–8).

        Many reasons could be listed for the gospel's worth, but the worth of the gospel is epitomized at the burial scene of the body of a saint of God. The priceless value of the pearl of great price soars to new heights in the understanding of the saved loved ones of the deceased—and 10,000 times more for the one who has gone to be with the Lord.

b. Christians share the gospel because of a desire to please Christ (5:9).

c. Christians share the gospel because of respect for the judgment seat of Christ (5:10).

d. Christians share the gospel because we know what it is to fear the Lord (5:11).

e. Christians share the gospel because of the compelling love of Christ (5:14).

f. Christians share the gospel because of a different worldview (5:16).

   i. It is based on how we regard Christ.

   ii. It is based on how we regard one who is in Christ.

   iii. It is based on how God makes the difference.

WEEK 44

Your Most Strategic Investment

Why, How, and What to Pray for Your Spiritual Leaders
Romans 15:30–33
By Dr. Daniel Henderson

Introduction

The Enemy's Strategic Attack

We are in a spiritual battle for the souls of men. Our spiritual leaders are on the front line of this battle and face constant attacks.

A Call to Counterattack

Paul knew that prayer was essential to spiritual victory. He constantly prayed for his disciples (Rom. 1:9; Phil. 1:4; Col. 1:3; 1 Thess. 3:10; 2 Thess. 1:11; 2 Tim. 1:3; Philem. 4). He also requested prayer for his life and ministry (2 Cor. 1:8–11; also Eph. 6:18, 19; Col. 4:2–4; 1 Thess. 5:25; 2 Thess. 3:1).

In Romans 15 Paul wrote that he planned to deliver a love offering to the Jewish believers in Jerusalem as he completed his collections among the Gentile churches. Afterward he hoped to visit the believers in Rome, then travel to Spain to preach the gospel. Paul urged the believers in Rome to pray for him, with specific instruction on why, how, and what they should pray as they engaged in their most strategic investment of focused intercession.

1. Why We Must Pray for Christian Leaders (v. 30)

We can do the right things for the wrong reasons. Prayer is the right thing to do. Paul gives us solid motives for our obedient intercession.

Our Duty to Pray

Paul began this appeal by saying, "Now I beg you, brethren." He used the Greek term *parakaleo*, which means "to call to one's side"[53] As he also did in 1 Timothy 2:1–3, Paul urges Christians to intercede for leaders. Knowing it is our duty to do so, we should pray.

Our Regard for Christ

Beyond duty, we must have overarching desire. This desire is rooted in our esteem and worship of Christ. Paul compelled the Romans to pray "through the Lord Jesus Christ" (Rom. 15:30). Not only are we only able to pray by Christ's provision (Heb. 7:25; 10:20–22), but also we are motivated to pray because of Christ's person—His glory, His name, and His renown.

Our Love for the Spirit

Paul also calls us to pray "through the love of the Spirit" (Rom. 15:30). The most literal rendering for this is "by your love for the Holy Spirit."[54] Our love for the person and power of the Holy Spirit motivates us to pray for the demonstration of the Spirit in the lives and ministries of our spiritual leaders.

2. How We Must Pray for Christian Leaders (v. 30b)

Paul requested of the Roman believers, "Strive together with me in prayers to God for me." This reflects the intense nature of prayer due to the seriousness of the spiritual battle we face. He called on his readers to contend with spiritual adversaries as they fought and strained on their knees. (See John 18:36; 1 Cor. 9:25; Col. 4:12; 1 Tim. 4:10; 6:12; 2 Tim 4:7)

3. What to Pray for Christian Leaders (vv. 31, 32)

a. Prayers for *protection*.

"[Pray] that I may be delivered from those in Judea who do not believe," Paul asked of his Roman followers (v. 31). He was referring to hostile Jews who hated him and wanted to murder him. His journey back to Jerusalem was risky, as Paul would face

---

[53] W. E. Vine, *Vine's Expository Dictionary of Biblical Words* (Nashville: Thomas Nelson, 1985).

[54] John MacArthur, *Romans* (Chicago: Moody Press, 1991, 1996), 350.

"chains and tribulations" there (see Acts 20:22–24). Today our spiritual leaders may not face human persecution as Paul did, but the devil constantly bombards our leaders with dangers, toils, and snares.

b. Prayers for *prosperity*.

"[Pray] that my service for Jerusalem may be acceptable to the saints" Paul continued in verse 31. Knowing the divisions and distrust between Gentile and Jewish believers, he understood the risk that his gift might be rejected or his motives questioned.

c. Prayers for *provision*.

Paul's third request was, "[Pray] that I may come to you with joy by the will of God, and may be refreshed together with you" (v. 32). Knowing the trials and strain of his leadership assignment, he asked the believers to pray for his joy and refreshment in their midst once he arrived.

Conclusion: The Outcome of Our Most Strategic Investment?

The results of these prayers for Paul are described in Acts 21:15—28:31. God used the Roman government to protect Paul from the murderous plots of the Jewish opponents (Acts 21:30— 23:24). God also protected Paul from shipwreck and snakebite as he traveled to Rome (Acts 27:1—28:16). The Jewish believers in Jerusalem gladly accepted the love offering (Acts 21:17). While under house arrest in Rome, many believers came to Paul and likely refreshed him, as is specifically stated of a man named Onesiphorus (2 Tim. 1:16).

The result for us is described "Now the God of peace be with you all" (Rom. 15:33). As we earnestly pray for the needs and ministries of our spiritual leaders, we will come to know the God of peace and experience the peace of God in our hearts and in our midst (Phil. 4:6, 7).

SUGGESTED ORDER OF WORSHIP

Prelude—Instrumentalists

> NBH 120 *Made Me Glad*

Call to Praise—Congregation

> NBH 14 *I Will Bless the Lord* (1x in F)
>
> NBH 121 *Everlasting God* (2x in Bb)
>
> NBH 122 *O God, Our Help in Ages Past* (vv. 1–4 in Bb, v. 6 in C)

Prayer of Praise—Pastoral Staff

Welcome—**Pastoral Staff**

Song of Welcome (*meet and greet*)—Congregation

> NBH 37 *Blessed Be the Lord God Almighty* (1x in Bb, 1x in C)

Worship and Praise—Congregation

> NBH 36 *I Exalt Thee* (chorus, 1x in F)
>
> NBH 133 *Shout to the Lord* (2x in Bb)

Offertory Prayer—Pastoral Staff

Offertory Praise

> NBH 85 *God Will Make a Way* (1x in G)
>
> NBH 535 *I Am Thine O Lord* (chorus, v. 3, chorus in G)
>
> NBH 85 *God Will Make a Way* (starting w/ "He will be my guide," in G)

Sermon—Pastor

Hymn of Invitation—Congregation

> NBH 473 *Just a Closer Walk with Thee* (as needed)

Benediction Hymn—Congregation

> NBH 8 *Bless the Lord, O My Soul* (1x in G, 1x in Ab)

Postlude—Instrumentalists

NBH 66 *Open the Eyes of My Heart*

KEY:

NBH: New Baptist Hymnal (2008)

WEEK 44

The True and False Shepherd

John 10:1–6
by Robert Murray M'Cheyne

1. The False Shepherd

   a. Who the False Shepherd Is

   It is evident that he speaks of one great false shepherd, and I have no doubt that it means the great false shepherd, the god of this world, who is continually trying to climb over the wall into the sheepfold. Now, Satan has got three ways in which he attacks the sheepfold.

   i. By the Antichrist (2 Thess. 2:8)

   ii. By the world

   iii. By false teachers (2 Cor. 11:13–15)

   b. The Marks of the False Shepherd

   i. The great mark of false shepherds is that they enter not by the door (10:1).

   ii. The mark of every false shepherd is, he is not saved himself (10:9).

   c. The Object of the False Shepherd (10:10)

   i. Steal

   ii. Kill

   iii. Destroy

2. The True Shepherd (10:2, 5)

   The Shepherd of the sheep is Christ Himself. The marks of the Shepherd of the sheep:

   a. He that entereth in by the door is the shepherd of the sheep (10:2).

    b. He calls his own sheep by name (10:3).

    c. He goes before them (10:4).

Christ never asked a sheep to go where He never went Himself. He has borne all that He calls his sheep to bear.

WEEK 44

Living a Fruitful Christian Life

Matthew 7; John 15
By Mark Smith

The twenty-first-century church has got to prepare itself to do what God wants it to do. We have to engage in an ongoing process of pursuing Christlikeness. We have to pray more, train more, and do more. We have to be filled with the Holy Spirit as never before, because God desires every Christian to be a fruitful Christian, and every church to be a fruitful church.

What does it mean to be a fruitful Christian (John 15:1–5, 11)? Fruitfulness is exhibiting the active, positive attitudes of Jesus Christ, which will be evidenced by the fruit that is produced (Gal. 5:22, 23).

1. Fruitfulness will identify the obedient Christian (Matt. 7:15, 16).

2. Fruitfulness is required for the obedient Christian (Matt. 7:17–20).

3. Fruitfulness is assured for the obedient Christian (John 15:16).

4. Fruitfulness will produce joy for the obedient Christian (John 15:11).

Most people think happiness should be the main pursuit of life. But Jesus is saying that when we are connected to the vine, we will produce fruit, and when we produce fruit, joy will be the inevitable result. Joy is not the pursuit; joy is the *result* of living a fruitful Christian life.

WEEK 45

Wake Up and Pray!

Genesis 1:1–3; Colossians 4:2
By Dr. Daniel Henderson

Introduction

We face a constant dilemma of prayer-less living and sleepy praying. Prayerlessness is our declaration of independence from God, and it is easy in our society with so many human resources to live on Christian autopilot as we neglect real prayer. Further, when we do pray, we can be very sleepy and lethargic about this high and holy calling.

Most of us have fallen asleep while praying. Perhaps you've been involved in prayer times that soon became supplication siestas. Like Peter, James, and John in the garden, who kept napping while they should have been praying (Matt. 26:36–44), we need to heed the words of Jesus, "Could you not watch with Me one hour? Watch and pray, lest you enter into temptation. The spirit indeed is willing, but the flesh is weak" (Matt. 26:40, 41).

When Paul wrote to the young New Testament churches, he said much about prayer. He commanded the saints to gather collectively in passionate, Spirit-guided, energized prayer as he challenged them to stay awake and alert (Eph. 6:20; Col. 4:2; 1 Pet. 4:7). God is not the author of boredom, especially when we are conversing with Him.[55]

The Possibilities of Creative Prayer

The opening verses of Genesis not only describe the beginning moments of creation but also lay a foundation for God's design for us to relate to Him.

---

[55] Daniel Henderson, *PRAYzing! Creative Prayer Experiences from A to Z* (Colorado Springs, CO: NavPress, 2007) 21. This book teaches extensively on creative prayer, along with twenty-six stories of how creative prayer can happen in a group context. We need fresh motivation for creative and engaging prayer. We need to declare war on sleepy prayer meetings.

1. We always pray to a creative God.

The English Bible opens with these words, "In the beginning, God created." This first action in all of human history is also the original description of His character. God is creative. A. W. Tozer states, "What comes into our minds when we think about God is the most important thing about us."[56] Our prayers should always begin with great thoughts about God, even as Jesus taught in His model prayer (Matt. 6:9). When we pray, we should have a high view of God as Father, Provider, Protector, and Guide, among His many other attributes. We must also worship Him in His creativity. This sets a positive *expectancy* in our prayers.

2. We should pray from the creative Word.

The creation account records that when God unleashed His creative power, He did so by speaking ("And God said"). Today, His creative insight, direction, and language for prayer still come from His written, inspired word. The most mature prayer warriors have learned to pray from an open Bible, talking to God in His words. This provides creative exploration in prayer.

Eugene Peterson says it well:

> Prayer is language used to respond to the most that has been said to us with the potential for saying all that is in us ... Prayer is dangerous ... it moves our language into potencies we are unaccustomed to and unprepared for ... We restore prayer to its context in God's word. Prayer is not something we think up to get God's attention or enlist his favor. Prayer is answering speech. The first word is God's word. Prayer is a human word and is never the first word, never the primary word, never the initiating and shaping word simply because we are never first; never primary ... the first word everywhere and always is God's word to us, not ours to him.[57]

3. We can pray by the creative Spirit.

In Genesis 1:2 the triune God looked over a formless, dark, and

---

[56] A.W. Tozer, *The Knowledge of the Holy* (New York, Harper One, 1978) 1.

[57] Eugene Peterson, *Working the Angles* (Grand Rapids: Eerdmans, 1987), 44, 47.

empty mass. The Spirit of God hovered over the amorphous abyss of raging, chaotic waters. Suddenly, at the will and voice of God, light appeared. Soon all that we know existed in order and beauty through the power of God's Spirit.

That same Spirit leads us in our prayers and inspires deep understanding as we pray (Rom. 8:14, 26, 27). First Corinthians 2:9–12 reminds us that "eye has not seen, nor ear heard, nor have entered into the heart of man the things which God has prepared for those who love Him. But God has revealed them to us through His Spirit ... that we might know the things that have been freely given to us by God."

This is our assurance for the energy we can experience for creative prayer.

4. We can pray in a creative way.

Going back to Genesis we discover God's design in creating humanity with these words: "Let Us make man in Our image, according to Our likeness" (1:26). We must conclude that this "image" entails a profound and abounding creativity as we recognize that one of Adam's first assignments was to name all the animals.

Conclusion

So, when you pray, be creative, just like God. It is who He is in you. It is what He made you to do. He is not the author of boredom, especially when we are conversing with Him.

SUGGESTED ORDER OF WORSHIP

Prelude—Instrumentalist

    NBH 13 *Joyful, Joyful, We Adore Thee*

Call to Worship—PT or Ensemble

    NBH 59 *Mighty Is Our God* (2x in Bb)

    NBH 141 *When Morning Gilds the Skies* (vv. 1–3 in Bb)

Call to Prayer and Worship—Pastor

Worship in Song—Congregation

> NBH 60 *To Him Who Sits on the Throne* (2x in Bb)
>
> NBH 447 *It Is Well with My Soul* (chorus, v. 1, chorus, v. 3, chorus in Bb, v. 4 in C)
>
> NBH 446 *Blessed Assurance, Jesus Is Mine* (chorus, v. 1, chorus, v. 3, chorus in C)

Welcome—Pastoral Staff

Welcome Song *(meet and greet)*—Pastoral Staff

> NBH 151 *Bless His Holy Name* (chorus, v. 1, chorus, v. 2, chorus, v. 3, chorus in Eb)
>
> NBH 142 *Worthy, You Are Worthy* (vv. 1 and 2 in Eb, v. 3 in F)
>
> NBH 130 *Here I Am to Worship* (v. 1, chorus, v. 2, chorus in F)

Offertory Prayer—Pastoral Staff

Offertory Praise—Solo, PT or Ensemble

> NBH 119 *There Is a Balm in Gilead* (chorus, v. 1, chorus, v. 2, chorus in F)

Message—Pastor

Hymn of Response

> NBH 433 *I Surrender All* (as needed in C)

Benediction Hymn

> NBH 301 *Crown Him King of Kings* (1x in Ab)

Postlude—Instrumentalist

> NBH 14 *I Will Bless the Lord* (1x in F)

KEY:

NBH: New Baptist Hymnal (2008)

WEEK 45

Where Are Your Sins?

Job 13:23; Psalm 51:2; 1 John 1:7; Romans 3:25
By John Charles Ryle, DD, Lord Bishop of Liverpool

1. You have many sins (Rom. 10:12; James 3:2; 1 John 1:8).

    a. Go and examine the law of God, as expounded by the Son of God Himself (1 Sam. 16:7; Prov. 24:9).

    b. Turn to the history of your own life, and try it by the standard of this holy law.

    c. Turn to the history of your own heart.

2. It is of the utmost importance to have our sins cleansed away.

    a. There is a God above you.

        i. This God is a God of infinite holiness.

        ii. He is a God of infinite knowledge.

        iii. He is a God of infinite power.

    b. Death is before you.

    c. Resurrection and judgment await you.

3. You cannot cleanse away your own sins.

    a. It will not cleanse away your sins to be sorry for them.

    b. It will not cleanse away your sins to mend your life.

    c. It will not cleanse away your sins to become diligent in the use of the forms and ordinances of religion.

    d. It will not cleanse away your sins to look to man for help.

4. The blood of Jesus Christ can cleanse away all your sins.

    a. It was blood that had been long covenanted and promised.

    b. It was blood that had been long typified and prefigured.

    c. It was blood that was of infinite merit and value in the sight of God.

5. Faith is absolutely necessary, and the only thing necessary, in order to give you an interest in the cleansing blood of Christ.

Where are your sins?

WEEK 45

How God Builds a Champion

Selected Scriptures
By Mark Smith

The Olympic champion weight lifter is being interviewed by the announcer, and he is asked the question, "What were your keys to becoming a gold medal champion?" Without a doubt, the proud athlete will talk about commitment, perseverance, diet, and training. If he's honest, he'll talk about getting a few breaks along the way, too.

Being a champion for God has nothing to do with luck, chance, or fate. God has some keys for every Christian who wants to be great, for His glory. The same keys to greatness apply to being a champion church as well.

1. Who we are is more important than what we do (Acts 1:4–8).

2. Being healthy comes before being busy (Acts 2:41–47).

3. Power from God accomplishes more than the resources of man (Acts 3:1–10).

4. Spiritual service must not replace spiritual growth (Acts 6:1–7).

WEEK 46

The Dynamic of Prayer

Matthew 6:1, 5–8
By Dr. Jerry Sutton

As Jesus moves into His middle section of the Sermon on the Mount, He tells His hearers, "Take heed that you do not do your charitable deeds before men, to be seen by them. Otherwise you have no reward from your Father in heaven" (v. 1). Here, Jesus introduces the concept of motive, why we do what we do in the spiritual arena. He addresses the issues of giving (vv. 1–4), prayer (vv. 5–15), and fasting (vv. 16–18). He concludes by emphasizing the importance of laying up treasures in heaven.

In the portion on prayer, He addresses two dimensions. First, He addresses the dynamics of prayer, particularly identifying the concepts of the authentic and the counterfeit. Second, He paints a word picture of the Father's design for prayer. He says simply, "Pray in this manner" (or "pattern"). This is not so much a prayer to be prayed as it is a pattern or design to be followed. Consider, therefore, the dynamics of prayer.

Notice the repetition of the phrase "when you pray" (vv. 5–7). This recurring phrase provides a convenient outline for our study of the dynamics of prayer. Consider Jesus' teaching:

First, Jesus tells us not to pray like the hypocrites (v. 5). The word *hypocrite* is traditionally translated as a "play actor." Such a person is utterly devoid of sincerity.

Yet, what I notice is that both the hypocrite and the authentic believer pray. The issue is not the presence of prayer but the motive that drives prayer. Jesus explains that the hypocrite loves to pray. But he loves to pray standing in the synagogue and on the street corner." Why in these places? So he can be seen by men. His motive is the affirmation of fellow human beings, and not the ear of God. Of these hypocrites Jesus says, "They have their reward in full." If your motive is the applause of men, you'd best enjoy it, because that is all the reward you will get. So, if we are going to pray aright, we must not pray with the impure motive of being seen and heard by others.

Second, we are to direct our prayer to our Father in heaven (v. 6). When you pray, Jesus says, there is a right way. Now, He is not discrediting public prayer, but rather, He is helping us see that the true motive in prayer is to speak strictly to our heavenly Father, whose ear is ever attentive to the voice of His children. So, Jesus provides guidelines that facilitate this essential.

Jesus tells us to go into our rooms and shut the doors (v. 6). When we are alone, we are together with God. By being alone we are in fact in a position to be in God's presence without distractions.

Now we are to pray to our Father, who is in the secret place. Perhaps no one else is aware of us being alone with God, but God is absolutely attentive. He longs for you to enter this secret place of prayer!

The result is that our Father, who sees in secret, will reward us openly. From the mouth of Jesus, this is an accomplished fact, a promise waiting to be embraced, a journey just waiting for your entrance. He will reward you openly!

Third, Jesus warns us to avoid the use of meaningless repetition in our prayer (v. 7). In fact, His counsel is that when we pray, we are not to use "vain repetitions," like those of the unbeliever. Put content in your prayer. Be specific in your prayer. God, who knows and understands, waits for you.

When blind Bartimaeus cried out, "Jesus, Son of David, have mercy on me," he got nowhere. When Jesus asked him, "What do you want?" he responded, "I want to see." When he got specific, God responded, and his sight was restored! (See Mark 10:46–52.) God wants us to be specific in our prayers.

When Jesus instructs the person of prayer not to use "vain repetition" He explains the reason. They think they will be heard for their many words. Then Jesus tells us that the Father does not answer prayer based upon the volume of our words, but because of the attitude of our hearts as we utterly depend upon Him in our human helplessness.

Jesus then exhorts us to pray with a word of confident comfort, "Your Father knows the things you have need of before you ask" (v. 8).

So here is God's design for prayer. We are to pray with the motive of being heard by God. We are to pray expecting God alone to answer our prayer. And we are to pray, being specific about our needs, understanding that the Father knows before we even ask.

SUGGESTED ORDER OF WORSHIP

The Dynamic of Prayer

Prelude—Instrumentalists

NBH 625 *I Will Sing of the Mercies of the Lord*

Call to Praise—Congregation

NBH 424 *I Must Tell Jesus* (v. 1, chorus, v. 2, chorus, v. 4, chorus in D)

NBH 279 *There Is a Redeemer* (v. 1, chorus, v. 2, chorus, v. 3, chorus in D)

Prayer of Praise—Pastoral Staff

Welcome—Pastoral Staff

Song of Welcome (*meet and greet*)—Congregation

NBH 453 *Leaning on the Everlasting Arms* (v. 1, chorus, v. 3, chorus in G)

Worship and Praise—Congregation

NBH 162 *Wonderful, Merciful Savior* (v. 1, chorus, v. 2, chorus, v. 3, chorus in Bb)

NBH 37 *Blessed Be the Lord God Almighty* (1x in Bb, 1x in C)

NBH 218 *That's Why We Praise Him* (chorus, v. 1, chorus, v. 2, chorus in C)

Offertory Prayer—Pastoral Staff

Offertory Praise—Congregation

NBH 426 *Open Our Eyes, Lord* (vv. 1 and 2 in D)

NBH 450 *Precious Lord, Take My Hand* (2x in G)

Sermon—Pastor

The Dynamic of Prayer

Hymn of Invitation—Congregation

    NBH 411 *Come Just as You Are* (as needed)

Benediction Hymn—Congregation

    NBH 151 *Bless His Holy Name* (2x in Eb)

Postlude—Instrumentalists

    NBH 20 *Great and Mighty* (2x in Eb)

KEY:

NBH: New Baptist Hymnal (2008)

WEEK 46

Victory over the World Through Faith

1 John 5:4
By Charles G. Finney

1. What is it to overcome the world?

 a. It is to get above the spirit of covetousness, which possesses the men of the world.

 b. Overcoming the world implies rising above its engrossments.

 c. Overcoming the world implies overcoming the fear of the world.

 d. Overcoming the world implies overcoming a state of worldly anxiety.

 e. The victory under consideration implies that we cease to be enslaved and in bondage to the world in any of its forms.

2. Who are those that overcome the world?

 Our text gives the ready answer: "Whatever is born of God overcomes the world."

3. Why do believers overcome the world?

 I answer, this victory over the world results as naturally from the spiritual or heavenly birth, as coming into bondage to the world results from the natural birth.

4. How is this victory over the world achieved?

 Believing in God, and having realizing impressions of His truth and character made upon our mind by the Holy Ghost given to those who truly believe, we gain the victory over the world.

WEEK 46

Shopping for Salvation

Colossians 2:4–10
By Rev. Mark Smith

Imagine this scenario. A vacuum cleaner salesman shows up at your door. You let him in. Next thing you know, he's showing you his "very best" vacuum cleaner. He *even* says it's so good that your family's allergies will clear up, and dust particles will flee in fear of the self-propelled, 350-horsepower Mighty Mite, with a four-barrel carburetor and twin cams. You think to yourself, *If I buy this, my mother-in-law will be amazed at what a flawless housekeeper I've become*. And all for the bargain price of $2,100, *including* the carpet cleaning system!

Now, fast-forward. It's twenty years later, and you still can't bring yourself to buy another vacuum cleaner, in spite of the fact that now you're not strong enough to lift the Mighty Mite out of the closet. Admit it: you were deceived by a smooth talker. He was a great salesman; you were a lousy buyer.

A lot of people today are saying some pretty right-sounding stuff about how to know God and find the meaning of life. When it comes to falling for the world's slick marketing techniques about life, remember three tried-and-true consumer axioms:

1. Get it in writing (v. 4).

2. Let the buyer beware (v. 8).

3. Watch out for the old bait and switch (vv. 9, 10).

WEEK 47

The Design of Prayer

Matthew 6:9–15
By Dr. Jerry Sutton

After Jesus lays out the dynamics of prayer in verses 5–8, He shifts focus, helping us learn the proper pattern for prayer. This is not so much a prayer to be prayed as it is a pattern to be followed. If the "many words" of the heathen will not facilitate effective prayer (v. 7), then what will? Here Jesus lays out the design, or pattern, to follow in prayer. He includes six components.

First, we initiate prayer with praise (v. 9). "Our Father in heaven, hallowed be Your name." Prayer begins by focusing not on ourselves but God. When we pray, we pray to the God who created both us and the world in which we live. He understands us and desires only what is in our best interest. Praise acknowledges God for who He is and not simply for what He can or might do. Jesus' words acknowledge that He is our Father and that we approach Him as His children!

Second, we incorporate His priorities (v. 10). "Your kingdom come. Your will be done." In short, we acknowledge our subservience to His agenda. Recall words that follow, where Jesus said, "But seek first [of priority] the kingdom of God ... and all these [other] things shall be added to you" (v. 33). Jesus primarily was concerned with ushering in a new kingdom, where He is the King! The kingdom of God has come wherever the will of God is accomplished. So here we see the standing priority of God in prayer that the will of God would be done on earth, just as it is done in heaven. As we pray, we seek to adjust our own lives to be in the center of God's will. Where the will of God is accomplished, the kingdom of God is established!

So, how do we know the will of God? As we get into the Word and pray, He will help us see His general will. For example, 1 Thessalonians 4:3 says, "This is the will of God, your sanctification." The Bible contains numerous references to the will of God. Scripture testifies that when we walk in obedience to God's general will, He will, by His spirit, reveal for us His specific will. Yet, we are called to walk by faith and not sight, which is not always easy. So we've entered into His presence (courts) with praise (see Psalm 100:4), and we've acknowledged His priorities as our own. What next?

Third, we bring before Him our need of provision (v. 11). Recall that Jesus has already said, "Your Father knows the things you have need of before you ask Him" (v. 8). So this component of prayer is not telling God something He does not know; it is confessing our specific needs to the Father and expressing a trusting dependence on Him and His ability to provide for what we need. When Jesus instructed us to pray, "Give us this day our daily bread," He was saying, "Trust God for today! What do you need? Ask Him to provide. Understand that anything large enough to worry about is big enough to pray about."

Fourth, we make sure that our connection with Him is unbroken through purity (v. 12). Jesus puts it this way, "And forgive us our debts, as we forgive our debtors." Jesus here is dealing with our moral obligations. And this portion of prayer is actually an expansion of what He has taught us in chapter 5. God forgives us based on the finished work of Christ on the Cross and our confession. See 1 John 1:9. In turn, we, too, should forgive. Understand that this encompasses personal offenses and does not necessarily let a serious offender escape accountability for his actions, particularly when the gravity of his offense is damaging to more than the individual offended.

Coupled with this, Jesus instructs us to pray, "And do not lead us into temptation, but deliver us from the evil one" (v. 13a). As we forgive and are forgiven, both the horizontal and vertical dimensions, we are still vulnerable to temptation and the schemes of the evil one. Pray that God leads you away from both!

Fifth, Jesus concludes the pattern by bringing us into His perspective: "For [God's] is the kingdom and the power and the glory forever" (v. 13b). We acknowledge that we are players on His stage in His world. He is not simply a player on our stage in our world.

Finally, Jesus wraps up His instruction on prayer by reminding us of two essential principles, forgiveness and faith. Prayer is contingent on our willingness to forgive and is predicated on faith. Will we trust God to be God in our lives and in our world?

SUGGESTED ORDER OF WORSHIP

The Design of Prayer

Prelude—Instrumentalist

NBH 498 *I Will Call Upon the Lord* (2x in C)

Call to Prayer—Pastoral Staff

Welcome—Pastoral Staff

NBH 347 *Lord, I Lift Your Name on High* (2x in G)

NBH 381 *Make Me A Servant* (2x in G)

NBH 423 *I Need Thee Every Hour* (v. 1, chorus, v. 2, chorus, v. 5, chorus in G)

NBH 285 *I Will Sing of My Redeemer* (chorus only in G)

Baptismal Celebration—Pastoral Staff

Prayer of Commitment—Pastoral Staff

NBH 534 *Take My Life and Let It Be* (vv. 1–4 in F)

Scripture Reading from Matthew 6:5–13 (*Please have prepared for IMAG*)

And when you pray, you shall not be like the hypocrites. For they love to pray standing in the synagogues and on the corners of the streets, that they may be seen by men. Assuredly, I say to you, they have their reward. But you, when you pray, go into your room, and when you have shut your door, pray to your Father who is in the secret place; and your Father who sees in secret will reward you openly. And when you pray, do not use vain repetitions as the heathen do. For they think that they will be heard for their many words. Therefore do not be like them. For your Father knows the things you have need of before you ask Him. In this manner, therefore, pray:

Our Father in heaven,
Hallowed be Your name.
Your kingdom come.
Your will be done
On earth as it is in heaven.
Give us this day our daily bread.
And forgive us our debts,
As we forgive our debtors.
And do not lead us into temptation,
But deliver us from the evil one.
For Yours is the kingdom and the power and the glory forever. Amen."

Prayer of Thanksgiving—Pastor

Offertory Praise—Solo with PT Ensemble

> NBH 431 *The Lord's Prayer*

Message—Pastor

> *The Design of Prayer*

Hymn of Response/Invitation

> NBH 460 *His Strength Is Perfect* (2x in F)

Benediction Hymn—Congregation

> NBH 599 *Soon and Very Soon* (1x in G)

Postlude—Instrumentalist

> NBH 4 *Almighty* (2x in F)

KEY:

NBH: New Baptist Hymnal (2008)

WEEK 47

Delight in the Will of God

Psalm 40:8
By Dr. John A. Broadus

1. In one sense, the will of God will always be done, whether we do His will or not.

    We are compelled to speak of God's will in terms applicable to our own. This is done in Scripture. There are three distinct senses in which this term is employed.

    First, the will of *purpose*—it is always done (Dan. 4:35).

    Next, the will of *desire*, or wish, which is not always done. For inscrutable reasons He permits free agents to act counter to His wish: "How often I wanted ... but you were not willing" (Luke 13:34); "Not willing that any should perish" (2 Pet. 3:9); "Who desires all men to be saved" (1 Tim. 2:4).

    Last, will of *command*, the wish of one in authority, when expressed, becomes a command. Every command of God is our solemn duty to obey—but, alas! It is not always done. Of course, it is human imperfection that makes these distinctions necessary, and they must not be pushed too far—yet they are, within limits, just distinctions, and should be borne in mind.

2. We should always do God's will, even if it be not with delight.

    We seldom, if ever, do anything with perfectly correct motives and feelings. Yes, we should always do God's will, even if it is not a delight. And often, the painful effort will change to pleasure; the duty commenced reluctantly will become a sweet joy! Yet, do not condition obedience upon its becoming delightful. It is the will of my God? Then His will I must do.

3. We should delight to do God's will.

    We may be led to it ...

a. By sense of right

b. By feelings of interest

c. By feelings of benevolence

d. By feelings of gratitude

WEEK 47

Ready for Revival

John 15:1–11
By Rev. Mark Smith

Some people have a strange idea of commitment. In Matthew 28:19, 20, Jesus gave us the Great Commission, where we are told to do three things: *go*, *baptize*, and *teach*. Throughout the New Testament, we read a recurring theme that a true follower of Jesus Christ has totally committed him- or herself to walking in the footsteps of Jesus—to thinking as Jesus thought, doing what Jesus did, and producing what Jesus produced.

1. A revived Christian has staying power (John 15:7).

2. A revived Christian obeys God (Matt. 7:21).

3. A revived Christian is an encourager (Heb. 13:3).

4. A revived Christian is accountable (John 15:10).

5. A revived Christian produces results (John 15:5).

6. A revived Christian glorifies God (John 15:7, 8).

7. A revived Christian has joy (John 15:11).

Being a revived disciple of Jesus Christ is about following His example: Jesus will never ask you to do anything He has not done; He will never ask you to go through anything He has not already endured; He will never require anything of you that He has not already demanded of Himself.

WEEK 48

The Confessions of Christmas

Gabriel's Christmas Confession

Luke 1:26–28

By Dr. Jerry Sutton

Paul tells us that Jesus "witnessed the good confession before Pontius Pilate" (1 Tim. 6:13). A *confession* is a word of affirmation, truth, and significance. Surprisingly, the Christmas story records a number of good confessions concerning the Lord Jesus Christ.

The first confession I draw your attention to is Gabriel's confession to Mary about Jesus. Scripture tells us that Gabriel was "sent" (Matt. 6:26). This word has the same root from which we get the word *apostle*, or one who is sent with a message. What was Gabriel's confessional message to Mary?

First, he told her, "Your circumstances are a matter for rejoicing" (v. 28, paraphrased). No doubt this sudden appearance and announcement from Gabriel terrified Mary. Yet, in spite of the shock, the message was positive—"You are highly favored, because the Lord is with you!" What an incredible announcement! The phrase "highly favored one" means she was a recipient of grace and divine favor.

Second, he told her that she did not need to be afraid. He then explained why: "You have found favor with God" (v. 30). It seems that a typical response to the presence of the supernatural is fear. Abraham, Isaac, Moses, and in the Christmas story, Joseph and the shepherds, all heard these same words of comfort: "You do not need to be afraid!"

Third, Gabriel told Mary, "You will have a Son" (vv. 31–33). In his confessional announcement, the angel provided six affirmations concerning this Son.

1. "You shall call His name Jesus" (v. 31). The angel told Mary that His name would be Jesus. This is the same thing that Joseph was told in the dream recorded in Matthew: "You shall call His name Jesus, for

He will save His people from their sins" (Matt. 1:21).

2. "He will be great" (v. 32.) This concerns His significance. No doubt, He is the most significant personality in human and divine history. After all, He is God, come in the flesh! And the work He was to perform, the Atonement, would be the most strategic in the history of humanity.

3. "He ... will be called the Son of the Highest" (v. 32). Recall that Psalm 2:7–8 tells us, "The Lord has said to Me, 'You are My Son, today I have begotten You. Ask of Me, and I will give you the nations for your inheritance and the end of the earth for your possession." What David wrote about in the Psalms, Gabriel announced to Mary!

4. "The Lord God will give Him the the throne of His father David" (v. 32). This looks back to the prophetic word from Isaiah, "Of the increase of His government and peace there will be no end. Upon the throne of David and over His kingdom, to order it and establish it with judgment and justice from that time forward, even forever" (9:7).

5. "He will reign over the house of Jacob" (v. 33). In short, Jesus is Israel's promised Messiah! They need not look for, nor expect, another!

6. "Of His kingdom there will be no end" (v. 33). Many kingdoms over the course of human history will come and go, but Christ's kingdom will have no end. See Daniel 7:13, 14. No matter what forces are arrayed against God's kingdom, it is indestructible!

Fourth, Gabriel announced to Mary that God Himself would cause all of this to happen (vv. 34–37). In fact, when Mary asked, "How can this be?" the angel simply said, "With God nothing will be impossible" (v. 37).

If Gabriel said all of this to Mary in her day, what is he saying that applies to us today? Consider these truths:

First, because God's presence is constant, we can have joy. This is an inner quality of contentment that results from the Spirit's work in our lives. Jesus tells us that it is the result of "abiding" or "remaining" in Him (John 15:11). Paul identifies joy as one of the fruits of the Spirit (Gal. 5:22, 23).

Second, because of God's presence, we need not live in fear. In His public ministry Jesus often said, "Fear not!" His love in us can overcome our fear. Knowing that our lives are in God's hands, we need not live in fear.

Third, understand that God the Father has sent a Savior for you, and His name is Jesus! John tells us that "as many as received Him [Jesus], to them He [God the Father] gave the right to become children of God, to those who believe in His name" (John 1:12). Has there been a time when you have placed your faith and trust in Jesus Christ?

And finally, we need to understand that nothing is impossible with God. You have no problem, difficulty, stronghold, sin, or habit that is too strong for God to have victory over.

SUGGESTED ORDER OF WORSHIP

The Confessions of Christmas

Prelude—Instrumental Group

NBH [[need name of hymn]]

Scripture Reading from 2 Corinthians 4:1–12—Pastoral Staff

Therefore, since we have this ministry, as we have received mercy, we do not lose heart. But we have renounced the hidden things of shame, not walking in craftiness nor handling the word of God deceitfully, but by manifestation of the truth commending ourselves to every man's conscience in the sight of God. But even if our gospel is veiled, it is veiled to those who are perishing, whose minds the god of this age has blinded, who do not believe, lest the light of the gospel of the glory of Christ, who is the image of God, should shine on them. For we do not preach ourselves, but Christ Jesus the Lord, and ourselves your bondservants for Jesus' sake. For it is the God who commanded light to shine out of darkness, who has shone in our hearts to give the light of the knowledge of the glory of God in the face of Jesus Christ. But we have this treasure in earthen vessels, that the excellence of the power may be of God and not of us. We are hard-pressed on every side, yet not crushed; we are perplexed, but not in despair; persecuted, but not forsaken; struck down, but not destroyed—always carrying about in the body the dying of the Lord Jesus, that the life of Jesus also may be manifested in our body. For we who live are always delivered to death for Jesus' sake, that the life of Jesus also may be manifested in our mortal flesh. So then death is working in us, but life in you.

Worship and Praise—Congregation

> NBH 204 *All Is Well*—PT Ensemble

Prayer of Worship—Pastoral Staff

Welcome—Pastoral Staff

Song of Welcome (*meet and greet*)—Congregation

> NBH 176 *Come, Thou Long Expected Jesus* (vv. 1 and 2 in F)

> NBH 214 *Isn't He* (2x in G)

> NBH 201 *Emmanuel* (2x in C)

> NBH 218 *That's Why We Praise Him* (v. 1, chorus, v. 2, chorus in C)

Testimony of Praise (2-minute video)

Offertory Prayer—Pastoral Staff

Offertory Praise—PT Ensemble

> NBH 200 *One Small Child* (in F)

Message—Pastor

> *Gabriel's Christmas Confession*

Hymn of Invitation—Congregation

    NBH 413 *Turn Your Eyes upon Jesus* (as needed)

Benediction Hymn—Congregation

    NBH 147 *Jesus, What a Wonder You Are* (1x in F)

Postlude—Instrumental Group

    NBH 181 *Joy to the World* (2x in D)

KEY:

NBH: New Baptist Hymnal (2008)

WEEK 48

As I Have Loved

John 13:34, 35
By Alexander MacLaren

Wishes from dying lips are sacred. They sink deep into memories and mold faithful lives.

1. The New Scope of the New Commandment

When the words were spoken, the then-known civilized Western world was cleft by great, deep gulfs of separation, like the crevasses in a glacier, by the side of which our racial animosities and class differences are merely superficial cracks on the surface. Language, religion, national animosities, differences of condition, and saddest of all, difference of sex, split the world up into alien fragments. The new commandment made a new thing, and the world wondered.

The very same principle which makes this love to one another imperative upon all disciples, makes it equally imperative upon every follower of Jesus Christ to embrace in a real affection all whom Jesus so loved as to die for them.

2. The Example of the New Commandment: "as I have loved you"

What do we see there?

a. The activity of love

b. The self-forgetfulness of love

c. The self-sacrifice of love

3. The Motive Power for Obedience to the Commandment

That is as new as all the rest. That "as" expresses the manner of the love, but it also expresses the motive and the power. It might be translated into the equivalent "in the fashion in which," or it might be translated into the equivalent "since—I have loved you."

WEEK 48

If I Would Love

John 14:23–31
By Rev. Mark Smith

There is great hope in what Jesus is saying to His disciples, but there is great sadness in the circumstances. His disciples are soon going to leave the camaraderie of the Upper Room and enter the uncertainty of Gethsemane and Calvary. Jesus knows these will be among the last words His dearest followers will hear Him say before some terrible things begin to happen. What will hold them together? What will bring them back from the brink of despair? What will cause them to explode with power after facing their greatest fears?

1. The Journey of Jesus (v. 28)

   a. Back to the Father

   b. Bringing sinners to Himself

   c. Exalted (Is. 53:2–10a)

2. The Building of Our Faith (v. 29)

3. The Defeat of Satan (v. 30)

4. The Demonstration of Love (v. 31)

Jesus said, "Let us go." Imagine the scene in the Upper Room. Do you see the concern on the disciples' faces? Can you sense the anxiety in their hearts? When Jesus said, "Let us go," it was more than a command to leave the room; it was a battle cry. The battle of the ages was about to begin, and the future of every human being ever born was on the line. The preparation time was over. The pep talk had been completed. And Jesus is still saying, "Let us go."

WEEK 49

The Confessions of Christmas

Elizabeth's Christmas Confession

Luke 1:39–45
By Dr. Jerry Sutton

We continue in our study of Christmas confessions with an examination of Elizabeth's words directed toward Mary. Luke tells us that after she learned that she was with child by the Holy Spirit, Mary made a visit to see her cousin Elizabeth (1:39, 40), who was also pregnant and would soon give birth to John the Baptist. No doubt part of Mary's human motivation was to escape the condemnation and shame that accompanied the town gossips about this "unwed" mother.

When Mary came into Elizabeth's presence, the unborn John leaped in her womb (v. 41). Luke further tells us under divine inspiration that Elizabeth was "filled with the Holy Spirit" (v. 41). Minimally, this spiritual condition gave Elizabeth a supernatural understanding of the significance of her guest. Himself under the influence of the Spirit, Luke wrote that Elizabeth's next words were exclaimed "with a loud voice." So, what is it that Elizabeth said to Mary?

First, she said, "Blessed are you among women" (v. 42). The word *blessed* is a perfect passive participle, which means it is something that has happened in the past by an outside force and that has abiding results in the present and future. This is the same thing that Gabriel said to Mary in Luke 1:28. *Blessed* means "spoken well of," "prospered," or "praised."

In short, Elizabeth was saying to Mary, "You are a blessed woman! And not just blessed, but blessed more than other women."

No doubt this affirmation sounded like music to Mary's ears, since much of what she had heard up to this time sounded more like curses and condemnation.

Second, Elizabeth told Mary, "Blessed is the fruit of your womb" (v. 42). The same confession she had made about Mary, she now made about the unborn baby Jesus. No doubt, Jesus will be the most blessed man who ever walked the earth. He was blessed, and He who was blessed from birth would bless the entire human race. In fact, Zacharias, the father of John the Baptist declared, "Blessed is the Lord God of Israel, for He has visited and redeemed His people, and has raised up a horn of salvation for us in the house of His servant David" (vv. 68, 69). And Zacharias was grateful that his son, John, would be this horn of salvation's prophet or forerunner (v. 76).

Third, Elizabeth told Mary, "You are the mother of [the] Lord" (v. 43). In fact, she said, "You are the mother of *my* Lord" [emphasis added]. This truth did not come from Elizabeth's keen intellect but from divine revelation. It was a truth divinely revealed from heaven, not passed along through human communication. God revealed this truth to Mary, Joseph, and now to Elizabeth. In turn, Elizabeth affirmed this truth to Mary. She, indeed, was carrying God's Son!

Fourth, "Blessed is she who believed" (v. 45). Interestingly, Luke uses a different word for "blessed" at this juncture. Whereas the state of blessedness noted in verse 42 was supernaturally bestowed, with no initiative or effort required on the part of the one blessed, the "blessing" here is different. It is propositional: you will be blessed if, when, and because you believe. Here, Mary's faith is the critical component. The word *blessed* is the same as that used in the Beatitudes. It depicts a condition of spiritual well-being, satisfaction, and contentedness. Here, Elizabeth was saying to Mary, "You had full confidence in the angel's message."

So, this was Elizabeth's confession to Mary. Yet, the abiding concern is, what does this say to us? Consider several concluding implications:

First, with Christmas God invaded history. When Jesus, God's Son, came to this earth, God was launching a counterattack to redeem lost humanity. When Adam and Eve sinned against God, the entire human race fell under the curse of sin. All people, by virtue of their sinful nature (predisposition to sin), were separated from God. Jesus came to restore this broken relationship.

Second, like Mary, we, too, can be blessed and experience the favor of God. In one sense, we are all cursed due to the presence of sin in our lives. At the same time we are created in the image of God. Sin has marred that image and caused us to be less than God intended. Yet, like Mary, we are blessed because of God's initiative. Motivated by

His love of humanity, God sent His Son, Jesus, to offer His free gift of salvation to anyone who will receive Him!

Third, this Christmas story tells us that we are blessed because of what God has done. It is initiated and sustained by the power of God. The question now is, will you trust God to demonstrate His power in you?

And fourth, the key to entering into this state of blessing is belief, or faith. Faith is the key that unlocks God's storehouse of blessing! Simply put, will you, in childlike faith, place your trust in Christ alone?

SUGGESTED ORDER OF WORSHIP

Prelude—Instrumentalist

NBH 13 *Joyful, Joyful, We Adore Thee*

Call to Worship—PT or Ensemble

NBH 176 *Come, Thou Long-Expected Jesus* (vv. 1 and 2 in F)

NBH 184 *Angels We Have Heard on High* (v. 1, chorus, v. 3, chorus in F, v. 4, chorus in G)

Call to Prayer and Worship—Pastor

Welcome—Pastoral Staff

Welcome Song (*meet and greet*)—Congregation

NBH 197 *Sing We Now of Christmas* (vv, 1–5 in D with a tag)

NBH 217 *Thou Didst Leave Thy Throne* (vv. 1, 2, 4, 5, in D)

NBH 213 *Infant Holy, Infant Lowly* (vv. 1 and 2 in G)

Offertory Prayer—Pastoral Staff

Offertory Praise—Solo, PT or Ensemble

NBH 189 *Child in the Manger* (vv. 1–3 in Bb)

Message—Pastor

Hymn of Response

> NBH 143 *You Are My All in All* (as needed in F)

Benediction Hymn—Congregation

> NBH 301 *Crown Him King of Kings* (1x in Ab)

Postlude—Instrumentalist

> NBH 199 *O Come, All Ye Faithful*

KEY:

NBH: New Baptist Hymnal (2008)

WEEK 49

Paths of Disappointment

Ecclesiastes 1:2
By Robert G. Lee

Thirty-seven times the word *vanity* occurs in the Book of Ecclesiastes. Moreover, vanity is the key word of the Book of Ecclesiastes, the keynote to its dirgelike message.

They are not the words of a man who walked a few paths, but the words of a man who walked many paths.

1. The Path of Wisdom (Eccl. 1:17)

    Mere human wisdom never satisfies. Even if we knew all things, there are many things we never would and never could know. Millions of things we do not know. Write down all we know; it will be a small volume. Write down all we do not know of things in the heavens and things in the earth and things under the earth; it would be a large library of many shelves and many large volumes.

2. The Path of Wine (Eccl. 2:3)

3. The Path of Wealth (Eccl. 5:9–15)

    No man can buy a contented heart. Money is powerless to furnish this. No man can purchase with riches a soul at peace with God. No man can pay in money the price of the hope of immortality and of a meeting in the Great Beyond. No man can find in riches the purchase price of God's favor or the realization of eternal salvation.

4. The Path of Works (Eccl. 2:4–6)

    He did mighty things in the matter of building cities and other great public works. He accomplished such things as multitudes have expected to provide satisfaction for life's labors. But when he had finished all his great works, he looked out upon them and cried, "Vanity of vanities[!]"

5. The Path of Women (1 Kin. 11:1–8; Prov. 9:13–18; 31:3; Eccl. 2:8;)

Many times Solomon doubtless proved all this, for he was a married man. And yet, because he left God out and reckoned not with his laws in relation to women, he found the path of women a path of great disappointments.

Our One Hope

But God is ever the God of the second chance. It is ever the providence of His mercy, if we will turn from our wicked ways, to reverse the curse of sin. Then—do this. Through Jesus, who died for you—do this. With faith in the Christ who bore our sins in His own body on the tree (1 Pet. 2:24), and died the just for the unjust that He might bring us to God (1 Pet. 3:18)—embrace the Cross now.

WEEK 49

Dangerous Distractions and Slippery Side Streets

Col. 2:8–19

By Mark Smith

When you were growing up, did you ever know any kids who were called "hyperactive"? Now they call it ADD, or ADHD, or something like that. Whatever you call it, it adds up to one distracted kid. When you're trying to be a good student, or when you're learning to drive a car, you realize that being distracted can be a dangerous thing. Being distracted is bad for your spiritual life too.

Paul warns Christians about three distractions, or side streets, that can hurt our relationship with Jesus Christ:

1. The Philosophy of the Godless (vv. 8–10)

2. The Legalism of the Insecure (vv. 11–17)

    a. Not circumcision

    b. Not the law

    c. Not special holy days

3. The Distraction of the Supernatural (vv. 18, 19)

A man who won't ask for directions makes a lot of wrong turns. He might see some impressive sights or some pretty scenery, but he's still lost. If you want to get on the right track spiritually and stay there, you need a personal relationship with Jesus Christ, and a worldview that is based on the Word of God.

WEEK 50

The Confessions of Christmas

The Angel's Christmas Confession

Luke 2:8–18

By Dr. Jerry Sutton

It is just like God to announce the greatest news to those whom society has overlooked. Shepherds were considered the lowest of the low in first-century Judea. Yet in spite of their low standing in the eyes of man, God favored and blessed them by including them in the unfolding events of the very first Christmas.

For the shepherds, the first Christmas was simply another day and night. Yet in the midst of the ordinary, God broke through in supernatural glory. Luke puts it this way: "And behold, an angel of the Lord stood before them, and the glory of the Lord shone around them, and they were greatly afraid" (2:9). Now notice what the angel said in his Christmas confession to the shepherds of Bethlehem.

First, "Do not be afraid" (v. 10). Fear seemed to be a common response to an angel's appearance. Yet at the same time, we need to understand that fear was also a common experience in this first Christmas. Mary no doubt feared the ostracism of those who did not understand her special circumstances; Joseph perhaps feared the responsibility of caring for both a wife and a child; Herod feared being displaced; all Jerusalem feared Herod and his cruelty; the wise men feared Herod's wrath; and here, the shepherds feared the angel of the Lord. From whatever source fear came, the declaration from the angel was, "Do not be afraid!"

Second, he proclaimed the good tidings (news) of great joy for all people (v. 10). This message, this good news, would result in great joy for everyone. The extent of this good news is to every member of the human race. The point is, this event producing great joy is for the entire human race, not a predetermined, select few.

Third, he announced that a Savior had been born that very day in

Bethlehem (the city of David), and that He is "Christ the Lord" (v. 11). The angel was specific in his announced confession. The who of the confession is Christ the Lord. The where of the confession is Bethlehem. The when of the confession is today! The *what* of the confession is that a Savior has been born! Notice that the angel was clear that He is Christ—this word means the pronounced Messiah—and Lord—a term in context reserved for deity! He is God invading planet Earth and the human race in the form of a baby!

Fourth, here is how you can identify Him! (v. 12). And the angel described the unique circumstances of Jesus' first hours and days as an infant. "You will find a Babe wrapped in swaddling cloths, lying in a manger." Luke tells us that this was a "sign" to the shepherds. In short, God was giving the shepherds a ringside seat at the most phenomenal event to date in human history.

After a great finale of praise, the shepherds acted on their newfound knowledge. Luke relates their resolve—"Let us now go to Bethlehem and see this thing that has come to pass, which the Lord has made known to us" (v. 15). And he concluded, "And they came with haste and found Mary and Joseph, and the Babe lying in a manger" (v. 16).

Luke noted that upon their return to Bethlehem, "they made widely known the saying which was told them concerning this Child" (v. 17). Then he recorded the reaction of those who heard: they "marveled at those things which were told them by the shepherds."

Now, in light of this confession, this angelic announcement to the shepherds, what is the angel saying to and for us?

First, God cares for the overlooked, the dispossessed, the outcasts, and the nobodies of this world. Whereas the world may have assessed these shepherds as of no value, God thought enough of them to invite them to the Savior's birthday! Here are people, created in the image of God, for whom Christ would die. Perhaps we're all reminded that God gives grace to the humble!

Second, the angel's announcement is for all people. All have sinned, all are lost, and all are separated from God because of their sin. And the good news is that now all people have the hope of a Savior available to them! This gospel is good news for everyone!

Third, we see here that God keeps His promises. Scripture contains numerous prophecies and promises concerning a coming Messiah. Micah 5:2 is fulfilled here. What is true for this one prophesy is true for hundreds of others. God keeps His promises, and He will keep His promises to you!

And finally, if you want to know God, He will help you find Him. When the shepherds heard the good news, they wanted to see and know Jesus. And the Father gave them specific instructions on how to find the Savior. He will do the same for you!

SUGGESTED ORDER OF WORSHIP

The Angel's Christmas Confession

Prelude—Instrumentalists

NBH 182 *Go, Tell It on the Mountain* (2x in F)

Welcome—Pastoral Staff

Call to Praise—Congregation

Proclaim the Word, from Luke 2:16–20

And they came with haste and found Mary and Joseph, and the Babe lying in a manger. Now when they had seen Him, they made widely known the saying which was told them concerning this Child. And all those who heard it marveled at those things which were told them by the shepherds. But Mary kept all these things and pondered them in her heart. Then the shepherds returned, glorifying and praising God for all the things that they had heard and seen, as it was told them.

Worship and Praise—Congregation

NBH 182 *Go, Tell It on the Mountain* (2x in F)

NBH 179 *Angels, from the Realms of Glory* (vv. 1, 2 in A, v. 4 with chorus in Bb)

CH 260 *Worthy, You Are Worthy* (3x in Eb, 1 x in F)

Offertory Prayer—Pastoral Staff (Prayer of praise for provisions)

Offertory Praise—Worship Leader and Congregation

> NBH 312 *Jesus, Your Name* (3x in C)

> NBH 201 *Emmanuel*—(2x in C)

Worship and Praise—Congregation

Scripture Reading from Luke 2:8–14

> Now there were in the same country shepherds living out in the fields, keeping watch over their flock by night. And behold, an angel of the Lord stood before them, and the glory of the Lord shone around them, and they were greatly afraid. Then the angel said to them, "Do not be afraid, for behold, I bring you good tidings of great joy which will be to all people. For there is born to you this day in the city of David a Savior, who is Christ the Lord. And this will be the sign to you: You will find a Babe wrapped in swaddling cloths, lying in a manger." And suddenly there was with the angel a multitude of the heavenly host praising God and saying: "Glory to God in the highest, and on earth peace, goodwill toward men!"

> CH 269 *How Great Our Joy* (vv. 1, 2, 4 and transition)

> CH 270 *Joy to the World* (vv. 1, 2, 4 and transition)

> CH 271 *Joyful, Joyful, We Adore You* (vv. 1 and 2 in G)

Sermon—Pastor

> *The Angel's Christmas Confession*

Hymn of Invitation—Congregation

> NBH 411 *Come Just as You Are* (as needed)

Benediction Hymn—Congregation

> NBH 151 *Bless His Holy Name* (2x in Eb)

Postlude—Instrumentalists

KEY:

CH: Celebration Hymnal (Word Music/Integrity Music, Nashville, TN)

NBH: New Baptist Hymnal (2008)

WEEK 50

The Almost Christian

Acts 26:28
By George Whitefield

1. What Is Meant by "An Almost Christian"

   a. An almost Christian, if we consider him in respect to his duty to God, is one that halts between two opinions; that wavers between Christ and the world; that would reconcile God and mammon, light and darkness, Christ and Belial.

   b. If you consider him in respect to his neighbor, he is one that is strictly just to all; but then this does not proceed from any love to God or regard to man, but only through a principle of self-love, because he knows dishonesty will spoil his reputation, and consequently hinder his thriving in the world.

   c. He is one that depends much upon being negatively good, and contents himself with the consciousness of having done no one any harm.

2. The Reasons Why So Many Are No More Than Almost Christians

   a. A false notion of religion

   b. A servile fear of man

   c. A reigning love of money

   d. Too great a love for sensual pleasures

   e. A fickleness and instability of temper.

   They looked upon religion merely for novelty, as something which pleased them for a while; but after their curiosity was satisfied, they laid it aside again.

3. The Folly of Being No More Than an Almost Christian

   a. It is ineffectual to salvation.

   b. It is very prejudicial (*disadvantageous* or *harmful*) to that of others. An almost Christian is one of the most hurtful creatures in the world; he is a wolf in sheep's clothing. It is the greatest instance of ingratitude we can express toward our Lord and Master Jesus Christ.

WEEK 50

How God Makes Nothing into Everything

2 Kings 4:1–7
By Rev. Mark Smith

One of the most exciting times in an auto race is a moment near the end of some races when the announcer on television points out that the lead driver has chosen not to make one more pit stop, even though he is dangerously low on fuel. If the fuel holds out, he will win; if the tank goes empty, he will lose. It's as simple as that.

More than a few of these drivers run out of gas and lose a lot of prize money and points in the standings. There is something about a car sitting still on a racetrack, completely empty, while the rest of the drivers whiz by. It must be a helpless feeling for the driver too. At that point, there is nothing he can do to fill the emptiness in his tank.

There was a woman in the Bible who was almost empty—both spiritually and economically. If she ran out of what little oil she had, she would be helpless. She seemed to have no means of getting filled again. But God was on the way, both with His provision, and a great spiritual lesson.

1. The Need (vv. 1, 2)

    Her husband was dead; her sons were to be taken from her as security against her debts; her only resource was almost exhausted.

2. The Instructions (v. 4)

3. The Result (vv. 5–7)

WEEK 51

The Confessions of Christmas

Simon's Christmas Confession

Luke 2:25–35

By Dr. Jerry Sutton

When Jesus was eight days old, Mary and Joseph carried Him into Jerusalem's temple for the circumcision ceremony. Luke says that they came "to do for Him according to the custom of the law" (v. 27). As they entered into the temple complex, they encountered a very special elderly gentleman named Simeon, who was just and devout.

He was waiting for the "Consolation of Israel" (v. 25). This phrase refers to the prophetic promise depicting the messianic hope. In Isaiah 40:1, God said in describing the one who would come, "Comfort My people!" The word Luke used for *Consolation* is the same one Jesus used in John 14:16 (KJV) to tell His disciples that the Father would send them "another *Comforter*" (the Holy Spirit).

The Spirit had revealed to Simeon that "he would not see death before he had seen the Lord's Christ" (v. 26). So day after day, perhaps year after year, Simeon was looking, anticipating, wondering if today might be the day. Then one day the Spirit whispered into his heart, *Today is the day; go to the temple now.*

When Simeon arrived, he was looking for this coming Messiah. When that supernatural moment occurred, Simeon took up the baby in his arms and blessed, or praised, God. Then Simeon made his good confession about Jesus. What did he say?

"My eyes have seen Your salvation" (v. 30).

According to Luke, God had prepared this event, and all people will see it (v. 31). Simeon communicated the implications. He, Jesus, would be a light for revelation to the Gentiles (v. 32a). To the mass of humanity, who lived in spiritual darkness, a great light had come.

And to the Jews, He would be the glory of Israel (v. 32b). And He is the fulfillment and culmination of all the law and the prophets. He is the fulfillment of the promises of God. He is the hope of the world.

Specifically, this baby would be a dividing line. Simeon told Mary, "This Child is destined for the fall and rising of many in Israel, and for a sign which will be spoken against ... that the thoughts of many hearts may be revealed" (vv. 34, 35). Simeon was telling us that Jesus has come to save, yet those who refuse and resist Him will be lost. But for now, Simeon had seen God's salvation. He did have a word of warning for Mary, though: "A sword will pierce your heart also"—in other words, "This will be incredibly painful for you," no doubt referring to the Cross.

"According to Your word ..." (v. 29)

Luke tells us that the Spirit was active in Simeon's life. The Spirit had revealed God's plan and God's will to Simeon. And now, Simeon had come to the temple complex "by the Spirit" or under the Spirit's direction (v. 27). As Simeon followed the Spirit's leading, he was brought to Jesus. God's desire for us is that we be sensitive to the Spirit's leading.

The Old Testament is rich with the promises and prophecies of the coming Messiah. With the coming of Christ, God the Father was fulfilling these ancient promises. Yet on a more personal note, Simeon had received promises and assurances that were more immediate. And to Simeon, God kept His promises. He was promised (v. 26) that he would not see death until he had seen the Lord's Christ (or Messiah). And now, he was holding and blessing the fulfillment of that promise. All things, both prophesied in Scripture and promised personally to Simeon, came to pass, "according to [God's] Word."

"Lord, now You are letting Your servant depart in peace" (vv. 29, 30)

Simeon said, "Lord, now You are letting Your servant depart in peace ... for my eyes have seen Your salvation." So, when is a person ready to die? When he has made his peace with God. When there is no unfinished business. When there are no unrighted wrongs. When God says it's time.

Now, what does Simeon say to us?

First, he tells us that a Savior has come. In short, Jesus came to save the lost. He came to save us. After all, Luke tells us that Jesus came to seek and save that which is lost (19:10).

Second, he demonstrates that God can and will be active in our lives, just as he was in Simeon's. God has taken the initiative; now the issue is, will we respond? Will we cooperate with Him?

Third, he reminds us that God keeps His promises. So, will we claim the promises of God? Will we stand on the promises of God? Will we walk by faith?

And fourth, he tells us that we, too, can die in peace. Because there is nothing so sure as death, and nothing so unsure as time, it is incumbent upon us to respond now. In Paul's words, "Now is the day of salvation" (2 Cor. 6:2).

SUGGESTED ORDER OF WORSHIP

Simon's Christmas Confession

Prelude—Instrumental Group

NBH 197 *Sing We Now of Christmas*

Welcome and Announcements—Pastoral Staff

Welcome Song

NBH 347 *Lord, I Lift Your Name on High* (2x in G)

Baptismal Celebration—Pastor

Prayer of Worship—Pastor

Call to Worship—Congregation

NBH 192 *Hark! The Herald Angels Sing* (v. 1, chorus, v. 3, chorus in F)

NBH 184 *Angels We Have Heard on High* (v. 1, chorus in F, v. 4, chorus in G)

NBH 191 *The Birthday of a King* (v. 1, chorus, v. 2, chorus in G)

NBH 194 *O Holy Night* (v. 1, chorus, v. 3, chorus in C)

Offertory Prayer—Pastoral Staff

Offertory Praise—Congregation

>   NBH 206 *Silent Night! Holy Night* (vv. 1, 3, 4 in Bb)

>   NBH 207 *What Can I Give Him?* (2x in Bb)

Christmas Scripture Reading from Luke 2:25–33; Galatians 4:4–7—Pastor

And behold, there was a man in Jerusalem whose name was Simeon, and this man was just and devout, waiting for the Consolation of Israel, and the Holy Spirit was upon him. And it had been revealed to him by the Holy Spirit that he would not see death before he had seen the Lord's Christ. So he came by the Spirit into the temple. And when the parents brought in the Child Jesus, to do for Him according to the custom of the law, he took Him up in his arms and blessed God and said: "Lord, now You are letting Your servant depart in peace, according to Your word; for my eyes have seen Your salvation which You have prepared before the face of all peoples, a light to bring revelation to the Gentiles, and the glory of Your people Israel." And Joseph and His mother marveled at those things which were spoken of Him. . . .

But when the fullness of the time had come, God sent forth His Son, born of a woman, born under the law, to redeem those who were under the law, that we might receive the adoption as sons. And because you are sons, God has sent forth the Spirit of His Son into your hearts, crying out, "Abba, Father!" Therefore you are no longer a slave but a son, and if a son, then an heir of God through Christ.

>   NBH 199 *O Come All Ye Faithful* (1x in G, 1 x in Ab)

Message—Pastor

Simon's Christmas Confession

Hymn of Response/Invitation—Congregation

NBH 207 *What Can I Give Him?* (2x in Bb)

Benediction Hymn—Congregation

NBH 211 *I Have Seen the Light* (2x in G)

Postlude—Instrumentalist

NBH 202 *How Great Our Joy* (2x in G minor)

KEY:

NBH: New Baptist Hymnal (2008)

WEEK 51

Christ the Way, the Truth, and the Life

John 14:6
Robert Murray M'Cheyne

1. *Christ is the Way.* "I am the way; no man cometh," etc. The whole Bible bears witness that by nature we have no way to the Father. We are by nature full of sin, and God is by nature infinitely holy— that is, He shrinks away from sin. Just as the sensitive plant, by its very nature, shrinks away from the touch of a human hand, so God, by His very nature, shrinks away from the touch of sin. He is everlastingly separate from sinners; He is of purer eyes than to behold iniquity.

2. *Christ is the Truth.* The whole Bible, and the whole of experience, bear witness that by nature we are ignorant of *the truth*. No doubt there are many truths which an unconverted man does know. He may know the truths of mathematics and arithmetic—he may know many of the common everyday truths; but still it cannot be said that an unconverted man knows *the truth*, for Christ is the truth.

3. *Christ is the life.* The whole Bible bears witness that by nature we are dead in trespasses and sins—that we are as unable to walk holily in the world as a dead man is unable to rise and walk.

From *Memoir and Remains of the Rev. Robert Murray M'Cheyne,* by Andrew A. Bonar

WEEK 51

I Am Not Ashamed

Romans 1:16–18
By Mark Smith

Shame has become a relative term in our world. The same things that brought shame upon a person or family fifty years ago are, in most cases, not the same things that would bring shame today.

Paul declares openly, "I am not ashamed of the gospel." Why would an early Christian be tempted to be ashamed of the gospel?

1. Jesus was crucified—the most shameful form of public punishment.

2. Being a Christian was upsetting every norm of Jewish culture, religion, and society.

There is much to celebrate about the gospel. The gospel is about verses 16, 17):

1. Redemption (v. 16b)

2. Revelation (v. 17): "For in it [the gospel] the righteousness of God is revealed from faith to faith."

3. Reconciliation (v. 17): It is righteousness of God:

   a. Bought by God

   b. Brought by God

4. Relationship (v. 17b): "The just shall live by faith."

The gospel is not something to be ashamed of. However, there is shame in *rejecting* the gospel (v. 18.)

WEEK 52

A Christmas Communion

The End of the Year ...

The Beginning of All Things

Revelation 19:11ff.

Adapted from a Sermon by Dr. Calvin Miller

Introduction

Behold this cup, from which we shall shortly drink. It symbolizes not just the obedience of Christ. It stands even more for the cosmic purposes of God, and Jesus locked in on their plan of world redemption. The beginning of God's cosmic plan reads like this:

> In the beginning was the Word, and the Word was with God, and the Word was God. He was in the beginning with God. All things were made through Him, and without Him nothing was made that was made. In Him was life, and the life was the light of men. (John 1:1–4)

When we encounter Jesus, at the season in which December fades into the New Year, we just can't leave Him that "sweet little Jesus boy" we celebrate in December. A fresh, new year demands a fresh, new look at the Christ. The Baby of December is the Lord of His own coming, the King of kings, and the Lord of lords. In January he is the Ransom of the church, the victorious Captain of History.

> Now I saw heaven opened, and behold, a white horse. And He who sat on him was called Faithful and True, and in righteousness He judges and makes war. His eyes were like a flame of fire, and on His head were many crowns. He had a name written that no one knew except Himself. He was

clothed with a robe dipped in blood, and His name is called The Word of God. And the armies in heaven, clothed in fine linen, white and clean, followed Him on white horses. Now out of His mouth goes a sharp sword, that with it He should strike the nations. And He Himself will rule them with a rod of iron. He Himself treads the winepress of the fierceness and wrath of Almighty God. And He has on His robe and on His thigh a name written: KING OF KINGS AND LORD OF LORDS (Rev. 19:11–16)

At this time of the year, it is no sin to be taken with the advent of the infant Jesus. But we must remember that His sweet nativity is not all of the story. This infant Jesus isn't a mere mythology of angels, shepherds, and Eastern kings. John points out that the baby has now grown into the Commander of eternity, the Cosmic Redeemer Jesus.

The Galactic Size of God

Here we have the cosmology of the astronomers greatly reduced. Sci-fi author Isaac Asimov said that if you took the sun and shrank it down to a ball one foot in diameter, you could reduce our solar system to minute proportions. With a one-foot-diameter sun, Mercury, the sun's nearest planet, would be less than one-half inch across. If that one-foot sun were located here in the pulpit where I am standing, Mercury, that one-half-inch planet, would travel in an orbit that eclipsed the auditorium fourteen pews back. Venus would be about an inch in diameter and cut its orbit seventy-eight feet distant from right here. Earth would be just over an inch in size. Jupiter would ride three blocks away, and Pluto ... well, you get the point.

When I start realizing what this means in terms of the galactic size of God, I am amazed that such a small, marble-sized planet as our own should ever have captured the loving attention of a great God. Why would Jesus bother saving such a tiny renegade planet in the midst of such a minute solar system.

It is the minute mechanics of our annual orbit around the sun that caused author Calvin Miller to write in *The Singer*:

Earthmaker set earth spinning on its way,
And said, "Give me your vast infinity[,] my son:
I'll wrap it in a bit of clay,
Then enter Terra microscopically
To love the little souls who weep away
Their lives." I will," I said, "set Terra free."
And then I fell asleep, and all awareness fled.
I felt my very being shrinking down.
My vastness fled away. In dwindling dread,
All size decayed. The Universe around
Drew back. I woke upon a tiny bed
In one of Terra's smaller towns.[58]

God in the Cosmos

In the beginning days of the space program, a rather arrogant Soviet cosmonaut, Yuri Gagarin, came back from one of his orbital flights, shouting, "I flew, I flew, I flew!" At one of his more excited moments, he cried "I am an eagle! I am an eagle!" Then, reportedly, he ventured crassly into the world of theology and cried. "I have been into space and have not seen God anywhere out there. Therefore there can be no God!"

How refreshing it must have been, on a Christmas Eve just a few years later, when the crew of *Apollo VIII* began circling the moon for the first time (man had not landed there yet, but they had made it into lunar orbit), and pilot William Anders read to all who were viewing by television, "In the beginning God created the heaven and the earth."[59]

What a wonderful statement to say that this world is not here by accident. It came to be with God's forming fingers shaping it into purpose and into being. But John saw it all when he cried, without ever having left the planet to get the bird's eye view of the cosmonauts, "In the beginning was the Word, and all things were made by Him, *the Cosmic, intergalactic Word.*"

---

[58] Calvin Miller, *The Singer Trilogy* (Downers Grove, IL: IVP, 1975, 1977, 1979, 1990), 109 (*The Singer*).

[59] "The Apollo 8 Christmas Eve Broadcast," http://nssdc.gsfc.nasa.gov/planetary/lunar/apollo8_xmas.html.

Jesus, Faithful and True

Consider the names given to the Christ of Revelation 19: The first of those names is "Faithful," which means that between Jesus and His Father, there has never been a point of contention. Whatever God asked of Jesus, Jesus did. The second name is "True," which in Greek means "undiluted." Everything that Jesus said was absolutely the way it was; the way he lived was the way every life should be lived. Nothing false ever proceeded from His redeeming heart.

He was faithful! He was true!

But even more than this, he was the founder of a new Order, the Order of the Saving Blood! He will come on a white horse, conquering all His foes, to judge the nation with a rod of iron. And on his vestment and thigh is His double name, FAITHFUL AND TRUE.

Who would not bow before such a king?

It is said that Queen Victoria once went to hear a performance of *Messiah*. It was agreed ahead of time that because she was queen and because it was so hard to stand in her royal regalia, she need not honor the custom of standing at the singing of the "Hallelujah" chorus. But even as that great chorus began to swell—"For the Lord God omnipotent reigneth ... King of kings, and Lord of lords"—she was so overwhelmed that she not only stood but took the crown of England from her head in humility to offer it symbolically to Jesus, the FAITHFUL AND TRUE.

Conclusion

What does it mean to call Jesus "Faithful and True"? It means two things. First, as obedience and integrity were the substance of his soul, they must be the substance of your own. Second what it means to call Jesus Lord is to remember all that He went through to purchase your redemption. All God wants to have of you, you dare not call unreasonable. Jesus has a right to all of our lives, and nothing that He asks is unreasonable. No burden is too heavy to carry in His service if that is what He requires.

In a cathedral in Lubeck, Germany, is this inscription:

Thus speaketh Christ Our Lord to us:
Ye call me master and obey me not;
Ye call me light and see me not;
Ye call me the way and walk me not;
Ye call me life and desire me not;
Ye call me wise and follow me not;
Ye call me fair and love me not;
Ye call me all me eternal and seek me not;
Ye call me gracious and trust me not;
Ye call me noble and serve me not;
Ye call me mighty and honor me not;
Ye call me just and fear me not;
If I condemn you, blame me not.[60]

And so we lift the cup, this hour! He bled; we drink. He was broken; we eat.

He died; we live!

In the beginning was the Word, cosmic, galactic, redeeming. All heaven owned was mortgaged to build a cup and a loaf, and call you to your remembrance. It was all for you.

Like Victoria of old, we stand with bowed heads and each lift a crown that was never ours. And we each hold a cup He gave us on the night He left Gethsemane in resolve and became for us poor sinners the Commander of the Cross, Faithful and True.

SUGGESTED ORDER OF WORSHIP

Prelude—Instrumental

Joy to the World

Christmas Greeting—Pastor and Pastor's Wife Together

Joy to the World ...

Mary Had a Baby—Solo

---

[60] D. B. Wartermulder and G. K. Rrodel, *Advent Christmas* (Philadelphia: Fortress Press, 1973), 12.

Reading of Scripture from Psalm 46:1–11—Chairman of Deacons and Wife

> God is our refuge and strength,
>> A very present help in trouble.
>>> Therefore we will not fear,
> Even though the earth be removed,
>> And though the mountains be carried into the midst
>> of the sea;
> Though its waters roar and be troubled,
>> Though the mountains shake with its swelling. Selah
>
> There is a river whose streams shall make glad the city of God,
>> The holy place of the tabernacle of the Most High.
> God is in the midst of her, she shall not be moved;
>> God shall help her, just at the break of dawn.
> The nations raged, the kingdoms were moved;
>> He uttered His voice, the earth melted.
> The LORD of hosts is with us;
>> The God of Jacob is our refuge. Selah
>
> Come, behold the works of the LORD,
>> Who has made desolations in the earth.
> He makes wars cease to the end of the earth;
>> He breaks the bow and cuts the spear in two;
>>> He burns the chariot in the fire.
> Be still, and know that I am God;
>> I will be exalted among the nations,
>>> I will be exalted in the earth!
> The LORD of hosts is with us;
>> The God of Jacob is our refuge. Selah

Christmas Testimony (3-minute video)

> *I Wonder as I Wander*—Ensemble

Prayer of Thanksgiving—Chairman of Trustees

Beautiful Baby—Ladies Ensemble

Reading of Scripture from Isaiah 40—Pastor and Congregation

Pastor:

"Comfort, yes, comfort My people!" says your God.

Congregation:

The voice of one crying in the wilderness: "Prepare the way of the LORD."

Pastor:

"Make straight in the desert a highway for our God.... The glory of the LORD shall be revealed,

Congregation:

"And all flesh shall see it together; for the mouth of the LORD has spoken."

Pastor:

He will feed His flock like a shepherd; He will gather the lambs with His arm,

Congregation:

And carry them in His bosom, and gently lead those who are with young.

CH 270 *Joy to the World* (vv. 1, 2, 4)—Congregation

Prayer of Praise—Sunday School Superintendent

The Lord Has Come ...

CH 278 *Angels We Have Heard on High* (vv. 1, 3, 4)—Congregation

Reading of Scripture from Luke 2:8–14—President of Women's Ministry

Now there were in the same country shepherds living out in the fields, keeping watch over their flock by night. And behold, an angel of the Lord stood before them, and the glory of the Lord shone around them, and they were greatly afraid. Then the angel said to them, "Do not be afraid, for behold, I bring you good tidings of great joy which will be to all people. For there is born to you this day in the city of David a Savior, who is Christ the Lord. And this will be the sign to you: You will find a Babe wrapped in swaddling cloths, lying in a manger." And suddenly there was with the angel a multitude of the heavenly host praising God and saying: "Glory to God in the highest, and on earth peace, goodwill toward men!"

> CH 277 *Hark, the Herald Angels Sing* (vv. 1–3)— Congregation

Reading of Scripture from Luke 2:15–30—Associate Pastor

So it was, when the angels had gone away from them into heaven, that the shepherds said to one another, "Let us now go to Bethlehem and see this thing that has come to pass, which the Lord has made known to us." And they came with haste and found Mary and Joseph, and the Babe lying in a manger. Now when they had seen Him, they made widely known the saying which was told them concerning this Child. And all those who heard it marveled at those things which were told them by the shepherds. But Mary kept all these things and pondered them in her heart. Then the shepherds returned, glorifying and praising God for all the things that they had heard and seen, as it was told them.

... Let Heaven and Nature Sing!

CH 265 *The First Noel* (vv 1, 6)—Congregation

Reading of Scripture from Matthew 1:18–23

Now the birth of Jesus Christ was as follows: After His mother Mary was betrothed to Joseph, before they came together, she was found with child of the Holy Spirit. Then Joseph her husband, being a just man, and not wanting to make her a public example, was minded to put her away secretly. But while he thought about these things, behold, an angel of the Lord appeared to him in a dream, saying, "Joseph, son of David, do not be afraid to take to you Mary your wife, for that which is conceived in her is of the Holy Spirit. And she will bring forth a Son, and you shall call His name JESUS, for He will save His people from their sins." So all this was done that it might be fulfilled which was spoken by the Lord through the prophet, saying: "Behold, the virgin shall be with child, and bear a Son, and they shall call His name Immanuel," which is translated, "God with us."

O Holy Night—Solo on verses, congregation on chorus

Offering of Praise and Worship—Pastor

Infant Holy, Infant Lowly—Soloist

Away in a Manger—Instrumental Solo

Christmas Message—Pastor

Hymn of Invitation—Congregation

CH 253 *Silent Night, Holy Night* (vv. 1–3)

Prayer of Blessing and Thanksgiving—Pastor

CH 249 *O Come All Ye Faithful* (v. 1, chorus, v. 2, chorus, v. 3, chorus)—Congregation

Postlude—Instrumental

God Rest, Ye Merry Gentlemen

KEY:

CH: Celebration Hymnal (Word Music/Integrity Music, Nashville, TN)

WEEK 52

Christmas Eve Service

The Perfect Gift

John 3:16
By Dr. Kent Spann

Have you found the perfect gift for all the people on your list? Have you ever received the perfect gift?

God has the perfect gift for you this Christmas.

1. God gave us the perfect gift of love: "For God so loved the world . . . ."

   a. He gave us the perfect gift of His unlimited love (1 John 3:1).

   b. He gave us the perfect gift of His unending love (Jer. 31:3).

   c. He gave us the perfect gift of His unconditional love (1 John 4:19).

   d. He gave us the perfect gift of His undeserved love (Rom. 5:8).

2. God gave us the perfect gift of His Son: "that he gave His only begotten Son"

   Isaiah 9:6:

   a. He is called Wonderful.

   b. He is our Counselor.

   c. He is the Mighty God.

   d. He is the Everlasting Father.

   e. He is the Prince of Peace.

3. God gave us the perfect gift of faith: "that whoever believes in Him . . ."

   My friends, even the faith we have in Christ is a gift from God. In Ephesians 2:8, 9, the phrase "and that not of yourselves; it is the gift of God" connects with faith. The faith that we exercise is even a gift from God. Apart from God's work in our hearts, we would have never been able to believe.

4. God gave us the perfect gift of eternal life: "... should not perish but have everlasting life."

    a. He gave us the perfect gift of unending life.

    b. He gave us the perfect gift of a better life.

    c. He gave us the perfect gift of a relationship with God.

WEEK 52

Wise Men Still Seek Him

Matthew 2:1–12
By Rev. Mark Smith

As we consider these verses in Matthew chapter 2, it's important to know that the wise men weren't looking for Jesus the Messiah, or even Jesus the Savior. They were looking for a newborn, earthly king. God used a new star as a sign of His birth, because people in that day believed that when a king was born, a new star would appear. God sent the star, and the kings went out, seeking a king.

Three truths about seeking and finding Jesus:

1. Wise men don't seek Jesus.

   Spiritually speaking, nobody looks for Jesus. It is Jesus who is looking for you (John 6:44; 12:32).

2. You can't find Jesus without faith.

   There are times in life when you'd better get evidence before you believe. However, it is impossible to come to God on that basis (Eph. 2:8; Heb. 11:6; 11:1).

3. Those who are wise will find Him (Ps. 32:8; Prov. 2:6).

   God gave the kings from the East enough wisdom to follow the star and find the King of kings. This Christmas, He wants to give you enough faith to follow the star and find the Savior.

FUNERAL MESSAGE

A Most Significant Day

Ecclesiastes 3:1–8, especially 1, 2, and 4
By Dr. Dave Earley

> *This message is appropriate to give at the memorial service for a believer in Jesus Christ. This message is most effective when made most personal. It is designed to minister to the saved and preach the gospel to the lost. When you read the words "the deceased" you should fill in the name of the believer in Jesus Christ who has gone to be with the Lord.*

Introduction

Today is not just an ordinary day for any of us. Today marks one of those special times and seasons of life. Most of us do not come to the funeral home very often. We do not wrestle with the reality of death frequently. There are several special aspects about us being gathered here today. Today is a significant time for several reasons:

1. Today marks a time of rejoicing (Ps. 16:11; 2 Cor. 5:8; Rev. 21:4).

For us it is a day of sorrow and grief, but do not forget that for the deceased today marks a time of rejoicing. They are truly in a much better place, experiencing a much higher quality of life. There is no more sickness, pain, sorrow, or tears. Today, for the deceased, is a commencement exercise to a better life. Today is their graduation into glory.

2. Today marks a time of remembering.

These beautiful flowers, the lovely music, our presence here today are in honor of the life of the deceased. Today is a day for remembering them. We are fortunate in that there are so many good memories of the deceased. *[It is appropriate to share positive memories about the deceased at this time.]*

3. Today also marks a time for grieving (Eccl. 3:4).

The preacher of Ecclesiastes says that there is a "time to mourn." Losing someone we love produces genuine pain and grief. While we have tears of joy, we also have tears of sadness. Those who've walked this road know that grieving is a common process that takes several forms and progresses through several stages. The key to successfully moving through is choosing to take each one to God.

a. A sense of shock, numbness, and often denial

Just a few days ago, the deceased was right here with us. Now they are gone. It may feel like a shock. Death should shock us. God's original plan was for lives without death, but when sin entered into the world, death came with it. So death should shock us, and it does. Take your shock to God today.

b. Feelings of anger and resentment

Death also often provokes feelings of anger. We feel anger at death, anger at sin, anger at people, anger at self, anger at sickness, and sometimes anger toward God. The important thing is to not stay angry. Choose to use this event as a prod to draw you closer to God and not away from Him.

c. Guilt

Death may cause us to feel guilty. There are two kinds of guilt: real guilt and false guilt. Real guilt is the loving touch of God calling you to confess specific sin and change in an area of your life. If you have such guilt, realize that "if we confess our sins, [God] is faithful and just to forgive us of our sins and to cleanse us from all unrighteousness" (1 John 1:9).

False guilt is a vague accusation that you don't measure up. It is also based on untruths. Take your guilt, real or false, to God today. He loves you, will forgive you, and will cleanse you.

d. Loss, loneliness, sorrow, emptiness, pain

The departure of the deceased will leave a great hole. If you have not yet felt the deep sense of loss and pain, you will. You will miss them. This hole is a clear call to run to God. Ultimately He alone can fill the holes in our hearts. Take your loss and pain to God.

4. Today is a time for examination (2 Cor. 13:5; Rom. 14:12; Heb. 9:27).

Funerals are reminders of the reality of death, the certainty of death, and the inevitability of examination. We should prepare ourselves for death, because "after this the judgment" (Heb. 9:27).

Let me ask you, are you in the faith? Have you trusted Christ to be your Savior?

Are we living with eternity in view? No one has a guarantee of tomorrow. We could be here next week doing your funeral. Would we have the hope of knowing you would be in heaven? Would we have the confidence that you would do well on your exam?

Conclusion

Are you ready for your final examination? Will you see the deceased in heaven? How can you know for sure that you are saved?

A—Admit you are a sinner and need God.

B—Believe in Jesus Christ. That He lived a sinless life, died for you, rose again.

C—Call upon Him to save you; commit your life to Him.

D—Determine to begin doing everything He says.

FUNERAL MESSAGE

Anchors in Death

Romans 8:28–39

By Dr. Kent Spann

Death brings chaos and confusion. In the midst of the chaos and confusion, we need an anchor to throw out that will secure us.

Today, I want us to focus our attention on a marvelous portion of Scripture in Romans 8. In this portion are found two anchors that stabilize and comfort us in the face of our or another's death, or for that matter any circumstance we face.

First Anchor: God's Unfailing Purposes (8:28–34)

Paul tells us in these verses that what God begins at our salvation, He will finish!

We all have numerous projects that we start but never finish. When we die, there will still be projects and things that didn't get finished. Not so with God, because what God begins, He finishes. See Philippians 1:6.

I would like to lift some powerful truths from these verses that will bring comfort to you today.

1. God is sovereign in our salvation (8:28–30).

   One hundred percent of those who are His will finish as His. In verses 29 and 30 we see the same number He foreknew were predestined, and the same exact number He predestined were called, and the same number He called were justified, and the same number He justified were glorified.

2. God paid the ultimate price for our salvation (8:31, 32).

   This was not some cheap, two-bit salvation.

   If He paid the ultimate price to save us, wouldn't it make sense that He would do whatever is necessary or needed to take care of us?

John Bunyan, who wrote *Pilgrim's Progress*, sat at his desk in deep depression, wondering if he could go on, worrying about the future, when Romans 8:31 came to his rescue:

> I remember that I was sitting in a neighbor's home, and was very sad, that word came suddenly to me. "What shall we say to these things? If God be for us, who can be against us?" That was a help to me.

3. God protects those who belong to Him (8:33, 34).

That is why Paul is able to say what he does in verse 28. Bishop Anders Nygren has written:

> Just as the present aeon is to be followed by eternity, it has already been preceded by an eternity. Only when we see our present existence set in God's activity, which goes from eternity to eternity, do we get it in right perspective. Then man comes to see that everything that comes to the Christian in this life—and consequently the sufferings of the present life too—must work together for good to him.[61]

God's unfailing purposes secured the one we honor today, and it will for you as well if you lean upon God.

---

[61] R. Kent Hughes, *Romans: Righteousness from Heaven* (Crossway, 1991), 167.

FUNERAL MESSAGE

Memorial Service for a Senior Saint

Psalm 16

By Dr. Carl Barrington

The emotions of those already in heaven are expressed to us by David in Psalm 16, where he says to God, "In Your presence is fullness of joy" (v. 11). The apostle Paul had a similar vision from God as he tells about a man who died and was taken up to heaven and who heard "inexpressible words, which it is not lawful for a man to utter" in 2 Corinthians 12:4.

We aren't given the specifics of what either man experienced, but one thing is very clear. In the presence of God, both King David and the apostle Paul knew that we would experience pure joy and wonder.

[Name], who we remember today, trusted in Jesus Christ as his Lord and Savior and has made the transition from this world to the next, and has exchanged his citizenship from the USA to the K.O.G.—the Kingdom of God!

He can now experience what many of us have looked forward to for a long time. Just as it says in the old hymn, "when by His grace, I shall look on His face, that will be glory, be glory for me."

Thoughts of heaven and an eternity in the service of God are wonderful to think about and talk about. But [Name] has passed from this life, in faith, and is now experiencing with new eyes what his heart had told him was true for many years.

God's Word says that those who make a decision to trust in Jesus Christ as Lord and Savior can fully understand those words of Paul, "For I know whom I have believed and am persuaded that He is able to keep what I have committed to Him until that Day" (2 Tim. 1:12).

The testimony of senior citizens who have been faithful to the Lord is the greatest prize of Christianity. Satan doesn't have any happy older men and women. But to those who have trusted in the Lord, things are different. Through the prophet Isaiah, God tells us about the special relationship He has with senior citizens. In Isaiah 46:4, He says, "Even to your old age, I am He, and even to gray hairs I will carry you! I have made, and I will bear; even I will carry, and will deliver you."

The reward we will receive as His obedient servants is to hear Him tell us, "Well done, good and faithful servant; you were faithful over a few things, I will make you ruler over many things. Enter into the joy of your [L]ord!" (Matt. 25:21).

Can we be confident that those who have passed from this life, who have trusted in Jesus Christ as Lord and Savior, are with Him in heaven right now? Yes we can! Paul told the church in Thessalonica that Christians don't have to grieve like the unbelievers, because for the unbelievers there is no hope.

As Christians, though, we have assurance, because we know the truth in the words of the old hymn by Edward Mote: "My hope is built on nothing less, than Jesus' blood and righteousness." But, even with this truth, Jesus knew that worry and uncertainty would creep into our lives as a liar. To remind us all, He told His disciples in John 14:1–3, "Let not your heart be troubled; you believe in God, believe also in Me. In My Father's house are many mansions; if it were not so, I would have told you. I go to prepare a place for you. And if I go and prepare a place for you, I will come again and receive you to Myself; that where I am, there you may be also."

I know that we will sincerely miss [Name], but I can promise you that the very worst thing that can happen between two children of God is temporary separation. One day, all of you who have asked Jesus Christ to save you from your sins will see your fellow Christians again. To them it will seem as if just a little time has passed. If they could speak to you now, they would say, "Please don't cry for me. Cry if you need to, but only because of the temporary separation. We *can* all be together again."

Whether it happens or not is related to the biggest question of life. Who is Jesus Christ? Who is He to you? Is He a great man, God's Son, the founder of a great world religion? Or, is He *your* Savior, *your* Lord, and *your* friend?

Do you know Him more as a baby in a manger and a man dying on the Cross, or as the one *rising* from the tomb and *living* in you as a personally invited guest? Because if you really do *know* Him, they one day when you stand before Him, He will acknowledge that He knows you, too, and welcome you into eternity, just as He did with

[*Name*] a few days ago. As we remember [*Name*] today, remember that each human soul lives forever. Physical death is merely the point of transition between a few years here on the earth and an eternity with or without God. Let's pray.

WORSHIP SERVICES

SUGGESTED ORDER OF WORSHIP

Ordination Service for Ministers
"Christ the Example of Ministers"

Prelude—Instrumental Group

NBH 7

Welcome—Pastoral Staff

Prayer of Worship—Pastoral Staff

Worship and Praise—Congregation

NBH 5 *How Great Is Our God* (2x in Bb)

NBH 162 *Wonderful, Merciful Savior* (v. 1, chorus, v. 2, chorus, v. 3, chorus in Bb)

NBH 6 *How Great Thou Art* (chorus, v. 1, chorus, v. 4, chorus in Bb)

NBH 133 *Shout to the Lord* (2x in Bb)

Challenge from the Chairman of the Ordination Committee

Message—Pastor

Christ, the Example of Ministers

Prayer of Commission—Ordination Committee

Hymn of Response/Invitation—Congregation

NBH 18 *Glorify Thy Name* (as needed)

Benediction Hymn—Congregation

NBH 8 *Bless the Lord, O My Soul*

Postlude—Instrumental Group

    NBH 13 *Joyful, Joyful, We Adore Thee*

KEY:

NBH: New Baptist Hymnal (2008)

SUGGESTED ORDER OF WORSHIP

Baby Dedication

Prelude—Instrumental

    NBH 150 *This is the Day*

Prayer of Worship—Associate Pastor

Praise and Worship

    NBH 655 *The Family Prayer Song* (2x in G)

Responsive Reading

Pastor:

As for me and my house, we will serve the Lord.

Congregation:

Train up a child in the way he should go and when he is old he will not depart.

Pastor:

Whoever welcomes this little child in My name welcomes Me.

Grandparents:

Let the little children come to me ... for the kingdom of heaven belongs to such as these.

Pastor:

You have prepared praise from the mouths of children and nursing infants.

Parents:

Neither height nor depth, nor anything else ... will be able to separate us from the love of God.

Song of Dedication—Congregation

> NBH 654 *A Christian Home* (vv. 1–4 in F)

Presentation of Children—Pastor

> NBH 650 *Praise Him, All Ye Little Children* (vv. 1–3 in D)

> NBH 651 *Jesus Loves the Little Children* (2x in G)

Dedication of Children—Pastor

Commitment from Parents to Help Nurture this child

Commitment from Grandparents to Help Nurture This Child

Commitment from Congregation to Help Nurture This Child

Prayer of Dedication—Pastor

> NBH 652 *Jesus Loves Me* (v. 1, chorus, v. 2. chorus in C)

Song of Thanksgiving—Congregation

> NBH 149 *Praise Him, Praise Him* (v. 1, chorus, v. 3, chorus in G)

Postlude—Instrumental

> NBH 655 *The Family Prayer Song* (chorus only in G)

KEY:

NBH: New Baptist Hymnal (2008)

SUGGESTED ORDER OF WORSHIP

Christmas Eve Communion Service

Prelude—Instrumentalists

NBH 190 *He Is Born* (2x in F)

Prayer of Praise—Pastoral Staff Asking Blessing for the Evening

Welcome—Pastoral Staff

Song of Welcome (*meet and greet*)—Congregation

NBH 181 *Joy to the World* (vv.1 and 2 in D, v. 4 in Eb)

Prayer of Worship and Praise—Pastoral Staff

NBH 180 *The First Noel* (v. 1, chorus, v. 4, chorus, chorus in D)

Communion

Scripture Reading from Matthew 26:26–30—Pastor

And as they were eating, Jesus took bread, blessed and broke it, and gave it to the disciples and said, "Take, eat; this is My body." Then He took the cup, and gave thanks, and gave it to them, saying, "Drink from it, all of you. For this is My blood of the new covenant, which is shed for many for the remission of sins. But I say to you, I will not drink of this fruit of the vine from now on until that day when I drink it new with you in My Father's kingdom." And when they had sung a hymn, they went out to the Mount of Olives.

Sharing of the Bread

NBH 220 *Tell Me the Story of Jesus* (vv. 1 and 3 in D)

NBH 124 *Who Is He in Yonder Stall?* (v. 1, chorus, v. 2, chorus, v. 3, chorus, v. 4, chorus)

Prayer of Thanksgiving for the Bread

Sharing of the Cup

> NBH 402 *A Communion Hymn for Christmas* (vv. 1, 3, 4, and 5 in D)

> NBH 209 *Mary, Did You Know?* (v. 1, chorus, v. 3, chorus in B-minor)

Prayer of Thanksgiving for the Cup

Worship and Praise—Congregation

> NBH 175 *O Come, O Come, Emmanuel* (v. 1, chorus, v. 3, chorus, v. 4, chorus in E-minor)

> NBH 198 *What Child Is This?* (v. 3, chorus in E-minor)

Missions Video

Offertory Prayer for the Nations—Pastoral Staff

Offertory Praise—Solo and PT Ensemble

> NBH 191 *The Birthday of the King* (v. 1, chorus, v. 2, chorus in G)

Message—Pastor

Hymn of Invitation—Instrumentalists

> NBH 552 *My Jesus, I Love Thee* (as needed in F)

Lighting the Candles—Congregation

> NBH 206 *Silent Night, Holy Night* (vv. 1, 3, and 4 in Bb)

Hymn of Benediction—Congregation

> *NBH 184 Angels* We Have Heard on High

Postlude—Instrumentalists

> *God Rest Ye Merry Gentlemen*

KEY:

NBH: New Baptist Hymnal (2008)

SHARPENING YOUR PREACHING SKILLS

How to Prepare Sermons with Pizzazz!

By Dr. Carl Barrington

Let's face it. After many years in the same pulpit, we all fight the tendency to do things in the same old way. Perhaps you always preach through books of the Bible, or maybe you preach fifty-two consecutive topical sermons. Give your congregation a break and give yourself a challenge by attempting something brand-new! Get outside your comfort zone and learn to preach on well-known topics in an entirely new way. Add a little pizzazz by rethinking the familiar.

1. Rewrite a parable to retain biblical meaning, but with modern-day characters and situations.

    Examples: the parable of the rich, young fool in Luke 12:13–21, the parable of the great banquet in Luke 14:15–24, or the parable of the shrewd manager in Luke 16:1–18. These are timeless stories. Simply create a twenty-first-century version of the same story, exchanging the particulars, but retaining Jesus' original message. If you have people in your church interested in drama, this would be an excellent opportunity to involve more people in the service.

    Options are:

    a. Present the parable yourself in the form of a monologue.

    b. Have a church member do the same thing.

    c. Have actors portray each person in the story (usually only two or three in most parables).

2. Consider a sermon that you already have outlined in your mind. What kind of character would make this sermon come alive?

    a. Create an "opposite character." I have a character I call the Reverend Pharis C. Priestly, who never seems to understand grace and always responds with a legalistic point of view. Whenever my church hears me become him in a sermon, they always understand that whatever "Rev. Priestly" suggests, they should do the opposite.

b. Create seasonal characters, like "Football Fan," who regularly gets his priorities out of whack during football season, or "Secular Christmas Man," who loves the sparkling lights of December, but who forgets why we celebrate on December 25.

c. Write out appropriate questions for congregational members to ask at preordained times during the sermon. This will always get the attention of your congregation. People are so unprepared for anyone other than the pastor to speak during the sermon half-hour that they will listen more attentively than ever. For example: you are preaching on Romans 1, and questions may arise regarding what will happen to those who have never heard the name of Jesus. Or, you are preaching on 1 Corinthians 12, and questions arise regarding the spiritual gifts that may not be manifest in your church or denomination. Expect and anticipate these questions, and deal with them straightforwardly.

3. Create or expand on a character who is mentioned only peripherally in Scripture.

For example: the young servant girl who convinced Naaman to go to Elisha in 2 Kings 5, or the mother/father of the bride at the wedding feast at Cana in John 2:1–11, or possible insight into the mind of Judas as he waited to betray Jesus in Luke 22:1–6, or what Balaam might have done after returning home in Numbers 22–24. An especially humorous one is to have a real-life husband and wife engage in a one-sided conversation between Elizabeth and mute Zacharias while awaiting the birth of their future son. An extremely serious and dramatic dialogue can be imagined between Herodias and Herod after the murder of John the Baptist.

4. Listen to a variety of both secular and Christian music and media to come up with songs and video clips that can be used before, during, and after a sermon on a particular topic. For example: play "Material Girl" by Madonna before leading a youth Bible study on values and

living life as a Christian in a majority non-Christian world, or play "At Seventeen" by Janis Ian, or "Dust in the Wind" by Kansas before Bible study on the meaning that life has for Christians and the lack of meaning that most non-Christians experience at many times during life. If you watch movies or television, constantly be on the lookout for scenes that can be shown in church to make your point from popular culture. (Be sure not to violate copyright laws, however.) You may already be aware of the excellent series based on *The Andy Griffith Show* that many groups have used in church and small-group Bible study.

5. Prepare a creative sermon outline on one of the following topics (even if you're not sure how you will use it): "Does God Really Care About What I Think?" or "How Can I Know What God's Will Is for My Life?" or "The Life of King David: How Starting Well and Finishing Well Are Two Different Things." This is especially good for pastors who *never* preach topical sermons. Sometimes the best way out of a rut is to simply jump out.

This list is by no means exhaustive. Even if creativity doesn't come easily to you, be bold and try something new. As long as you are faithful to Scripture, your congregation will almost certainly learn new truths about familiar scriptures. Emphasize the application section of these sermons, and your congregation may leave your worship service ready to be of service to both their Lord *and* their little corner of the world!

SHARPENING YOUR PREACHING SKILLS

How to Preach on Prayer

By Dr. Daniel Henderson

I have often said that prayer is the most often talked-about and least practiced discipline of the Christian faith. This truth poses both the danger and the opportunity of preaching on prayer. On one hand, more information and inspiration about prayer can lead to a widening of the gap between learning and obedience. Conversely, sermons on prayer that are coupled with application and practice can motivate and equip your people to become a true house of prayer as Jesus described (Luke 19:46) and Paul instructed (1 Tim. 2:1–3).

In striking the balance between preaching and practice, our deep longing for our people is reflected in Jesus' words: "If you know these things, blessed are you if you do them" (John 13:17). Our goal for preaching on prayer is not just to increase knowledge or stimulate warm emotion. Our ultimate aim is a church culture marked by the regular, biblical, passionate engagement in both private and corporate prayer for the glory of Christ.

Preaching on the people of prayer sparks motivation. Most of us learn best by the example of others. The Bible presents many stories of both Old and New Testament saints who prayed with honesty and spiritual resolve. A "Portraits of Prayer" approach allows the congregation to embrace the personal struggles, enduring faith, and candid vocabulary of real people with a "nature like ours" (James 5:17) who prayed in and through the problems of life. One valuable resource to stimulate thought about the many examples of prayer is the classic *All the Prayers of the Bible* by Herbert Lockyer (Grand Rapids: Zondervan, 1959).

Preaching on the patterns of prayer provides tools. Certainly, we cannot reduce prayer to predictable formulas or mindless mechanics. However, the Bible gives many patterns for prayer that can help Christians find practical handles for the principles of prayer. Of course, the great pattern Jesus gave in His model prayer is one that should be taught and modeled regularly. The Psalms present many valuable prayer patterns, as do some of the great prayers of biblical characters like Daniel (Dan. 9:1–23), Mary (Luke 1:46–51), and Paul (Eph. 1:3–14; 3:14–21).

Preaching on the promises of prayer increases faith. Our preaching on the subject of prayer must ultimately stimulate the faith of the congregation in believing God for great things, for without this faith it is impossible to please God, even in our praying (Heb. 11:6). However, it is vital that we present these promises in context, clearly teaching any requisite conditions, and not offered as some "genie bottle" that can be stroked haphazardly to produce instant results.

For example, John 15:7, 8 says, "If you abide in Me, and My words abide in you, you will ask what you desire, and it shall be done for you. By this My Father is glorified, that you bear much fruit; so you will be My disciples." The conditions for this promise involve a commitment to spiritual intimacy and biblical hunger. The goal of this promise is the glory of the Father through our fruitful lives of genuine discipleship.

During my twenty-five years as a senior pastor, I found that an annual series on prayer kept the priority of prayer central in the life of the church. A rotation of the above themes (people, patterns, and promises) proved to be a balanced and motivating approach.

Engaging in the practice of prayer creates a praying church. A great concern in this article is not simply the need for more information on prayer from the pulpit, but real leadership in prayer in conjunction with our teaching. In spite of the plethora of prayer books and devotionals in our modern society, it is still rare to find a true "praying church." This is partly because many pastors are more comfortable preaching on prayer than modeling prayer among the people. The point is that we should strive to couple, even surpass, our preaching on prayer with the actual practice and modeling of prayer in the regular course of church life.

One pastoral colleague confessed to me that he preached on prayer every Sunday for an entire year. His observation was that the sermons did little to increase the practice of prayer in his church. He then began to lead his people in regular gatherings of prayer, modeling the principles and practices of prayer, and the prayer level of this church increased significantly. We must remember it was Jesus' model (i.e., "as he was praying" in Luke 11:1) that motivated the disciples to want to learn more about prayer. His message followed his model. Messages without modeling can cause our people to have an affection for the romantic notion of prayer but fall very short in the biblical practice of prayer.

As we seek to clearly present the great doctrines and precepts of prayer, we do well to heed the penetrating words of Charles Spurgeon: "The minister who does not earnestly pray over his work must surely be a vain and conceited man ... he limps in his ministry like the lame man in the Proverbs 'whose legs were not equal' for his praying is shorter than his preaching."

As a college student, I remember listening to a motivational message by Charles "Tremendous" Jones. He made a statement that continues to challenge me to this day: "All the truth in the world will do you little good until God brings a person across your path and you are able to see that truth in action. Suddenly, that truth becomes a driving force in your life." As preachers, we long to deliver biblical, accurate, and applicable messages on the subject of prayer. We also must ask the Lord for the grace to make the message of prayer a driving force in the lives of our people as we show them how to pray, both from the pulpit and on our knees.

SHARPENING YOUR PREACHING SKILLS

Preparing Your Flock to Share Christ with Mr. Skeptic

by Michael R. Licona, PhD

Thirteen years into my marriage, I needed help. Marriage had, to that point, been a profound disappointment. My wife and I could not understand each other's needs. Then we read Gary Chapman's *The Five Love Languages*, a book that would be a game changer in our marriage. Chapman's premise is that there are five general ways in which we communicate to our spouses that we love them (i.e., gift giving, words of affirmation, physical affection, acts of service, quality time) and that one or two of them are the ways that an individual hears most clearly that he or she is loved by his or her spouse. (If you identify more than two of the above as strong needs for yourself, you're needy and should get some help!) Other than my own selfishness, I had attempted to communicate my love for Debbie by the love language in which *I* preferred to be loved. And she did the same. As you may guess, the problem is that we each have different love languages. The results were that both of us had been telling the other, "I love you," but the message was in a language the other couldn't hear. Once we understood each other's love languages, we could effectively communicate love to the other, and our marriage experienced a dramatic improvement that occurred almost overnight.

A similar principle applies to sharing the gospel. There are gospel languages. One believes because an authority in his life taught him that the gospel is true, while another believes because of someone's testimony of how Christ has changed her life. But there are others who don't care about testimonies or what their parents or teachers taught. For these, only the facts will do, and someone's testimony will be of little persuasive value.

During the last few decades we have watched the West become a post-

Christian culture where Christianity is not only no longer the default religion but where it is actually the religion that receives the most abuse without apology from the major media and secular academic institutions. The time has never been greater in the West for pastors to teach a rational defense of the Christian faith to their members. This is a field called *apologetics*. The term comes from the Greek word *apologia*, meaning "a rational defense." First Peter 3:15 instructs Christians to be ready always to "give a defense" (*apologia*) to everyone who asks you to give an account of the hope in you. This has become an increasingly difficult task.

In the 1970–80s, Josh McDowell and Norman Geisler provided wonderful apologetic resources that were more than adequate for defending the Christian faith against skeptics, including many professors on university campuses. The advent of the Internet, where data became available in quantities unthinkable in the previous decade, has resulted in a seemingly infinite number of discussions incorporating new data and requiring both greater specialization and carefully nuanced arguments to survive in cyberworld, the classroom, and the office.

It's therefore of no surprise to observe that a number of pastors are now intimidated by apologetics due to the volume of data with which one must now familiarize himself. It's not necessarily that pastors are unable to engage in academic thinking as much as that they already have too much on their plates without adding the daunting task of rigorous research in a different field and because they are comfortable doing and teaching evangelism as they always have. This is certainly understandable. However, such pause is unnecessary, and many churches are missing out on some great blessings God has and wants to give as a result. Therefore, I contend that *every pastor can have a more fruitful and enjoyable ministry by observing the three Rs of apologetics*.

The first R concerns the *reason* for training your flock in apologetics. It's apostolic. Peter commanded believers to use apologetics when called upon. How will church members do this unless they are trained? The pastor is ultimately responsible to see to it that his flock receives adequate training. If he is so inclined, he can conduct the training. If not, he can usually find a member who is attracted to apologetics and who will be happy to provide training in a Sunday school or small-group setting. And don't forget that your youth group needs the training in preparation for what they will face in the university classroom! It's also interesting to observe that the apostles used different methods for sharing the gospel with different cultures. The beginning verses of Acts 17 inform us that it was Paul's habit to go into the synagogues every Sabbath and, *using the Scriptures*, show that the Messiah had to suffer, die, and rise from the dead. Later on in the same chapter we find Paul speaking to the intellectuals in Athens. During his presentation Paul never made so much as a single appeal to the Scriptures. Different from the Jews in the synagogues, those in Athens did not share Paul's belief in the authority of the Scriptures. So, he instead used *their literature* to illustrate his point. But the message of God's revealing Himself through the resurrection of His Son, Jesus, remained a constant. Just as Jesus changed the tone of his message according to whether his audience was a rich man who was truly seeking eternal life (Mark 10:17–22) or a group of stiff-necked Pharisees (Matt. 12:22–45), Paul was willing to adjust the method by which he shared the gospel according to his audience. His objective was to communicate effectively (1 Cor. 9:19–23).

The second R concerns *recommendations* for training your flock in apologetics. Prepare them for *real* challenges. More harm than good may be done by providing a halfhearted and inadequate apologetic that no longer works in the real world. Weak arguments will be easily defeated by today's skeptical high school student who has engaged in countless hours of discussion of religious matters in Internet chat rooms and may result in fostering doubts about Christianity's truth in the mind of the defeated church member. Therefore, use updated resources that are readily available for training in apologetics. If you're one of those who have developed an interest in apologetics and have read extensively in the area, be very careful not to overload your flock with too much information too quickly. Don't use a single sermon to provide four major arguments for God's existence. Break it up into four sermons. Your flock will get much more out of your messages, and you'll reap four sermons from your work instead of only one!

The third R concerns *resources* for training your flock in apologetics. There is now a wealth of fantastic resources on apologetics, many of which are turnkey solutions. The North American Mission Board has created a quality Web site with articles supporting the Christian worldview and written by leading scholars and scientists: www.4truth. net. The website exists in five languages at the time I write this. Of even more interest is that this site has a private page providing more than forty PowerPoint presentations for pastors, Sunday school teachers, and youth/collegiate ministers. These are available for free download in eleven languages! Go to www.4truth.net/ppts. Download, read through them a few times, and you're ready to deliver your next message. These can be a great help on those weeks when numerous emergencies pop up and you don't have enough time to prepare a sermon.

Lee Strobel and Gary Poole have created a number of apologetics resources for small groups based on Strobel's best-selling books *The Case for Christ*, *The Case for Faith*, and *The Case for a Creator* (Grand Rapids: Zondervan). Each is a DVD with six sessions and includes a participant's guide with open-ended discussion questions that lead to group interaction and discussion. Leaders only need to facilitate the discussion and cue up the DVD for showing at the appropriate times. No previous knowledge on the subjects discussed is required.

The information age has brought many discoveries that support the truth of the Christian worldview. And there are many quality resources, many of which are turnkey, that allow pastors to equip their flocks adequately and easily. Neglecting one's responsibility in this area will only hurt the sheep we have been commissioned to protect. However, giving attention to the important topic of apologetics will increase the fruitfulness of one's ministry. And this added fruit will be accompanied by joy and amazement!

SHEPHERDING GOD'S PEOPLE

Myths and Maxims in Conflict Resolution

By Dr. Rich Halcombe

Conflict is one of the hardest things pastors and church leaders have to face. It's emotionally draining, can result in hurt feelings and people exiting the church. The good news is that each of us can learn how to manage conflict well, to get good results for the church in general and the individuals involved. Handling conflict well requires the best of who God wants us to be and can be a time of great growth.

It's fair to say all churches experience conflict. If we think our church is beyond conflict or has outgrown conflict or won't have any conflict, it says more about our ability to perceive conflict than it does the presence or the potential of it. It is true that some churches have less conflict than others. The churches with lesser levels of locking horns are those who address divisive issues quickly and wisely over time.

The Bible props up the premise that churches experience conflict. The second time the word *church* is mentioned in the Bible (Matt. 18:15–17), it is within the context of conflict and a way to resolve it. Moses, the great liberator of God's people, had his share of conflicts. Korah and his cohorts were just one example. Even the apostle Paul could have sung, "Nobody knows the trouble I've seen" when he saw the conflict brewing in the church at Philippi. He addressed the brouhaha in Philippians 4:2 when he says, "I implore Euodia and I implore Syntyche to be of the same mind in the Lord." Leaders know that griping and complaining and arguing and conflict aren't good. It tears at morale, creates dissension, and impedes the progress of the church. And, as leaders, we also know that it is part and parcel of our responsibility to deal with conflict in a way that builds the body and lessens the likelihood of conflict in the future. What's harder to know is the best way to deal with those potentially explosive situations. Here are some myths and maxims when entering those perplexities.

MYTH #1: Your approach to conflict is based on your personality and background. It's more colored by your character than it is conditioned by your nature or nurture. The way you handle conflict is your choice. It may be a well-considered response or a knee-jerk reaction, yet it's a choice nonetheless. And it's best to choose your response based on the particular situation. Tendencies need not be activities. Each person possesses the God-given capacity to act how he so chooses. As Christian leaders, we are called to act wisely, humbly and gently.

MYTH #2: You have to have firsthand information before you deal with the situation. Often God gives us a heads-up when something is brewing. If someone tells us there's a problem, we don't have to hear the same story from that certain person before we address the issue. God is letting us know, through that person, that we have a big problem. What do you do? If it is of a serious nature, you call and schedule a meeting with the person who was mentioned. You open the meeting with something like, "You know, this may sound crazy, but, I heard that someone in our church has a major problem with the way I'm handling [fill in the blank]. And what's even crazier is that your name was attached to it. Can you help me understand that?" Contrary to popular belief, you don't have to tell where you heard it. If there is an issue you personally need to address, it could come up in this conversation, and you can make adjustments in your own ministry, if need be. At the very least, the potential complainer knows that those kinds of things are taken seriously, whether he/she said anything or not. And if he/she didn't say anything, you haven't accused anybody, but you have addressed the issue. And if the issue does arise, you deal with it in that meeting. Awareness, not firsthand information, is our clue that we are responsible to handle it.

Now a couple of principles, or maxims, to help us deal with conflict constructively.

MAXIM #1: A little sooner is better than a lot later. The best way to handle conflict is early. Here are a few reasons to handle it sooner rather than later.

The earlier conflict is addressed:

- the less emotion is attached to it, making it easier to address
- the fewer people are involved, reducing the spread of the hurt or offense

- the less damage is done, making it easier to overcome
- the more likely it is for the result to be good, which is what we all want!

MAXIM #2: The best strategy in any conflict is to be non-anxious. Your emotional demeanor is the one most important factor in dealing with difficulty. If you are relaxed, it relaxes others around the room. If you are tight, it tightens the already tense. The Bible prescribes this in Galatians 6:1: "Brethren, if a man is overtaken in any trespass, you who are spiritual restore such a one in a spirit of gentleness, considering yourself lest you also be tempted." Note we are commanded "how" to approach a sinning brother: gently. Even when it's serious, we don't have to be angry, and it's much better if we aren't. One good way to reduce the anxiety is to inject humor in the discussion. It relieves the tension and shows that this one issue needn't be the end of the world (or the end of the relationship).

The main key that has worked well for so many is to seek wisdom. Study what the Scriptures say about it, ask God for it, and hang around godly people to learn it. The Bible makes a strong correlation between producing peace and having wisdom. And as He increases our wisdom, we are better prepared to deal with conflict as it comes. And it will come.

SHEPHERDING GOD'S PEOPLE

From the Pew to the Pulpit

By Tony Brown

I have been asked to write an article entitled "From the Pew to the Pulpit" as a way of providing feedback to pastors as they prepare to lead their congregations from the pulpit. I am currently senior vice president at a retail organization, with responsibility for almost two thousand employees and a budget of over $100 million. In the ministry, I have served as a deacon for more than twenty years and assisted administratively throughout the church. I have had the privilege of being a member of various size congregations during the past thirty years. The size of worship attendance varied from fifty to more than five thousand. I have also ministered very closely with the senior pastors at multiple churches. The following article comes from a sincere desire to encourage pastors in the calling on their lives to lead the church.

First, the power of a pastor's preaching is preceded by his personal touch on the congregation. Members need to spend time directly with their pastor in order to feel a connection on a personal level. I have seen this work effectively for pastors in several ways. Some stay after the Sunday morning service and talk as long as the people stay around. This could add up to an hour after the end of the service, but it gives personal time to the members. Many choose to stand at the door and shake hands as the congregation exits. Others will greet the crowd as they arrive for worship service. This small gesture of a personal connection to the pastor creates a bond of trust with the congregation. Regardless of how it is accomplished, Sunday morning is your best opportunity to connect with your membership—maximize your impact!

Second, a personal touch from the pastor should be followed by transparency in the pulpit. Growing in Christ is a lifelong journey—

eventually all will struggle at some point. Dr. Jerry Falwell often said, "You are either in a crisis, just exiting a crisis, or about to have a crisis." Obviously, discretion is a key, but when a pastor shares some of his own challenges, it then encourages others to follow the model of their pastor in seeking a closer relationship with Christ. People like to see the human aspect of their pastor, and this helps you connect with them on a personal level from the pulpit. You will be amazed at the impact of showing your vulnerability. I have seen that in my career and feel it does transfer into church leadership.

Teaching is a third aspect that people are looking for from the pulpit. Most of your congregation will only go as deep as you take them on a weekly basis. Do not hesitate to take your congregation deeper in the study of God's Word on Sunday morning. Trust the Holy Spirit to speak to individuals through His Word. Do not try and preach someone else's message. It may seem strange to make this statement in a preaching resource book, but I feel that it is a fitting point. I have visited churches in the past where it was obvious that the pastor was using another's message. If you do not own the message, then it will not connect with those listening. Personalize the message with your fingerprint as the Spirit leads. You can weave some of your personal experiences that tie to the subject or even show some of your struggles as previously discussed regarding transparency.

I personally feel the congregation also shares responsibility in effective teaching. They need to be prepared and ready to learn. Encourage members to take notes during the service. I prefer using a small notebook each week rather than the note section of the bulletin. I find it helpful to refer back to previous sermons, but I would always throw out my bulletin with the important notes. Another option is to insert an outline with blanks for the congregation to fill in as you preach. However, this could also lead the note taker to easily dispose of the notes once he or she goes home. If a member has the perspective that each Sunday is a teaching moment similar to a college lecture, it may elevate the overall experience in worship.

Finally, a worship experience should result in transformation of the congregation. According to Romans 12:2, transformation comes from renewing of the mind. Renewal begins by becoming engaged in the worship service. The congregation will normally model the attentiveness of the staff during the service. When the staff is not engaged in the service, they are setting a poor example for others to follow. This can be seen by pastors whispering to each other, not paying attention to what is happening on the platform, or in some way drawing attention to themselves instead of the service. A worship service that feels tense is very apparent to the congregation. However, a Spirit-led worship experience prepares both heart and mind to receive the message. The Word of God can then penetrate and begin its transforming work.

As a Christ follower, I want to feel closer to Him after participating in a worship service. Although I realize that I am ultimately responsible for the closeness of my relationship with the Lord, the role of the pastor is to create the best environment for the member to worship. I am continually challenging myself and my staff at work. We have adopted the acronym ARFI— Always Room For Improvement. With this as our mantra, we are rarely satisfied with our current state. Once you stop improving, you become stale.

In conclusion, my encouragement to pastors is to include the following as part of your sermon preparation;

- Touching your congregation
- Transparency from the pulpit
- Teaching deeply
- Transforming

Thank you for your service to His kingdom purposes!

SHEPHERDING GOD'S PEOPLE

The Lost Art of Encouragement

Robert P. Uhle, MA, LPCC-S, LSW

One morning, early along in my marriage, an amazing thing happened. I discovered black socks differentiated and sorted, bundled in pairs in my sock drawer. Being nearly color-blind when it comes to navies and blacks, and being the disorganized type, last-minute fellow that I am, to me this was a remarkable thing. What a great gift! My new bride saved me the time of having to find and match socks as I was scampering out the door with a piece of toast in my mouth and coffee in my hand.

The week passed, and so did my socks. My drawer emptied, I hurriedly called downstairs with, admittedly, some irritation in my voice, I asked (*exhorted*) Linda to bundle socks for me once again. The following morning, along with my ritualistic onslaught of last-minute chaos, came another request (*exhortation*), followed, of course, by similar results—no socks in the drawer. The next day, I proceeded to *tell* Linda that I wanted her to once again *bless me* with bundled socks. Alas, and not surprisingly, no bundled socks appeared. Additional less-than-kind requests (*demands*) followed, until I finally decided that bundled socks were not worth the stress on my marriage. I dropped it. A month or so passed. Lo and behold, what should appear in my drawer but bundled black socks! Sitting on the end of the bed, pulling up my socks, I began laughing aloud. It was bizarre just how much pleasure I derived from Linda's simple act of thoughtfulness. She made life just a little less chaotic and a bit more manageable. This time, when I went downstairs, I shared this with her, kissed her on the cheek, and said thanks. Guess what has appeared in my drawer with great regularity, from then to this present day? That's right, black socks ... in bundles, no less! And guess what I tell her when I run out and that sock drawer has no more bundles in it? That's right again, not a darn thing! I say *nothing*! I have learned that which is just expected or demanded, can never be given.

Whatever happened to the lost art of encouragement? It seems like we've decided it is more efficient to just correct people, or to criticize them into submission, rather than to encourage them toward good works. As a Christian therapist, I get to see the results of people who, from a very young age, have been the product of mostly well-intentioned persistent exhortation. Once filled with promise and competence, these folks who often come into counseling complaining of depression or anxiety, lack self-confidence, but are often judgmental toward others. Over the course of their history, they'd received a steady dose of correction, generally lacking in encouragement. Coming from my own perfectionistic upbringing, my tendencies are toward my personal default mode to just be very critical. When I as the father/husband walked in the door of my home after a long day, and all I could seem to notice were the toys on the floor not yet put away, and dishes left undone in the sink, I'd go into a tirade. Not, "Nice to see you," or "How was your day?" or "Hey, where are my two favorite girls?!" Instead I'd fail to notice the one thousand awesome things that were addressed amazingly well in the midst of an otherwise hectic, chaotic, and exhausting day for my wife and my daughter. Let me tell you, they *really* looked forward to my coming home!

When exactly did we quit affirming and encouraging one another? Psychologist Larry Koenig illustrates the power of encouragement by discussing two of the most difficult developmental tasks we will ever be asked to master in our lifetimes—walking and talking.[62]

When one of our cherubs makes an attempt at letting go of the table edge to launch into their first few solo steps, nobody corrects a toddler. Instead, we go ballistic! We note their valiant effort, and what follows is that we affirm. What results is they experience the fact that people believe in them, and then they pull themselves up and try even harder. For adults, it seems we somehow believe we've outgrown the need for such childish encouragement. We see encouragement as being soft, coddling, or wishy-washy. After all, why beat around the bush when we can just lay it on the line? The apostle Paul, however, understood this encouragement thing well when he consoled, comforted, encouraged,

---

[62] Larry Koenig, *Happily Married for a Lifetime* (Baton Rouge, LA: Smart Family Press, 2000).

and exhorted others on to doing good deeds. William Barclay references the encouragement term that Paul uses as being *paraklēsis*, which implies "coming alongside another."

Paraklēsis is more than soothing sympathy; it is encouragement. It is the help which not only puts an arm around a person, but also sends them out to face the lion; it not only wipes away the tears, but enables them to face the world with steady eyes." Comfort + Strength = *Paraklesis*[63]

What you and I need is for someone to come alongside and engage us in such a way that we feel understood, and yet also challenged. There is dignity and respect in this. It delivers the message, "Though you need assistance or correction here, I believe in you." This message inspires us on to greater things. Once we have experienced this, first from Jesus, and then from another, He asks us to go and do likewise. He *parakaleos* us in order for us to *parakaleo* others; that we might become agents of change in our families and beyond, for our spouses, children, parents, parishioners, neighbors, and in our communities.

A servant of the Lord must not quarrel but be gentle to all, able to teach, patient, in humility correcting those who are in opposition, if God perhaps will grant them repentance, so that they may know the truth, and that they may come to their senses and escape the snare of the devil.

—2 Timothy 2:24–26

---

[63] William Barclay, *The Letters to the Philippians, Colossians, and Thessalonians: The Daily Bible Study Series*, rev. ed., ed. James Martin (Philadelphia: Westminster Press, 1975), 83.

SHEPHERDING THE SHEPHERD

Mentoring: Passing Along the Faith

By Thad Franz

Therefore take heed to yourselves and to all the flock, among
which the Holy Spirit has made you overseers, to shepherd the
church of God which He purchased with His own blood.
—Acts 20:28

Paul shows us a few things from this verse that are worth pointing out as we look into leaders effectively mentoring men within the church body. First, Paul was talking to a group of elders, leaders from a particular fellowship. Shepherding does not fall solely on the senior pastor or pastoral staff, but on a body of leaders. This group can be different depending on the church, whether they're called elders, deacons, committee chairs, or other types of leaders. This was also a reminder to the leaders of this church to oversee and help shepherd the church. Pastoral care and leadership within the local church are there to help guide and guard the church congregation. These are leaders that don't have their own agenda, but do according to God's will. The above verse states, "among which the Holy Spirit has made you overseers"—the Holy Spirit directs and gives power to run an effective church. So how do we get to the point where we have a group of leaders, including the pastor(s), running an effective church? How does this become a team effort and not just the pastor's job to shepherd the church?

Mentoring others within the church body is essential for the success of any church. To mentor is to develop a relationship with someone who has the wisdom, experience, and skill to lead while walking closely with God. Since there is always more we can learn, we are always in need of a mentor. Mentors don't hold in what they have learned from God, but they give to others who have not yet experienced at the same level they have. This is exactly what Paul was trying to communicate to Timothy. Second Timothy 2:2 says, "And the things that you have heard from me among many witnesses, commit these to faithful men who will be able to teach others also." Paul wanted to make sure that the Christian teachings and beliefs were spread abroad through other believers. This, in essence, is paying it forward.

I'll give you a good example. I have been a member of a men's small group consisting of about ten men, including our senior pastor. We gather together on a weekly basis together to discuss a book, work through a Bible study, or simply have a devoted prayer time. We also have fellowships together outside the church where we can even further develop our relationships with one another. During our meeting time, even though our pastor has been a participant within the small group, he has not been the only one leading the group time. Each man has been mentored not only by the pastor, but by others within the group. Since each man is in a different place in his life, we have all learned from each other's knowledge and experiences to be better leaders within our congregation.

The whole shepherding process within the church is a commitment that takes time. In order to see the blessings and benefits of a true leader come to fruition, first there must be consistent time invested in the relationship. A time to meet, to talk, and to listen is essential in the mentoring relationship. Listening and asking the appropriate questions will help find out the needs of the person and know what will be the best way to guide the person. Lifting up the mentored in prayer is another vital part of the shepherding process. Praying for your Timothy consistently can not only directly affect his life spiritually, but also have an impact on how God directs you to mentor in the future.

Mentors shepherd by counseling, teaching, challenging, guiding, and other ways, but the prime way is through modeling. Paul again shares in 1 Corinthians 4:16, 17, "Therefore I urge you, imitate me. For this reason I have sent Timothy to you, who is my beloved and faithful son in the Lord, who will remind you of my ways in Christ, as I teach everywhere in every church." If you don't model the characteristics of Christ, as Paul did here, then it will be hard for others to emulate Christ's likeness. One main area where Christlikeness needs to be modeled in a mentoring relationship is the area of humility. In order to effectively mentor someone, you usually have to step out of your comfort zone to meet them where they are. This could mean both in the spiritual and practical sense. As mentors, we need to stay girded in God's grace and look to Him as the source of wisdom, not to ourselves or our own agenda. If the mentored can see this example of humility, they will see the importance of pursuing a more intimate relationship with God, not just with the mentor. We can share all of our skill and experience, but only God grants the mentored the power and purpose to apply the knowledge and become effective leaders with the hope of one day God appointing them to teach and mentor others.

SHEPHERDING THE SHEPHERD

Understanding Servant Evangelism

The Biblical Example

When Jesus met His first disciples along the shores of the Sea of Galilee, He called them to do more than simply leave their nets behind. His call was an invitation to be involved in both evangelism and discipleship. Ultimately, this same call would become an entreaty to live a radical new life. This life demanded total commitment to the servant example of Christ.

Thus, the disciples' spiritual rebirth was so profound and joyful that they could not possibly keep it to themselves. As new creations, their faith overflowed into every aspect of their lives. Both their relationship with the heavenly Father and the way they viewed the unredeemed around them were forever transformed.

The disciples spent three years walking with Jesus, learning what it meant to be channels of His love, grace, and servanthood. In His role as both evangelist and mentor, He modeled for them, and for us, what it meant to be His agents of hope in a misguided, sinful, and hurting world.

Through His witness, Jesus demonstrated that every dimension of life was included in the Father's redemptive concern. While He was primarily concerned with the salvation of one's eternal spiritual souls, He forbade us to ignore physical and emotional needs.

Think about it: Jesus' model of evangelism combines both a ministry of compassionate servanthood with a strong verbal witness. This is why Jesus is most commonly recorded in the Gospels proclaiming the good news of salvation and forgiveness, then moving into the crowds to touch and to heal (see Matt. 4:23–25).

Probably His greatest verbal expression of this concept is found in Mark 10:42–45. In response to the entitlement mentality of James and John, who desired to sit at the right and left of Jesus when He came into His glory, He responds, "You know that those who are considered rulers of the Gentiles lord it over them, and their great ones exercise authority over them. Yet it shall not be so among you; but whoever desires to become great among you shall be your servant. And whoever of you desires to be first shall be slave of all. For even the Son of Man did not come to be served, but to serve, and to give His life a ransom for many."

Every Christ follower should be deeply convicted by the instruction to become a "servant" and "slave of all." Just as Jesus washed the feet of the disciples, Christians are to do the same for a hurting world that is dying to see authentic examples of a loving Savior! In the end, Christians must understand that an unbelieving world will not believe what we say about Christ and faith, until they first see the truth manifested through His followers. In a sense, we are implored by the biblical example to wrap our faith in the flesh of daily living.

What Is Servant Evangelism?

Servant evangelism is a combination of simple acts of kindness and intentional personal evangelism. It involves intentionally sharing Christ by consistently modeling biblical servanthood.

The concept is as old as the New Testament. Like many profound truths, this one is so simple it is easily missed: Get a group of believers, say, for instance at a local church, and begin practicing simple acts of kindness with an intentional aim toward evangelism. In many cases, such acts of kindness open the door for the greatest act of kindness a Christian can give: the gospel.

Understand what kindness means. It does not mean telling people what they want to hear so they will feel good about themselves. Servant evangelism involves more than mere acts of kindness. There are valuable ministries, such as taking a loaf of bread to newcomers, and others, which are helpful, but they are not explicitly evangelistic. Servant evangelism is intentionally evangelistic, though by no means does it seek to coerce in a negative sense. When doing an act of kindness, the witness says, "I am doing this to show the love of Jesus in a practical way." Then, as the Holy Spirit opens the door, usually through the individual responding, "Why are you doing this or that?" the one performing the act of servanthood has a captive audience and proceeds to share his conversion testimony, coupled with the gospel presentation. If the other person is not open for discussion, the witness goes no further, except to offer a gospel tract, literature, or prayer. However, experience reveals that servant evangelism results in gospel conversations more than twice as often as simply presenting Christ to a stranger.

Keep in mind, *servant evangelism means intentionally sharing Christ by modeling biblical servanthood.*

Some believers have gone door-to-door, giving away free lightbulbs: "You'll probably have a lightbulb go out sometime, so here's one," they say. "By the way, did you know that Jesus said He is the light of the world?" It is amazing to see how responsive people become as the result of a simple gift or act of servanthood.

The same testimonies can be multiplied one hundredfold across America and the world by congregations, student ministries, etc., and many others who have adopted servant evangelism as a mode of intentionally sowing and reaping the gospel seed. Whether feeding quarters into a washing machine at a Laundromat to share the gospel, washing car windshields at the mall, giving away coffee or sodas at local stores, going door-to-door with packages of microwave popcorn with the note attached "Pop in and see us sometime," or providing free gift wrapping for a local store at Christmas, servant evangelism provides an effective, if not essential, approach to intentionally sharing one's faith in today's contemporary culture.

Five Servant Evangelism Projects That Work

Gas Buy-Down

Secure a local gas station and buy down every gallon of gas that is sold from 11 a.m. to 1 p.m. by .25 per gallon up to 20 gallons. If the gas is $3.00 per gallon, it would be sold for $2.75 per gallon, and the church will make up the difference. Church members will pump the gas and wash windshields.

Adopt Local Public Schools

Take fresh donuts to the teacher's lounge each week. Volunteer to take up tickets for sporting events, or feed the teachers for free on in-service days. You can also provide free tutoring, school supplies, clothing, and shoes for needy students.

In addition, provide donuts and coffee for the bus drivers early in the morning. One local church planter chose to do this just to let them know how much their services were appreciated. It actually caused such a stir of goodwill among the drivers that the local paper chose to highlight the church planter's servant spirit and heart for people. The result was the birth of a new congregation!

Dollar Car Washes

Rather than the alternative of free car washes, we have found that using a dollar bill is much more effective. As a car drives up, the person is told to hold on to his dollar until the car wash is complete to make sure the quality is good. When the wash is done and the person tries to pay, he is greeted with a polite refusal and an envelope containing one dollar, several ideas how to use it as a blessing for someone else, and the charge to pass it on.

Adopt Your Neighborhood

Begin by praying for your unchurched neighbors by name. Follow up by preparing "free" meals, mow yards, rake leaves, shovel snow, deliver 9-volt batteries for smoke detectors, etc.

Use Intentional Connection Cards

The connection cards can say something as simple as, "We just wanted you to know that we care." On the back is a small map to the church and any pertinent information. The cards are good for any SE activity; however, when utilized by Christians when anonymously paying someone's bill in a restaurant, or paying for the car behind you in a drive-through line at a fast-food restaurant, it is an effective way to plant seeds. This also works in Starbucks, Sonic, or any number of other opportunities.[64]

Go to www.servantevangelism.com for numerous other ideas.

---

[64] Taken from the book *Innovate Church* by Jonathan Falwell, General Editor (Nashville: Broadman & Holman, 2008), 139–40.

SHEPHERDING THE SHEPHERD

Help! I'm Burned-Out!

By Dr. Kent Spann

Help! I'm burned out! Those are not the words you want to hear coming out of your mouth, especially if you are the senior pastor of your church. According to the statistics I read, 1,500 pastors leave their churches every month. One of the top three reasons is burnout.

Help! I'm burned out! I never thought those words would come out of my mouth until November 2009, when I told my deacon body that I was burned out, depleted, and empty. I had hit the proverbial wall. There was simply nothing left in the tank. I couldn't keep going the way I was going.

Those words were hard for me to say, but I had to say them. They were hard to say because a "godly" person doesn't burn out. Burnout only happens to the unspiritual, not someone who loves God and His Word and who seeks Him. But that is exactly where I found myself. I couldn't hide it any longer. My family knew it, and the people in the congregation were getting a sense that something was wrong.

What I found as I plunged into the abyss of my burnout was that I was not alone. I didn't find 1,500 pastors, but I found many pastors. In fact, as I spent time with other pastors, some being leaders of very prominent churches and ministries, I discovered that many of them had gone through a similar experience. I also came to realize that burnout afflicts more than the 1,500 pastors documented in studies. Not all cases of burnout are reported because it comes in many forms. Burned out pastors speak in the language of Zion to make their burnout sound spiritual.

- *I feel God leading me to another church.* The truth is, sometimes guys are burned out and are looking for another church.
- *I am going through a dark night of the soul.* "The dark night of the soul" is

a term used especially among the mystics to describe a spiritual crisis in one's journey with God. St. John of the Cross made it popular. I believe people experience a dark night of the soul in their Christian journey. My contention is that many confuse the dark night of the soul with simple burnout.

Those are just a few of the ways we can spiritualize burnout. Realizing that burnout is a common experience didn't alleviate my pain, but it sure took away the sting of guilt and shame.

I didn't have to talk to pastors or read studies on clergy burnout to discover it is a common experience. The Word of God tells the stories of people who experienced burnout. Moses was on the path to burnout (Ex. 18:13–18); Elijah flamed out after Mount Carmel (1 Kin. 19:1–18); David wrote of burnout experiences (Psalms); and Jeremiah the prophet grew weary to the point that he wanted to quit.

What Is Burnout?

It is emotional and physical exhaustion. Christina Maslach, professor of psychology at the University of California at Berkeley, in her book *Burnout: The Cost of Caring* (n.p.: Malor Books, 2003), describes it as

> a state of physical, emotional and mental exhaustion marked by physical depletion and chronic fatigue, feelings of helplessness and hopelessness, and by development of a negative self-concept and negative attitudes towards work, life and other people.

Herbert J. Freudenberger, in *Burn Out: The High Cost of Achievement* (n.p., Anchor Press, 1980), defines it as

> the extinction of motivation or incentive, especially where one's devotion to a cause or relationship fails to produce the desired results.

In simple terms it is the inability and/or the desire to keep on going. Being very similar to depression, it is difficult to distinguish the two at times.

What Leads to Burnout?

The causes of burnout abound in the ministry. Our profession is full of potholes that will bring down even the heartiest of soul.

- The trials of life (2 Cor. 11:23–27)

    Everyone has trials, but sometimes they are so great that it leaves a person exhausted and depleted (2 Cor. 1:8, 9).

- The daily pressure of ministry (2 Cor. 11:28)

    As Paul pointed out, for those in the ministry there is the daily pressure of the church. It can be a 24/7 pressure.

- Compassion fatigue (Mark 6:30, 31)

    Compassion fatigue is the cumulative outcome of caring too much and too long with no end in sight. It is common among doctors and nurses, but nowhere is it more common than among pastors. A pastor's world is caring for people with needs—unending needs.

- Inability to admit to limitations or set boundaries (Luke 4:42, 43)

    Most ministers find it very hard to set boundaries because they feel it is their job to meet the needs of the flock. The most lacking word in a minister's vocabulary is No. Even Christ had to say no at times (Luke 4:42, 43).

- Unrealistic expectations set by the congregation, but most often by the pastor (Luke 10:38–42)

- Poor fit between one's gifting and the demands of the job (1 Cor. 12)

- Neglect of one's spiritual life (1 Tim. 4:9–16)

- Fear, such as persistent anxiety about life (Matt. 6:25–32; 13:22) or the fear of man (Prov. 29:25)

- Perfectionism

    Here I am not talking about spiritual perfectionism; rather, I am talking about people who live under the pressure to get everything excessively right down to the last detale (it is bothering you perfectionists that the word is misspelled isn't it?).

- Failure to rest

- Physical rest (Ps. 127:2)
- Rest from labors (Ex. 20:8–11)
- Spiritual rest (Matt. 11:28–30; Heb. 4:1–13)

What Can We Do to Avoid Burnout?

There are many things that a pastor can do to help avoid burnout.

- Maintain your walk with Christ through the spiritual disciplines (2 Pet. 3:18; Jude 17–23).
- Learn to set boundaries (Acts 6:1–7).
- Take regular time off—days off, vacation, sabbaticals, etc. (Is. 58:13, 14; Mark 6:31).
- Maintain good health through exercise and proper diet (1 Kin. 19:5, 6; 1 Cor. 6:19, 20; 3 John 3:2).
- Laugh, and enjoy life (Prov. 17:22).
- Build a team around you (Ex. 18:17–26).
- Practice silence and solitude (Ps. 46:10).

These things can help, but they are no guarantee you will never hit burnout or hit the wall. After all, we do live in a fallen world (1 John 2:15, 16) in frail bodies (2 Cor. 4:7).

How to Recover from Burnout

Some of you reading this article may already be in the thralls of burnout. Many of the things I shared on how to avoid burnout will help, but there are some essential things you must do in addition to the above.

1. Admit you are burned out.

This is a huge step in the process of recovery. Pretending you aren't burned out or denying you are burned out is a recipe for physical, emotional, mental, and spiritual burnout. I am convinced that many of the pastors who end up in adulterous affairs were burned out first but didn't deal with the burnout, which then led to the affair.

2. Get help.

Find a counselor in your town who can help you. There are also great programs for pastors who are burned out. I attended a three-week program at Alongside Ministries in Michigan (www. alongsidecares.net), which was a godsend.

3. Find a pastor (preferably pastors) you can pray and share with.

The greatest danger is isolationism. Don't fall prey to it. You need the ministry of the body of Christ.

4. Share your condition with your leadership.

Most churches are going to support and do what they can to help you. What keeps most ministers from sharing their burnout with leadership is fear or pride. When I shared my condition with my leadership, they told me to take a sabbatical. While on my sabbatical, the church ministered to me through prayers and cards (I have a file full of cards that church members sent to me during my time off).

Certainly if you are going through a difficult time with your church, and that is partly the cause of your burnout, then you may not be able to share it. In that case talk to your denominational leadership.

5. Take time off from the ministry.

I didn't say quit the ministry; just take extended time off from the ministry. If you don't take time off, you will probably end up quitting the ministry. You have got to rest.

6. Let God minister to you physically, emotionally, mentally, and spiritually.

He is the Lord who heals (Ex. 15:26). One of the most moving scenes is when Jesus restored Peter, broken Peter, in the context of intimate fellowship (John 21:1–19).

7. Be patient with the process.

If a person has a major heart attack or a transplant, we know there will be a long period of recovery; why do we think it would be any less for those recovering from burnout? Don't expect to just jump back into the saddle. Pace yourself.

The Good News

The good news is you can recover from periods of burnout. That is the message of grace!

> Come to Me, all you who labor and are heavy laden, and I will give you rest. Take My yoke upon you and learn from Me, for I am gentle and lowly in heart, and you will find rest for your souls. For My yoke is easy and My burden is light. (Matt. 11:28–30)

May you discover His rest for your soul.

A HERO OF THE FAITH

Dr. J. Edwin Orr

Written by Dr. Doug Munton

The Michael Jordan of the history of spiritual awakenings was a short, wiry, enthusiastic little man named James Edwin Orr. His exhaustive writing and powerful preaching and teaching on the subject of revival made Orr a legend in the field.

J. Edwin Orr was born in 1912 in Northern Ireland. As a boy he came to faith in Jesus Christ and as a teenager he felt a call to preach and evangelize. This call led to a ministry as an itinerant evangelist and soon young Edwin Orr was traveling the world preaching the gospel message. He traveled by faith with almost no resources and few contacts across many parts of the world. The message he preached was one of salvation and full surrender to the lordship of Christ. Orr wrote numerous books chronicling these journeys of faith.

After additional education (Orr earned several degrees over the course of his life, including a PhD from Oxford) Orr joined the faculty of the newly formed School of World Missions at Fuller Theological Seminary. He found great joy in teaching and also an open door for more opportunities to continue to speak and write.

Today, Orr is probably best remembered for his extensive research and writing in the field of spiritual awakenings. He authored numerous books on the history of these times of revival. His books uncovered the neglected stories of God's work in revitalizing believers, especially in the last few centuries. He told of the exciting stories of God's work on every continent. Many books were devoted to the massive but less-known story of the awakening of 1858, sometimes called "the Prayer Revival."

Orr helped the church immensely through his definition of revival. He typically used the words "revival" and "spiritual awakening" interchangeably. He preferred the term "spiritual awakening" because of the use of the term "revival" in the Western world as an evangelistic campaign. He noted that this resulted in churches having the contradiction of holding "revivals" where no one was revived.

In his later writings, Orr sometimes made a distinction between the two terms. He used "revival" as something that "rejuvenates the family of God" and "spiritual awakening" as that which "rocks the surrounding community."[65]

Usually, however, Orr used the terms interchangeably and gave the following definition of revival or awakening. He said, "An Evangelical Awakening is a movement of the Holy Spirit bringing about a revival of New Testament Christianity in the Church of Christ and in its related community."[66]

J. Edwin Orr's definition of revival made several things clear. Revival, he noted, was from the Holy Spirit and not from man. This countered the belief of many historians who saw revival as merely the result of sociological explanations. Orr knew revival came from God and not merely as the result of changes in societal patterns.

Second, Orr believed that revival brought the church back into right fellowship with the Bible and with the Lord. Real revival, he often noted, involves genuine repentance of sin and restoration of a right relationship with the Lord. It always leads to a full surrender of one's will to the lordship of Christ.

While Orr believed revival always resulted in the desire to reach lost people, he also believed it to be more than merely evangelistic work. Revival, he believed, was more than evangelism but always resulted in evangelism.

The research J. Edwin Orr did on the subject of awakenings was a tremendous benefit to the evangelical world. He brought to light many of the great movements of God in history which had begun to fade from the collective memory of the church. He reminded believers of the great and mighty works God had performed in days gone by and how those mighty works had changed the course of history.

It is important to note, however, that Orr was more than a historian. He was also an exceptional preacher. He preached with great vigor and enthusiasm. His passion for God's Word and for God's people was extraordinary. Few men have been so keenly used by God to open the

---

[65] J. Edwin Orr, "Revival That Rocked the World," *Moody Monthly*, June 1986, 68.

[66] J. Edwin Orr, *The Fervent Prayer: The Worldwide Impact of the Great Awakening of 1858* (Chicago: Moody Press, 1974), vii.

eyes of the church to what God wants to do in bringing life and passion to the body of Christ.

The preaching of Orr was captivating. His delivery was filled with quirky humor and bold directness. He was willing to "step on toes" and focus on the need for repentance. Yet he was also warm and loving in his presentation. He spoke as one who longed for God and for godliness. His wit was disarming, his style was engaging, and his message was penetrating.

Orr died in 1987 while preaching at Ridgecrest Conference Center in North Carolina. Fittingly, his final message was on praying for spiritual awakening.

Preachers of this generation would do well to learn from J. Edwin Orr. His combination of scholarship and passion serve as a model. His great faith and gentle, humble spirit instruct us still today. May his great ministry stir the next generation to seek revival that changes lives and impacts the world.

See July 31, August 7, and August 14 for samples of Dr. Orr's sermons.

A HERO OF THE FAITH

Dr. George W. Truett

Written by Josh Saefkow

George Washington Truett is perhaps one of the most notable preachers in Southern Baptist life. Truett was born in Clay County, North Carolina, in the spring of 1867. His heritage is speckled with ministers of the gospel, as his grandfather and his great-uncle would take the pulpit. One of the most significant things about Truett's childhood and conversion was his mother. Mary Truett would often be found in solitude and prayer over her family. The influence of his parents and brother, who was deaf, would set the trajectory for George's life as he faced his teenage years. Some say the reason George was so highly skilled in being an orator was because he would carefully articulate each word to his younger brother. By the age of eighteen, he completed his studies at Hayesville Academy and immediately began teaching. While trying to pay for college, Truett opened a school in Hiawassee, Georgia, and employed only three teachers. He taught in a one-room public school, and the student body eventually numbered more than three hundred. It was during this two-year apprenticeship that George was converted.

The conversion experience of Truett was at the age of nineteen, when an evangelist extended his crusade for another week. It was during this week that Truett felt the Holy Spirit beckoning his soul. The preacher asked the congregation to open their Bibles to Hebrews 10:38: "Now the just shall live by faith; but if anyone draws back, My soul has no pleasure in him." By the time the sermon had concluded, many people were making their way down to the altar, and Truett was one of them. Truett says of his conversion experience, "I was glad to be in the company going forward. I could draw back no longer."

This new convert was hungry and eager to win souls for the gospel of Christ. Truett's life could be defined as the title of his great work, *A Quest for Souls*. He surprised himself at how zealous he was after his first sermon. Truett said:

As I spoke, I was fairly carried away with passionate concern for the salvation of that congregation, everyone of whom I knew, in that house crowded to the doors. I went down the aisle pleading with the people upon the right hand and the left. Then it suddenly dawned upon me, what a spectacle I must have made of myself, and in unspeakable humiliation I sat down. Very soon, I hurried out of the building and went down the country road as fast as I could walk, to my country home, and to my bed.[67]

It is comforting for us to know that spiritual giants such as Truett had moments like these as well.

He was a teacher who possessed extraordinary gifts. One time while preaching, Truett, being led of the Spirit, told his friends to bring him the worst sinner they could find. His friends brought back a hardhearted, half-paralyzed man who listened to Truett and was gloriously redeemed!

In 1889 the Truett family moved to Texas, where George became very active in the church at Whitewright, Texas. The people began instantly to invite him to be their pastor, but he continuously told them no. His desire was to practice law, and he was beginning to prepare himself for that journey. In 1890 Truett's plans would change dramatically at a church service on a Saturday night. He told of the event:

And when they got through with all the rest of the church conference, at the close of the minister's sermon, the oldest deacon, then quite frail in health, rose up and began to talk deliberately and very solemnly. I thought, "What a remarkable talk he is making—perhaps he thinks this is his last talk." Presently, I became disturbed by it. He said to the church in conference: "There is such a thing as a church duty when the whole church must act. There is such a thing as an individual duty, when the individual, detached from every other individual, must face duty for himself; but it is my deep conviction, as it is yours—for we have talked much

---

[67] Powhatan W. James, *George W. Truett: A Biography* (New York: Macmillian Co, 1945), 25, 26; also used in Clyde E. Fant Jr. and William M. Pinson, *Twenty Centuries of Great Preaching*, vol. 8 (Waco, TX: Word, 1971), 131.

one with another—that this church has a church duty to perform, and that we have waited late and long to get about it. I move, therefore, that this church call to a presbytery to ordain Brother George W. Truett to the full work of the gospel ministry."

It was promptly seconded and I immediately got the floor and implored them to desist. I said, "You have me appalled; you simply have me appalled!" And then one after another talked, and the tears ran down their cheeks and they said, "Brother George, we have a deep conviction that you ought to be preaching." Again I appealed to them and said, "Wait six months, wait six months!" And they said, "We won't wait six hours. We are called to do this thing now and we are going ahead with it. We are moved by a deep conviction that it is the will of God. We dare not wait. We must follow our convictions.

There I was, against a whole church, against a church profoundly moved. There was not a dry eye in the house— one of the supremely solemn hours in the church's life. I was thrown into the stream, and just had to swim.[68]

This would only be the beginning of what God would have in mind for George W. Truett. As churches would begin calling this young man to come be their pastor, there was one that was particularly persistent.

The First Baptist Church of Dallas, Texas, called Truett to be their pastor, and he gracefully declined. Yet, they sensed this was the will of God and pursued him once more. The church was deeply in debt and had only 715 members. God began to give Truett a deep burden within his soul to be with the people in Dallas. His young spirit, enthusiasm, and love for the Lord would capture the hearts of First Baptist. The once-struggling church springboarded into a healthy, vibrant organism. The debt was chiseled away, and many joined the growing church. Truett's ministry grew to more than seven thousand every Sunday morning. Truett's popularity grew on the national level as well. In 1927 he was elected president of the Southern Baptist Convention and served in that position for three years. His ministry was powerful, and God was blessing the people of First Baptist.

---

[68] Ibid., 48, 49.

It was at this precise moment when George struggled with leaving the ministry. Several months prior, Truett had accidently shot one of his closest friends, the chief of police, on a hunting trip. After many days of praying and crying, he could not stand in the pulpit and preach again. God, in His divine fashion, revealed himself to Truett in a dream, saying, *You are My man from now on.* That day Truett returned to the pulpit, and other churches canceled their services so that their members could go hear him preach.

Truly, Truett may be recognized as the prince of preachers. His preaching style was like a locomotive that would rattle one's heart in fear and reverence of the Lord God. The preacher's voice was powerful. He usually began by speaking in low tones; his voice began to rise as the sermon progressed and would stay passionate until the conclusion of his sermon. He was about six feet tall and weighed around two hundred pounds. His tall stature and powerful voice would command a holy hush in any congregation before which he stood.

After a forty-seven-year tenure as pastor of First Baptist Church, George W. Truett was called home in the summer of 1944. After many months of sickness and pain, Truett's last reading, *With the Sorrowing*; the corner of one page was turned down to mark his place. Truett jotted these words in the margin: "And there shall be no more death, neither sorrow, nor crying neither shall there be any more pain: for the former things are passed away."[69]

George Truett dedicated his life to the Lord Jesus Christ and showed what God is willing to do with one man who says, "Lord, here am I. Send me."

---

[69] Fant and Pinson, *Twenty Centuries*, 142.

BABY DEDICATION REGISTRATION

Infant's Name: _____

Significance of Given Names: _____

Date of Birth: _____

Siblings: _____

Maternal Grandparents: _____

Paternal Grandparents: _____

Life Verse: _____

Date of Dedication: _____

BAPTISMS/ CONFIRMATIONS

Date   Name   Notes

_____   _____   _____

_____   _____   _____

_____   _____   _____

_____   _____   _____

_____   _____   _____

_____   _____   _____

_____   _____   _____

_____   _____   _____

_____   _____   _____

_____   _____   _____

_____   _____   _____

_____   _____   _____

_____   _____   _____

_____   _____   _____

_____   _____   _____

_____   _____   _____

_____   _____   _____

_____   _____   _____

FUNERAL REGISTRATION

Name of Deceased: _____

Age: _____

Religious Affiliation: _____

Survivors: _____

Spouse: _____

Parents: _____

Children: _____

Siblings: _____

Grandchildren: _____

Date of Death: _____

Time and Place of Visitation: _____

Date of Funeral or Memorial Service: _____

Funeral Home Responsible: _____

Location of Funeral or Memorial Service: _____

Scripture Used: _____ Hymns Used: _____

Eulogy by: _____

Other Minister(s) Assisting: _____

Pallbearers: _____

_____

_____

Date of Interment: _____ Place of Interment: _____

Graveside Service: _____ No _____

FUNERALS LOG

Date	Name of Deceased	Scripture Used

MARRIAGES LOG

Date	Bride	Groom

SERMONS PREACHED

Date	Text	Title/Subject
_____	_____	_____
_____	_____	_____
_____	_____	_____
_____	_____	_____
_____	_____	_____
_____	_____	_____
_____	_____	_____
_____	_____	_____
_____	_____	_____
_____	_____	_____
_____	_____	_____
_____	_____	_____
_____	_____	_____
_____	_____	_____
_____	_____	_____
_____	_____	_____
_____	_____	_____
_____	_____	_____

SERMONS PREACHED

Date	Text	Title/Subject

SERMONS PREACHED

Date	Text	Title/Subject

SERMONS PREACHED

Date	Text	Title/Subject
_____	_____	_____
_____	_____	_____
_____	_____	_____
_____	_____	_____
_____	_____	_____
_____	_____	_____
_____	_____	_____
_____	_____	_____
_____	_____	_____
_____	_____	_____
_____	_____	_____
_____	_____	_____
_____	_____	_____
_____	_____	_____
_____	_____	_____
_____	_____	_____
_____	_____	_____
_____	_____	_____

WEDDING REGISTRATION

Date of Wedding: _____

Location of Wedding: _____

Bride: _____

Religious Affiliation: _____

Bride's Parents: _____

Groom: _____

Religious Affiliation: _____

Groom's Parents: _____

Ceremony to Be Planned by Minister: _____ By Couple: _____

Other Minister(s) Assisting: _____

Maid/Matron of Honor: _____

Best Man: _____

Wedding Planner: _____

Date of Rehearsal: _____

Reception Open to All Wedding Guests: ____ By Invitation Only: ____

Location of Reception: _____

Photos to Be Taken during Ceremony: _____ After Ceremony _____

Other: _____

Date of Counseling: _____

Date of Registration: _____

NOTES

NOTES

NOTES

NOTES

NOTES

NOTES

NOTES

NOTES

NOTES

NOTES

NOTES

NOTES

NOTES

CPSIA information can be obtained
at www.ICGtesting.com
Printed in the USA
LVHW092149031122
732354LV00028B/1154